USS Constellation

USS Constellation

FROM FRIGATE TO SLOOP OF WAR

GEOFFREY M. FOOTNER

Naval Institute Press
Annapolis, Maryland

Naval Institute Press
291 Wood Road
Annapolis, MD 21402

Library of Congress Cataloging-in-Publication Data
    Footner, Geoffrey M. (Geoffrey Marsh), 1923–
    USS Constellation: from frigate to sloop of war / Geoffrey M. Footner.
        p.   cm.
    Includes bibliographical references and index.
    ISBN 1-55750-284-6
    1. Constellation (Frigate)—History. I. Title.
    VA65.C68 F66 2002
    359.8'32'0973—dc21

                                                                    2002004274

Printed in the United States of America on acid-free paper ⊗
10 09 08 07 06 05 04 03   9 8 7 6 5 4 3 2
First printing

Contents

PREFACE

Controversy tracked the noble ship USS *Constellation* since the day that President George Washington announced that one of the nation's first six frigates would be built in Maryland. Washington's detractors ignored the fact that the Continental frigate *Virginia* was built in Fells Point, Baltimore's original harbor district, as critics, most from north of Chesapeake Bay, voiced the warning that skilled mechanics for such a grand project could not be found in the Tidewater, though the region in 1794 built the world's finest schooners and brigantines.

Originally, Joshua Humphreys prepared drafts for six frigates with plans for two ships, *Constellation* and *Congress,* of about twelve hundred tons burden. Humphreys' draft for the other four created a new class of powerful warships. Ultimately, five of the six were built: three large ships, *Constitution, United States,* and *President,* and the two smaller frigates named above.

Before construction of *Constellation* began at David Stodder's shipyard on the eastern edge of Fells Point, the War Department, with Washington's consent, appointed Capt. Thomas Truxtun—a commercial captain, ex-privateer, merchant, and adventurer—her future captain and sent him to Harris Creek as superintendent of the project. When the navy commissioned the five original frigates, it was the naval architect and shipbuilder Joshua Humphreys and Truxtun of the *Constellation* who emerged as the principal players in the drama surrounding the building of the first ships drafted for the United States Navy and employed first in a brief undeclared war with France.

Captain Truxtun, David Stodder, and Joshua Humphreys argued their project to completion through three years of construction delays and rising costs. Following *Constellation*'s launch on 7 September 1797, Truxtun voiced a series of complaints concerning his ship, several the results of changes he demanded during her construction and several that may not have been flaws at all. Unfortunately, by meddling with *Constellation*'s plans and with her builder during construction, Truxtun's demands and complaints inflicted on the ship a reputation for instability, causing a series of modifications that continued for decades.

Constellation's operational records, comments about her sailing qualities, the later rebuilds, information from journals and ship logs never compiled before for publication, and navy yard reports and plans relating to this ship have been gathered to present a reasonably complete historical and architectural study of the ship. My story is a portrait of a beautiful ship fighting for her place in history. It is also the story of a ship built of a different model and the recurring fight against the heavy hands of a parade of commanders, constructors, and administrators who endeavored to make her more like a traditional gun platform. Though many American naval officers admired *Constellation,* her smaller size and unique sailing qualities (her plain sister, USS *Congress,* sailed in her shadow) made her the frigate that ambitious officers sought to step beyond to reach command of a frigate-44 or a battleship of the line.

To enrich the setting and establish focus to the story, the history of *Constellation* is placed in proper perspective in the periods that she served the nation. This then is the story of a wooden sailing ship in her contemporary setting, connected by her operations to several related subjects—international relations and national politics, naval architecture, ship technology, navy repair policies, and her missions at sea in light of naval administration on shore.

I use the expression "to rebuild" in the same sense that naval administrators, politicians, and constructors used it in the wooden-ship navy in the first half of the nineteenth century: a major repair, sometimes so great that the work involved redesigning and/or replacing a ship's hull. There exists a rich lode of documentation concerning the navy's administration of this policy between 1800 and 1854, much of it previously unpublished. Included are data concerning *Constellation*'s rebuilds of 1812, of 1829, and again in 1839, during which major modifications were made to her hull dimensions and shape prior to 1853. These included greater breadth, reduced tumble home, reduction in her draft, new spars plans, a round stern, and a new rudder assembly.

In the public's mind, U.S. Frigate *Constitution* is a symbol of might and power—a ship of iron sides. The smaller *Constellation,* with her beautiful form, placed first on the firing line, was for decades a ship to cherish. Thoughtful naval officers respected the ships' differences.

Addressing the controversy concerning the provenance of the U.S. Frigate *Constellation* and the U.S. Sloop of War *Constellation* would be a far worthier undertaking if naval historians had a well-grounded understanding of U.S. Navy administration between the War of 1812 and the Civil War. The fact is, the study of that period of naval history can be as dull as the study of any similar period of military history during which guns are fired only at practice or in duels. Most of the best men left the navy and most of those who remained were better sailor-lawyers/politicians than hands-on commanders of ships and men.

The *Constellation* controversy is a particularly strange tale as Howard I. Chapelle single-handedly created it. He successfully manipulated his story to fit with the existing mood of his potential opponents, as at the time—post–World War II—the United States Navy's disinterest and disaffection for the subject of old wooden ships gave him little opposition. His charges, though wild, were ignored by most and considered unimportant by others. Why he chose to push so hard a thesis that many nineteenth-century navy ships were built illegally remains beyond comprehension.

The modern navy establishment and its historians continue to neglect *Constellation*. She remains today a second-class ship that the navy ignores in favor of one of Joshua Humphreys' larger frigate-44s, USS *Constitution*. But they should never forget the role the smaller ship played in establishing freedom of the seas for the American merchant service. And she is the only Humphreys ship to face an opponent of equal or more powerful armament. When rated a second-class frigate and commanded by Captain Truxtun, she engaged *La Vengeance* and fought the French frigate to a draw. Her accomplishment forced the French and English navies to recognize that, thanks to Mr. Humphreys, the small American navy had positioned itself on the cutting edge of naval warfare.

The questions concerning *Constellation* are important today because Maryland interests have finally saved her from burial at sea despite the navy's neglect. It is fitting that the ship's history and provenance are fully investigated and paraded in the records of American naval history. Hopefully, the history of *Constellation* will, in the future, sit on shelves next to books about the great warships *Bonhomie Richard*, *Hyder Ally*, *Constitution*, *United States*, *President*, *Hornet*, *Wasp*, *Peacock*, and *Enterprize*. I quote a paragraph from the closing pages of *Fouled Anchors*, a recent report on *Constellation* by Dana Wegner and others from the David Taylor Research Center, U.S. Navy Department: "An exhaustive search made by the team of the historical record produced no genuine evidence either in drawings or documents to link the two *Constellations* other than in name only. The two ships were conceived by two different naval constructors in separate centuries to different sets of naval requirements. It appears that a deliberate attempt by perhaps one person was made to link the two *Constellations* by forging historical records." The nine chapters that follow covering *Constellation*'s history contradict this paragraph and the conclusion it seeks to convey.

As Chapelle devoted only a few paragraphs of his total writings to the *Constellation* controversy, he is a minor figure in the reconstruction of the ship's story. This is particularly the case as Chapelle, the draftsman, did not comply with the rules of writing history. On the other hand, to refute more recent nonhistorical theses about *Constellation,* as frigate and sloop of war, this book covers all the evidence—evidence that other writers say does not exist. Obviously, disinterest, personal agendas, and laziness are the enemies of truth, for there exists a multitude of historical documents undisturbed by any forger or for that matter by any revisionist. A forger is easy to stigmatize because he is a criminal, but are those researchers in naval history who knowingly mislead others by their omissions of historical evidence any less reprehensible? In the process of preparing this manuscript, the story divided itself into six general categories I wanted to investigate:

1. Did John Lenthall design a new ship in 1853 or did he only make specific modifications to *Constellation*'s hull? I trace the modifications made to *Constellation*'s original draft that began in David Stodder's yard and continued through four rebuilds.
2. To support the conclusion to question one, can it be proved that preexisting framing or flooring was used in the rebuild of 1853–54 to guarantee the integrity of her rebuilt hull and her unbroken lineage?
3. In addition to reused timbers, did the navy return to the ship materials and equipment taken from the ship-frigate when she entered Gosport's ordinary in 1845 after she was rebuilt and razeed?
4. Are affirmative answers to questions one, two, and three supported by the flow of official documents generated by contemporary officials of the Navy Department and others in the executive branch of the government?
5. What new sailing ships did the navy design, build, and launch after 1845? Did Congress authorize a new ship at any time to replace the U.S. Frigate *Constellation*?
6. Did the interaction between the executive branch (including the Navy Department) and Congress support the premise that the navy rebuilt *Constellation* in 1812, 1829, 1839, and 1853?

If the answers to these questions are provided in the chapters that follow and if they are appropriately supported by official records and other related contemporary documents, then this book should be sufficient to favorably close the case concerning the ship *Constellation*'s provenance. Of course, I anticipate that other writers may want to question my sources or interpretations of them.

Acknowledgments

$\mathcal{W}$hen I began this project, I was subjected to a number of shots across my bow—from friendly fire and others less friendly—warning me that the *Constellation* controversy had mortally wounded better maritime writers than I. Approaching the subject with a great sense of apprehension, I took heart immediately when I realized that during more than a half century of bitter arguing over the provenance of the USS *Constellation,* no one had written a physical history of her long life. A close associate suggested that since I walked the same streets as the shipwrights who built the ship-frigate and drank and talked in coffee shops and taverns located in buildings where similar establishments existed in 1794, when Fells Point celebrated George Washington's decision to build one of the nation's first navy ships here, that perhaps I was too emotionally involved to make *Constellation* a subject of study. There is no question that I am driven to solve the riddle of her past; however, I am convinced that the most captivating reason to write the story of *Constellation*'s unique position in naval history is simply because, like Mount Everest, she is here. So I set aside other projects to prepare this story.

Not specifically trained in naval history and for that matter having had no great interest in military activities of any kind once my own naval experiences ended, I took on the project to rehabilitate the history of USS *Constellation.* I believed in the work of William M. P. Dunne, who fought her battle often virtually alone in later years. His logic made sense. The basic premise upon which Howard I. Chapelle built his thesis did not. But unlike Howard Chapelle, Bill Dunne never had enough time to make his argument. He tried to cover too many subjects and to teach too many of us who pestered him with complicated questions on naval architecture or maritime history. In his study of *Constellation,* Bill made some mistakes, unknowingly used some fake documents, misinterpreted some data, but never wavered in his ultimate conclusion that in several areas of study the sloop of war *Constellation* and the frigate *Constellation* were linked, creating an architectural, physical, documentary, and sentimental bond of provenance as strong as that of any surviving wooden naval ship in existence in 2002. If Bill, the old warrior, and Brina J. Agranat, a historian just beginning her career, had had time for collaboration, this book would not need to be written.

Bill brought to my attention the graduate thesis Brina Agranat prepared for a master of arts in maritime history at East Carolina University. This paper, which is a pilgrimage into nineteenth-century naval administration, cleared my mind of the lesser writings of better known authors of our navy's history. Like so many experiments in scholarly investigation, Ms. Agranat's paper reaches conclusions she did not expect when she started her project. This makes it even more profound and reasonable. It is also a testimonial to her advisers at East Carolina University, who reluctantly allowed her to pursue the truth about *Constellation*'s provenance.

Unfortunately, death took away Dr. Dunne and Ms. Agranat. It would be wrong for me not to acknowledge my debt to them. Our conclusions are similar, and many of their ideas and sources helped me develop the chapters that follow. I enjoy the pleasure of acknowledging their contributions and dedicate this project to them.

There is a third individual whose work during the preparation of this manuscript requires my very special acknowledgment. The fact is, I could not have written a good story—a complete story—without his counsel, his experience, and his marvelous talents. I refer to William L. Crothers, author of the book *The American-Built Clipper Ship*. I say simply and sincerely, if there are any maritime historians out there who do not have this book in their reference library, they do not have a library. The wonderful drawings in my book came from Bill Crothers. The drawings can be shared with my readers; what they will not see are the marvelous letters chock full of advice he wrote for two years as we struggled to bring into focus the series of modifications through which *Constellation* suffered as commanders and constructors labored to change her from a sea eagle into an ordinary navy ship.

Frederick C. Leiner, who takes care of a family and a career but still finds time to be a good naval historian, read and corrected almost everything I ever wrote for publication. My debt to him is not possible to calculate. Tom Price, a friend of two generations of our family, did sketches and offered professional advice; I acknowledge also Professor Gregory White of the United States Naval Academy for invaluable lessons in naval architecture. The staff of the Nimitz Library at the Naval Academy in Annapolis, Maryland, but particularly the staff of the Special Collections Branch, allowed me to work there in quiet seclusion and were always ready to help me find another book or manuscript. To them I am grateful. The staff of Old Navy History at the National Archives never failed me with their advice and guidance; I wish to thank, too, the regional archivists at College Park, Maryland, and Waltham, Massachusetts.

Easy access to records held in other countries is an expensive problem to solve. Though the Internet makes research overseas more affordable, nothing surpasses the advantage of having friends in a distant country, particularly if language is a problem. I could not travel overseas during the preparation of this manuscript, but I was lucky to have had the wonderful assistance of Yves Poupard in Paris and Jacqueline Caron in Rochefort. Their work enriches this book. Vincent Poupard directed our Internet communications in English. I know Yves Poupard well and someday I hope to meet the other two, who helped unselfishly.

USS Constellation

One

Mr. Humphreys' Frigates

*F*or several years during his administration, Pres. George Washington ignored his fellow Americans' demands to free seamen held by the Barbary nations of North Africa. He had no choice as his country had no navy. The United States' political leaders, including the two men who would follow Washington to the presidency, John Adams and Thomas Jefferson, agreed that, without a navy, America could not stop acts of piracy by Barbary corsairs. Both men wrote, while serving as ministers to London and Paris long before 1794, the year Congress authorized Joshua Humphreys' frigates, that America needed a navy, and there is no record that they altered their positions. Jefferson wrote to Adams that he thought the country should build a fleet of at least 150 guns and that it was proper to establish a small marine force "even if we buy peace with the Algerines."[1] John Adams responded that he agreed with Jefferson that a navy was necessary, adding that he was willing to go to great lengths to promote it "whether or not it is used against the Algerines."[2]

Jefferson, following his appointment by President Washington to his cabinet as secretary of state, restated America's problem with the Algerines in a report to Congress dated 30 December 1790. He explained that the administration's problem with Algiers was not so much continuing attacks on American vessels passing into the Mediterranean Sea at Gibraltar but rather the embarrassment of having captured American seamen held in slavery there. Most American trade to southern Europe via the Mediterranean Sea had died out after 1783. Jefferson noted that Algerine naval forces consisted of light vessels, swift but not able to withstand a broadside from a frigate.[3] On 22 February 1791, the Senate passed a resolution that authorized President Washington to enter into negotiations to settle disputes with the Barbary nations by paying tribute or a ransom to free the country's merchant seamen held in slavery.[4]

Subsequently, an increase in privateer activity by Barbary corsairs, probably initiated as an attempt to raise the ante, followed this decision. The immediate increase in corsair activity spurred Congress in 1794 to authorize funds for the nation's first naval ships.[5]

Even following the escalation of Algerine corsair activity, few influential Americans favored answering these new attacks with force. America's fast-growing overseas trade, concentrated in the West Indies and on the transatlantic trade route, increasingly placed U.S. ships on collision courses with France and England, at war with each other once again after 1793. America's neutral trade increased each year in tonnage and value and merchant profits soared, mostly at the expense of the merchant ships of those nations. America's powerful mercantile group pressured Washington's administration to protect its vast stake as more and more American vessels sailed into turbulent West Indies waters controlled by the Royal Navy and infiltrated by an increasing number of privateers, most French-owned. America's West Indies carrying trade to Europe drove the nation's naval policies and diverted attention from the humane problem of American seamen held as slaves in remote Africa. As French and British forces captured more and more American merchant vessels, all claiming the privilege of neutrality, Washington's administration pressed forward efforts to negotiate tribute payments to North African nations while at the same time starting a campaign in Congress for money to build warships.

In March 1794 mounting losses of American ships in the transshipment trade prompted President Washington to ask Congress to declare a thirty-day embargo on foreign trade. The political undercurrent producing this action was the president's growing awareness, as the intensity of the conflict between Great Britain and France grew, that America was increasingly in danger of involvement in a European conflict. The embargo also served to focus attention on plans for a navy as the Federalist administration continued to coax the legislative branch to recognize the nation's responsibility to protect its growing commercial shipping community. Unable to gain immediate support from Congress for a naval force to protect American shipping against attacks by the Royal Navy and the ever-increasing swarm of French privateers, Washington's administration constantly pushed forward the fiction that a U.S. Navy would be used to fight the Barbary corsairs. The act Congress eventually passed authorizing the nation's first frigates stipulated that if the nation negotiated peace with Algiers, work on the ships would cease.[6]

Joshua Humphreys laid out his ideas for the U.S. Navy's first ships months before he made preliminary design drafts. These ideas are contained in his frequently quoted letter to Robert Morris, dated 6 January 1794. Here he set forth his ideas for a navy consisting of large two-decked ships, rated frigates, such as the U.S. Frigate *United States,* the ship eventually awarded to him after he was appointed naval constructor at the port of Philadelphia in 1794. He confided to Morris that, in view of the nation's weak naval position, he favored a small fleet of large, fast, and heavily armed ships, actually super frigates or, in modern terms, pocket battleships. Humphreys wrote that ships armed with only 12- or 18-pounders would not fill the need should America be drawn into a war with a European nation or even the Algerines. He recommended that no ships built should have keels under 150 feet in length or main broadsides of less than 24-pounders.[7]

Thomas Fitzsimmons, chairman of the House of Representatives naval committee studying proposals for a shipbuilding program, originally recommended four large frigates of forty-four guns and two smaller ships of twenty-four guns.[8] The fact that the Navy Act, when passed, included two 36-gun ships along with four 44-gun ships represented the wish of Congress and was not the result of a compromise among Secretary of War Henry Knox's advisers. The secretary did not form a committee of Philadelphia shipbuilders to review drafts prepared by Humphreys until after Congress passed the enabling act on 27 March 1794.[9]

Knox and his shipbuilding committee, which included John Wharton, Thomas Penrose, John Powers, and Colonel Marsh, settled the final dimensions and specifications of the 44-gun ships between April first and fifteenth. Then Humphreys added the committee's suggested modifications to his draft of the 44-gun ships. After finishing these revisions, he prepared a second draft and model for the two smaller ships, frigate E, later named *Constellation,* which was awarded to Maryland, and frigate F, *Congress,* eventually built at Portsmouth, New Hampshire. He drafted the smaller ships on the same model as the four authorized super frigates, *United States, Constitution,* and *President,* and a fourth ship never constructed. When commissioned, the *Constellation* class of frigates compared in size to the fourth class of heavy British frigates. Humphreys' specifications for *Constellation* and *Congress* did not alter their main broadsides of 24-pound guns, the same weight he planned for the *Constitution* class and in line with his earlier recommendations to Robert Morris and Henry Knox.[10]

Fame rests easily with U.S. Frigate *Constitution,* but her smaller sister frigate, *Constellation,* though she also has survived to modern times, suffered the ravages of continuous controversy. The act of Congress authorizing the first frigates provided the foundation for conflict when legislators decreed that Joshua Humphreys must draft the country's first frigates in two models of virtually the same design but of different dimensions. President Washington himself nurtured the seeds of recurring discontent by insisting that the ships would be built in six ports, assigning *Constellation* to Fells Point, a small village not yet part of Baltimore, and in 1794 the home of a swarming hive of shipbuilders of Chesapeake Bay pilot boat schooners.[11]

The War Department organized an administrative structure to control the building program at the six ports awarded contracts. Secretary of War Henry Knox, in cooperation with Secretary of the Treasury Alexander Hamilton, appointed naval agents at each port. Knox, after consultation with President Washington, who selected the ports and assigned each ship, appointed naval constructors and ordered the ships' future commanders, also selected by the president, to the yards designated to build their ships. The War Office handled major purchases with the Treasury Department and provided a forum for questions and answers concerning materials, purchasing, and changes in the ships' design or construction specifications. Constructors and commanders referred proposed modifications in design or specifications to the War Office, which passed these inquiries and alterations to Humphreys for determination. Once Knox and his committee approved Humphreys' drafts, the War Office gave him final authority over modifications to them or the specifications. After these men and procedures were in place, Knox hired Joshua Fox, an English immigrant trained as a shipwright and draftsman, to help Humphreys prepare builders' drafts and lay them down in a mold loft.[12]

During the winter of 1794, as the Navy Act progressed through Congress, French and British attacks on American merchant vessels in the West Indies escalated. Political unrest in Fells Point directed against England reached a dangerous level with the declaration of Washington's trade embargo in March. A mob led by David Stodder threatened the life of a British captain detained in port and tarred and feathered a seaman. Taken before Judge Samuel Chase, Stodder refused to pay bond and Chase ordered him jailed. Hopeful that President Washington would award the building of a frigate locally, Robert Oliver, John Smith, and other pillars of Baltimore's merchant circle offered themselves as security, but Stodder continued to resist their pleas to give himself up to the court. Finally, Capt. John O' Donnell, who brought the ship *Pallas* with Baltimore's first Chinese cargo to Fells Point in 1785 for the account of Robert Morris, pleaded successfully with the shipbuilder to surrender himself to Judge Chase and a crisis was avoided.[13]

Hate for the British and particularly the Royal Navy grew in intensity in Baltimore and Fells Point with the passing years. Both towns had commercially important French immigrant populations, and close commercial relations between the larger merchants of Baltimore with French commercial cities like Bordeaux placed its political establishment awkwardly out of step with the nationally dominant Federalist Party. Washington insisted on having one ship built in Maryland because of the state's contributions during the American War of Independence and because of a practical need to eliminate sectionalism. The complications of national politics became irrelevant as simpler passions directed against Great Britain's trade policies, superheated by the issue of impressment of local seamen, controlled

Baltimore politics. The arrogance of the growing British practice of kidnapping at sea raised the tempo of reactive anger to the level of politics of insurrection at Fells Point, igniting mob violence. While impressment was always a burning issue in Chesapeake Bay ports, northern maritime centers tolerated it to a greater degree since British imports of manufactured goods played a more important part in that region's foreign trade. Chesapeake Bay states, though out of step with Federalist policies that seemed more and more designed to placate England, managed to maintain their strong ties with President Washington, who did not waver in his determination to have *Constellation* built in Maryland.

When Secretary Knox appointed David Stodder *Constellation*'s naval constructor effective 24 July 1794, he was Fells Point's most important shipbuilder. Admittedly, at this date, the group of shipwrights in Fells Point was small; they routinely provided Baltimore merchants with only a minor portion of their ship requirements. Stodder may have been Fells Point's only shipbuilder experienced enough for the project. The *Constellation*'s draft called for a ship of a size far exceeding the tonnage of any vessel previously built on Chesapeake Bay.[14]

Fueled by heavy demand for Baltimore schooners from local merchants and overseas buyers, principally the French, a startling growth occurred in Fells Point's shipbuilding production in 1792. With the rebellion of San Domingo's (now Haiti's) slave population that year and the renewal of French-British conflict in 1793, French demand for fast schooners, which they armed as privateers and blockade runners, quickly turned all of Chesapeake Bay into a center of shipbuilding, with Fells Point leading the way. New shipyards filled open spaces on its waterfront and artisans' shops lined the village's streets behind the yards.

Shipwrights moved into Fells Point from all parts of Tidewater to build a new type of vessel, the offshore pilot schooner, a large version of the region's famous pilot boat, which previously had been a baycraft. The pilot schooner had recently gained great favor in the West Indies because of its speed; local shipbuilders in 1794 were unable to fill the demand from French island possessions, which were in upheaval and under attack by the Royal Navy. Simultaneously merchants and plantation owners in the Caribbean possessions of other nations bought these schooners as war between the great powers of Europe placed inhabitants of many West Indies islands on the verge of starvation; war, privateering, and piracy made the whole region dangerous for shipping, particularly for vessels of neutral nations. Because of a complete breakdown in normal channels of supply, Baltimore merchants could not fill the demand for flour, bread, and other food products. They raked in huge profits as their own fast Baltimore schooners, reaching two hundred tons burden, sailed between Fells Point and the islands, delivering food products and returning with coffee and sugar. Most of the coffee and sugar imported from the Caribbean, upon reaching

Fells Point, entered United States customs under bond, as merchants quickly arranged for transatlantic vessels to move it to Europe. Under the rules of the carrying trade established by European nations owning possessions overseas, ships of neutral flag could carry colonial cargoes only after tropical goods established legal identity as American products by passing through customs at a United States port.[15]

William Priest, an English actor visiting Baltimore in 1794, estimated its population at twenty thousand and said that Fells Point was the fourth most important port in the nation. John Harriott, a visiting mariner, wrote that the cost of living there exceeded that of London, Bristol, or Liverpool. John Davis found the place remarkable for its commerce in ships and their cargoes as "crews wait not even until twilight to fly to the polluted arms of the white, black and yellow harlots."[16] When Thomas Truxtun arrived in August 1794, he found Fells Point a booming shipbuilding community with shortages of labor and mechanics and great competition for timber and materials. As a result of the exploding local growth in shipbuilding, the cost of building the smaller *Constellation* would exceed that of *Constitution*.[17]

David Stodder established his shipyard at the close of the Revolutionary War on leased land about one-half mile east of Fells Point, where Harris Creek flows into the Patapsco River. He later purchased the ten acres in 1787 which encompassed his shipyard.[18] In the years between the Revolutionary War and 1794 Stodder built large, full, traditionally burdensome ships such as *Hester, Goliath,* and *Prosperity.* He also built Capt. John O'Donnell's *Chesapeake* in 1789, the first Fells Point ship to sail to Calcutta.[19] Moreover, Stodder built the ship *Samson.* This vessel gained fame when owned by Capt. Joshua Barney in 1792. Barney chose to trade with San Domingo (Haiti) at the height of the slave insurrection on the French island and had several harrowing experiences, including capture by a British privateer and later by a Royal Navy frigate.[20] The ships Stodder built were probably the largest commercial ships constructed in Fells Point prior to the time he became naval constructor for *Constellation.*

Constellation was not the first Joshua Humphreys–designed navy ship constructed by a Fells Point shipbuilder, nor was she the first frigate built there. During the American War of Independence, the Marine Committee of the Continental Congress assigned the frigate *Virginia* to George Wells, a Fells Point builder, who may have gained his early shipbuilding experience in Philadelphia. Moreover, there is evidence that the Continental Congress originally planned to have one or more of this fleet of frigates, drafted by Humphreys, built on Elizabeth River at Gosport, near Norfolk, and that David Stodder moved to Hampton Roads to build the ships. When that did not happen, Stodder moved into Fells Point, though the year of his arrival in Maryland has not been established.[21]

Stodder had had other government shipbuilding contracts before *Constellation.* Secretary of the Treasury Alexander Hamilton awarded him a revenue cutter, the schooner *Active,* in 1791, one of the first built for the Treasury's Revenue Service on Chesapeake Bay. This schooner was modeled after the successful Virginia revenue schooner *Liberty,* built for the state's service following the Revolutionary War. These schooners took their design from the Chesapeake Bay pilot boat. The navies of Virginia and Maryland used armed versions of the model with great success against British privateers on Chesapeake Bay during the Revolutionary War. After the British defeat and when peace returned to the bay, Virginia formed its revenue service with schooners from its successful state navy fleet. Most of the Treasury's Revenue Service boats from 1791 forward were built on the Chesapeake Bay pilot boat model.[22]

Active is believed to be the first pilot-boat model schooner built by David Stodder.[23] When commercial demand for large offshore versions of the pilot schooner developed in 1792, Stodder, like all other builders at Fells Point, built them for sale to local buyers and in the West Indies. At first shipwrights referred to them as schooners, pilot-boat built; as their fame quickly spread along the East Coast of the United States and in the West Indies, the larger ones became known as Baltimore schooners. Baltimore's merchants, including Jeremiah Yellott and Robert Oliver, among the region's most respected ship owners, purchased Baltimore schooners from David Stodder. Oliver and Yellott jointly owned the pilot schooner *Active* (84 feet by 22 feet by 7 inches by 10 feet 2 inches), which Stodder built in 1794 just prior to receiving his appointment as navy constructor. Though his contract with the War Office forbade him from taking private contracts, Stodder's name appears as builder of the pilot schooner *Vulpes* in 1795 and *Punch* in 1797, both built during the period he served as naval constructor. It is possible that he arranged to build these pilot schooners near his home at 9 Philpot Street in Fells Point with the assistance of his slaves. According to the U.S. Census Report, he owned seventeen in 1800.[24]

Thomas Truxtun, mariner, merchant, former privateer, and a newcomer to government service, arrived in Baltimore from Philadelphia in August 1794 to supervise the construction of *Constellation,* the ship he eventually would command. Some historians have written that Stodder's difficult personality made him the most controversial of those involved with the Baltimore project. Truxtun's position as superintendent of the project and commander of the 36-gun ship required him to rise above the squabbles and become the calming leader at the Fells Point location, which teemed with labor and material problems. He failed to rise to the occasion. The faulty leadership and limited capacities Truxtun brought to his role as supervisor resulted from his inability to expand the limits of his vision; his life was grounded in the narrow experiences of a mariner-merchant who searched the world for opportunities for personal gain. As leader of the *Constellation* project, he brought a narrow understanding of naval ship design and construction that, combined with a

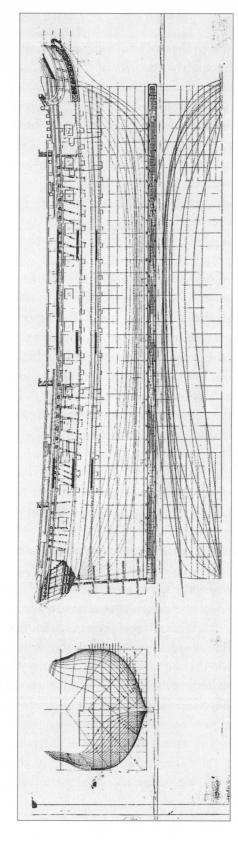

Figure 1.1. U.S. Frigate *Constellation/Congress.* A redrawing of William Doughty's original draft, 1794–1795. M.T. Watson, Bureau of Ships, 7 September 1944. *National Archives*

large ego, could have destroyed the project had not Secretary Knox's system of checks on his authority kept him somewhat in harness.[25]

The commissions conferred on the commander-supervisors by Secretary Knox for the administration gave them no authority over naval agents, who purchased materials and engaged artisans and laborers for naval constructors. Moreover, Truxtun and the other superintendents could not directly interfere with the builders' plans or activities. As the eyes and ears of the government, Truxtun was required to keep check on Stodder's compliance with Humphreys' drafts, offsets, and molds.[26] Truxtun's clashes with Stodder intensified following the arrival of William Doughty's copy of Humphreys' draft the third week in February 1795 (fig. 1.1).[27]

Truxtun, though he would win some skirmishes, eventually lost the battle to control *Constellation*'s construction site. His defeat came about because the two shipbuilders most concerned with the ship, Humphreys and Stodder, did not disagree in any major way with the inherent contents of Joshua Humphreys' drafts. Unfortunately, neither Secretary Knox nor his successor, Timothy Pickering, or even Humphreys, who, at times, made concessions on modifications of the draft and specifications, always resisted the bombastic commander. But his disruptive influence diminished somewhat following a failed attempt to seize control over the project, which undermined his position with the administration in Philadelphia. Truxtun's vanity and his argumentative, impudent, and opportunistic nature neutralized the contributions he brought to the program. Sadly, because of his overblown sense of self-importance, he tarnished his medals and caused his supporters to turn away from him, though his accomplishments will not be overlooked here.

In the end, Truxtun did not affect in any significant way Stodder's determination to adhere to Humphreys' draft of *Constellation*, once the builder understood that the compromises of naval architecture presented in the draft were acceptable and realistic. Stodder and Humphreys brought to the frigate project similar training and experience in the art of building ships designed for speed under sail. A concern for speed in navy ships at that time disturbed traditional navalists, Yankee shipbuilders, and ex–Royal Navy trainees such as Josiah Fox, Thomas Truxtun, and later Thomas Tingey, a threesome of ex-Englishmen who affected the sailing performances of a number of U.S. Navy vessels. Concurrence of the builder of *Constellation*, Stodder, with her designer, Humphreys, that America's frigates should be drafted with a balance of size and speed resulted in Stodder's building a 36-gun ship that compared in several design aspects to ships engaged in Middle Atlantic commerce. These ships were themselves built on a modified design of the smaller fore and aft vessels of the exporters of the two great bays, modeled as they were on the dynamics of survival at sea and the requirements of specific trades.

The bond between Stodder and Humphreys that most maritime historians and naval architects overlook grew from their knowledge of the common shipping requirements of the Chesapeake and Delaware bays. For generations the composition of the foreign commerce to the two bays remained strikingly similar. The two shipbuilders did not disagree on the manner of drafting for speed, as their livelihood depended on their ability to adjust for it. Or, to put it another way, Humphreys may have gotten his ideas for the size of his frigates from razeed French navy battleships of the line, but his experiments with speed came from a need to satisfy a large group of commercial customers. The ship owners who purchased vessels from Stodder and Humphreys were exporters of Maryland and Pennsylvania grain products.

One important result of the cantankerous relationship between Stodder and Truxtun was, no doubt, that *Constellation,* as built, may be the ship whose performance most closely represents the hoped-for goals of Joshua Humphreys' draft. But if this occurred accidentally, as the fallout of disagreements between Truxtun and Humphreys and Truxtun and Stodder (with Josiah Fox fueling the fire), it also happened to some extent because the ships built at other ports did not benefit from similar adversarial relationships between builder and commander. Humphreys' drafts for each of the four ships built north of the Chesapeake Bay—*United States, President, Constitution,* and *Congress*—may have been compromised accidentally because, as built, each reflects the idiosyncrasies of regional artisans as well as each commander's preferences.

Agreeable relationships between navy constructors of these ships and the commanders acting as supervisors of construction, unlike at Fells Point, may have unconsciously or knowingly modified Humphreys' draft as they built ships according to a lifetime of prior building experience. Even a happy collaboration between Humphreys and Captain Barry, father of the navy, affected the sailing qualities of U.S. Frigate *United States,* built under Humphreys' supervision. This subject is largely academic because the record of performances of the ship-frigates is too subjective and controlled by variables never made comparable because of the always changing conditions at sea.

Stodder understood Humphreys' goals, as his own experiences required him to change from a builder of burdensome Yankee-type ships to vessels more architecturally balanced for speed and capacity. What greater incentive for a builder than to adhere to drafts prepared by a colleague whose goals he understands and in whose plans he recognized the circumstances or characteristics the Philadelphian drafted for his ship-frigates. And what greater admission of defeat could Truxtun have voiced in the end than when he admitted to James McHenry just before *Constellation*'s launching that it would have been better if all the frigates had been built north of Chesapeake Bay?[28]

Truxtun arrived at Baltimore with the secretary of war's orders directing him to concentrate his attention on two specific aspects of the frigate's construction—control of the quality of the materials purchased for use in the ship and close observance of Stodder's compliance to the draft prepared under the supervision of Humphreys. With his jurisdiction limited to those aspects of the project, Truxtun had no control over purchasing and pricing of materials, locally the job of the Baltimore naval agents Joseph and Samuel Sterett. He had no control over the progress of construction because he lacked authority over the hiring of artisans or laborers, including the number employed at any particular time. Stodder selected the men he wanted, and the naval agents arranged employment terms and handled the payroll. Therefore Truxtun's primary responsibility to the War Office required him to determine that the constructor did not deviate from Humphreys' plan—in the case of *Constellation,* the builder's draft prepared by William Doughty.[29]

Truxtun received midshipman training in the Royal Navy. He supported British traditional navalist views on warship design. His awareness of Humphreys' ideas for the first frigates of the U.S. Navy had not made him agreeable to the plans as his early training in Britain's navy impressed upon him the advantages of fleet power over speed. Though he arrived in Baltimore from Philadelphia, the nation's capital in 1794 and his own base of operations, and was a long-term friend and client of Joshua Humphreys, he came prepared to do battle with the man who is recognized as America's first important naval architect.

The drafts Humphreys created for America's first frigates serve as his memoirs. His memorials are the U.S. Frigate *Constitution,* rebuilt many times, and the Fells Point–built USS *Constellation,* modified and rebuilt three times, then razeed from frigate to sloop of war in 1853–54. Both ships are afloat in 2001 and recently restored. As the twenty-first century opens, even after John Lenthall's profound modifications in 1853, the swelling contours and symmetrical hull of U.S. Frigate *Constellation*'s original form—a shape that can be traced back to Humphreys' original draft—still caresses the eyes, particularly for those who benefited from the opportunity to observe the shape of her full hull prior to her relaunching in 1998 following her last extensive rebuild.

Because of Joshua Humphreys' reputation as a naval architect and his experience stretching back to the Revolutionary War, the Federalist administration of George Washington selected him to prepare plans and advise the government through the initial creative period of planning during which the young nation planned and built its first naval fleet. Given the political climate, in which sectionalism limited the appeal of a single point of view, input by several minds complicated the planning phase under the direction of Secretary of War Henry Knox. (There was no Navy Department until 1798.)[30]

In view of the fundamental weakness of the young national government, Humphreys may or may not have dominated the debate that preceded the adoption of a final draft of the first frigates, but his basic ideas on design survived the process. While compromise was an element in the final drafting of the ships, it would be rash to conclude that Washington's administration, made up principally of those men who led the country to independence twenty years earlier, failed to place their confidence in the shipbuilder who played an important role in drafting the Confederation's fleet of frigates during the American War of Independence. There can be no doubt that Joshua Humphreys' presence filled a unique role at the birth of the nation's navy. There are ample archival records that confirm his role as designer of the navy's first ships, which eventually included five frigates.[31]

Once President Washington, with advice from Henry Knox and Alexander Hamilton, completed the selection of ports, naval agents, captains, and naval constructors, the frigate project started with great hope and enthusiasm in the summer of 1794. Stodder moved quickly to secure his shipyard, now a government facility leased to the War Department for $400 per year. During the first months of the construction period, which eventually extended over more than three years, Stodder prepared his yard for the immense job ahead. Because of the prevalence of theft, he moved quickly to prepare to receive incoming materials. A clerk's office, covered sheds, and other facilities such as shops for artisans and a complete blacksmith's shop had to be constructed before a keel could be laid. The naval agents, Joseph and Samuel Sterett, appointed John Hamilton clerk of the Navy Yard.[32]

Shortly after Knox approved Humphreys' draft and model, he appointed the shipbuilder navy constructor at Philadelphia, where *United States* was scheduled to be built. Left without an experienced adviser, Knox brought Josiah Fox into the War Department effective 16 July 1794 with the title of clerk and a salary of $500.[33] Fox, trained at Royal Navy shipbuilding facilities, had emigrated from England to Philadelphia the year previously, hoping to find opportunities for advancing a career in shipbuilding in the United States. Fox had a good resumé and important connections. It should be pointed out that he proved to be an excellent draftsman and a fair naval architect. Like many ambitious men who preceded him to America, Fox, though intelligent and clever, endeavored to advance his lot by shouldering his way into the developing naval scene at Philadelphia, using influence as leverage against established professionals such as Joshua Humphreys. Burdened by his own high regard for his untested qualifications and abilities in naval architecture, Fox, when assigned to more mundane tasks, proved to be opinionated, politically fractious, and uninspired at handling administrative matters necessary to move the frigate project forward. In 1809, while Fox served as navy constructor at the Washington Navy Yard, Thomas Tingey, another Royal Navy–trained Englishman, fired him and Fox moved west and out of navy circles.[34]

As in the case of Thomas Truxtun, Fox's early Royal Navy training imposed limitations on his ability to adjust to the pragmatism that prevailed at the conception of the U.S. Navy. Early in May 1794, Fox made a verbal presentation to Knox, listing several aspects of the frigate drafts or models that he thought would adversely affect the ships' performance at sea and under conditions of warfare. Knox documented this list and passed it along to John Wharton, who served on his frigate planning committee.[35] Fox's criticisms will be treated later in this chapter when *Constellation*'s draft and construction specifications are examined in detail. Here, it is sufficient to write that Humphreys dismissed out of hand the importance of Fox's contributions, writing that Fox had nothing to do with the planning of the draft or model of the frigates, only with copying them.[36]

As time passed, several of the Englishman's acts, which are fully documented, reveal some of the mistakes of his seesaw career. His first recorded transgression, committed early in his relationship with Humphreys and before Knox hired him, demonstrated his inability to control the insubordinate nature that dogged him throughout his navy career. Humphreys wrote that Fox, while helping him revise the 44-gun ship drafts to include the Knox committee's suggestions, altered the master draft "according to his own opinion which was so foreign from my ideas that I set it aside." In correspondence with his family, Fox, certainly a man inclined to brag or perhaps mildly handicapped by megalomania, wrote his brother that Secretary Knox hired him to prepare the drawings for six frigates, though the secretary had not hired him until after Knox had accepted Humphreys' draft. His position, according to both Knox and Humphreys, limited him to copying drawings or drafts previously prepared by Joshua Humphreys.[37]

Following Fox's appointment to the navy section of the War Office in mid-July, Knox loaned him to Humphreys, who assigned him to immediately start laying down the 44-gun ships in the mold loft and complete builders' drafts of that model for the various constructors, as the large frigates had priority over the 36-gun model. Knox and Humphreys found it necessary to pressure Fox to complete the preparation of these molds. After assigning William Doughty, clerk of Humphreys' yard at Philadelphia, to assist Fox, the two draftsmen completed the molds and copies of Humphreys' draft of the 44s in November 1794.

Rough molds reached John T. Morgan in Georgia in October. Knox had detached Morgan, originally nominated to build the fourth 44-gun ship at Gosport, and sent him to Georgia to supervise live oakers cutting timber for the ships. In a letter to Humphreys dated 21 October, Morgan claimed that the specifications did not provide the measurements needed and the molds received so far frightened him because of the size of the timbers. Shortly after that, Humphreys and Captains Barry and Truxtun voted to change the original specifications for the ships' floors and rising timbers from white oak to live oak, a decision that brought the program to a halt on several occasions for want of frame timbers and that contributed to delaying the launchings by more than two years.[38]

Humphreys, as is confirmed by his correspondence, drew the draft and prepared specifications of the 36-gun ships during the period that Fox and Doughty made the molds and copied plans for the larger frigates in the summer and fall of 1794. An impatient Truxtun, probably realizing that the 44s had been given priority, sent a Fells Point carpenter, Thomas Rouse, to Humphreys in Philadelphia and asked him to put him to work preparing *Constellation*'s molds. Responding to Truxtun's request, Humphreys, with or without Rouse's assistance, laid down the 36-gun ship in his mold loft late in 1794. The Sterett brothers, naval agents for *Constellation* at Baltimore, received the Doughty copy of Humphreys' draft of the 36-gun ship on or about 20 February 1795.[39]

General Knox in his report to Congress on the state of the frigate project optimistically predicted that the ships would be afloat in 1795. An observer at the navy yard on Harris Creek as the second year of the project opened in January 1795 would find Stodder and his workers still building sheds and a blacksmith shop, though materials purchased for the ship had begun to arrive in a steady flow. A vessel delivered the yard's first shipment of live oak timber consisting of ninety-three pieces on 17 January. Stodder requisitioned it immediately upon arrival. By that date, the molds that Humphreys, assisted by Rouse, made late in 1794 for the 36-gun ship had arrived at Fells Point.[40]

Humphreys approved several changes in hull specifications early on, and there is no reason to assume that further changes did not occur during the first year of construction. He concurred with the commanders' request to alter specifications for floors and rising timbers, originally of white oak, to live oak as previously mentioned. On the other hand, he decided that the deadwood over the keel could be white oak rather than live oak. In still another modification, Humphreys ordered the throats of the frame's floors of the 36-gun ships reduced to 19 inches and the sir-marks to 13 inches but allowed no changes in the frames at the level of the port sills. Most of these early modifications developed during the mold lofting process.[41]

As activity at Harris Creek increased, it became clear that the navy yard would manufacture or dress most of the ship's materials on the site. Stodder and his foreman, John Kirkwood, sent woodcutters into southern Maryland forests to cut white oak logs. When these logs arrived at the yard, the yard clerk, John Hamilton, arranged storage for seasoning. Later, Stodder sawed, hewed, or dressed all timber received. A second shipment of live oak timber consisting of 187 pieces arrived on 20 March 1795. Shortly after that, Morris Job, Stodder's blacksmith, took possession of his shop and commenced receiving iron bars and steel which he would be expected to shape into the required sizes for fastenings. A War Office circular arrived in March, reversing a previous one, ordering live oak used for deadwood. Though materials continued to be logged into the yard by Hamilton, as the winter changed into spring, the only ship carpenter work accomplished so far consisted of dressing 280 pieces of live oak timber that arrived during the previous months. On 1 April, Stodder continued building storage sheds in the yard. Pine and oak logs arrived from his men working in Maryland's forests. Truxtun, if present in Baltimore, had been relatively quiet. That was about to change.[42]

It would be appropriate to summarize Stodder's relationship with Thomas Truxtun, Joshua Humphreys, and Josiah Fox, now employed at the War Office to liaison between the constructors and captains at the yards. Secretary Pickering replaced Knox at the end of 1794. Joshua Humphreys, whom Knox had authorized to settle disputes or questions raised by constructors or commanders, had to defend his authority to Pickering because after Knox retired Fox attempted to undermine his position. Despite Fox's claims to the contrary, the record is clear that he had no hand in the planning or preparation of *Constellation*'s draft, the original having been the work of Humphreys, who also prepared her offsets and molds with the help of Thomas Rouse, a Fells Point ship carpenter. Moreover, Humphreys assigned William Doughty the task of copying the original draft of the 36-gun ship, which Pickering sent to the Sterett brothers.

Not unexpectedly, a close relationship developed between Thomas Truxtun and Josiah Fox based on their common disapproval of *Constellation*'s draft. Their characters, similar in many ways, inevitably produced an alliance that attempted to upset the developing working relationship between Humphreys and Stodder, a closeness developing from common experiences in drafting and building ships designed to lift bulky cargoes and the newer designs being built to outsail more burdensome ships under most weather conditions.

In the search for speed under sail, what common drafting and building experiences did Humphreys and Stodder share? Which naval architectural circumstances relating to vessel speed did Humphreys' final draft give *Constellation* and the other navy frigates? How do we know that Humphreys drafted and Stodder built *Constellation* from past experience and had not been influenced by French ships or those of any other nation insofar as speed? The answer to the last question is in the record. If Humphreys had taken more than the idea of a super frigate from the French navy, Truxtun and Fox would have applauded his draft. The answers to the first two questions are more complex. Answers will be uncovered from the records of American naval history.[43]

Several generations after the American colonies occupied North America's Atlantic coast from the Carolinas to New England, the Tidewater region, having turned away from tobacco for the most part, and the valley of the great Susquehanna River, spreading over vast tracts of fertile land west of Philadelphia, became the bread-basket of New England. The Middle Atlantic region also served Britain's colonies from Nova Scotia and Bermuda to the island possessions of the West Indies. On the rich island plantations of the Caribbean, owners who had grown wealthy shipping sugar and coffee to Europe had become dependent on imported food from middle North America. During America's War of Independence, the Middle Atlantic states fed Washington's forces and sent schooners to the West Indies with flour, returning with guns and powder. Even following American independence, British and French colonies and those of other nations remained dependent upon Pennsylvania, Delaware, Maryland, and Virginia for grain and flour, so much so that they waved navigation laws to keep America's sloops and schooners moving with grain, flour, and other food products on the trade route that had become the lifeline between ports of the Delaware and Chesapeake bays and a hundred island destinations.[44]

Builders of schooners and sloops on Chesapeake and Delaware bays improved their vessels to cut passage time in an effort to minimize two long-term problems that seriously affected profits of the regions' exporters: high marine insurance rates covering loss of vessels to enemy action or piracy and loss of perishable cargo. Shipping from cold or cool northern seas into southern warm waters made spoilage by heat and humidity a constant threat. The only answer was to cut passage time, which forced the region's shipwrights to build faster vessels.

Long before the American War of Independence, small schooners appeared on Chesapeake Bay and hauled grain from plantation landings to flour mills. The numbers grew into a great fleet of baycraft as the demand for grain and flour increased. By 1794, these schooners, and some sloops, reached two hundred tons burden. Shipwrights, starting with the dimensional proportions and models of the regions' pilot boats and ferries, increased dimensions (and cargo capacity) as exporters placed these ships on the outside trade route between Middle Atlantic ports and the West Indies. Though most naval historians are familiar with the fast grain schooners of the Chesapeake Bay, Philadelphia exporters, too, reached into central Pennsylvania, Delaware, and northern Maryland for cargoes of grain and flour for shipment to the West Indies under the same risks and conditions. Joshua Humphreys and his associate shipbuilders did not grow up unaware of the shape of those indispensable sloops and schooners.

Successful adaptation of the pilot schooner into a commercial success did not happen overnight. During the Revolutionary War, when Humphreys, a bright young shipbuilder, crafted his reputation, pilot boat schooners hauling cargo around Delaware and Chesapeake bays became the principal means by which the Middle Atlantic grain growers of America supplied Washington's army and American cities and towns, including Philadelphia. Shipwrights built pilot schooners like *Greyhound*—captured by British privateers and recaptured by Capt. Henry Geddes—large enough to carry seventy-nine hogshead of tobacco to the West Indies and return with arms and powder. Armed pilot schooners of Maryland, Virginia, and Pennsylvania's navies successfully fought British occupation and privateer activity in the Middle Atlantic region.[45]

Pilot schooners built in Maryland and Virginia from 1750 forward developed a fairly standard design that builders adhered to regardless of their location in the Middle Atlantic region. Shipwrights worked out the principal naval architectural characteristics of their fore and aft craft by keeping fairly constant proportions between the principal dimensions of the pilot boat as larger models were built. Though dimensions of baycraft and offshore models differed substantially, shipwrights maintained ratios between their length, depth, and breadth, and the shape of their hulls varied only slightly though the shipwrights who built them lived hundreds of miles apart. Their sails plans did not vary either. Of relatively long length and rather shallow depth of hold, with rising bottoms endowed with full cheeks, these craft, mostly schooners, gained initial stability with relatively ample breadth and less than extreme deadrise, combined with low freeboard and a single flush deck which placed the center of gravity below the waterline when properly ballasted. Raking bows and stern and a long keel that dragged significantly from bow to stern are among the pilot schooner's dominant characteristics. These schooners sat low in the water with enough initial stability for a delicate baiance that supported tall raking masts and a cloud of sails. Below the waterline, sharp ends and a cod head and mackerel tail shape with a long run of the tapering hull to a keel that dragged made the model extremely responsive, with a weatherly helm that allowed the model to point up better than pursuing vessels of any design or rig or size.[46]

As a result of unrest in the West Indies, offshore pilot schooners (and a few single deck brigantines) replaced more burdensome vessels after 1792. Every shipwright on Chesapeake Bay built these schooners at the time President Washington made the decision to build *United States* at Philadelphia, *Constellation* in Maryland, and a 44-gun ship at Hampton Roads. While it is certain that the popularity of pilot schooners did not influence Washington's decision, one may be just as sure that their sudden success, when speed counted, had not gone unnoticed by shipwrights in the region stretching from Philadelphia to ports as far south as South Carolina.

Though under his contract with the War Office Joshua Humphreys could not accept commercial contracts while building the frigate *United States*, the Department of State used Humphreys' experience to advise and coordinate the design and construction of a small fleet of warships for the dey of Algiers. The costs were paid partly from money appropriated by Congress as tribute and the remainder by Algerine funds. The vessels built included the frigate *Crescent* and three schooners, including a pilot schooner *Hamdullah,* built by Richard Spencer at St. Michaels, Maryland. Also built at that time for the dey's account was the brigantine *Hassan Bashaw,* by a draft prepared by Samuel Humphreys, the son of Joshua. Benjamin or Nathan Hutton and Samuel Humphreys built the gun-brig in Joshua Humphreys' shipyard, which, of course, in 1798 was still partly leased to the Navy Department. Howard I. Chapelle describes her as built on the model, somewhat modified, of pilot boat schooners then coming to the attention of the maritime world. This light warship measured 93 feet 2 inches length overall by 27 feet breadth by 11 feet 6 inches depth of hold.[47]

Though admittedly no comprehensive investigation took place, the author of several books on the U.S. Navy, Fletcher Pratt, writing in the 1940s, is the only naval historian I have discovered who suggested that the pilot schooner served as an inspiration for Joshua Humphreys' draft of the ship-frigates. Nor has anyone noted that that Joshua Humphreys had *Hassan Bashaw* built under his supervision in Philadelphia at the time he launched *United States.* Pratt suggests that for his large frigates to show speed in light winds, Humphreys provided them with breadth of the same dimension as ordinary (smaller) frigates. This would make them unstable but, wrote Pratt, the shipbuilder had frequently observed Baltimore clippers (pilot schooners) ghosting through Delaware Bay, long, slim vessels, fish-shaped along the run, and raked sharp at bow and stern. Pratt said that pilot schooners had a turn of speed like nothing on earth; that they were the product of generations of ingenious builders who added an inch here, took one off there, until in the ideal test tank of their landlocked bays they found just the point at which speed, stability, and capacity joined in a "marriage á trois."[48]

Pratt's enthusiastic observation went unnoticed in the main. A half century later another iconoclast, William M. P. Dunne, related the pilot schooner design to *Constellation.* In 1993 I sent Dunne, who was then preparing a paper rebutting a navy report that claimed the navy built a new *Constellation* in 1853–54, line drawings of the letter of marque pilot schooner *Grecian,* built by Thomas Kemp at Fells Point during the War of 1812. He wrote that upon examining the drawings he saw for the first time the hull shape of a Chesapeake Bay pilot schooner.

Dunne remarked that the first concept to strike him was the radical amount of drag to the keel. A Yankee, Dunne grudgingly admitted that *Grecian's* bow shape preceded Herreshoff's *Gloriana* and Tom McManus's *James S. Steele* by more than sixty years.[49] "The plan removes deadwood forward and the steeply angled stern post cuts it out considerably aft." He thought that *Grecian* had less deadrise than one would expect. He closed his letter with the comment that he would expect her to go to windward like a bitch and, with accentuated drag, turn on a dime. Still, Dunne wrote, with such deadrise, *Grecian* would be a complete failure as a gun platform in stormy weather. On that point, Dunne's insight had already proven correct during *Constellation*'s battle with *l'Insurgente* in 1799.[50]

Make no mistake, Humphreys did not design his super frigates, including *Constellation,* like pilot schooners. The brigantine *Hassan Bashaw* and *Constellation* were built as warships, not for hauling grain to the tropics. But by comparing *Hassan Bashaw*—built along the lines of the pilot schooner—and *Constellation*'s draft, we will be studying examples of vessels with designs influenced by the shape of the pilot schooner's hull. Clearly Humphreys looked no further than his own backyard to find examples of the speed he strove for in his super frigates. The source of Joshua Humphreys' and David Stodder's experience building ships of war that sailed fast out of harm's way or could overtake another ship of equal or lesser size came from their training and experience drafting and building commercial vessels in home waters. Dunne did not make the connection between Humphreys' past shipbuilding experiences with "the Baltimore frigate's raked bow and sleeker silhouette." He attributed those features to "David Stodder's extensive experience with the narrow-bodied low-slung hulls of Chesapeake Bay pilot schooners." It is closer to reality to point out that Stodder and Humphreys shared past experiences with speed that caused their approach to *Constellation* to be not merely compatible but complementary. That probably caused the Fells Point–built ship to be constructed differently than Humphreys' other ship-frigates.[51]

Back in Philadelphia in the spring of 1794, while Humphreys conducted conferences with Knox's advisers to finalize the draft of the ship-frigates, Josiah Fox gained the secretary's ear. Presumably verbally, as his papers do not contain a contemporary version in his hand, he gave Knox several suggestions for revising Humphreys' draft for the super frigates. Knox transcribed this list of alleged flaws in a letter to John Wharton dated 12 May 1794. The same list is contained in a letter from Humphreys to Knox of the same date. The contents of the two letters provide a breakdown of the specific aspects of Humphreys' draft, making it possible to examine the viability of the suggestions made by Pratt and Dunne that *Constellation*'s model included naval architectural characteristics of the Chesapeake Bay pilot schooner. It would be those influences in Humphreys' draft that Fox would have opposed. My assumption is based on the premise that Fox would oppose any plan that affected the stability of warships as gun platforms.[52]

I do not imply that Fox approved Humphreys' approach to the composition of a small U.S. Navy that consisted of super frigates. He voiced his disapproval of that idea, too.[53] But there can be no doubt of the position Fox took on any plan of Humphreys to compromise the stability of the frigates in order to make them faster (under certain conditions). Knox's outline of the specific aspects of Humphreys'

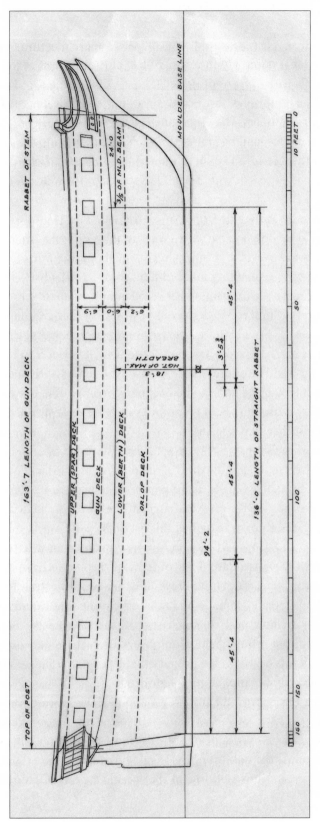

Figure 1.2. USF *Constellation*'s sheer plan, drawn in accordance with J. Humphreys' specifications, 1795. *William L. Crothers*

draft to which Fox objected is the key to isolating the naval architectural circumstances that relate to speed. They will be characteristics or compromises for speed that will appear to be common in Humphreys' frigate model, *Hassan Bashaw,* and the pilot schooner model. The reader should bear in mind that the concern here is not whether Fox's claim to have drafted *Constellation* and the other frigates is true. It is, rather, whether there is any factual basis to the theory that Humphreys' draft, insofar as it strives for speed, is the result of the influence of the most prominent local craft, the pilot schooner. I use Fox's objections to the Humphreys draft to demonstrate the point.

Knox's letter to Wharton dealing with Fox's suggested changes to Humphreys' draft summarized the 44-gun ship's planned dimensions as of the date of the letter, 12 May 1794. In it he wrote that Humphreys' 44-gun ship measurements as of that date were keel, 147 feet, beam, 43 feet, and hold, 14 feet; the ship measured 7 feet between decks and had a 7-foot waist, with 3 feet of deadrise at two-thirds of the floor (presumably at the dead flat). Humphreys adjusted these figures when he drew his final draft. He did not begin to draw that plan until the final dimensions of the 44-gun frigates were fixed, so only one set of dimensions appears for the *Constellation* class.[54]

Knox asked Wharton to review the criticisms presented by Fox relating to Humphreys' draft. Fox objected principally to the specific aspects of the draft designed to increase the frigates' speed under the conditions Humphreys felt necessary. The connection between Fox's criticisms and the frigates' designed speed is analyzed below. An examination of the Englishman's objections to Humphreys' draft with its compromises in stability and storage space to gain ship speed will reveal the influence of the Chesapeake Bay pilot schooner model on Humphreys' plans.

1. Fox's first question asked whether long ships require their extreme breadth as far forward (as in Humphreys' draft) proportionately as shorter vessels. And where was the proper place in long ships for the dead flat (midship section) to be placed? Examining figure 1.2, a redrawing of the sheer plan of the *Constellation,* the reader will observe that Humphreys located the ship's dead flat on the keel, straight rabbet, two-thirds the distance, plus 3 feet by $5^3/4$ inches, forward of the stern post, and therefore, less than one-third abaft the forward rabbet of the keel. Checking the comparable position of the dead flat of the *Hassan Bashaw,* a gun brigantine, modeled on the pilot schooner plan and drafted by Samuel Humphreys, the location of the dead flat is approximately one-third the distance abaft the rabbet of the keel. With maximum breadth well forward of the center line of the hull, a broad full bow, raked below the waterline, the frigate and the brigantine's hull taper through long runs and fine after-sections. The similar position of the dead flat of the two warships confirms the existence of a naval architectural relationship between the pilot schooner model, *Hassan Bashaw,* and *Constellation.*[55]

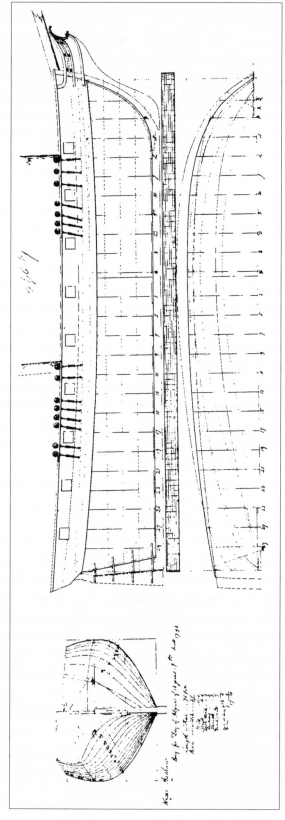

Figure 1.3. Gun brigantine *Hassan Bashaw*, drafted and built by Samuel Humphreys, Philadelphia Navy Yard, 1798. *John Lenthall Collection, Franklin Institute*

2. Fox questioned Humphreys' designed deadrise for the frigates, that is, the rise of the bottom of the hull above the horizontal. He thought it excessive. Humphreys' original plan for the 44-gun ships specified deadrise of 3 feet at a line two-thirds out from the centerline of the half body section at the dead flat. According to the working draft of the *Constellation* prepared by William Doughty, Humphreys set her deadrise at 2 feet, 7¹/₂ inches. This forms an angle of approximately 22 degrees above the horizontal. *Hassan Bashaw*'s angle of deadrise measured approximately 25 degrees. It may be observed that the significant deadrise of both vessels is firm at the turn of the bilges, an additional feature of Chesapeake Bay pilot schooners. The similarities in the manner that the Humphreys, father and son, treated the lower portion of the hulls of *Hassan Bashaw* and *Constellation* may be observed in the brigantine's plan and in figure 1.3, a drawing of *Constellation*'s half-body midship section (fig. 1.4). In all models, including the pilot schooner, the treatment of deadrise was similar.[56]

3. The third question raised by Fox concerning Humphreys' design dealt with the position of the wales, a component relating to hull strength, not speed, and therefore not pertinent to an analysis of the source of Humphreys' inspiration or influence in drafting fast ship-frigates. If Fox referred to the position of the wales in relation to the height of the extreme breadth line above the base line, then this is a circumstance of naval architecture affecting *Constellation*'s design. Humphreys' specifications stated that the height of the line "is the upper edge of the second wale from below," which he fixed at 21 feet above the base line at the stem and 24 feet 7¹/₄ inches above the base line at the transom. The difference in the two measurements, 2 feet 4³/₄ inches, is the amount of drag that Humphreys designed for his frigates. The drag of the keel from bow to stern is an important characteristic of the pilot schooner model affecting leeway, maneuverability, and weatherliness.

4. Fox questioned the proportional relationship between the depth of hold of Humphreys' frigates and their breadth, a relationship that could affect stability and vessel speed. Fox's objection directed attention to the weight of armament that the smaller class of ship-frigates could carry and still remain stable under various weather conditions. He expressed doubt that ships like *Constellation* had the breadth to avoid being crank under certain sailing conditions. While Fox's criticism proved to have merit, particularly in *Constellation*'s case during the period her main battery consisted of 24-pounders, nevertheless, her performance under various conditions identified her as a fast ship. Neither *Constellation*'s nor *Hassan Bashaw*'s drafts (nor their performance under sail as gun platforms) can be compared with small pilot schooners with different missions at sea. Still it is safe to conclude that when Humphreys drafted the frigates for speed, having less beam in relation to other dimensions would be one of his naval architectural compromises. Fox's fears played out in John Lenthall's analysis fifty years later, when the navy constructor informed the secretary of the navy that insufficient displacement contributed to *Constellation*'s chronic instability. One

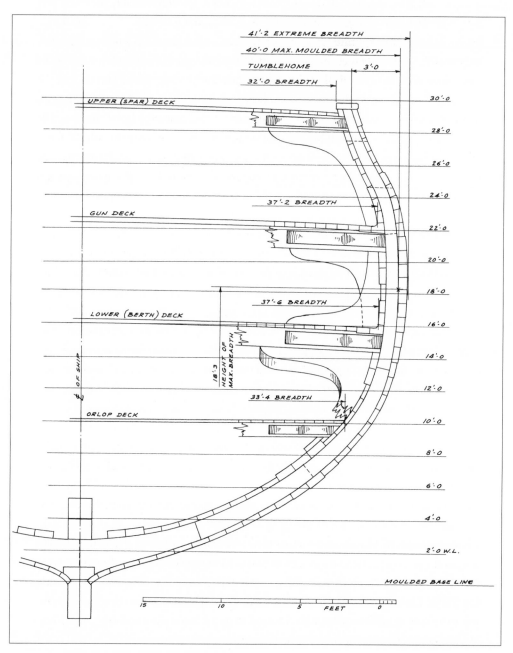

41'·2 EXTREME BREADTH

40'·0 MAX. MOULDED BREADTH

TUMBLEHOME

3'·0

32'·0 BREADTH

UPPER (SPAR) DECK

30'·0

28'·0

26'·0

24'·0

37'·2 BREADTH

GUN DECK

22'·0

20'·0

18'·0

37'·6 BREADTH

LOWER (BERTH) DECK

16'·0

14'·0

16'·3 HEIGHT OF MAX. BREADTH

℄ OF SHIP

33'·4 BREADTH

12'·0

ORLOP DECK

10'·0

8'·0

6'·0

4'·0

2'·0 W.L.

MOULDED BASE LINE

15   10   5   FEET   0

Figure 1.4. USF *Constellation*'s midship section, drawn in accordance with J. Humphreys' specifications, 1795. *William L. Crothers*

can conclude, therefore, that in this aspect of her design, the ship's stability problems may have originated from the same source as those of pilot schooners.[57]

5. Fox suggested to Knox that Humphreys drafted the ship-frigates too long—presumably he meant in relation to their breadth. Length is the dimension particularly associated with speed. *Constellation* measured 163 feet 7 inches at the level of the gun deck under the congressional method of measure of length overall for a multideck ship, that is, a straight line measure from the rabbet of the stem to the forward edge of the post. The ship-frigate's extreme molded breadth was 40 feet and her maximum breadth 41 feet 2 inches. Humphreys set length of keel for tonnage at 136 feet. To repeat, *Hassan Bashaw* measured 93 feet 2 inches by 27 feet by 11 feet 6 inches. The long hulls of the two warships included a significant amount of rake to the bows and some rake at the post.

   Both brigantine and ship-frigate had keels that dragged, which caused their hulls to be deeper aft than forward. Hulls tapered abaft dead flat sections placed well forward on the keel, to concave-shaped after-sections. These characteristics, including long length, all duplicated in the drafts of pilot schooners, provided Humphreys' warships with speed but also made them less stable than Royal Navy gun platforms that Fox worked on prior to emigrating to America.[58]

6. Fox directed attention to the fact that he believed Humphreys' draft made the frigates' fore body and after body disproportionate to each other. He suggested that buoyancy was distributed improperly, that even with a broad full bow Humphreys' model, with extreme beam far forward, and cutaway rake in the bow, lacked sufficient buoyancy forward. The "cod's head and mackerel tail" hull shape represented the current limit of naval architecture advance in 1800, and while affecting vessel speed at upper levels in heavy weather because of wake wave resistance created by the shape, it represented current thought. During the nineteenth century, as the body of knowledge on the effects of water friction and wave drag increased, naval architects moved the dead flat section aft closer to midship and abandoned the full bow in favor of the sharper clipper ship bow. Like Truxtun, Fox probably objected to the lack of storage space created by Humphreys' model. The pilot schooner design, with less wetted surface, increased vessel speed compared to bulkier contemporary vessels, particularly in lighter winds. With this knowledge of regional craft, Humphreys realized his goal of drafting and building faster ship-frigates under certain conditions. Later, John Lenthall would redesign *Constellation* to lessen the effect of excessive wave drag at higher speeds with the modifications he introduced in 1853, representing advances in naval architectural science over the previous fifty years.[59]

Secretary Knox's advisory group did not accept Fox's objections. The degree of attention his changes received and their effect on the final version of Humphreys' draft may be judged to be unimportant, just as Humphreys claimed. Humphreys did reduce the dimension for the keel of the 44-gun ship-frigate from 147 feet to 145 feet and made an increase in depth of hold and perhaps other adjustments. Overall, the modifications proved to be slight and gave Fox no justification for claiming authorship of the ship-frigates' draft.

Fox bounced back quickly and when Knox left office in 1794 he commenced a campaign to convince the new secretary of war, Timothy Pickering, of the indispensable value of his services. Pickering appointed him assistant naval constructor to replace shipwright Morgan, who would be assigned to Georgia to break the live oak timber jam.[60] Before Fox left Philadelphia for Gosport to work on *Chesapeake,* he hatched a plan that had as its goal displacing Humphreys as the arbitrator of questions, problems, and controversies originating with the builders and the supervising commanders, and particularly directed toward elevating Captain Truxtun to a position in which he could control the decision-making process at Stodder's yard. With his new standing with Pickering, Fox hoped to substitute himself for Humphreys and gain control of the frigate program. It was a bold plan shabbily executed. While the evidence does not reveal whether Truxtun was an informed participant, once Fox set his plan into motion, the self-serving commander fell in with it.[61]

On 2 April 1795, some weeks after Fox learned he would go to Hampton Roads, he sent Truxtun a letter telling of his meeting with an unidentified informer who claimed to have been in company with David Stodder and who quoted the builder as saying that he had seen the draft of the frigates, which he despised. Then, Fox alleged, Stodder told the informer that he knew how to draft and model the frigates much better than the persons employed by the secretary of war. The informant went on to say, according to Fox, that Stodder had revealed that he would not build the frigate at Baltimore to agree with either the draft or War Office instructions. Instead he would do just as he pleased and would not pay any attention to the molds or bevellings sent to him. And, he, Stodder, would refuse to obey directions from any person appointed to superintend *Constellation.*[62]

Truxtun immediately protested to Secretary Pickering and demanded that he receive authority over Stodder that would allow him to control construction of *Constellation.* This was an attempt to force a revision in the procedures requiring that in the future the naval constructor would comply with Captain Truxtun's orders. But despite a partiality to Fox that his letters show, Pickering could not be stampeded into changes that would have restricted Stodder's authority over construction and his direct access to Humphreys concerning modifications. The secretary ordered Stodder to follow the draft and specifications and to seek advice from the War Office for modifications, which as before would be forwarded to Humphreys. The Fox conspiracy failed.[63]

After the dust settled at Stodder's yard, Truxtun wrote Humphreys demanding that Stodder build the frigate according to the directions of the War Office. However, Fox made still another attempt to divert control from Humphreys over changes in the draft. The temporary replacement for Morgan at Gosport stopped over in Baltimore on his way to Hampton Roads. This produced a letter of protest from Humphreys, who wrote Pickering that he questioned the propriety of Fox calling at Baltimore with a letter of introduction. This letter, evidently originating with Pickering, stated that Fox should be contacted should they (Truxtun and Stodder) want information on any point respecting the molds or putting the frames together. From that time forward neither Truxtun nor Fox seemed to have interfered with Stodder or War Office procedures, though both Stodder and Truxtun suggested other modifications to Humphreys' draft and specifications.[64]

As spring passed into summer, ending the first year of construction, Stodder began to work on *Constellation*'s keel, having completed its foundation. Due to the great problems getting materials for six frigates collected, the War Office tried to direct materials into Baltimore and Philadelphia. This did not work well as too much material already filled the pipelines. In preparation for receiving additional live oak timber from Morgan in Georgia, Stodder made and forwarded him a set of molds for the 36-gun ship. Isaac Garretson replaced Hamilton as clerk of Stodder's yard. Later, the navy appointed Garretson purser of *Constellation* under Captain Truxtun and he stayed on to serve the navy many years.[65]

In September Pickering's office sent a hopeful letter to Congress that *Constellation*'s frame would soon be raised, but as it happened, Stodder did not requisition the three white oak logs for her keel until October. He continued this work through to the end of 1795, reporting to Pickering in December that he had completed *Constellation*'s keel on blocks, the three pieces scarfed and bolted together. In the same report to Congress Pickering laid out his difficulties acquiring live oak for six ships simultaneously; as a result, deliveries were being concentrated at Philadelphia and Baltimore. President Washington reported that negotiation with Algiers had been concluded successfully, placing the future of the frigate program in doubt. Rumors arriving in Baltimore from Philadelphia suggested that Washington would push Congress to authorize work to continue on three of the six frigates.[66]

Thomas Truxtun decided that his ship, *Constellation,* must be one of the three to be completed. He wrote Fox, who had returned to the War Department in Philadelphia, that to mount a successful campaign to accomplish his goal he would have to give up his commercial activities. The captain traded for his own account with two ships he owned outright, *Delaware* and *Friends Adventure.* After May 1795, he shared ownership in the snow *John and Joseph* with naval agents Joseph and Samuel Sterett and William Patterson, another merchant headquartered at Baltimore with extensive wharves and warehouses at Fells Point. He did not eliminate his interest in either *Friends Adventure* or *John and Joseph*.[67]

After Congress ratified the Algerine Treaty, the original 1794 act authorizing the ship-frigates became defunct and Washington suspended work at the yards 15 March 1796. As it happened, two weeks later Garretson received the first shipment of live oak timbers in twelve months. Truxtun, anxious to know the fate of *Constellation*, wrote Fox that they had just received a shipment of eighty-eight pieces of timber and forty hands were employed in the yard. Stodder lost a cargo of the precious timber in January when a vessel destined for his yard blew ashore on Martha's Vineyard. Congress passed the Act of 20 April 1796, which allowed the administration to complete ships at Philadelphia, Boston, and Baltimore, so work continued at Harris Creek without a break.[68]

The live oak timber jam seemed to break just as Congress reduced the number of ships under construction to three. Only a week after the arrival of a cargo in March, Captain Goodwin's and Captain Stodder's schooners arrived at the yard's dock with 202 pieces of live oak timber. Garretson received many cedar top timbers in April 1796. Following the arrival of another cargo of live oak in Capt. E. Stodder's schooner 30 June, which totaled 137 pieces, David Stodder wrote the War Office listing piece by piece the floor and futtock pieces still needed for the frame. His list included the numbers of eleven floor pieces, seven third futtocks on both sides of the frame, fifty-six stanchions, eight counter timbers, ten breast hooks, two cant top timbers, and one stemson piece needed. The War Office dispatched Fox to the closed-down yards to gather up pieces of live oak and get them transported to Harris Creek. In July Garretson received fifty-seven pieces, in August he received additional shipments of five, seventeen, and sixty-eight pieces, and finally, in September, another small shipment consisting of five pieces, which may have completed Stodder's needs for *Constellation*'s frame. The smaller shipments probably came to Baltimore from the closed yards.[69]

Through the summer and fall of 1796, as the live oak timber flowed into Baltimore from Georgia and the closed yards, activity by all classes of artisans increased. Rum requisitions, though not a precise measure of yard activity, jumped to over a hundred gallons per allocation. John Weaver, the lead blockmaker of 9 Fell Street, working on blocks for ship's rigging with James Hardy of 44 Alisanna Street of Fells Point, began work on her rigging, making lines out of cordage made at William Smith's ropewalk, adjacent to the yard. John Leahy of Triplet's Alley, Fells Point, a cooper, was at work on the ship's tanks and casks. William Jacobs, dean of local sailmakers, began to requisition bolts of sailcloth from the yard clerk, Garretson, during the spring and summer months. Silas Engle built *Constellation*'s boats; Garretson received three of them—a long boat, pinnace, and jolly boat—in December 1796. For the first time, after the passage of two years, yard employment peaked. The yard had received most of the necessary materials. With *Constellation*'s guns ready for inspection, Stodder promised delivery during the month of May 1797.[70]

James McHenry, who served as Washington's last of three secretaries of war, was the president's fourth choice for the position after he elevated Pickering to secretary of state. His contemporaries judged him incompetent, which may be one of the reasons that Josiah Fox returned to the War Office; his management of the Gosport Yard had lasted less than one year when Congress decided that construction on *Chesapeake* would be curtailed. During the summer of 1796 Fox traveled to the three northern yards directing and redirecting live oak timber as an expeditor. Though Truxtun and McHenry exhibited concern and impatience with Stodder, the building of *Constellation* moved forward toward a launch date. Truxtun, never able to keep from interfering, convinced McHenry that Humphreys' revolutionary strengthening members, called diagonal riders, were unwarranted, and received the secretary's permission to leave them out of *Constellation*. Truxtun reasoned that her sharp, narrow hull, already providing limited storage space, would carry less than four months' provisions with the riders installed.[71]

A cold winter in 1797 slowed work at the navy yard. In January, Jacobs, the sailmaker, requisitioned 10,249 yards of sailcloth from Garretson as Stodder and his carpenters worked on her main deck knees, clamps, and deck beams while others fastened *Constellation*'s lower deck planks. Congressman Parker reported to the House of Representatives that bad weather would delay *Constitution, United States,* and *Constellation* beyond the War Department's current target date, 1 May, despite McHenry's report to the contrary. Then Truxtun reported to McHenry in March that progress had been slow over the winter, and promised him a detailed report from Stodder in a few days, but he did not believe the ship would be ready before July. John Adams replaced George Washington as president. The nation moved toward confrontation with France.[72]

When Stodder did report on 20 April, he blamed slow deliveries of materials for the delay of *Constellation*'s launching date. He also blamed the naval agents for the high cost of the ship, writing that he could have furnished materials at least "100 percent" cheaper and saved greatly on labor, too, as he would have built the ship during the year's long days.[73] The harder McHenry pushed Truxtun and Stodder to get the ship ready, the more bad news he got. In May Truxtun reported that *Constellation* would not be launched before August. Truxtun endeavored to escape direct responsibility for delays, pointing out to the agitated secretary he was never satisfied with his "anomalous position"; even so he had by his conduct and independent spirit tried to bend the efforts of all concerned to building the best possible frigate in the shortest possible time. Then he reminded McHenry that he had told Knox in the beginning that no ship-frigates should be built south of Philadelphia. At the time Knox responded that they knew it would cost 25 percent more, but George Washington wanted to distribute the money throughout the Union.[74]

Stodder reported to the War Office 16 June that *Constellation* would be launched in July and ready to sail in August. McHenry passed this information to Congress along with the news that the ship's guns were tested and ready to be put aboard. The 24-pounders were cast at the Cecilton Furnace, but McHenry requisitioned the lighter 12-pounders for the ship from Fort Whetstone, situated at the entrance to Baltimore harbor. Then McHenry renamed the fort for himself. When the middle of August arrived with no launch, McHenry wrote bitterly about the delays. Finally, when a September date seemed firm, McHenry ordered Humphreys to Baltimore to supervise the launching.[75]

The *Telegraphie,* a newspaper published in Fells Point, reported several days before the launch in the matter-of-fact manner of a normal waterfront event that after three long years of delays, changes, mistakes, and worry, wind and weather and tide permitting, U.S. Frigate *Constellation* was to be launched 7 September.[76]

A gentleman from England visiting the yard wrote that he thought *Constellation* was encumbered with too much woodwork, but otherwise she was a fine vessel, built with beautiful wood, evergreen oak and cedar.[77] Joshua Humphreys selected William Rush, a Philadelphia artist, to sculpture the ship-frigates' figureheads and stern ornaments. For *Constellation*'s figurehead Rush carved a female head crested in fire with her waist encircled with the zone and signs of the zodiac, her hair and drapery loose and flowing, her right arm and head elevated, and her left arm resting lightly on a large sphere on which the constellation was rising. Her feet were on a rock, part of which Rush carved into a crude pyramid, allegorical of the rapid and natural union of the states. The center of the stern carving consisted of a large sphere with other carvings covering the completely flat surface of the ship's huge transom.[78]

Before departing for the navy yard early on the morning of 7 September, the day of the launching, Captain Truxtun took a heavy dose of calomel pills to keep his bowels open. From prior experience he knew it would prove a somber day as a yellow fever epidemic spread through Fells Point, held aloft by the late summer's hot, humid air, which hung like a curtain of death over the Point and Baltimore. At nine o'clock, two hundred laborers formed squads along the length of the ways upon which *Constellation*'s keel rested on blocks. A crowd gathered outside the yard upon a hill just to the east of the navy yard. Other family groups gathered on the Patapsco River in various commercial craft, oyster boats, and rowboats, too frightened, because of the epidemic, to draw close to a neighbor's craft, too curious, in this port town, to stay away.[79]

Armed guards kept everyone out of the yard. The accounts of the day mention no visiting dignitaries. The workman began to pound in wedges, lifting the ship's keel to free the blocks upon which it rested. The *Federal Gazette* reported that everything being complete, all the blocks now removed and every man out from under the ship, with her hull standing on almost nothing but the slippery tallow, an order was given to knock away the last stanchion. In silence, *Constellation* moved slowly down her ways and came to rest a mere one hundred yards from shore. Only then did the crowd break its silence with a resounding cheer.[80]

Two

A WARSHIP OF A DIFFERENT MODEL

$\mathscr{U}$. S. Frigate *Constellation* entered life afloat on 7 September 1797. As it happened, when the Boston Navy Yard launched *Constitution* on 21 October, both the *United States* and *Constellation* had preceded her launch, Humphreys having been first with *United States* on 10 May.[1] With James McHenry in charge of the War Office, it had been a hurry up and wait situation as he placed *Constellation* in ordinary after ordering builder Stodder to finish fitting her out in the fall of 1797 as quickly as possible. Stodder, Captain Truxtun, and others composing an inspection team warned McHenry that as the ship rested on her bottom at the navy yard wharf at low tide they feared that damage could occur.[2] McHenry reported to Congress on 26 December of *Constellation*'s readiness to leave the Patapsco River.[3]

Following that long-awaited announcement, Congress launched an inevitable investigation into the cost of *Constellation.* The unfortunate McHenry had the job of explaining why the smaller frigate required three years to build and why she cost more than the other ship-frigates built despite her smaller size. The secretary emphasized in his report to Congress that the costs of all the ships rose because the government wanted each built at a different port; in addition, Congress's decision to build two models added further to the cost, he claimed. McHenry recited all of the problems and extra costs that developed because of decisions made to use a large proportion of live oak in *Constellation*'s frame and hull. He reported the loss of two shiploads of live oak at sea and the resultant difficulties and additional cost of molding frame timber and other live oak pieces for the smaller ship from timber originally cut for larger frigates. McHenry estimated that up to 40 percent of the live oak shipped to the navy yard at Harris Creek proved to be larger than the molds made for the model. As a result of these problems *Constellation*'s frame (pieces) did not all get into the yard until October 1796. McHenry closed the report by reminding Congress that extreme weather during the winter of 1797 and yellow fever in September and October further delayed completion of *Constellation.*[4] In the meantime, McHenry ordered Captain Truxtun back to his ship to take her out of ordinary and into deeper water. Of greater importance to Truxtun, the secretary ordered him to take aboard her cannon and provisions and make arrangements for shipping a crew. [5]

McHenry forwarded a copy of his report prepared for Livingston along with other documents concerning the investigation of *Constellation* to Truxtun, which produced a long response from the captain. Since one of the subjects of Livingston's critical inquiry covered the high cost of building *Constellation* under Truxtun's supervision, the captain's letter summarized his frustrations, his personal sacrifices, the mistakes of others, and the impotent position imposed on him by the procedures originally set up by Secretary Knox, which he protested but failed to have amended when Secretary Pickering replaced the general in 1795. This part of the captain's defense referred to the Fox-Truxtun conspiracy to give him authority to control the project by subjecting the naval agents and David Stodder to his orders.

After reminding all yet again of his warning to Knox in 1794 that a ship-frigate should not be built at Fells Point, Truxtun complained in his defense to McHenry that he found prices of local materials exorbitant, laborers and artificers indolent, and that the builder, Stodder, since it would be his last ship, made the most of it. Truxtun, always on the attack in his defense, wrote that he quickly became disgusted with everyone engaged in the business. He closed this tirade to McHenry with the sly comment that perhaps he had been fortunate that Pickering never gave him the authority he had requested in April 1795. Truxtun's self-serving letter claimed that he saved the government thousands of dollars and never touched a shilling of public money or derived any advantage from the building of the ship. He pointed out that he sacrificed money and time attending to the ship over almost four years, not as commander, but "as a director to the arrangements for the Carpenters, Rigger, Joiner and every other tradesmen, for they were alike ignorant of such business, though otherwise good workmen." (It is not easy to interpret this statement as Truxtun had no authority over hiring workmen or selecting tradesmen, and also claimed that he never took any public money.) He closed the letter to McHenry by blasting the naval agents Joseph and Samuel Sterett for their mishandling of purchasing and accounting as well for setting up poor controls over the materials held at the navy yard. In a letter denying any responsibility in the shipyard, Capt. Thomas Truxtun protested too much and against all, except Josiah Fox, with whom he kept his close association. [6]

Suddenly, everyone's attention was diverted as President Adams ordered mobilization of the navy. A bill creating a separate Navy Department cleared Congress

30 April 1798. As the administration searched for the department's first secretary of the navy, the highly criticized McHenry leaned heavily on Alexander Hamilton, still treasury secretary, for guidance as he faced the formidable task of getting the country's small fleet provisioned, crewed, and to sea while waiting for a navy secretary to accept the new office.[7] Finally, with a newly organized department managed by a savvy secretary, Benjamin Stoddert, serving a new president who seemed more eager than his predecessor, George Washington, to choose sides, John Adams moved the young nation toward an undeclared war against its former ally, France, and into an inevitable alliance with its former master, England. To many it seemed as if the world had turned upside down. When President Adams decided to move against French armed corsairs, USF *Constellation*, with the ever-complaining Captain Truxtun in command, became the first of Mr. Humphreys' frigates commissioned and to put to sea. After preliminary sea trials inside Chesapeake Bay, Captain Truxtun in *Constellation* stood out of Hampton Roads 26 June 1798. His ship was the second United States Navy vessel to reach the open sea, USS *Ganges*, a converted merchant ship under the command of Richard Dale, having already reached her assigned patrol grounds off Delaware Bay when *Constellation* cleared Cape Henry. Truxtun noted in his journal on 2 July that he had that day hailed a Boston schooner and learned that USF *Constitution* would not be at sea before two weeks.[8]

Truxtun reported before departing Norfolk that *Constellation* went through the water with great swiftness down Chesapeake Bay, but he had been shocked to discover on departure from the Patapsco River that her draft exceeded 22 feet. He would not be able to clear Charleston's bar and enter that harbor, or any other one south of Chesapeake Bay.[9] His orders, signed by Benjamin Stoddert, the nation's first secretary of the navy, covered this first cruise, which would be a coastwise run from Cape Henry to a position off Charleston, as at that time national policy toward France was limited to driving the country's corsairs off the coast of the United States.[10]

Truxtun and his ship received their first real test on the Fourth of July as *Constellation* ran into an Atlantic hurricane. Winds began to blow on 3 July and increased after meridian, continuing to blow harder through the night as Truxtun took in her sails one by one. At 8:00 A.M., with the winds now blowing violently from the north and at full hurricane force, *Constellation* ran before the storm on bare poles. Truxtun noted that his ship took in much water. He attributed the leaks to faulty caulking, rather than to alterations in the ship's specifications that he insisted on having done at Stodder's navy yard.

Truxtun's demands to McHenry, who was totally unaware of the effect of his acquiescence to the captain, had resulted in orders to Humphreys to allow substitution of oak beams and decks as replacement for pitch pine and to the elimination of innovative diagonal riders. The combination of pine beams and diagonal riders would have provided *Constellation*'s forward end with greater durability, strength, and resiliency under all weather conditions. By not adhering to Humphreys' specifications, *Constellation*'s decks, under strain in a pounding sea, now opened, allowing water to seep into her lower decks and hold.[11] Once at Charleston, Truxtun reported back to the War Office (evidently still unaware that Stoddert headed a new Navy Department) that the cruise down from Hampton Roads proved that *Constellation* behaved well in all sorts of weather and sailed fast, though he did add that his ship needed caulking.[12] His mail caught up with him there: he received word from Stoddert that Congress had extended the limits of the navy's cruising area and his next cruise would be to convoy American merchant ships to Havana.[13]

Captain Truxtun in *Constellation* returned to Hampton Roads on 15 August from his first cruise, which he considered a sea trial.[14] He had commenced complaining about his ship as soon as she hit the water. He felt strongly that Humphreys' faulty draft placed *Constellation*'s point of extreme breadth (the dead flat section) too far forward and that this caused an unusual disparity between her draft forward, which he measured following her launch at 13 feet 3 inches forward and 18 feet 6 inches aft. This mistake in design, according to Truxtun, gave *Constellation* and the larger frigates a depth of draft too great to enter most East Coast ports. Also, he pointed out that he found it necessary to place her ballast far forward in the ship to gain proper sailing trim.

Contemporaries claimed that *Constellation* had a problem shared by no other Humphreys frigate regardless of size: her draft of water exceeded 22 feet and equaled that of the larger frigates. Actually, Captain Murray recorded that she drew 22 feet 6 inches, the same as U.S. Frigate *United States*. Truxtun lamented the practical supply problems of so sharp a ship; more important, though, her extreme draft confirmed the presence of an architectural or construction variance of the Fells Point–built ship from the other ship-frigates. Had *Constellation*'s sharp and raked bow, substantial deadrise, and extreme breadth well forward in the ship as drafted by Humphreys and built by Stodder produced a ship that compromised her stability so much that she would never satisfy the requirements of a naval ship? The answer to this question is complicated by the subjective nature of much of the testimony on record.[15]

Captain Truxtun did not complain about his ship's speed. Like a child, he mixed his cries of dissatisfaction with shouts of pride as he related the virtues of his ship to Secretary Stoddert. Though he grumbled about *Constellation* being so sharp she could carry no more than four months of provisions, he could not contain his enthusiasm for her speed. He was surprised that she took so little ballast compared to British and French frigates. The 36-gun ships of those nations averaged three hundred tons less but had greater breadth relative to *Constellation* and could not be compared to her. He modestly wrote Stoddert that there had been so much bragging by the commanders of *United States* and *Constitution* that he hesitated to report on the sailing performance of *Constellation*. However, he managed to overcome his reluctance enough to say that "in no instance of chace [*sic,* chase] during the cruise was half our canvass necessary to overhaul the fastest sailing vessel we met," including (Baltimore) flyers, he claimed. Truxtun continued to brag that should he meet *United States* or *Constitution,* the secretary should not be surprised if he learned that *Constellation* outsailed them both. Then Truxtun gave his ship the ultimate compliment, informing Stoddert that *Constellation* was, in every situation, "the easiest ship I was ever in."[16]

In this same report to Stoddert made on his return to Hampton Roads, Truxtun pointed out that the ship needed a crew of 330 men to man her properly. The captain was thinking ahead to the number of men he would need to capture French armed vessels and to get the prize ships safely in port. With a view toward his ship's ability to fight an enemy successfully, he suggested to Stoddert that stability could be a problem because twenty-eight 24-pounders and the height of *Constellation's* fall masts—just 27 feet less than those found in an English 64-gun ship—resulted in a combined weight that could affect the fighting trim of his ship. The question raised by Truxtun's dialogue would be repeated over and over: Did Humphreys' draft and Stodder's method of construction produce unique problems for this ship, or did she carry too much weight too high, creating a reputation for being crank that stuck even after her guns and rig had been reduced in weight and size?[17]

In September 1799, several months after *Constellation* fought and captured the French frigate *l'Insurgente,* James Buchanan, a Baltimore ship owner, observed USS *Maryland,* a subscription ship built by Fells Point shipwright William Price for the United States Navy and then at anchor at Fells Point. He wrote Secretary of State Pickering that USS *Maryland's* design was flawed; the sloop of war's hull swam too low in the water, bringing her gun ports to the water's edge—"a fault that *Constellation* had in a great degree and indeed every American man of war I have yet seen which I am sorry for as it makes them always crank or tender or even dangerous either in a gale of wind or in a battle if there is any sea going or observing an enemy, compels [the American ships] to fight their lee guns."[18]

Buchanan's remarks provide substance to Dr. Dunne's thesis that Stodder built *Constellation* with particularly fine lines at her ends and greater deadrise, which resulted in a warship with an uncommonly sharp hull.[19] Buchanan's comments referring to Truxtun's problems fighting *l'Insurgente* during a gale and centered on his concern with *Constellation's* deep draft aft suggest, too, that Stodder laid her keel in a manner that caused it to drag downward from bow to stern in excess of lines of Humphreys' draft, with the result that the ship sat too low in the water when fully provisioned and in trim. *Constellation's* relatively limited breadth and depth in comparison to her length, a characteristic noted by Truxtun, Buchanan, and other contemporary observers, provides credence to the conclusion that Humphreys' choice of naval architectural elements enumerated as objectionable by Fox not only survived as drafted by Humphreys but may have been exaggerated by David Stodder in the course of building the ship under the prevailing conditions at his navy yard.

Though the Federalist administration of John Adams publicly attributed the decision to break off diplomatic relations with France in 1798 to the infamous XYZ affair, the real reasons for the growing hostility between the two former allies grew out of implementation of the terms of the Jay Treaty, which France interpreted as a commercial alliance between England and the United States. At the same time, much of the American good feeling toward its fellow republic dissipated as France mounted an intense *course de guerre* by her privateers and navy ships against American vessels, particularly in the West Indies carrying trade. America's bellicose attitude increased as the number of frigates and other ships built or acquired expanded the country's naval force until it exceeded the number of French navy ships in the West Indies in 1799, the Royal Navy having previously taken control of the region's seas. By the middle of October 1798, three Humphreys frigates and five converted merchant ships (*Ganges,* the sixth conversion, had been taken out of naval service for repairs) entered naval service. Secretary Stoddert supplemented this force with five revenue cutters.[20] In one of the classic errors of American naval history, Stoddert pushed for additional frigates and other large navy ships, though they proved too slow to overhaul French privateer schooners, now over two hundred tons in burden and able to point to windward so well that square-rigged ships soon dropped under the horizon in a chase. Even Truxtun recognized the need to take armed Baltimore schooners into the United States Navy to successfully chase down French privateer schooners, many of which had also been built on Chesapeake Bay.[21]

After *United States* (Barry) and *Constitution* (Nicholson) joined *Constellation* and French privateers withdrew from American coastal waters, Stoddert ordered Truxtun to take *Constellation* into the Caribbean Sea with a convoy destined for the Spanish colony of Cuba. The secretary notified Truxtun that Baltimore merchants had a large amount of specie at Havana which he was authorized to transport back to America as naval freight. This consignment may have been the first specie carried by a United States Navy ship, and though reports do not mention a fee, Truxtun most certainly received his first monetary commission as a commander as he was bound to follow precedent set by officers of the Royal Navy, who retained for their benefit this perk of command. *Constellation* convoyed fifteen American merchant vessels to Havana and returned to American coastal waters with a fleet of forty-five American vessels, though storms separated the fleet before the ships reached their destinations. *Constellation* anchored off the Tail of the Shoe in Hampton Roads 25 October in ten fathoms.[22]

Truxtun's previous reports to Stoddert stated that no French corsairs cruised in American waters, and upon his return from Cuba he notified the secretary that French privateer operations around that island proved to be insignificant and could be handled by a schooner and a brig. Stoddert responded with the news that *Constellation* could expect new orders shortly that would take her to the West Indies. This expansion of naval operations would force the navy to form into squadrons and set up supply bases to support their operations, cut off as they would be from the mainland of the United States. Among the naval vessels assigned to Truxtun's squadron was USS *Retaliation,* the former French privateer schooner of the Baltimore model. Commodore Truxtun chose Basseterre Roads at St. Kitts as his base for the ships assigned to him. He arrived off St. Kitts on 18 January 1799.

Once in the West Indies, the wily captain assigned his squadron to convoy duty as he concentrated on training his crew to prepare his ship to take any rich prizes that he could flush out in the game of hide and seek that was bound to follow. Stoddert had notified him of an intelligence report locating one or more French frigates at Guadeloupe. The secretary suggested that Truxtun may have reason to join up with Captain Barry in *United States,* but Truxtun had no intention of sharing his prizes with another commodore.[23]

British colonial administrators at St. Kitts incorrectly reported to Truxtun that the French frigate *l'Insurgente* had returned to France, when actually the ship, under command of Citizen Capt. Michel Pierre Barreaut, had recently completed a three-month cruise and returned to her base at Guadeloupe. Barreaut captured five merchant ships during the course of that cruise. When *Constellation* sighted *l'Insurgente* sailing east of the island of Nevis on a northwesterly course at meridian, 9 February, the French frigate's current cruise had commenced the previous day. Barreaut's orders, issued by Gen. Étienne Desfourneaux, administrator for the Republic of France at Guadeloupe, instructed him to pursue merchant ships belonging to the enemies of France, including privateers and other armed vessels, but to avoid all ships of superior or equal armament. He instructed Barreaut to cruise in *l'Insurgente* in an area from St. Croix to the east of Barbados, waters through which British ships traveled to make landfall on voyages from Europe.

Desfourneaux specifically warned him to avoid warships of equal or larger size. Barreaut claimed after his battle with *Constellation* that General Desfourneaux also ordered him not to fire on American warships. *L'Insurgente,* reputed to be a fast sailer, arrived from France in the fall of 1798, most likely after an overhaul there. Several months later, at the time of the engagement with *Constellation,* her condition may be presumed to have been good, since Truxtun placed her in his squadron at St. Kitts after making battle repairs.[24]

Commodore Truxtun, having established a base, dispatched his other ships with a convoy for North America in early February 1799. Then he sailed *Constellation* to Guadeloupe where he stood off the harbor at Basse Terre and challenged a French frigate and a corvette to come out. Though Secretary Stoddert's orders could be interpreted as ambiguous since they never instructed his captains to seek and destroy French navy ships, the secretary did authorize action against French naval ships in his more informal communications with Truxtun. Previous to his arrival off the French island, Stoddert informed Truxtun that he had intelligence concerning the arrival of the French ships and suggested that he join up with Captain Barry's squadron if a situation developed. Then the secretary coyly suggested that it would be glorious if Truxtun captured a frigate. When *Constellation*'s provocative challenge received no response, Truxtun sailed north to Barbuda searching for French privateers.[25]

Prior to meridian on the morning of 9 February, with the island of Nevis about fifteen to eighteen miles ahead on the far horizon, Truxtun set *Constellation* on a southwesterly course to pass south of that island and into Basseterre Roads at St. Kitts, her base. At meridian, a lookout reported a large ship to westward. *Constellation* made chase. Truxtun wrote in his journal that the weather on the ninth and tenth of February was unsettled and with squalls as his ship plowed through head seas, though the wind blew from the east. Running free, Truxtun altered course to head off the unidentified warship, which he judged to be on a northerly course with a distance of about nine miles separating the two ships.[26]

When Captain Barreaut's lookout picked up *Constellation*'s sails on the horizon at 12:30, 9 February, meridian time, he had *l'Insurgente* on a course of north-north-east with *Constellation* to windward, bearing northeast of his ship. After a half-hour, with the unidentified ship closing, the French captain ordered his helmsman to fall off to the west to pass between St. Kitts and the island of Saba. Captain Barreaut was inclined to flee as he ordered the helm to come up on a course for St. Eustatius, the Dutch free port of haven. There followed a period of trepidation on board *l'Insurgente* as Barreaut hesitated between running for the neutral port or clearing his ship for action. Though General Desfourneaux's orders admonished him to avoid the risk of losing his ship to one of larger or even equal armament, Barreaut claimed later in his report of the battle that he mistook *Constellation* as a British corvette or sloop of war. But as the French captain also reported disagreements among the ship's officers concerning the proper course of action, indecision appears to have prevailed aboard the French ship.

Barreaut testified at an inquiry conducted at Lorient in the autumn of 1799 that Desfourneaux ordered him not to fire on American warships. But he admitted that as he dealt with his ship's options, his indecision concerning the flag and size of the oncoming ship contributed to the confusion. After a delay, he ordered his officers to maneuver *l'Insurgente* into a position to challenge *Constellation,* which was now overhauling him, both ships under full sail in gale force winds. Following a series of false signals, Barreaut identified *l'Insurgente* as French but claimed at his trial that while the approaching ship flew the American flag, hoisted after other signals went unanswered, Truxtun never confirmed the identity of his ship by firing a gun to windward. Certainly Barreaut played directly into Truxtun's plan to attack, which never wavered as *Constellation* bore down on the French ship.[27]

After about a half an hour of the chase, Captain Barreaut worked his ship up to windward. Now sailing on the starboard tack, close hauled, he attempted to stay above the onrushing *Constellation.* Truxtun correctly interpreted the French frigate's maneuver as aggressive. At 1:30 P.M., Truxtun cleared his ship for action. At about that time a squall hit the ships and carried away *l'Insurgente*'s top mainmast as her crew worked to take in the frigate's topgallant sails. She bore away before the wind as the crew worked to clear her decks of debris, setting a course toward St. Eustatius once again. First fleeing *Constellation,* then changing course once again, Barreaut seemed bewildered as he made contradictory maneuvers, some evidently in deference to his junior officers.

Though it did not seem he could possibly fail to understand Truxtun's intent, Barreaut neither opened fire with his two long 18-pound stern guns nor did he continue to flee. Inexplicably, the French commander ordered his ship hauled up again on the wind to a heading north-northeast, which brought *l'Insurgente* up on a starboard tack once again and fully exposed to take the onrushing *Constellation*'s broadside. Truxtun had his frigate, a new ship with a well drilled crew, fine-tuned for battle. The sparse record makes uncertain an answer concerning *l'Insurgente*'s preparedness, condition, and readiness for battle as well as the morale of her officers and crew. Without a doubt, however, Captain Barreaut displayed a lack of resourcefulness which affected his ability to command.[28]

Thoughtful contemporary politicians would probably have concluded that the French captain erred by not surrendering his ship to Truxtun and let the legal challenges be sorted out in admiralty court, procedures that France and Great Britain followed when they took neutral ships into custody for possible infractions of contraband laws. It should be borne in mind that the nations involved had not declared war and neither commander had specific orders to attack each other's national ships.

The secretary of the navy's orders to Truxtun covering his second cruise escalated the undeclared war by placing the U.S. Navy in the West Indies war zone. Stoddert allowed his navy ships to "fall in with French cruisers" and to conduct active operations for "the protection of our commerce, and for the capture or destruction of French armed vessels." His orders reflected the decision of the Adams administration not to declare war and to limit American action to French armed ships. In this manner, the Adams administration hoped to place the action against France's armed cruisers on firm ground because French privateers, not French navy ships, captured hundreds of American merchant vessels between 1795 and 1798. Truxtun's attack on *l'Insurgente* swept away the hypocrisies of the Adams administration's foreign policy, exposing it as a policy of appeasement toward England.[29]

That President Adams decided to carry the war to the crippled French colonies to placate the Royal Navy and thereby protect New England's commerce with England has strong logic. At the very least, since the U.S. Navy did not take similar action against the Royal Navy and British privateers, also active against the American merchant vessels, the American government held itself open to the charge of supporting a policy toward Great Britain in the hope that it would foster stability in its transatlantic trade to Britain and with the neutral nations of Europe to the detriment of France. Stoddert bolstered this policy by issuing orders to American commanders that admonished them not to protect American commercial vessels from capture by the British; the legitimacy of that action would be determined by British admiralty courts. Commodore Truxtun, by design or by chance, became the com-

USF *Constellation* chasing French frigate *l'Insurgente* west of St. Kitts, 9 February 1799. Original engraving by E. Savage. *Naval Historical Foundation*

mander best suited to forge an alliance with the Royal Navy by unleashing his aggressions on the remnants of the French navy in the West Indies, already decimated by the British fleet. While the British thanked him and presented the victorious American captain with a medal, they never treated the United States Navy as an ally in its Quasi War with France.[30]

Truxtun does not mention in his journal when he realized that he had *l'Insurgente* in his grasp, yet it is known that he marked this ship for special attention and had previously registered disappointment when he heard she had returned to France. At the beginning of the frigate-building program, President Washington appointed Capt. Joshua Barney, second to John Paul Jones in fame for his Revolutionary War exploits, senior to Truxtun when he selected the original captains to command America's first frigates; Barney would be commander of *Constitution* and Truxtun, the last captain on the seniority list, received *Constellation*. For complex reasons, which are not part of this story, Barney declined the presidential appointment and proceeded to France in July 1794 to collect moneys owed him by the French government for commercial shipments of grain and flour. During the years leading up to the undeclared war between the United States and France, Barney, like many other mariners and anti-Federalists, hated the Royal Navy and favored the French cause when war between the two great European powers broke out once again in 1793.[31]

Forced to linger in France in near bankruptcy as the French government delayed payments of its debts, Barney recouped his finances by owning and operating privateer vessels based in France, their activities directed against British merchant ships in European waters. French friends as well as friends in the French republican government pushed Barney to accept a command in the French navy, which would offer him an opportunity to return to action against the Royal Navy. After the American Federalist administration negotiated and signed the Jay Treaty with England, the United States' relationship with France deteriorated. Barney detested the British. With the Federalists in control of the American government in 1796, Barney entered the French navy to fight the country that he considered America's real enemy—England.[32]

Because he was a sailor of fortune in the service of France, hired to fight the hated British, the Federalist Party in America began a campaign to label Barney a traitor. Given command of two French frigates, one new, named *La Harmonie,* and the other named *La Railleuse,* Barney sailed from Rochefort 28 May 1796 for St. Domingo to take charge of the country's naval forces there. The following fall a hurricane almost destroyed his frigates, but Barney managed to save both ships and get back to his base, Cap Français. He found the island population without food. Provided with two other frigates, *Medusa* and another named *l'Insurgente,* he departed for Chesapeake

Bay with only his good name and credit to offer in return for grain to feed the starving islanders. *L'Insurgente* needed repairs badly at that time and before he could load grain, the hero of the American Revolution arranged for the French frigates to be overhauled at Norfolk. Miraculously, the Marylander got his grain and eluded a British blockade of Chesapeake Bay, returning to St. Domingo in *l'Insurgente* with *Medusa* in company, both ships loaded with relief supplies.[33]

Prior to 1798, that is, before the Federalists decided to take aggressive action against the French in an undeclared war, the party's newspapers questioned Barney's patriotism. However, by the time President Adams authorized attacks on French armed vessels in June of that year, Barney had, in fact, returned to France and resigned from the French navy.[34] Truxtun associated a strike against *l'Insurgente* as a possible blow against Barney, so fractured had relations between Federalists and the pro-French Republican Party become. The party of Jefferson criticized the Jay Treaty as an alliance of convenience with England that brought America into a state of war against its former ally, France. When *Constellation* roared up on *l'Insurgente*'s stern the afternoon of 9 February 1799, Truxtun ignored Captain Barreaut's last-ditch effort to parley, leaving the commander of *Constellation* to ponder later: What if he found himself face to face with the renowned Joshua Barney, friend of Washington, Madison, Jefferson, and Monroe?[35]

Truxtun had another reason to refuse to parley with the captain of *l'Insurgente*. In November 1798 Captain Barreaut's ship arrived from France accompanied by the frigate *Volunteer,* carrying General Desfourneaux. Just off St. Kitts, *l'Insurgente* had fired on Lt. William Bainbridge in USS *Retaliation,* U.S. Navy schooner, forcing him to strike the American flag. *Retaliation* thus became the first national vessel lost by the young republic. Stoddert had previously assigned *Retaliation* to Truxtun's squadron, and Truxtun took her loss personally. The war escalated immediately after that event from one restricted to convoy duty for American merchant ships to orders from President Adams to fire on and capture armed French vessels. As Truxtun bore down on *l'Insurgente,* he sought revenge.[36]

Finally, prize money motivated Truxtun, once a privateer during the Revolutionary War, and he now prepared a naval attack on *l'Insurgente*. There would be reward money for commanders, officers, and crews of United States Navy ships under a prize system already in place. Such awards became navy practice immediately and were based on the size of navy vessels captured relative to the attacking vessel, plus the condition of each prize. Taken from Royal Navy practice, on which the rules and traditions of the early U.S. Navy were largely patterned, the system assured that huge bounties would accrue to American navy vessels for capturing enemy warships in addition to prize money received for capturing French armed private vessels. The amount received by each man would be determined by rank or rate.[37]

43

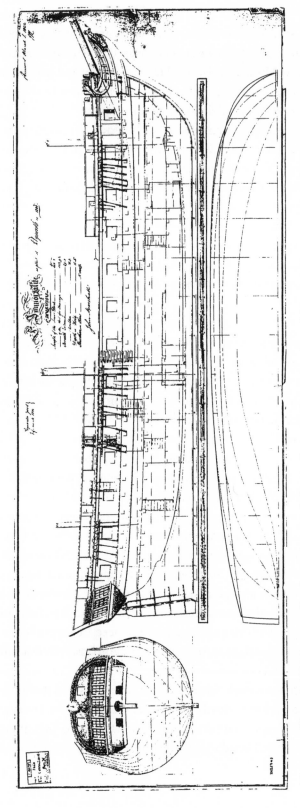

Figure 2.1. Plan of HMS *Immortalite*, formerly French frigate *l'Immortalite*, sister ship of *l'Insurgente*. Lines taken off at Plymouth in 1800 by John Mitchell. *National Maritime Museum*

The prize system, plus other perks of naval service such as carrying navy freight (specie), enriched lucky navy captains from the beginning of the navy until the Civil War. The hope of riches expressed later in his correspondence ran through Truxtun's mind as his ship prepared to fight *l'Insurgente.* It is doubtful that before his first battle, Truxtun mulled over the popular adulation that would follow victory or the political ramifications of a successful attack on a French frigate. During his life as a merchant captain and privateer, free of control but also unrewarded by fame, his mind-set going into battle against *l'Insurgente* probably stood closer to that of a pirate than to a patriot. Later, as a national hero, he demonstrated his lack of preparation for any role other than captain of a financially successful ship by his inability to handle fame.[38]

The French frigate was four years older than *Constellation,* yet when Capt. Joshua Barney commanded her in 1797, he found her badly in need of repairs. She returned to France in 1798 and presumably was overhauled before returning to the West Indies later that year with Captain Barreaut in command. Built by P. J. Penetreau at the port of Lorient, Brittany, in 1793, she entered service in 1794. *L'Insurgente*'s dimensions are available from three sources, all providing slightly different figures because each set represents a different nation's method of measuring ships.

The United States Navy, which purchased the ship from Captain Truxtun and *Constellation*'s crew, recorded her measurements as 147 feet 9 inches long at the level of the gun deck between stem and post. Her extreme breadth is listed in navy records as 37 feet 5 inches. French naval archives list *l'Insurgente*'s dimensions as 140 feet long and 35½ feet breadth, with no further explanations. The French measurements are very close to the American calculations, as the old French foot measured about 7 percent more than its English/American equivalent. The Royal Navy, which captured *l'Insurgente*'s sister ship, *Immortalite,* took off her lines at Plymouth in 1800, and recorded her dimensions of 145 feet 2 inches length and 39 feet 2 inches maximum breadth. French records list the two frigates, built at the same yard, as identical. Penetreau built *Immortalite* a year after *l'Insurgente.* There are no drawings of Truxtun's prize, but the plan of the British prize, *Immortalite,* is reproduced in figure 2.1.[39]

In dimensions, burden, and displacement, *Constellation* exceeded *l'Insurgente* in size. For instance, while the American frigate drew over 22 feet, fully provisioned and watered, the lighter French frigate drew about 14 feet. But the differences in firepower of the two ships illustrate the mismatch in which Barreaut found his ship engaged. At that time *Constellation*'s broadside consisted of twenty-eight 24-pounders and ten 12-pounders on her spar deck. *L'Insurgente* had two long 18-pound stern chasers, which Barreaut evidently never brought into action. His frigate's main broadside consisted of twenty-four 12-pounders, less than half the weight of Truxtun's gun deck battery. Though Truxtun later claimed that he had overwhelmed

45

a 40-gun frigate, the facts are that the combined weight of *l'Insurgente*'s guns totaled two-thirds of the weight of *Constellation*'s broadside.[40]

As the distance between the two ship decreased rapidly with the strong prevailing east wind blowing, Lady Luck carried the day for *Constellation*. There is little doubt that her heavy guns would vanquish the smaller ship, but gale conditions so hobbled the crank American ship that if the same gale had not taken out *l'Insurgente*'s main topmast, Truxtun may have experienced greater difficulty vanquishing his smaller foe.

At about 2:00 P.M., following the loss of *l'Insurgente*'s main topmast, the French frigate fell off the wind for a short interval to clear her deck of debris. Then, according to Lt. John Rodgers's report to the secretary of the navy, *l'Insurgente* hauled up within eight points of the wind on a starboard tack. Truxtun ordered his helmsmen to bring *Constellation* around too, but at about 3:00 P.M., with the wind blowing extremely hard and his ship heeling badly, Truxtun relinquished all efforts to gain the weather gage. In the gale winds, his ship's tall rig combined with the weight of her heavy guns caused *Constellation* to heel to such a degree that he could not bring his lee battery to bear on *l'Insurgente*. This problem could have made the difference between victory and defeat had Truxtun's opponent been equal in size and firepower. Truxtun ordered the helm to fall off to bring the ship up on the Frenchman's lee, which would allow Rodgers and his deck officers to work *Constellation*'s starboard guns. His decision to close under *l'Insurgente*'s lee would have proved a dangerous maneuver had the frigate not been so small and slow to respond following the loss of her topsails.[41]

Whatever Barreaut's final plan, he waited too long to execute it and now the horror of his position caused him to plead with Truxtun for a parley. Truxtun's privateer blood was on fire, and his lust for victory and its rewards caused him to ignore the French captain's shouts. *Constellation*'s commander ordered his lieutenants to direct their fire into *l'Insurgente*'s hull. Action commenced at 3:15 P.M., 9 February, meridian time, with a broadside from *Constellation*. *L'Insurgente* immediately answered Truxtun's with one of her own. Truxtun's guns wrought havoc to Barreaut's quarterdeck. The damage inflicted by the American frigate's guns and *l'Insurgente*'s loss of sails amidship allowed Truxtun to pour additional broadsides into the smaller ship and to rake her fore and aft. One well aimed shot entered the French ship through one of her stern ports, upsetting one large gun there, damaging the other, and killing eleven men. Barreaut fired three broadsides before he struck forty-five minutes later at 4:00 P.M., according to Lieutenant Rodgers, and at 4:30 P.M., according to Truxtun's report to the secretary of the navy.[42]

L'Insurgente suffered heavy casualties during the short battle: twenty-nine killed and forty-one wounded. A few days later, when Truxtun turned Captain Barreaut and his officers over to General Desfourneaux, the French administrator placed the defeated captain under arrest. In due time, he returned to Lorient and was ordered to face court-martial for the loss of his frigate. His officers testified against him, describing the captain's demeanor during the battle as that of a coward. That testimony apparently did not impress the court, however, because it acquitted Barreaut, though he never received another command at sea.

Truxtun reported insignificant casualties on board *Constellation.* Two men died, one when Lt. Andrew Sterett ran his sword through a crewman, Neil Harvey, for cowardice. Among the four wounded were Midn. James Macdonough, who lost a foot, a wound that ended his career; William Brown, a freeman of color from Fells Point, who enlisted in 1798, suffered a wound to the foot. He sailed as a powder monkey and remained aboard *Constellation* during her battle with *La Vengeance.*[43]

Without prior authority, Truxtun took his prize into the United States Navy and presented command of the frigate, now named *Insurgent,* to John Rodgers. Stoddert allowed the commodore some slack while *Constellation* and *Insurgent* remained in the West Indies. When the ships returned to Norfolk in June 1799, Stoddert relieved Rodgers but later gave him command of a new sloop of war, USS *Maryland.* When the ships arrived for repairs, Truxtun found himself a national hero. He pressured his friend, William Pennock, the naval agent, to set *l'Insurgente*'s value at $120,000, which the admiralty court at Norfolk accepted. Lieutenant Rodgers testified she had forty guns and a crew of 409 men. Before the court reached a decision on the final award, Secretary Stoddert stopped the charade and challenged Truxtun to contest his decision on behalf of the navy to pay *Constellation*'s crew $84,500, an amount he was prepared to offer. Truxtun did not challenge Stoddert's award. In the meantime, President Adams appointed Capt. Silas Talbot commander of *Constitution* and Truxtun challenged that appointment on the grounds that Talbot did not belong on President Washington's seniority list because he had not received a command when Congress delayed completion of two of the original frigates and canceled the sixth one. Truxtun demanded that the Adams administration allow him to leapfrog over Talbot and take command of the larger frigate. To enforce his demand, he resigned from the navy.[44]

Adams refused to cave in and Truxtun, coaxed by Stoddert, reversed his decision and rejoined *Constellation* at Hampton Roads. He headed out to the West Indies to corner another frigate which the secretary said had recently arrived from France. He did not have to wait long. Getting under way from St. Kitts on 31 January, he fell in with Capt. Alexander Murray in *Insurgent* with a convoy. Murray's foremast had sprung and Truxtun ordered him into St. Kitts for repairs. He then proceeded on a southerly course toward Guadeloupe.[45]

According to Truxtun's journal, with his ship beating up under Guadeloupe, on 1 February 1800, *Constellation*'s lookouts spotted a large ship. Truxtun hoisted English colors and gave chase. The unidentified ship sailed on a southwest course about fifteen miles southeast of *Constellation*. Captain Pitot in *La Vengeance* had been exercising his ship and crew in preparation for a return voyage to France when he observed the large ship approaching on a southerly course at 8:00 A.M. As his orders instructed him to avoid contact with enemy warships, Pitot, upon recognizing that the approaching ship was a frigate, set all sails and bore off to the southwest, but he noticed that the ship continued the chase. Certain of Truxtun's hostile intentions, Pitot cleared his ship for action. The French captain reported later that while he had the ship ready for battle, he was determined not to attack. At noon the wind fell, and *Constellation*, formerly gaining on what Truxtun had identified as a 54-gun frigate, now held her own in the chase. Both ships were running to leeward in a light southerly breeze. Truxtun began to worry that his wishes would not be gratified.[46]

During the remainder of the daylight hours, Pitot in *La Vengeance* held his own, but at nightfall, *Constellation* came up rapidly. According to the French captain, at 8:15 P.M. the enemy took a position on his starboard quarter at half range. The French crew placed two 18-pound guns in the stern and opened fire with the hope of disabling *Constellation* (still unidentified by Pitot). According to Truxtun these guns proved ineffective, so the French captain brought *La Vengeance* around into the wind and commenced firing broadsides into the approaching *Constellation*. Pitot reported that he maintained a violent pace of firing as his gunners concentrated their aim on *Constellation*'s masts and standing rigging. Their guns knocked out *Constellation*'s head sails and her fore topgallant sail, forcing Truxtun to drop back and repair his ship's damaged spars.[47]

According to the French captain's report, *Constellation* made quick repairs and by her superior speed did not permit him to avoid *Constellation*. Truxtun passed orders to his lieutenants to load the ship's main guns (18-pounders having replaced the 24-pounders in New York the previous summer) with double shot. As Truxtun reported it, he gained the weather quarter and once in position commenced "a close and as sharp an action, as ever was fought between two frigates," which continued into the night. Truxtun ordered *Constellation*'s gunners to take aim on the French frigate's hull.

Both ships maintained running courses until 10:10 P.M. when *La Vengeance* once again changed course to starboard and the two ships pounded away at each other for thirty-five minutes. *Constellation*, with her main battery guns from the quarter deck and forecastle and waist all firing, suddenly bore in on the French ship as if she intended to board or to rake her stern. The American ship rained grape and grenades on *La Vengeance*, forcing the French ship to haul off. They sailed board to board as Truxtun followed her around.[48]

Constellation remained the aggressor as *La Vengeance*'s captain continually endeavored to get clear of the attacking ship, having a number of passengers aboard,

Builder's model of French frigate *La Vengeance.* Photographed by G. Porte for the Minister de la Marine. *Naval Historical Foundation*

including thirty-five American prisoners, as well as an inexperienced crew, seventy-seven short of the ship's full complement. At midnight, after maintaining the engagement four hours, the two ships drifted apart, both having received such extensive damage to their rigging that they had become difficult to manage. Coyly, Truxtun suggests in his battle report that at this point he considered the Frenchman his prize but in reality the two ships drifted apart, each ship critically damaged. Truxtun could do nothing except watch his prey disappear into the night. Disaster struck *Constellation* soon after that when her complete main mast structure collapsed over the side, leaving Truxtun's ship in indefensible condition. Truxtun put his crew to work clearing the wreckage. His ship, vulnerable to attack even from a wounded opponent, forced Truxtun to bear away for the island of Jamaica, where he hoped the Royal Navy could provide repairs.[49]

As described by Captain Pitot in a detailed report, *Constellation* seemed to drift away sometime after midnight and because of the condition of his own ship's rigging he could not trim his sails and chase the American ship. He noted that his opponent hoisted and lowered lanterns, which suggested to him that she had anchored and now sought his assistance. This activity was probably Truxtun's crew clearing the fallen main mast from the deck. Coincidentally, *La Vengeance*'s main mast gave way and crashed straight forward onto the foremast and the bow of the French ship. Both frigates had fought to a point that rendered each helpless to attack or to defend herself or to even sail out of harm's way. Truxtun jury-rigged his ship and began a slow sail to Jamaica, while Pitot desperately kept his pumps working and carpenters struggled to plug the holes in her hull. Then he set his crew to repair rigging and to place his battery in condition to withstand another attack. Pitot noted that after an hour passed, *Constellation* drifted out of his vision and he saw her no more. The French captain praised the behavior of his undermanned crew who he said maintained precision order in the ship and a constant fire upon the attacker. *La Vengeance* gunners fired 742 rounds and four hundred cartridges at the enemy. His stated casualties consisted of twenty-eight dead and forty wounded, though France never provided an official count.[50]

Truxtun claimed that Pitot broke off the action and drifted out of sight, leaving him to believe that *Constellation* sank *La Vengeance*. In his report, Pitot stated that Truxtun drifted out of view and he could not follow his enemy. Both ships lost main masts, and the constant blasting away at *La Vengeance*'s hull by *Constellation*'s gunners left the French ship in danger of sinking. If battles that wreck ships and kill and maim so many may be considered magnificent, then the battle between *La Vengeance* and *Constellation* must be placed among the most noble ever fought by a wooden frigate of the United States Navy. It had the grandeur of an engagement fought between opponents of approximately equal size and firepower. *Constellation* is the only American wooden ship-frigate to fight an enemy near to or greater than her in size and in the weight of broadside. In ways surely not expected by Humphreys, *Constellation* fulfilled his and his country's greatest expectations.[51]

En route to Jamaica Truxtun fell in with USS *Enterprize* (John Shaw) and ordered him to take his schooner to Chesapeake Bay with dispatches. Truxtun hoped to get *Constellation*—in his own words, a complete wreck—refitted at the British island. In the meantime, Isaac Henty, *Constellation*'s surgeon, reported in a letter to a son dated 3 February that the ship's casualties totaled fifteen killed and twenty-five wounded, all badly. Supplementing his journal for 1 and 2 February 1800, which his clerk copied for transmittal to Stoddert, Truxtun wrote that the battle with *La Vengeance* ended in the complete dismantlement of *Constellation*.[52]

La Vengeance reached the Dutch island of Curaçao on 6 February. Pitot thought his recent engagement was with a Royal Navy ship, but the American consul on the island learned from an arriving vessel that *Constellation* had been his opponent. Benjamin Hammell Phillips, the American consul at Curaçao, reported to the State Department that French casualties totaled 160 men. He reported also that *La Vengeance* carried about $1 million in specie and other valuable cargo, information that must have been rather upsetting to Truxtun when it reached him. Phillips arranged to receive the thirty-six American prisoners still on board the French ship, all of whom had survived the recent battle. Dutch authorities refused to allow Captain Pitot to repair his ship in the island's harbor out of fear that such an act would destabilize the island, though a supply ship reached the French frigate in late March 1800. A French invasion of Curaçao occurred on 23 July 1800. The attacking force, which included a new crew for Pitot's ship, occupied the west side of the island at Rif and l'Othrabanda. During the French occupation, *La Vengeance* must have been repaired because she sailed before the French withdrew from the island.[53]

On 20 August 1800, *La Vengeance,* sailing between Puerto Rico and the Island of Mona, fell in with a Royal Navy three-masted schooner with lanteen sails, which, on observing the French frigate, fired warning shots to alert a Royal Navy frigate sailing off Mona Island. Once again Pitot attempted to escape what he thought might be a Royal Navy squadron. The Royal Navy frigate, later identified as the HMS *Seine,* took out after *La Vengeance,* sailing on a southerly course running free for the Caribbean Sea. Shortly after midnight, *La Vengeance* commenced firing her stern guns at the faster Royal Navy ship. Heavy firing by both ships followed as Pitot brought his ship up to bring his battery to bear. The British ship fell astern at 5:30 A.M. and once again Pitot attempted to escape. Firing resumed at 6:20 A.M. and ceased about an hour later. *La Vengeance* began to run low of shot and both ships had received considerable damage. When a third round of firing started, *La Vengeance* lost her mizzenmast, then her main topmast, and finally her foremast fell. Captain Pitot struck his colors. *La Vengeance* never made it back to Portsmouth, England, for repairs and for measuring; she stranded and broke up in the West Indies in 1801.[54]

According to British dimensions, *La Vengeance* measured 160 feet by 41¹/₂ feet. The Royal Navy classified her as a fourth-rate rate fifty. *La Vengeance*'s sister ship, *Resistance,* also captured by the Royal Navy and renamed *Fishguard,* measured, according to her draft, 160 feet 6 inches by 40 feet 8.72 inches and 1,182 tons burden. French records show that the sister ships, one built in 1793 and the other in 1794, measured 150 feet in length at the waterline, which is a measurement almost exactly equal to the British dimension of *Fishguard* (*Resistance*) when converted from French to English feet. The French and English measurements of breadth differ only slightly. According to French records *Resistance* and *La Vengeance* measured 39 French feet in breadth, which when converted to English feet equals 41.73 feet and suggests that all measurements of beam in the sources cited are for extreme breadth. With this information one may conclude that *Constellation* and *La Vengeance* were roughly equal in tons burden.[55]

Pierre Degay built *Resistance* (1793) and *La Vengeance* (1794) at Paimboeuf (Nantes), in Brittany. Degay's specifications called for a main battery of thirty

24-pound guns and twenty 12-pounders. Like *Constellation,* these ships had been drafted to carry heavier 24-pounders for their main broadside; like *Constellation,* too, when the ships opened fire at each other the night of 2 February, both mounted main batteries of twenty-eight 18-pound guns, though the French ship carried two additional 18-pounders as stern guns. *La Vengeance* had been designed to mount twenty 12-pounders on her upper deck, but during the engagement with *Constellation* her armament consisted of, in addition to the 18-pounders on her gun deck, fourteen 12-pounders and eight 36-pound carronades, for a total of fifty-two guns. *Constellation's* armament at the time she fought *La Vengeance* consisted of ten 24-pound carronades plus the twenty-eight 18-pounders, a total of thirty-eight guns. The weight of one of *Constellation's* broadsides totaled 372 pounds of iron. The weight of *La Vengeance's* broadside totaled 480 pounds. Since there were many efforts to puff up the figures to emphasize the magnitude of *Constellation's* handicap, these figures, which appeared in a Federalist journal, may be inflated. Nevertheless, it is certain that the faster *Constellation* fought a ship almost equal to her in tonnage and which had the capacity to fire about one hundred pounds more per broadside than *Constellation.* However, Truxtun bragged that his crew fired their guns more consistently than the patched-up crew of the French ship, short seventy-one hands.[56]

Captain Truxtun would never put Pitot's scalp on his belt, which annoyed him through the years following his second resignation. And he never stopped claiming that the Frenchman had struck and his ship was his prize. But he could not deny that what you cannot reach to claim will never be yours, as both ships, badly damaged, survived to fight again. No records survive providing the extent of *Constellation's* repairs.[57] Truxtun became a national hero and a roaring bore as he searched for adulation or slight from everyone he met. The Quasi War wound down quickly when the electors turned out Adams and brought in America's most influential Francophile, Thomas Jefferson, who served two terms as the country's third president.

Benjamin Stoddert, who ministered the young navy into a fairly potent force, now needed, like his most famous captain, to go home to Georgetown. Fortunately he could following Jefferson's election, and his ill-conceived plan to add a number of battleships of the line to the navy quickly collapsed. The navy's officer corps would wait a decade for the big ships, though Stoddert, the father of the United States Navy, initiated another naval policy that commanders accepted as readily as gold braid and broad pennants. Stoddert formed the first peacetime quasi–naval-diplomatic cruise, with its primary purpose of showing the American flag in far-off places. He ordered Capt. Alexander Murray in *Constellation* to cruise the route of ships returning from India, and he sent USS *Ganges* and *Connecticut* to patrol the straits off Batavia in the

Dutch East Indies. Orders changed and *Constellation* returned once again to the West Indies, but the assignments carried out by the other two ships marked the beginning of American naval imperialism.[58]

Constellation remained docked in New York while Stoddert pondered future strategy. President Adams was now a lame duck, having lost his office after a single term. Peace negotiations with France opened. On 30 December 1800 Stoddert ordered Murray in *Constellation* back to St. Kitts with dispatches for Truxtun, then commander of USF *President*.[59] On this short cruise, the gentlemanly Murray worked closely with French mariners and administrators as the two nations moved beyond the recent undeclared war.[60] *Constellation* returned to Newcastle on the Delaware River about 13 March 1801 and anchored off that town. A few days later, Stoddert suggested that he move his ship farther up the river. Murray complied, anchoring *Constellation* two miles below Fort Miffin in a "convenient place for any purpose." On 23 March Stoddert ordered Murray to pay off the crew, "keeping enough men necessary for the preservation of the ship. You will have the ship placed in a safe situation." Murray acknowledged these orders and brought the ship up to Philadelphia on the evening of 2 April. Murray questioned the fact that Stoddert had assigned no officers to the skeleton crew as he intended to take leave. Despite not receiving specific instructions, he left two lieutenants and a number of warrant officers on board, plus fifty marines.[61]

In the meantime, incoming President Jefferson appointed ex-Senator Samuel Smith of Baltimore acting secretary of the navy. At the time, the Jefferson administration intended to reduce the mission of the navy and Smith notified Murray that *Constellation* would be placed in ordinary at Washington, D.C. Thinking that Smith might not be aware of *Constellation*'s draft, he notified him that when fully provisioned she drew 22 feet 6 inches, the most of any ship in the navy, and that when lightened, she would still draw 19 or 20 feet.[62]

On 10 April an accident occurred that would place *Constellation* out of commission for six months. A distraught Murray reported to Smith that his ship had grounded in Philadelphia harbor on the hard rock and sand bottom of the Delaware River during a storm. The ship, with her deep draft, was pounded mercilessly until the tide receded, at which time, with an increasing percentage of her hull exposed, she fell over on her beam ends and soon filled with water. With the added weight of her guns, masts, spars, and wet sails, it proved to be a difficult and dangerous undertaking to bring her back to an upright position.[63]

The ship lay as she was, half sunk, for more than a week.[64] Joshua Humphreys took charge of the salvage operation; after a failure to lift her 20 April when a fifteen-inch cable parted, he was able to write Smith on 22 April that his crew had gotten *Constellation* upright the previous evening. Five pumps got the water down below the outside water level, which allowed Humphreys to conclude that the ship had not bilged. He got the ship completely pumped out over the following week, which allowed him to report to Smith that *Constellation* received no damage to her bottom. Murray shifted the ship to a wharf and began to discharge her equipment and supplies, including her sails and rigging.[65]

The Jefferson administration had previously decided to moor *Constellation* in ordinary in the Eastern Branch of the Potomac River, just outside of the new capital of Washington. As would become standard practice, Smith wanted minimum repairs done to the ship prior to her being laid up. Murray, who had announced himself as sympathetic to the Jefferson administration, pointed out that Stoddert ordered him to take his ship up to Philadelphia and to discharge all of his crew except the few retained as caretakers. Because of the present state of the ship, Murray wrote, the expense to make just the necessary repairs to sail her to the Potomac and the cost to obtain a crew for that purpose would be high. Further, *Constellation*'s captain told Smith that if she was not thoroughly dried out and repaired, the ship would rot out in twelve months. After conferring with Jefferson, Smith ordered Murray to remain with his ship at Philadelphia. Humphreys would supervise her repairs.[66]

According to a preliminary survey by Humphreys and Murray, the principal damage to the ship as a result of capsizing and flooding centered on her sails, rigging, and equipment, and much if not all of her canvas and cordage would need to be replaced. But Humphreys and Murray, after their joint inspection, found other heavy damage due to rot in *Constellation*'s hull from below the wales upward to the spar deck, where much of this timber needed to be replaced. This included some deck beams, the wales themselves, and planks above the wales inside and out, as well as gun deck, clamps, and waterways, all of which showed a great amount of rot. The surveyors recommended replacing all of the rotten beams and planks and warned Smith that more damage would be uncovered when they opened up the ship. They reported that *Constellation*'s frame appeared to be sound.[67]

Disruption in the affairs of the secretary's office (there were two acting secretaries before Robert Smith took the cabinet post) delayed work on *Constellation* until July. One of Humphreys' immediate problems concerned the hull's strength in its present condition, and he received authority to replace some planks to protect the shape of her hull. But in August when the ship was completely opened up workmen uncovered more decay and the Navy Department authorized a general repair of the ship. Humphreys placed master shipwright Nathaniel Hutton in charge of *Constellation*. In another decision concerning replacement of the ship's masts and spars, Humphreys decided to rerig *Constellation* as conservatively as her sister ship, USF *Congress*, and requested the dimensions of her masts and spars and her good and bad sailing qualities from Capt. Thomas Tingey at the new Washington Navy Yard.[68]

Finally, with a permanent secretary, Robert Smith, in office 12 September, Humphreys forwarded him a fairly complete report on the condition of *Constellation.* Humphreys had ordered the ship stripped of all defective planks. He informed Secretary Smith that he found most of her spar deck beams defective and had taken them out. He ordered all inside and outside planks including wales taken out down to her gun deck. Hutton removed some planking below her wales and her waterways because of defects, as well as some planks lower in the ship that showed rot and were to be replaced. Humphreys also discovered that Stodder had installed her air ports and water closet incorrectly, which caused increased damage to the ship. When the new secretary made the decision to repair *Constellation,* he rescinded the previous order to place her in ordinary at Washington and notified Murray that she would be returned to duty and that his ship's services would be required about 1 February 1802. *Constellation*'s next cruise would be to the Mediterranean Sea in a squadron under Commo. Richard V. Morris. Her mission would be to subdue or arrange monetary settlements with Barbary nations engaged in acts of piracy against nations failing to pay tribute.[69]

It seemed odd that Murray would request permission to increase *Constellation*'s main armament from thirty-eight to forty-four guns since the Barbary nations fought with gunboats and other light vessels. Smith pointed out that Truxtun removed her 24-pounders to gain stability. The addition of more guns would make her crank once again unless the diminution in the size of her spars would keep her duly poised. Smith also worried that the additional weight would increase her draft. But Murray put Smith's fears to rest by pointing out that on his previous cruise in *Constellation* he found the ship sufficiently stiff but, like all sharp-built ships, she laid over on her bearings until she bore the press of sail as well as any other ship. While the additional guns would add weight above the waterline, Murray pointed out that he ordered changes made to her masts and spars and upper works. In addition, the removal of storeroom walls and bulkheads allowed her to carry an additional month's supplies and to reduce ballast by thirty tons. He wanted the new 24-pound carronades, already available at the Philadelphia Navy Yard, mounted on the quarterdeck. Murray raised her crew to 320 men. Smith approved the request and *Constellation* became a 44-gun frigate.[70]

Murray reported 1 December that repairs resulting in the near rebuilding of *Constellation* from the water's edge upward would be finished in three weeks. The cost of the work totaled $30,551.76. And, though Smith ordered Murray to depart for Gibraltar as soon as possible because *Constellation* would be a relief ship, the captain, with the counsel of Captain Barry, postponed his departure from Philadelphia because of bad winter weather and low water in Delaware Bay. *Constellation* finally passed over the bar below Fort Miffin 27 February 1802.[71]

Stormy weather in the Atlantic Ocean at the approach to Gibraltar forced Murray to bypass that port for the Spanish port of Malaga, where he found USF *Essex* (Barron) and *Philadelphia* (Bainbridge) anchored on 30 April 1802. After watering *Constellation,* the three American frigates departed Malaga in company. The other captains reported to Murray that *Constellation* was out of sailing trim, drawing too much at the head. She drew 22 feet aft and 24 feet forward. On this occasion the weather allowed the three ships to enter Gibraltar and anchor. Midn. Thomas MacDonough wrote in the ship's log that while at anchor in the harbor, the carpenter department built a bulkhead around the forecastle. He gave no reason for the construction, but Murray probably ordered it built as a barrier against green water passing over *Constellation*'s bow as she pounded through the Atlantic Ocean and into the Mediterranean Sea, fighting headwinds. During the month of June *Constellation* cruised the Mediterranean Sea. She visited several ports and on 6 July arrived off of Tripoli where she took her blockading station along with the Swedish frigate *Thetis.* After this initial period inside the Mediterranean Sea, Captain Murray formed impressions of the effectiveness of American operations there and of the ultimate cost of gaining control over a fluid situation, which would ultimately require Smith to order the whole U.S. Navy to those distant waters.[72]

Constellation fought a running engagement with Tripolitan gunboats on 22 July, but because his ship's draft limited Murray's ability to maneuver close to the city's harbor, the situation gave the Tripolitan gunboats, firing 24-pounders, some advantage over the frigate, particularly during calm weather. *Constellation* received some damage to her yards but managed to fire close to two hundred rounds in the direction of the nine fleeing boats. Murray's purser, Keith Spence, referred to it as a brush rather than an engagement. He also pointed out that small, well-armed boats posed a danger to large ships when the wind faltered while they were close to land, a sort of prediction of the event that ended in the loss of *Philadelphia.* Murray confirmed later that he had inflicted some damage on the gunboats, killing eight men.[73]

Murray wrote Secretary Smith about his activities since his arrival on station at Tripoli. Reviewing his engagement with the Tripolitan gunboats, he alerted Smith to the news of the capture of an American brig and that its crew had been taken into Tripoli in spite of his blockade. This news plus the obvious conditions which allowed attacking gunboats to operate without the worry of interference from large ships convinced Murray that the American squadron, as currently composed, would be impotent under existing conditions. He recommended to Secretary Smith that frigates be replaced or supplemented by gunboats, schooners, and brigs.[74]

This sort of practical advice separated Murray from Secretary Smith and the younger and more aggressive American naval officers. During the Revolutionary War, Captain Murray became a true hero both at sea and in the Continental Army,

USF *Constellation* at Toulon, 1802. Painting by Antoine Roux. *Naval Historical Foundation*

and he learned well the limits and possibilities of warfare and appeasement. In another letter to Smith, following his thoughts on the blockade, he pointed out that though curtailment of payments of tribute was laudable, until the other nations banished such payments and joined America in a uniform effort to control piracy, it was prudent for the American government to suffer the indignity of tribute. This position isolated Murray. Next, he became embroiled in controversy with William Eaton, an aggressive Department of State representative active in clandestine activities in North Africa. All of these complicated political activities reach far beyond the scope of this book. But even before Murray in *Constellation* headed home to Chesapeake Bay, Smith ordered construction or purchase of a small fleet of Baltimore-type schooners and brigs for the U.S. Navy. The secretary also acquired gunboats in Naples and built others at Washington, Baltimore, and other American ports. It took years for the Jefferson administration to follow Murray's advice to get the navy out of the Mediterranean Sea and free of the naval quagmire in North Africa.[75]

Smith abruptly ordered Captain Murray to return to Washington. *Constellation* stood off Europa Point at meridian on 26 January 1803. After a tempestuous winter voyage, she entered Chesapeake Bay and proceeded up to St. Marys at the mouth of the Potomac River. He picked up a pilot who guided the ship to Greenleaf Point where she grounded in mud. *Constellation* then went into ordinary. Smith limited Captain Murray to coastal duty, his decision no doubt related to the old hero's objections to the extension of naval operations in North Africa as managed by the navy under Robert Smith.[76]

The nation did not receive the shocking news that Capt. William Bainbridge, the commander of USF *Philadelphia,* had run his ship on uncharted rocks near the entrance of Tripoli harbor until March 1804, though the incident occurred 1 November 1803. Ironically, the navy had lost its second ship to an enemy and the same man commanded both of them, the first being USS *Retaliation,* lost by Bainbridge to the French frigate *l'Insurgente.* Bainbridge put *Philadelphia* on submerged rocks four to five miles east of Tripoli in uncharted waters. At the time the American frigate was engaged in the pursuit of enemy gunboats. Bainbridge maintained the attack on them while running free before the wind toward the North African shoreline. *Philadelphia* struck rocks in twelve feet of water as Bainbridge attempted to beat off the beach, having passed the seven-fathom line. After the news reached Commo. Edward Preble in *Constitution* on 27 November, he wrote in his diary that *Philadelphia* had run on shore. Though she was badly damaged, with a cracked keel, the Tripolitans got her off 6 November and hauled her into the harbor. On the sixteenth of February 1804, the ketch USS *Intrepid,* under the command of Stephen Decatur, Jr., boarded *Philadelphia,* overwhelmed her small caretaker crew, and burned the ship.[77]

When Secretary Robert Smith received news of the loss of *Philadelphia,* he placed into motion orders to mobilize the portion of the U.S. Navy in ordinary at Washington, which consisted of the frigates *President, Congress, Essex,* and *Constellation.* He also prepared to send the USF *John Adams* to Commodore Preble with supplies. Smith's plan to mobilize most of the American naval ships in ordinary and send them thousand of miles into the Mediterranean Sea left the U.S. coast unprotected. President Jefferson's acquiescence to this course of action committed the navy fleet and its yearly budget to a single distant mission. This became particularly important because as a result of the postponement of ship maintenance, the navy found itself poorly prepared for the crisis with England that developed after the *Chesapeake-Leopard* affair and events leading up to the declaration of war in 1812.[78]

Master Comdt. Isaac Chauncey in the *John Adams* arrived at Gibraltar 22 July 1804, reporting that the frigates would have left Hampton Roads about 1 July. Smith gave Capt. Hugh Campbell command of *Constellation.* But Smith also conferred upon Capt. Samuel Barron command of all American forces in the Mediterranean Sea. Upon his arrival, the combined fleet consisted of the frigates *President, Congress, Constitution, Essex,* and *Constellation* and brigs *Siren* and *Argus.* Schooners *Vixen,*

Nautilus, and *Enterprize* would be commanded by Barron with a mission to coerce Tripoli into a treaty of peace.[79]

Constellation (Campbell), held up for want of cables, arrived at Hampton Roads 21 June, the last ship in Barron's squadron to report to him. *John Adams* (Chauncey) sailed 26 June and arrived at Gibraltar 22 July reporting that Barron's group had been scheduled to sail 1 July. In the meantime, Commo. Edward Preble offered through Richard O'Brien $40,000 for the bashaw, plus $10,000 to those officials of Tripoli who agreed to assist pushing forward successful negotiations for ransom of the crew of *Philadelphia.* Negotiations having failed and with full knowledge that his replacement had departed Hampton Roads for the Mediterranean Sea, Commodore Preble attacked Tripoli 3 August. The attack continued through 16 August and with no word from Barron's ships, a shortage of water and supplies forced Preble to send *Enterprize* to Malta to make arrangements for provisioning his attacking fleet. The attack resumed close-in as Preble anchored *Constitution* just outside Tripoli harbor about two and one-half miles from the bashaw's castle.

The smaller vessels of Preble's fleet including the gunboats entered Tripoli and took up positions at the entrance of the harbor, where they opened a strong attack. Preble moved *Constitution* into the harbor and commenced heavy fire on shipping, the town, and the bashaw's castle. Eventually, Preble positioned *Constitution* within the reach of grapeshot and pumped eleven broadsides into the bashaw's castle, town, and batteries. The action broke off as Preble's fleet withdrew to assess damage, resupply, and re-form. The wind shifted to the northeast on 5 September; on the seventh, Preble ordered his vessels to retire to Syracuse except *Constitution, Argus,* and *Vixen,* which remained off Tripoli to maintain the blockade. On 10 September, Barron in *President* with *Constellation* hove into sight. Shortly thereafter Preble returned to America, having been replaced by Captain Barron, his senior officer. The officers and crew of *Philadelphia* remained in the custody of the bashaw. American casualties were heavy and damage to vessels significant. While the action of young American officers and crewmen was brave and often brilliant, tactically speaking, Preble's raid on Tripoli failed to accomplish the desired result; Captain Bainbridge and his crew remained prisoners and Preble pulled back, leaving the bashaw unchallenged again that year. The frigates *President, Constitution,* and *Constellation* with *Argus* remained stationed off Tripoli. Richard O'Brien, assessing the U.S. Navy's situation, wrote that the frigates could not take Tripoli without the gunboats and it was too late in the season for the gunboats to return to action.[80]

During the winter of 1805 *Constellation* stood off Tripoli maintaining the blockade. Peace between Tripoli and America came in June 1805 as the result of a land and sea attack on Tripoli. Following a truce with the bashaw, *Constellation* picked up part of the crew of *Philadelphia* and a few days later she took aboard a marine detachment and others who participated in the successful march on Derne, which led up to the surrender of the bashaw. *Constellation* departed Derne 12 June. She leaked badly. By August, she took in over two feet of water per hour. Campbell complained to Commodore Rodgers that *Constellation* leaked a large amount of water in bad weather about the bow and very low down on her hull, causing the ship to be very wet inside her berth deck, storerooms, and coal hold.[81]

Commo. John Rodgers ordered a survey of *Constellation*'s condition. The board, consisting of Charles Stewart, Stephen Decatur Jr., and John Shaw, found *Constellation*'s bottom in such bad condition that the ship required a complete overhaul, and Rodgers decided to send her home immediately. Captain Campbell assumed command of *Essex* and Master Comdt. Charles Stewart became commander of *Constellation* 22 August. She arrived at Hampton Roads 9 November and was taken into ordinary at the Washington Navy Yard at the end of that month. The navy did not return the ship to service until 1812.[82]

Campaigns against the Barbary nations, carried out by the navy under Robert Smith, forced the secretary, under budgetary pressure, to ignore or postpone proper maintenance for the nation's small naval fleet. There had been exceptions. USF *Constitution* received substantial repairs over several years between 1803 and 1806. The record shows only the amount of money spent in those years; based on that amount, we can assume that *Constitution* received proper maintenance. She may have been the first navy vessel to be rebuilt. Preble reported to President Jefferson upon his return to America that his ship was rebuilt and coppered in 1803. However, the navy spent an additional $99,868 on repairs to *Constitution* in 1808 at New York. Another navy vessel that received repairs under Preble's command in the Mediterranean Sea was USS *Enterprize,* rebuilt at Venice in 1805.[83]

Smith reported to Congress in January 1806 that *Constitution* and *Chesapeake* were repaired and the frigates *Adams, Essex,* and *John Adams* fit for service, a category in which he also placed *Siren, Hornet, Argus, Vixen, Nautilus, Enterprize,* and the bombships *Spitfire* and *Vengeance,* as well as all gunboats. Smith admitted that the frigates *President, United States, Congress, New York, Boston,* and *Constellation* required repairs; the cost to repair them was impossible to calculate. In his report to Jefferson, Preble agreed that *Constitution,* repaired in 1803, would last seven years without material repairs. He confirmed that *President, United States, Essex, Congress, New York, Boston, Adams,* and *Constellation* needed repairs. In another section of his analysis of the navy's ships, Preble informed Jefferson that while both *Congress* and *Constellation* were fast sailers, he considered *Congress* the better of the two ships.[84]

Repairs charged to *Constellation* at Philadelphia in 1802 totaled $30,551.76. Additional charges to the ship included $6,954.51 for repairs performed in the Mediterranean Sea in 1802–3, when *Constellation* was under command of Alexander Murray. She received $8,016.43 in repairs while in ordinary at Washington in 1804. Emergency repairs performed in the Mediterranean Sea in 1805, authorized by Captain Campbell, totaled $9,499.96. And in 1806 at Washington, while she was again in ordinary, charges against her amounted to $1,073.40. There are no records covering the costs of repairing *Constellation*'s battle damage after her engagements with *l'Insurgente* and *La Vengeance*. Comparing the known cost of rebuilding and repairing *Constitution* and *Constellation* over approximately ten years of service, the repairs made to *Constitution* totaled $302,582 while known repair costs of *Constellation* totaled $56,096.06. If these figures are accurate for the maintenance programs for the two vessels over the period of service to 1809, it is not difficult to understand why *Constellation* would require a thorough rebuild in 1812.[85]

$\mathcal{T}hree$

Tingey's rebuild, 1812

Throughout President James Madison's first term, Secretary of the Navy Paul Hamilton created serious problems for his administration. A South Carolina planter and politician, he had little specific naval or maritime experience. For three years of his first term of office, he failed to mount a serious effort to prepare the navy for war. Hamilton's addiction to alcohol undercut his standing inside the government. As a result, the Navy Department did not present Congress with a mobilization plan until early in 1812. Two sections of Hamilton's presentation received approval in March of that year, less than three months before the Madison administration declared war.[1] The first major legislation affecting the navy's preparedness, named an Act Concerning the Naval Establishment, was passed by Congress on 30 March 1812. Congress rejected Hamilton's request for new ships, but the legislators appropriated $300,000 for immediate repairs for *Chesapeake, Constellation,* and *Adams.* In addition the bill authorized $600,000 to purchase ship timber.[2]

After the bill passed, Capt. Thomas Tingey, commandant of the Washington Navy Yard, ordered *Constellation* taken out of ordinary and the yard began repairs on the second-class frigate immediately. USS *Adams,* in a state of rot almost beyond repair according to Tingey, followed *Constellation* into the yard. Extensive alterations to her hull and a subsequent rebuild took place over the following eighteen months. Hauled out and with her hull cut at the dead flat frame, a new midbody section increased *Adams*'s length 15 feet. The yard launched the smaller ship a day or so after Christmas 1812, but Capt. Charles Morris did not accept her, ready for sea, until late in 1813. Even after he successfully evaded the British blockade of Chesapeake Bay in January 1814, Morris complained that the *Adams* became unmanageable under certain conditions.[3] *Chesapeake,* in ordinary at Boston, was hauled over to the Charlestown

Navy Yard and repaired under the supervision of Capt. William Bainbridge, commandant of the yard that was located near Boston.[4]

The act of 30 March 1812 allocated $600,000 for purchase of ship's timber over three years. It stipulated that the first contracts of timber must be "suitable for rebuilding the frigates *Philadelphia, General Greene, New York,* and *Boston.*" After Congress rejected Hamilton's request for new ships, the administration waited another nine months, that is, until 3 January 1813, before receiving congressional approval to expand the navy. Observers in Washington linked Congress's eventual passage of a bill authorizing ships of the line and frigates to the presence in Washington of U.S. Frigate *Constellation*'s new commander, Capt. Charles Stewart, during the autumn of 1812. Delayed getting to sea by a shortage of sailcloth and other equipment, he led the navy's lobbying group that pushed Congress for a permanent navy in which ships of the line and heavy frigates would assume a major role, thereby replacing Jefferson's unpopular gunboat navy.[5]

Commandant Tingey's major project to modify and rebuild the nation's oldest navy ship, *Constellation,* commenced in March 1812 at the Washington Navy Yard and continued through the summer and autumn months. No naval constructor worked at the yard, so it is not known who supervised the work as master builder. Robert Smith appointed Josiah Fox to the position of naval constructor in 1804 and fired him in 1809, most likely at the request of Captain Tingey. William Doughty became the naval constructor assigned to the Washington Navy Yard in 1813. No records survive of the scheduling or progress of repairs to either *Constellation* or *Adams;* not even the final completion date of the work on the frigate is known because the yard encountered many problems obtaining experienced personnel, materials, and ship's equipment. As a matter of fact, even after *Constellation* reached Hampton Roads in February 1813, she could not have left the bay on a cruise under wartime conditions without a spare set of sails and tested gunpowder. Congress committed $120,000 for her repair, a sum estimated to be less than one-half of the cost of a new second-class frigate rated thirty-six guns. Tingey reported that the yard dismantled *Constellation* down to her bottom timbers, replaced some of her live oak floors, then rebuilt the ship from that point upward. Since Tingey found only her keel and most of her original floor timbers intact and only her ordnance and some equipment reusable, one may conclude, in the absence of records, which were burned on the night of 24 August 1814, when Washington came under attack by British land forces, that the amount allocated by Congress proved to be insufficient.[6]

The Navy Department became aware of the deteriorating condition of *Constellation*'s hull in the spring of 1801 following the grounding and capsizing of the ship at Philadelphia in April of that year. Joshua Humphreys, still a navy constructor when the accident occurred, played a leading role in the dangerous but successful effort to pump out the ship and return her to an upright position. He then supervised her repairs. Over a decade later, in a letter dated 5 September 1812, Humphreys, in response to a request by Congressman Adam Seybert of Philadelphia for his opinions on the condition of the United States Navy and its role in the conflict recently declared, wrote a report covering various aspects of naval affairs.[7] The revered shipbuilder retired in 1812. Living on his farm but still a strong Federalist in his views on naval policy, he urged the congressman to support a strong navy. In response to the congressman's question concerning the premature rotting of ships built for the Quasi War between 1794 and 1800, Humphreys acknowledged that he knew of the problem and that its cause lay in the improper ventilation of the frigates and the failure to use salt to combat condensation trapped between ceiling and planking.[8]

Humphreys informed Seybert that when he examined *Constellation* in 1801 he found rot in the areas of the ship where beams and bulkheads restricted the movement of air. After uncovering the rotting planks and wales, he notified Secretary of the Navy Robert Smith that if these planks were not ripped off, "the frame will soon be destroyed."[9] An added complication that contributed to *Constellation*'s rotting condition, also reported to Smith at the time, resulted from constructor David Stodder's failure to install the frigate's air ports correctly. Humphreys closed them in the course of repairing *Constellation* following the Philadelphia accident.[10]

Continuing with the contents of the letter to Seybert, Humphreys acknowledged that he could not be sure whether *Constellation* received salt treatment in the fall of 1801 because Secretary Smith discharged him before he had completed work on the ship. The newly elected Jefferson administration scheduled the frigate for ordinary in October 1801, and as Smith seemed anxious to save money on repairs, Humphreys told Seybert that he doubted that the ship received his recommended treatment of salt.[11] Smith sent new orders to Capt. Alexander Murray, her commander, instructing him to prepare the ship for a cruise to the Mediterranean Sea, which arrived after Humphreys left the department.[12]

The cost of repairs charged to *Constellation* in 1801–2 at Philadelphia totaled $30,551.76, a significant amount but a pittance compared to the cost of rebuilding U.S. Frigate *Constitution* between 1803–4, which totaled $117,911, plus $84,802 charged to her for repairs performed in the Mediterranean Sea in 1805–6 and $99,809 expended in New York in 1808–9.[13] *Constellation*'s problems with rot continued to develop over the following decade, though Humphreys wrote that he had removed all rotten planks and beams uncovered in 1801. When Commo. Edward Preble reported to President Jefferson on the condition of the frigates in early January 1806, he said that *Constellation* required rebuilding from her wales up, which seemed to confirm Humphreys' prediction.[14]

Tingey put the torch to the shipyard as the British entered Washington 24 August 1814, and fire destroyed most of the yard's records. When Madison's government reoccupied the city, the British having retired to their ships and departed for Baltimore, William Jones, who followed Hamilton as secretary of the navy, received from Captain Tingey a clear and concise written report describing the rebuilding of *Constellation* under his supervision two years earlier. Tingey dated his summary 15 October 1814.[15]

Tingey's report, written in documentary form, stated:

The frigate *Constellation,* February, 1812, was brought to the wharf, and some of her floor timbers, replaced with new, from thence rebuilt up entirely new; being much improved by an extension of 14 inches more beam at the main breadth. Her hull being finished, she was masted and careened out on both sides; the new copper bolts which had been driven through her bottom all ring rivited [sic]; three new metal rudder braces fixed to her stern post and a new rudder made; new coppered with the exception of a few strakes near her keel; her interior joiners' work all new fitted complete; had entire new water casks, gun and cannonade carriages and apparatus, together with new masts, spars, rigging and cables, sails, boats, and all her stores. Was completely rigged, fitted for sea, and, in the fall of the year, left the yard a better ship than when first from the stocks, and sometimes so to be.

The political situation at Washington in 1812, Tingey's background, and old reports concerning *Constellation*'s performance under sail outlined in chapters 1 and 2, meld with Tingey's report, suggesting it is reasonable to accept it at face value.[16]

Figure 3.1 shows the U.S. Frigate *Constellation*'s midship section, redrawn to include the modifications made under Captain Tingey's supervision at the Washington Navy Yard in 1812. The half-body drawing illustrates her new dimensions following the rebuild and after fairing her lines and shows the frigate's new hull shape following the extension of her breadth by 14 inches. It is interesting to note that Franklin Buchanan, an officer serving on *Constellation* in 1815, recorded a series of measurements between points on her gun and spar decks. His measurements confirm that the modifications resulted from the increase in breadth. They also make clear that the yard did not alter the breadth of *Constellation*'s spar deck, which meant that Tingey altered her tumble home the full amount of the increase in the molded breadth of the half-body midship section by 7 inches. Readers are reminded that a number of letters, reports, and journal entries by the frigate's commanders between 1798 and 1805 alleged that the Fells Point–built ship possessed flaws as a result of Humphreys' radical design, which emphasized speed. Some of the ship's critics blamed David Stodder's crew of Fells Point shipwrights, who had been trained to build Chesapeake Bay pilot schooners. The critics charged that the shipwrights accentuated those aspects of Joshua Humphreys'

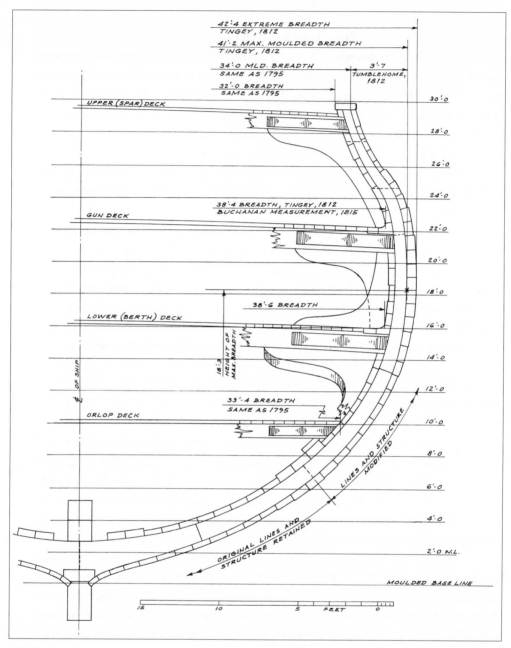

42'·4 EXTREME BREADTH
TINGEY, 1812

41'·2 MAX. MOULDED BREADTH
TINGEY, 1812

34'·0 MLD. BREADTH
SAME AS 1795

3'·7
TUMBLEHOME,
1812

32'·0 BREADTH
SAME AS 1795

UPPER (SPAR) DECK

30'·0

28'·0

26'·0

24'·0

GUN DECK

38'·4 BREADTH, TINGEY, 1812
BUCHANAN MEASUREMENT, 1815

22'·0

20'·0

18'·0

LOWER (BERTH) DECK

38'·6 BREADTH

16'·0

14'·0

18'·3 HEIGHT OF MAX. BREADTH

12'·0

OF SHIP

ORLOP DECK

33'·4 BREADTH
SAME AS 1795

10'·0

LINES AND STRUCTURE MODIFIED

8'·0

6'·0

ORIGINAL LINES AND
STRUCTURE RETAINED

4'·0

2'·0 W.L.

MOULDED BASE LINE

15   10   5   FEET   0

Figure 3.1. USF *Constellation*'s midship section, 1812, drawn in accordance with modifications reported by Capt. Thomas Tingey, 14 October 1814. *William L. Crothers*

draft attributed to the incomparable Baltimore schooners, which had been built in great numbers between 1792 and 1798.

Though on one hand it is difficult to accept the premise that shipwrights would undertake to revise the frigate's lines (there is documentation that confirms that David Stodder did not alter her dimensions), her sharply cut and raked stem and hollow lines below the waterline, a keel that dragged at the stern, substantial deadrise, and sharp lines aft gave *Constellation* a cruising draft aft of 22 feet 6 inches, this figure having been recorded by Capt. Alexander Murray in 1802. Since this is the same draft reported by the larger frigate, the Humphreys-built *United States,* it is probable that because of disorganization in the cutting and delivery of live oak timber, Stodder's shipwrights hewed or reworked a large percentage of *Constellation's* framing timber. If so, these circumstances could have led to the accentuation of the pronounced influence Chesapeake Bay craft already had exerted on Joshua Humphreys' draft for the frigates as discussed in chapter 1.[17] *Constellation's* first commander, Thomas Truxtun, complained that her excessive sharpness of body below the waterline caused the ship to roll in a crossing sea. Or had this reputation stuck because Truxtun originally overmasted and overgunned his ship? Another reported flaw in Humphreys' design or with Stodder's construction concerned *Constellation's* sharp ends, which provided the ship insufficient buoyancy in her bow and stern sections. Or did the excessive strain that opened her decks to leaks result from Truxtun's decision to eliminate diagonal riders, an internal innovation of Humphreys' original specifications?

Truxtun complained of *Constellation's* deep draft, as well as the great difference between her draft forward and at the post. At the beginning of *Constellation's* first cruise, the captain's journal noted that his ship was crank, but later the seriousness of this complaint varied from commander to commander and year to year. Certainly Truxtun was pleased with his ship's speed during *Constellation's* battles against two French frigates but was critical of her excessive heel. As *Constellation* bore down on *l'Insurgente,* gale winds forced him to approach the French frigate on her lee quarter as he could not bring *Constellation's* broadside to bear overtaking the French ship on the weather gage. Truxtun eliminated this problem after the battle by reducing the size of *Constellation's* guns and remasting her more conservatively. Neither Alexander Murray nor Hugh Campbell, the commanders succeeding Truxtun, complained that she heeled excessively, but Campbell verified that the ship took aboard too much water as her deck seams opened in a pounding sea.[18]

Certainly, *Constellation's* length combined with significant deadrise contributed to her speed, but the frigate's great draft when fully provisioned for a cruise caused her to settle deep in the water, restricting her efficiency as a gun platform. This criticism, levied against most Fells Point–built navy ships, really went to the heart of

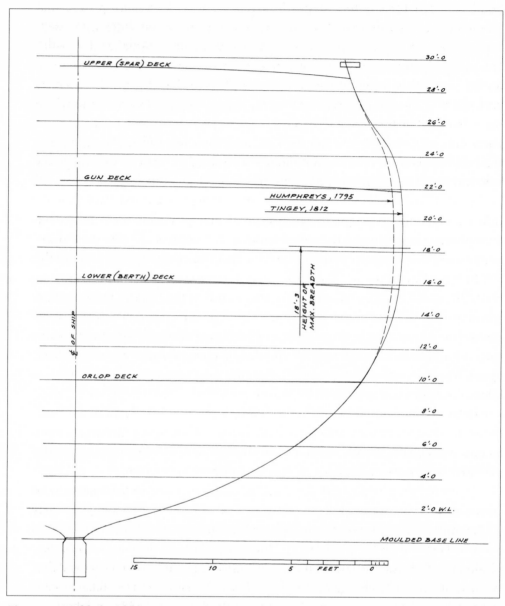

UPPER (SPAR) DECK

GUN DECK

HUMPHREYS, 1795

TINGEY, 1812

LOWER (BERTH) DECK

HEIGHT OF MAX. BREADTH

18'·3

ORLOP DECK

℄ OF SHIP

30'·0
28'·0
26'·0
24'·0
22'·0
20'·0
18'·0
16'·0
14'·0
12'·0
10'·0
8'·0
6'·0
4'·0
2'·0 W.L.
MOULDED BASE LINE

15   10   5   FEET   0

Figure 3.2. Molded midship sections of USF *Constellation* in 1795 and 1812, drawn in accordance with Humphreys' specifications and body plan, 1795, and Capt. Thomas Tingey's modifications report, 14 October 1814. *William L. Crothers*

Humphreys' draft and specifications and cannot be laid at the feet of Fells Point builders.[19] Truxtun's battles with *l'Insurgente* and *La Vengeance* proved that *Constellation*'s speed, maneuverability, and size allowed her commander, with a well-trained crew, to gain advantage over opponents of equal or smaller size just as Humphreys predicted. However, no commander ever received the opportunity of testing *Constellation*'s speed fleeing a larger ship.[20] There is no evidence that her deep keel, which dragged from bow to stern in the manner of a pilot schooner, provided her with extra bursts of speed or quicker response on a tack than her sister frigates. Forty-four years after she was launched and after three rebuilds, her "long leg" was the subject of comment by Lt. M. F. Maury, a knowledgeable critic of navy policy who was particularly critical of the high cost of repairs to older ships.[21]

Thomas Tingey, with his background and training in the Royal Navy, thought differently about the design of Navy ships as gun platforms than did Joshua Humphreys, who designed the Continental navy's frigates and saw them over-whelmed by the Royal Navy's more powerful ships. When *Constellation* entered the Washington Navy Yard for a rebuild, had Tingey seized the opportunity to redesign one of Humphreys' smaller frigates—a ship with a brilliant record, gained at least partially because of her speed? Did Tingey attack Humphreys' theories as had Josiah Fox, another Englishman trained by the Royal Navy, and Thomas Truxtun, once a Royal Navy midshipman? In ship design, no matter which is emphasized, speed or burden, there is always a need for compromise, as naval architecture is a sci-ence of balancing opposites. The Washington Navy Yard rebuilt or repaired *Constellation,* as well as *Enterprize, Nautilus, Hornet, John Adams,* and *Adams* between 1804 and 1813 under Josiah Fox's or Tingey's supervision. Reputedly, none of these vessels left the yard as fast as they sailed prior to entering it, following the extensive work performed under the two Englishmen's supervision.[22]

Tingey reported to Secretary Jones that he increased *Constellation*'s beam by 14 inches at the main breadth. Since there is no record of girdling or doubling the wales of the ship's hull, it must be concluded that the thickness of *Constellation*'s planks remained the same as those used when Humphreys replaced them in 1801. The con-clusion is that the yard increased the frigate's molded breadth by 14 inches and that because of a resulting change in hull shape, *Constellation*'s lines were refaired stem to stern. When he increased *Constellation*'s breadth, Tingey had addressed the ship's alleged instability, a reputation the ship gained principally as a result of Truxtun's complaints. Figure 3.2 shows *Constellation*'s change in shape at the dead flat frame as a result of the rebuild under Tingey's supervision.

Three years after the 1812 rebuild, Franklin Buchanan measured the ship and recorded her new dimensions. Unfortunately, he did not measure her beam at the point of her extreme breadth, most probably because its location at the ship's 18-feet

69

3-inch waterline level at the dead flat proved to be inaccessible.[23] Buchanan meas-ured the width of her gun deck as 38 feet 4 inches inside of ceiling, and his journal reveals that the corresponding dimension at this position in the ship measured exactly 14 inches greater at that waterline level than Humphreys' designed width of the gun deck in 1795. Here, then, is verification of the increase in *Constellation*'s molded beam at the point of her greatest breadth. And Buchanan's measurement proved that the increase extended upward from the level of the ship's maximum breadth at the upper edge of the second wale to the gun deck.[24]

Constructor Josiah Fox measured the location of *Constellation*'s dead flat frame or midsection at the Washington yard in 1806 and confirmed that David Stodder, during construction, conformed to the specifications of Humphreys' original builder's plans. I reached the conclusion that when Tingey's shipwrights increased *Constellation*'s beam in 1812, they increased it 14 inches at the original position of the ship's dead flat. Interpreting Tingey's expression "at the main breadth," with application of the definition of the preposition "at" from the Oxford American Dictionary as "a location" of the increase in beam, it follows that "main breadth" should be defined as the same as with the term "dead flat." Tingey's carpenters had modified the hull by increasing *Constellation*'s molded beam 14 inches at the loca-tion of the dead flat.[25] Surely, as no contemporary drawings survive other than Humphreys' draft, my critics will claim that measurements taken off by naval offi-cers and constructors reflect the idiosyncratic habits of individuals and are there-fore suspect. However, in this instance Franklin Buchanan moved up to the spar deck and measured its width, which proved to be exactly the same as the Humphreys/Doughty drawing of 1795. Tingey, to increase *Constellation*'s stability, had, by keeping the spar deck dimension unchanged, altered the ship's tumble home from 3 feet to 3 feet 7 inches. Buchanan's journal provides the data verifying the extent of Tingey's alterations to *Constellation*'s lines and the manner in which he carried them out during the course of the rebuild. Buchanan also measured and recorded *Constellation*'s length of keel, straight rabbet, at 140 feet. I found the offi-cer's measurement to be accurate, since it corresponds to Humphreys' original drawings, too.[26]

Accounts of the physical history of *Constellation* that claim the ship-frigate was destroyed in 1853 reject any interpretation of Tingey's report that concludes that the ship's molded beam increased 14 inches in 1812. In spite of the concise language of his report, subsequent accounts deny the facts of the rebuild as related above, though my conclusions, drawn from Tingey's report and verified by Buchanan's measure-ments, are clearly supported by the evidence of the ship's performance in the after-math of her rebuild at Washington. Confirmation of Tingey's changes in design are available from *Constellation*'s operating records. The ship's increased stability is con-

Table 3.1. Length of Selected Spars and Yards of USS *Constellation* in 1801 and 1813

Name	1801 Length	1813 Length
Fore Mast	86 ft., 6 ins.	94 ft.
Main Mast	96 ft.	104 ft.
Mizzen Mast	82 ft.	81 ft.
Bowsprit	60 ft.	60 ft.
Jib Boom	43 ft.	53 ft.
Flying Jib Boom	44 ft.	53 ft., 6 ins.
Foremast Yard	76 ft.	81 ft.
Mainmast Yard	84 ft.	94 ft.
Mizzenmast Yard	57 ft.	75 ft.
Fore Topsail Yard	54 ft.	62 ft., 2 ins.
Main Topsail Yard	60 ft.	70 ft., 6 ins.
Mizzen Topsail Yard	42 ft.	49 ft.
Boom	54 ft.	62 ft.
Gaff	40 ft.	40 ft.

Source: Length of *Constellation*'s masts in 1801 and length of selected yards: Chapelle, *History of the American Sailing Navy,* appendix, 483. Length of *Constellation*'s new masts in 1813 and length of selected new yards: Orders and Articles Book of Captain Charles Stewart, 1812–13, William Nelson Collection, New Jersey Historical Society, Newark, New Jersey.

firmed by information in Captain Stewart's Order and Articles Book, supplemented by his correspondence with Secretary Jones.

When Stewart arrived in Hampton Roads in early February 1813 and discovered a Royal Navy blockade that forced *Constellation* to flee into Elizabeth River, he wrote Jones that a dash for the open sea was not possible as *Constellation*'s sails were not ready, "her old ones being one third too small."[27] With this information, *Constellation*'s commander provided strong evidence of the frigate's improved stability. As a result of changes caused by remasting, *Constellation* required larger sails for her new masts and yards, which in 1813 were substantially larger than her previous rig. This information focuses on the ship's new stability in 1813, particularly in view of adjustments ordered by her designer, Joshua Humphreys, when he remasted her in 1801, reducing the length of her spars and yards.[28] Both masting plans survive, and a comparison of principal spars and yards of 1801 with those installed in the ship at Washington in 1812 is provided in table 3.1.

The increase in size of the ship's masts and yards in 1812 was extreme and as a matter of fact, her revised plan compared to that of U.S. Frigate *Java*, 44 guns, built at Fells Point in 1813–14. If *Constellation*'s commanders considered her crank before Joshua Humphreys rerigged her in 1801, her additional sail area in 1813 would have rendered her unmanageable unless Tingey materially altered her hull shape prior to replacing her masts and yards with new ones of greater length.[29]

An increase in *Constellation*'s molded breadth, which required refairing of the ship's lines, provided the ship with greater buoyancy and improved trim, both a result of a new fullness in the ship's hull. Captain Murray reported in 1802 that when fully loaded and ready for a cruise, *Constellation* drew 22 feet 6 inches. Capt. William Crane, her commander in 1817, wrote in the ship's log 7 June 1817 that after loading all provisions and 34,100 gallons of water, *Constellation*'s draft was 21 feet 7 inches.[30] Increased stability and buoyancy, then, resulted from the increase of *Constellation*'s molded breadth.

Captain Tingey closed out his report to Jones concerning *Constellation*'s rebuild with a flip bit of braggadocio directed at Joshua Humphreys and David Stodder. He stated that as a result of the rebuild under his supervision "she was a better ship than when first from the stocks." He could not prove this statement in October 1814, as the ship never left the Chesapeake Bay during the war. Of greater import was the unanswered question of whether or not Tingey had so altered the ship's hull that she would never again sail with the speed that Humphreys and Stodder built her for, keeping in mind that Tingey's and Humphreys' theories of naval architecture differed as they related to the mission of the U.S. Navy.

Constellation, fourteen years old in 1812, had undergone replacement of all frame pieces (futtocks) above the floor timbers as well as some individual floor pieces, according to Tingey's report. If decay was the principal reason for these repairs, this is not startling in view of the ship's physical history as summarized by Humphreys in 1812 in his letter to Congressman Seybert. Navy constructors calculated that wooden ship hulls built for naval service required replacement on an average every sixteen years.[31] However, Tingey's modifications to *Constellation* and other navy ships at the Washington Navy Yard, often extreme in extent and effect, initiated a United States Navy policy, which, crystallized under the Board of Commissioners, allowed hull modifications when rebuilding ships undergoing great repairs.

Constellation's battles in the Quasi War, her years of transatlantic service during the Barbary Wars, her Philadelphia accident, and her six idle years in ordinary, combined with the probability that she was built largely of green timber, provide a fairly reliable body of evidence that a survey then would have concluded that the repairs received by the ship in 1812 as reported by Tingey to Jones in 1814 were realistic. Tingey, reacting to a vacuum in leadership, took the opportunities presented by the condition of *Constellation* and *Adams* to redraft and rebuild them in 1812, thereby creating rebuilding policies that survived as long as the navy's wooden ships.

Tingey's report stated that, in addition to rebuilding the hull, he replaced much of the frigate's equipment, including spars, sails, gun carriages, cables, and rigging, a complete rebuild by any nineteenth-century definition. Congress originally provided $120,000, but the cost of the work probably far exceeded that amount (Jones reported a deficit in his repair budget of $218,130.83).[32] The practice of intermingling funds authorized by Congress originated during this period as great repairs for ships with congressional authorization (*Constellation, Adams,* and *Chesapeake*) or vessels undergoing repairs or rebuilds without specific authorization of Congress—*John Adams,* 1809, *Congress,* 1810, *Vixen,* 1810, *Hornet,* 1811, *Enterprize,* and *Nautilus* (the last two were repaired and rerigged as brigs)—created a foundation for the navy's pragmatic approach to rebuilding.[33]

Early in July 1812, with his ship, U.S. Frigate *Constitution,* moored at Annapolis, Capt. Isaac Hull, fearing a Royal Navy blockade of Chesapeake Bay even that early in the war, requested sailing orders from Secretary Paul Hamilton. After receiving them, Hull hurriedly signed on a crew and proceeded down the bay to Hampton Roads, clearing the Capes 12 July. Sailing up the coast toward New York, *Constitution* fell in with several ships of the Royal Navy 17 July. By well-organized measures taken over the next few days, Hull won the most important nonbattle of the war, escaping the enemy's ships, which included HMS *Guerrière.* As much of the struggle to save the ship took place on a calm ocean, Hull's crew expended great energy towing and kedging the American ship, a supreme effort that enabled *Constitution* to escape into Boston harbor on 28 July. After determining that the British squadron did not have his ship under blockade, Hull slipped out to sea 2 August and on 19 August fell in with *Guerrière,* previously a tormenter during the desperate pull for freedom. A vicious battle ensued until darkness separated the ships. The next morning, observing the shattered *Guerrière,* Hull knew that the war's first American naval victory belonged to him.[34]

Following the declaration of war with Great Britain 18 June 1812, Hamilton gave Capt. William Bainbridge a choice of remaining in Boston in charge of the navy yard or commanding a ship. Bainbridge, looking forward to action, notified the Navy Department that he wanted to return to active sea duty. Hamilton offered him command of U.S. Frigate *Constellation* but asked him to remain at the Charlestown Navy Yard while his ship was undergoing a great repair at the Washington Navy Yard. Bainbridge, dissatisfied with the appointment, used his seniority to bump Hull from his command of *Constitution.* When Hull reentered Boston harbor in late August following his victory over HMS *Guerrière,* Captain Bainbridge was there to take command of *Constitution.*[35] Hamilton's second choice to command U.S. Frigate *Constellation* fell to Capt. Charles Stewart. When Stewart arrived at Washington in late summer of 1812, *Constellation's* repairs had reached an advanced stage in the ship's comprehensive rebuild. At the time of Stewart's arrival, a blanket of apathy covered the disarray of an American government at war. Back on 3 June, before war was declared, Capt. John Rodgers, in a letter on naval strategy to Secretary Hamilton, outlined the special danger of a blockade to Chesapeake Bay and particularly to Norfolk and to shipping at Hampton Roads.[36] President Madison's administration, but particularly the military departments, seemed unable to digest the importance of Rodgers's foresight. They suffered a shared myopia that caused each future event to develop with an element of surprise.

Though Hull and Rodgers concluded months earlier that a blockade of Chesapeake Bay shipping by the Royal Navy was inevitable, Tingey made no arrangements to prepare *Constellation* sufficiently to get her out of Chesapeake Bay at the earliest possible time. Finally, on 11 October, after more than half a year in the yard, the navy recommissioned the frigate and hoisted her colors. A few days later Stewart received a letter from Hamilton urging him to make every effort to get to sea.[37] However, Captain Tingey's logistical problems at the yard caused by shortages of materials, equipment, and ordnance delayed the completion of *Constellation;* mechanics continued to work on her as she lay moored at a wharf.[38] On the morning of 6 November, with eight launches towing her, assisted by gunboats and laborers from the yard, the ship was hauled off downriver. At a position below Greenleaf Point, she stuck fast on a mud bar and moored. Gunboats delivered anchors, guns, and provisions, which the ship's booms hoisted aboard where she lay downstream. The supply operation continued right up to 26 November, the day of a grand party given by Captain Stewart for members of Congress and other dignitaries including the Madisons, the nation's First Family.[39] Capt. Charles Stewart knew his ship well. It was his second stint as the commanding officer of the frigate; he had replaced Hugh Campbell in 1805 when the Navy Department ordered *Constellation* home from the Mediterranean Sea and into ordinary at Washington. Earlier, Stewart had served as first lieutenant under Captain Murray during *Constellation*'s first cruise against the Barbary nations in 1802–3. One author rates Stewart the best of Preble's boys.[40]

It is closer to the facts contained in his service record to point out that as commander of the navy schooner USS *Experiment* at the end of the Quasi War Lieutenant Stewart learned seamanship, a commander's role, and the sweet taste of victory. *Experiment* and USS *Enterprize,* both Baltimore schooners, were built in 1799 for the navy, the latter at St. Michaels, Maryland, and the former at Fells Point by William Price. Stewart received high praise for his successful engagements with the French privateers *Diana* and *Deux Amis,* both of which defended themselves. He established his gallantry when he and his first officer, David Porter, in *Experiment,* standing in Mona Passage, east of Puerto Rico, observed the vessel *Eliza* foundering on the rocks. Lieutenant Porter, in *Experiment's* launch, successfully rescued sixty women and children and seven crew members, the stranded ship's officers having perished while attempting to gain the beach. Following his service in the Quasi War and the Barbary Wars, Captain Stewart joined the merchant service, then returned to the navy as America's second war with Great Britain loomed.[41]

Stewart's lingering stay in the vicinity of Washington, which lasted through the year until December 1812, creates the impression that Rodgers's and Hull's sense of urgency failed to incite in him a similar fear that a Royal Navy blockade of Chesapeake Bay was imminent. The problems of the Navy Department at that time suggest that Stewart lingered in Washington partially because he was involved in unofficial matters concerning the incumbent secretary. Throughout 1812 the administration's strategy for the navy failed to evolve. Hamilton and his assistant, Charles Goldsborough, hesitated to press forward with mobilization plans. The heavy responsibilities of preparation for war produced an increasingly debilitating effect on Hamilton. The secretary, often incapacitated by his addiction to alcohol, proved ineffective in presenting a program acceptable to Congress, which was unable to agree on the navy's role in a second war with Great Britain's powerful Royal Navy.[42]

Stewart had problems other than his lobbying role for the Navy Department. Tingey's operation of the Washington Navy Yard attracted criticism from him and from Capt. Charles Morris, commander of USS *Adams.* Stewart spent time looking for equipment and provisions for *Constellation.* He located sailcloth for his ship's sails. Once under way he complained to the secretary of the navy about the shoddy materials and workmanship of the yard. Morris also bitterly complained about work done on *Adams,* which held up her departure from Chesapeake Bay for over a year.[43]

Once it committed itself to the idea of mobilizing the United States Navy, Congress correctly authorized great repairs or rebuilds to existing ships. Legislators followed these initial commitments with legislation for the expansion of the navy in 1813. By this sequence of congressional actions the Navy Department and Congress operated in a fiscally conservative manner by establishing first an effective rebuilding policy for ships in ordinary. Rebuilding, always separate from expansion by the addition of new ships, never included unauthorized new construction; neither Congress nor the navy linked rebuilding with new construction. And neither Congress nor the navy blurred the legal separation of the two distinct operations, even in later years. While the navy rebuilt ships without obtaining congressional approval, it never built a new ship without prior authorization by Congress.[44]

Earlier examples of rebuilding or great repairs to navy ships exist, but the work on *Adams* and *Constellation,* which included the partial redrafting of both ships, provides a clear, broad definition of the rebuilding policy of the U.S. Navy. Even more than *Constellation,* Tingey's rebuild of *Adams* created a complete definition of rebuilding that was widely accepted by the navy and its critics, Congress, and most administrations after 1815. Rebuilding policies, formed under Tingey's tenure at the Washington Navy Yard, not only included changes in a vessel's hull lines, but set the precedent for costs of a great repair to approach the original cost of a ship; the rebuilt ship, in this case, was *Adams.*

When Tingey completed *Adams's* rebuild no one suggested then or has since that the rebuilt ship was a new ship, though Tingey added 15 feet to her length. Certainly, rebuilding *Adams* was not only an extreme example of rebuilding a navy ship, but once approved by Congress, with the navy's sentimental and grateful nod toward the nation's second president, this rebuild helped establish a pragmatic rebuilding policy then in process of development. Congress appropriated funds specifically designated to rebuild *Adams* and *Constellation* as well as for repairs to *Chesapeake* at Boston, a legislative practice repeated over and over again in its appropriations for the navy.[45] The frequency with which the navy gave advance notification to Congress of an intended rebuild of a specific ship is often overlooked.[46]

The history of America's sailing navy and its rebuilding policies, once fully developed, included a set of qualifying conditions, though a study of naval history reveals that all criteria for rebuilding a ship were not always present. A fluid policy became routine during the war. Later, budget limits, a cap on the number of men or ships on active duty, the navy's need for smaller ships, or a political or sentimental reason produced very flexible rebuilding decisions. Tingey's approach, which served as the basis of the policy in the U.S. Navy, proved similar to the early pragmatic policies of the Royal Navy.[47]

From 1812 until the end of the American wooden sailing navy, vessels were repaired, rebuilt, or built new. A simple, straightforward definition of a new wooden ship for the U.S. Navy is one authorized by an act of Congress, built with new materials and equipment and as an addition to the fleet. The normal definition for repairs in the service was those required by a vessel after a tour of duty, which could be as short as a month or as long as two years. The important qualifying terms here are "routine" and "normal wear and tear."

Rebuilding is a far more complicated concept because any explanation or definition of it in theory does not necessarily explain its practical application. It was, in the nineteenth century, a broad policy that varied according to changing conditions inside and outside the service, conditions that forced decisions based on an array of factors, including the navy's changing missions.

In the twentieth century, when most ships built were constructed of steel and plastic, the concept of the perishable wooden hull of 1812, partially redesigned and sometimes almost completely replaced, and then, following rebuilding, the original ship surviving, is not an easy nineteenth-century preservation concept to grasp. While there is no denying that the Navy Board of Commissioners under Capt. John Rodgers pushed the rebuilding process to a point that makes it difficult for the uninitiated naval architect not to question the process, the denial of the legitimacy of rebuilding usually results from the reader's inability to grasp the art of building wooden ships and repairing navy vessels in the nineteenth century, a reasonable problem hopefully overcome in the presentation of the historical record. If the existence and reality of the navy's rebuilding policies are denied forthwith, denial usually relates to an agenda quite separate from the historical record. Certainly twentieth-century naval architects raise questions concerning the nineteenth-century practice more than historians. But that is understandable because modern naval architects generally study only wooden-ship drawings. Historians examine documentation from congressional records, the executive branch, and shipyards; they study the practices, systems, and traditions of shipbuilding as well as shipbuilding techniques and operations, all of this accumulated documentary record compiled for a historical restatement of navy construction and repair policies in a contemporary setting.

Congress, with its hold on the government's purse, may have caused the navy to repair ships on occasion when a new ship would have produced a more effective navy. Though that may have happened, it is also true that experienced officers of the wooden sailing navy preferred repairing a well-designed ship in need of a complete rebuild rather than taking the risk of receiving command of a poorly designed new ship. But the navy built no ships under the guise of rebuilding without at least a sentimental attachment to a preexisting vessel. Sometimes, when rebuilding was controversial, the navy held discussions or obtained congressional approval before proceeding with a rebuild. More than any other factor, rebuilding policies of the nineteenth-century navy are under scrutiny today not because intrigue was exposed in the administration of the navy, but simply because the service made a hash out of repair programs as costs skyrocketed out of control in navy-operated repair yards.[48]

As a policy took shape during the terms of Robert Smith, Paul Hamilton, and William Jones, the secretary of the navy authorized rebuilding United States Navy vessels when one or more of the following conditions prevailed:

a. To save the cost of building a new ship
b. To retain ships in service, such as *Constitution, Macedonian,* and *Constellation,* as memorials to past events or for other sentimental or historical reasons
c. When the ship had performed exceptionally well

d. When authorized by congressional legislation (rebuilding did not generally require congressional approval)
e. To fill requirements of a specific mission
f. To use stockpiled materials and equipment
g. When Congress capped the number of personnel and vessels commissioned
h. When legislation allowed unneeded new ships to remain in the stocks, with funding spread over several decades
i. To introduce modifications or to modernize older vessels

Secretary of the Navy William Jones's report to Congress on 22 February 1814 presented an outline for the foundation of the U.S. Navy's ship rebuilding policy. He reported to Congress that during 1812 the navy purchased no timber authorized by the act of 30 March 1812. Early in 1813 Jones noted that, in compliance with Congress's instructions, the navy purchased $23,000 worth of live oak timber at Baltimore for rebuilding the ships *Philadelphia, General Greene, New York,* and *Boston.* He informed Congress that he issued orders to have this timber redistributed among the new navy ships under construction at Fells Point and Philadelphia because Congress failed to pass legislation authorizing rebuilding of the old frigates. Jones, faced with a controversial situation, tossed the responsibility back to Congress, a practice repeated later in the century by Secretary John Branch and supported by President Jackson. Jones's report to Congress stated that he rejected the opportunity to rebuild these ships as *Philadelphia* did not exist and *General Greene, New York,* and *Boston* were worthless hulks, and as "it would cost much more, in proportion to their value, to rebuild them than to build new frigates of a better class and of vastly superior construction."[49]

Secretary Jones's report highlights the underlying practicality of a well administered rebuilding policy. Also, his decision to use funds of different authorizations, a result of the redistribution of the timber purchased with one authorization and then transferred to another appropriation, in this instance to new ship accounts, became standard navy accounting practice as the service developed flexible reporting systems for funds covering new construction, repairs, rebuilds, and the stockpiling of timber. As the cost of new ships often spread across several fiscal years, Jones's precedent of mixing appropriations became fairly standard practice. However, intermingling of the navy's repair, rebuilding, and new ship accounts and funding authorizations caused criticism, wasted funding, and strained relations with Congress on occasion.[50] The Jones report highlighted the importance of controlling rogue rebuilding projects. The only reason to rebuild *Philadelphia* was questionable sentimentality attached to her loss at Tripoli. As for the other ships—*General Greene, New York,* and *Boston*—Jones believed none were of a superior design and all would cost more than similarly built new ships. As a result of these decisions it became apparent that he believed an improperly conceived rebuilding scheme wasted money, thereby setting a wise precedent. But that is not to say that similar ill-conceived projects such as *Philadelphia* were not promoted, considered, and approved in later years. Jones's action helped establish a checklist of conditions for rebuilding, leaving the final responsibility with the secretary of the navy, who after the war delegated these tasks to the Board of Commissioners to approve rebuilds on their own authority or to go to Congress when the rebuilding of the ship under consideration created political controversy.[51]

The conclusions drawn in this chapter require summation because of their bearing on future chapters of this book. First, and of foremost importance, rebuilding became a prominent policy of the U.S. Navy early in its existence and redrafting or redesigning ships in advance of major rebuilds became part of a process repeated over and over again as long as the navy supported wooden sailing vessels. As early as 1803, with the rebuilding of *Constitution* in 1803–4 at Boston, followed by the rebuilding of *Enterprize* at Venice in 1804–5, the navy routinely rebuilt vessels for a variety of reasons, correcting perceived flaws in design as a part of the routine.

No segment of *Constellation*'s long history is more important nor has any part of it raised more questions than Captain Tingey's rebuild of 1812. Opponents of the conclusion reached here, that Tingey increased the ship's extreme beam at the dead flat by extending her molded breadth 14 inches, have to this date failed to produce a single definitive document or contemporary drawing in support of an opinion that Tingey did not alter *Constellation*'s molded breadth, but rather that he increased her extreme beam by replacing the ship's 7-inch wales with wales 14 inches thick.

Tingey wrote that he built *Constellation* entirely new from her floors up. This made girdling of the ship totally unwarranted. Tingey did not write that he made *Constellation* as good as new, or like new, or almost new; he wrote, simply, that she was entirely new from the floors up. Tingey's new dimensions were verified by Franklin Buchanan, a brilliant, young, serious officer, who enjoyed a successful navy career. Captain Stewart's Signal Book proved that Tingey's alterations greatly enhanced the ship's stability. Captain Crane's 1817 log confirms *Constellation*'s improved buoyancy and trim. It follows then, that if the Gosport Navy Yard's naval constructor measured U.S. Frigate *Constellation* in 1853 prior to dismantling, her molded breadth, her extreme breadth, and her shape below the waterline as shown in figure 3.1 would be the approximately the same in 1853 as in 1813, unless, of course, another naval constructor redrafted and rebuilt the ship during another great repair in the period between 1812 and 1853. Later chapters will demonstrate that the navy did, indeed, rebuild or partially rebuild *Constellation* a total of four times while she remained in active naval service.[52]

Four

THE LUCKY CONSTELLATION

Seamen, many who claimed to be United States citizens, were an international migrant labor force of the early nineteenth century. Once at sea, masters or commanders, in view of the absence of international law, set rules based on self-interest. Many foreign sailors moved into the crews of American ships at this time because they believed that wages were higher, life as a right acknowledged, and freedom to leave normally an alternative. Be that fact or fiction, it was this migration of a significant number of foreigners, particularly British- and Irish-born, into the American merchant service and navy as an effect of a series of other events, that darkened the seas and led to America's declaration of war against Great Britain in June 1812.

The United States Merchant Marine grew significantly in the first decade of the nineteenth century. It expanded with great numbers of handsome and efficient ships sailed by good crews, whose owners lifted a greater and greater percentage of Western Hemisphere cargoes as war tore the European continent apart and exhausted its wealth and population. Troubles growing out of America's new international presence, which accompanied the rise of its shipping empire, were as predictable as the fall of sand in an hourglass.

As cracks in the system of French, Spanish, and British protective navigation laws deepened, private and public empires controlled by individuals began to crumble. The United States, rising with a volcanic force of new energy, revealed the North American continent as a place of hope and challenge on land and sea. As time passed and the inconclusive War of 1812 stumbled into history, the effects growing from it seemed infinitely more important than its causes. For seamen, impressment was a matter of relative danger, discomfort, and indignity. Along with the flow of thousands of British and Irish emigrants to America's expanding cities, a steady number of seamen left the Royal Navy and its incubator of ordinary seamen, the British merchant service, as they jumped ship in America and abroad in favor of American maritime trades. The loss of the Crown's mariners struck at the heart of the British military defense system, the Royal Navy. Behind the serious loss of manpower, a number of political and economic changes rattled the foundation of a European system that had run its course—though it was not dead yet by far in 1815, at war's end. As for the war itself, there was no winner or loser and impressment did not end immediately.

The kidnapping of seamen from American ships for the Royal Navy was just one reason for the War of 1812. The *Chesapeake-Leopard* affair off Hampton Roads in 1807 focused the nation's attention on the problem of impressment. Around waterfront wharves and taverns seamen experienced the work of press gangs for decades. Traditionally, at New England ports, with their larger and well-established British trade, the practice was tolerated as a necessary adjunct to the region's prosperous commerce with Great Britain. Powerless seamen accepted impressment as another inhumane aspect in the life of an itinerant mariner or they moved south to the booming harbor of Baltimore, where sailors and politicians thoroughly disliked the British nation and its bullying navy. The issue divided the country into sections.

The veteran captains of the navy's wars against the French and Barbary nations—Decatur, Bainbridge, Hull, Rodgers, Stewart, and some younger officers, too—descended on Washington one after another to gain a command as America's second war against the Royal Navy opened. Their message for Madison's government and Congress was that they wanted a ship of the line for each senior captain and a heavy frigate for each younger one. It took six months to lobby Congress to legislate approval of the new battleships and frigates, which would take another two years to build. That is the kind of war it was.

Writing two decades later, James Fenimore Cooper expressed the opinion that after the war began, the Royal Navy successfully blockaded three of the nation's eight frigates, but failed to prevent any sloops of war from getting to sea. He concluded his criticism of American naval policy during the War of 1812 with an observation that though the blockade could not be prevented, the navy failed to build and employ the types of ships that could pass the blockade and gain the open sea.[1]

Captain Hull quickly refitted USS *Constitution,* fourteen years old and not yet a famous ship, but one of the few navy ships ready for sea shortly after Madison's war opened. Hull left Chesapeake Bay quickly, haunted by the possibility that he could be blockaded and, if not that, then forced to relinquish his command to William Bainbridge, who tracked him from Boston to Washington by coach.

Senior officers promoted the notion that the U.S. Navy must expand, and all concurred with the conclusion that success for the navy depended on ships of the line (74s) and more large Humphreys frigates. Their arguments seemed self-serving, and, in the end, academic, because peace returned before a single new ship rated a frigate or larger entered service. After Bainbridge refused an appointment as commander of the rebuilt *Constellation,* Paul Hamilton presented the appointment to Charles Stewart. This dashing officer became the navy's unofficial lobbyist as down at the navy yard Captain Tingey and his mechanics struggled to rebuild *Constellation* and *Adams.* Later in 1812, Charles Morris and Isaac Hull joined Stewart and Tingey in Washington and this foursome formed the phalanx of the officer corps' effort to expand the navy.

Quickly Stewart discovered that he should not expect much help from the Navy Department. Paul Hamilton, an alcoholic, became his problem, not his ally. The national election of November 1812 provided President Madison with a mandate to fight the war, though an observer described his efforts up to that point as half measures. Madison himself was definitely a man not born to lead under these circumstances; he was timid and obstinate, both acting and yielding too late, a president wholly ignorant of what the military defense of America required. Madison, this observer wrote, was "beset and tossed about by intrigue."[2]

Following Captain Stewart's lavish party on *Constellation* 26 November, routine on board remained unhurried. Several days later Washington society excitedly received news of plans of yet another party. This time the sponsors invited Captain Stewart to be their guest of honor, along with Captains Morris and Hull. The ball's committee selected Tuesday, 8 December, for the affair.

Rumors of the capture of HMS *Macedonian* floated over the capitol that afternoon. The city's lights illuminated a sense of anticipation that spread through the hall as dancing began. At nine o'clock, a startling event unfolded in front of Washington's elite as Midn. Archibald Hamilton, son of the secretary, arrived and spread the tattered colors of Captain Decatur's prize, HMS *Macedonian,* on the floor of the ballroom. The whole assembly gathered around Mrs. Hamilton and her daughters as they greeted a son long absent at sea. A witness described it as a remarkably affecting moment. Then someone gathered up the flag and laid it at Mrs. Madison's feet.[3]

Probably, at this magic moment, the navy could have demanded anything and Congress would have approved its most lavish requests. It passed the administration's bill for expansion of the navy 23 December 1812.[4] Three days later, in London, the Crown's secretaries of war gathered to plan a strategy to relieve pressure on their forces on Canada's border with the United States. They dispatched orders to the admiralty to blockade Delaware and Chesapeake bays, and to commence raiding their communities and plantations. The mighty Royal Navy began to gather at

Bermuda, a development that Madison's government never considered would occur that early in the war. Fate began to tighten her embrace on *Constellation*.[5]

With the approval of an appropriation bill for four ships of the line (74s) and six heavy frigates, Stewart's work in Washington was complete. However, *Constellation* remained on the upper Potomac for the rest of December 1812 as she did not stand down the river to St. Marys at the river's mouth until the end of the month. The new secretary of the navy, William Jones, ordered Stewart to move his ship up to Annapolis to test her gunpowder as cold weather thickened the ice on the Potomac River.[6]

Weather forced Stewart to notify Secretary William Jones that icing conditions would force the ship to leave her exposed anchorage in Annapolis Roads. Also, he complained bitterly of the quality of work done to his ship under Tingey's supervision.[7] But Jones ordered Captain Stewart to continue to conduct tests on the ship's gunpowder.[8] However, exhibiting some impatience and real concern for his ship's safety, Stewart interrupted the testing and ordered *Constellation* to make sail for Hampton Roads. His sudden departure, before powder tests could be completed, a result of ice on the bay, hard on ship and crew, accounts for his fatal decision to flee Annapolis Roads. Because Stewart did not know that a vanguard of four Royal Navy frigates at that time approached the coast, his decision to sail to Hampton Roads set the stage for an episode that cost the navy an irreplaceable frigate for the duration of the war.[9]

Once under way Stewart had no alternative destination.[10] With no advance knowledge of the Royal Navy's almost simultaneous arrival at Cape Henry, the discovery of a blockade forming in front of him just as *Constellation* dropped anchor there proved a numbing shock to captain and crew. As a matter of fact Stewart wrote Jones despondently on 10 February that he felt "extremely at a loss what steps to pursue." Clearly exhibiting his depressed state of mind, he asked Jones for instructions and requested from him the "expectations of the government."[11]

Though other historians have written that Stewart intended to stand out to sea and begin an Atlantic Ocean cruise, this is improbable as her refit remained incomplete. Stewart received no orders beyond Annapolis from Secretary Jones, *Constellation* still needed her spare set of sails, and, of course, her sudden departure interrupted testing the ship's powder, its condition unknown.[12] In a letter to the secretary reporting his departure from Annapolis, Stewart failed to include his date of arrival at Hampton Roads. His report revealed only that "yesterday (4th) we discovered two sail of the line, three frigates, a brig and a schooner of the enemy working up (from the Capes) between Middle Ground and the Horseshoe for (Hampton) Roads." He left a gap of two days unaccounted for in his correspondence with Jones.[13]

George de la Roche, sailing master on board *Constellation*, entered in his journal that *Constellation* anchored in Hampton Roads 2 February and that the British fleet arrived off Cape Henry on the third. He wrote that on the latter date *Constellation* stood out to sea, but when off Cape Henry was chased back by four British frigates. Were these different versions of the same events the result of faulty memories, incorrect information, or a cover-up on Stewart's part?[14]

Captain Stewart's correspondence raises three questions. Why did he fail to inform Jones of his date of arrival at the Roads when he reported to him 5 February? How was it possible that he incorrectly identified the size and composition of the enemy fleet when he placed their position inside Cape Henry and *Constellation* aground off Willoughby Spit? Could British lookouts aboard Royal Navy frigates, almost one hundred feet above the sea, fail to sight *Constellation,* stranded on Willoughby Spit bar, if the lead frigate, *Maidstone,* as reported by Stewart, was observed to be "between the Middle Ground and the Horseshoe, at the entrance to Hampton Roads"? The evidence suggests that Stewart, aground on Willoughby Spit on the afternoon of 4 February and haunted by the realization that his emergency departure from Annapolis endangered his ship and his career, wrote a report to Jones with care not to bring criticism upon himself in view of the embarrassing developments. The *Norfolk Herald* reported 8 February that the Royal Navy ships, consisting of two 74s, three frigates, a brig, and a schooner, effectively blockaded the port, basically the same incorrect information that Stewart relayed to Jones.[15]

A reconstruction of events suggests that *Constellation* arrived off Horseshoe Shoals 3 February and anchored between Cape Henry and the Willoughby Spit, which marks the entrance to Hampton Roads. When the news of the British fleet arrived by pilot boat 4 February, Stewart hastily hoisted anchor and headed into Hampton Roads between the Horseshoe and the bar at the end of Willoughby Spit. Losing headway in a calm, the ship drifted onto the bar on the south side of the channel at low tide at about 2:00 P.M. 4 February. With the ship hard aground at the end of the spit, calls went out for assistance and several vessels responded. Moving quickly, the frigate's crew unloaded provisions and Stewart ordered her water started.[16]

The tide ran its cycle and with a flood running in, water rose under the lightened ship's bottom and she refloated at 6:00 P.M., after the sun had set. James Thomas, a Norfolk pilot, assisted Stewart and with Hampton Roads calm, *Constellation*'s boats towed her to the mouth of Elizabeth River. Once there, small craft, including the ship's boats with lanterns attached, lighted the twisting Elizabeth River channel as *Constellation,* under tow, proceeded upriver to an anchorage opposite Norfolk and Portsmouth, about four miles above Craney Island at the mouth of the river. Stewart's report to Jones makes clear that he never saw the enemy and that the enemy never saw *Constellation* because she was already inside Elizabeth River before the British frigates dropped anchor in Lynnhaven Bay.[17]

After remaining anchored in the vicinity of Norfolk for more than a month, *Constellation* got under way 9 March and, as Stewart reported to Jones, "went down to

Craney Island lite [*sic*]." Rear Adm. George Cockburn's squadron, consisting of four ships of the line, several frigates, and smaller vessels, arrived at Lynnhaven 3 and 4 March, joining HMS *Maidstone* and the three other frigates, which had arrived 4 February. Word of Stewart's probe reached Cockburn quickly, and he moved his ships of the line into Hampton Roads in two days, the fleet's progress somewhat slowed by the need to mark a channel. This huge display of Royal Navy power robbed Stewart of all hope of escape. At that point, gloomy concerning the defense of the ship and Norfolk, he turned his attention to stripping *Constellation* and to reorganizing the corps of gunboats, which he found to be in appalling condition and without trained crews.[18]

Stewart assessed his position and the chances that combined naval and militia operations could make a successful defense of the river, the frigate, and the towns of Norfolk and Portsmouth. His mood turned dark again as Virginia militiamen, asked to join the crews of navy gunboats, started slipping out of town. Further, Stewart lamented the fact that the army had built no fort or battery on Craney Island as the end of March approached. Though there existed a willingness on the part of Stewart as well as Captain Cassin at Gosport Navy Yard and local army and militia officers to mount a joint defense of the river and towns, this effort suffered from the lack of support at the higher level of Virginia's executive department and from the departments of the navy and army in Washington.[19]

With his return upriver following *Constellation*'s brief excursion to the mouth of Elizabeth River 9 March, Stewart concluded that he had no chance of escaping through Hampton Roads and the capes into the Atlantic Ocean. The ship must be stripped and made ready to withstand attack by British barges and boats. A well-organized naval defense coordinated with local military units would deter any fleet of small craft Cockburn mustered to carry the river at Craney Island. Stewart appointed Capt. William Tee of Portsmouth the navy's chief pilot and ordered him to block the channel off Lambert Point, which is opposite the island on the Norfolk side of the river. Tee accomplished this in short order, sealing the Royal Navy out and the *Constellation* inside Elizabeth River. Tee then sank additional vessels below *Constellation*'s new position, according to a Cockburn report.[20]

With *Constellation* once again anchored in the middle of the narrow channel opposite Norfolk, Stewart stationed ten gunboats, five on each side of the ship, their crews now consisting of officers and men of the frigate. With the boats in this position, their guns could maintain a flanking fire against any advancing British boats or barges. "A circle of booms, securely fastened, protected the gunboats from being boarded." The main deck guns of the frigate were housed and their ports shut. Stewart ordered no ropes hung over the side of the ship and stern ladders taken away and even the gangway cleats removed. "Boarding netting were made of twenty one thread ratlin stuff boiled in half made pitch, which rendered it so hard almost to defy the knife. Nail rods and and small chains were secured to the netting in lines about three feet apart."[21]

To guard against boarders, the crew spread netting outboard toward the yard arms, attaching it about twenty-five feet above the deck. "To the outer rope or ridge line of the netting, they secured pieces of kentledge, that by cutting lines, should the enemy get alongside, the boats and men would be snared beneath it. Pieces of kentledge were also suspended forward, from the sprit yard and bowsprit to prevent boats from lying under them, while netting was here hoisted to the fore stay." The main battery having been secured, carronades, stuffed to the muzzles with musket balls, were depressed to the nearest range to sweep around the ship. Her officers expressed confidence that *Constellation* could be defended against any attack by boats, and it was not expected that Cockburn would commit his ships to enter the river.[22]

Captain Stewart, working with Captain Cassin of Gosport Navy Yard, instituted a program of reconditioning the gunboats and training crews of officers and seamen from *Constellation* to man them. As the days passed, Cassin increased the effective fleet until it totaled twenty gunboats, almost all manned with crews from *Constellation*. Volunteers from Norfolk failed to muster as unemployed seamen deserted the blockaded town. Stewart acquired two tenders for cruising Hampton Roads as an early warning system and added the Norfolk pilot boat *Franklin* to his fleet of small craft.[23] All gunboats, because of their vulnerability, remained inside Elizabeth River, as he worried that an alert British ship could maneuver and successfully cut them out of the river if they ventured beyond its mouth. As the month of March passed, Stewart seemed to rouse himself from his dark despondency as he grew aware that a successful defense of Elizabeth River was not impossible. He requested Jones's permission to build a floating battery.[24]

Secretary Jones, writing from Washington on 27 March, expressed the urgency of a successful defense of Norfolk and *Constellation*. Tying up Admiral Cockburn and the majority of his fleet inside Chesapeake Bay provided leeway for the navy's other ships to breach the blockade and cruise the North Atlantic unfettered by a large portion of the enemy forces, thus subjecting British merchants ships as well as more vulnerable Royal Navy units to capture by one or more of the navy's powerful frigates. Jones described the situation to Stewart as one in which as the result of petty larceny warfare on Chesapeake Bay, America's gallant commanders scoured the ocean, gathering laurels in such abundance, and "in such rapid succession as to afford the enemy scarcely time to soothe the chagrin of one defeat before he is subjected to the mortification of another."[25]

The thought of capturing *Constellation* as a prize of war along with twenty-one or so merchant vessels with cargoes caught by the blockade in Elizabeth River, combined with the prospect of looting two port towns and of gaining wealth and fame, distorted the strategic planning of Admiral Warren and the rest of the British naval forces at Lynnhaven. From 3 March, when Cockburn arrived with his main force, until the battle of Craney Island 22 June, the admiralty raged at Admirals Warren and Cockburn for failing to spread their ships along the Atlantic coast, as much of Warren's fleet remained in Chesapeake Bay waiting for reinforcing troops for an invasion of Norfolk. Surely this concentration on Norfolk and *Constellation* frustrated for months the diversionary mission ordered by His Majesty's secretaries of war. They did not fail to inform Admiral Warren of their opinion of the situation with dispatches that contained the most elegant English irony and sarcasm.[26]

As Captain Stewart reached a conclusion that *Constellation*'s position on Elizabeth River made it impossible to break out, so too, Admiral Cockburn struggled with his own plans to enter the river with major units of his fleet. He ordered a sounding of the river's channel. Cockburn informed Warren that he never found deep water abreast of Craney Island, in spite of employing all boats of the squadron to assist and buoy off the channel in Elizabeth River. Bribing a local pilot in his custody, Cockburn's party, forced to work at night, failed to locate the course of the channel. The American pilot insisted that there was not enough water to carry the flats with more than twelve feet and that the channel carried just three and one-half fathoms abreast of Craney Island. Cockburn gave up "all further idea of carrying the ships into Elizabeth River."[27]

In early April, boats from HMS *Victorious* chased the Baltimore schooner *Flight* into the main channel, where she grounded on Horseshoe Shoal. A sudden squall hit the schooner and the British boat crews tried to get her off. Gale winds destroyed *Flight*, but her master, Matthew Kelly, one of the great letter of marque captains out of Fells Point, and his crew managed to get ashore. The crews of the British boats lost control of their craft, the gale blowing three ashore, and another fell into the hands of a launch from *Constellation*. One of *Constellation*'s prisoners, a Royal Navy midshipman, told Stewart of Cockburn's extensive search for the main channel of Elizabeth River. He confirmed that the captured American pilot found only nineteen feet of water between Sewell Point and Craney Island, but revealed that Admiral Warren wanted to send ships into the river anyway, that is, until he discovered that *Constellation* had taken a new position four miles farther up the river.[28]

Perhaps the British midshipman's other news—that units of the Duke of Wellington's forces in Portugal would be transferred to Chesapeake Bay in the months ahead—disturbed Stewart the most. As one of the U.S. Navy's senior captains, he believed that his position earned him the right to leave his current situation whenever a suitable command opened up. Patriotism as a force overriding personal considerations rarely existed at that time in the United States, still basically a confederation of states after twenty-three years of existence under a constitution. While

Stewart felt a sense of duty, it was a duty centered on his own career, not the nation's fate. As a mariner and a naval officer, his assignment as custodian of a ship blockaded for the duration of the war could not be expected of him by the government in Washington.[29]

William Jones, the Philadelphia merchant who became secretary of the navy after Hamilton stepped down, and given the job of directing the United States Navy during the war, agreed with Stewart that *Constellation*'s position at Norfolk was hopeless. He wrote *Constellation* off as a ship of war and so notified Stewart. The river, Craney Island, the United States Army units assigned to the region, and the State of Virginia and its militia, the frigate, the navy yard, and all other local assets must be knitted together locally to save Norfolk, Portsmouth, and the Gosport Navy Yard, Jones wrote. He told Stewart bluntly not to expect help from Washington.[30]

While Stewart mulled over his personal misfortune, spring brought a change in weather and the return of Warren's raiding group from the upper bay. Stewart's most immediate problem concerned the U. S. Army's failure to fortify Craney Island. Jones approved his request to build a floating battery and to manufacture fire chests and fit out fire vessels. He denied him authority to build batteries on Craney Island, citing the normal interservice separation of authority. Also, Jones denied Stewart any assistance manning gunboats, though Stewart seems to have already handled this problem by assigning his ship's officers and seamen to them. This move stripped *Constellation* of her crew, but the overall plan of defense provided for several of the gunboats to proceed upriver and re-form on the frigate's flanks should Craney Island fall to the enemy. Crews of the remaining gun boats would leave them, taking battle stations on the ship and manning the carronades on her spar deck.[31]

Charles Stewart's black mood continued to dominate his actions and on or about 20 April he wrote Jones an undated letter, laced with self-pity, tracing how a series of unfortunate circumstances forced "us" into Elizabeth River from which escape became impossible because of the great odds the enemy placed against *Constellation*. In this letter, which Jones recorded receiving on 22 April, Stewart, oddly continuing to employ the collective "us," begged the secretary not to forget him should the position of commander of *Constitution* open up. He advised the secretary to lay up *Constellation* and transfer her crew to the Norfolk gunboats permanently. If this was done, he wrote, "the ship won't collect oysters and mussels." Counting marines, *Constellation*'s crew stood at 345 officers and men.[32]

Stewart's determination to leave *Constellation* at that particular time would be judged today as an act of a self-centered officer who, knowing well that a battle would shortly occur, exhibited a complete lack of awareness of or concern for his ship and crew, particularly when he moved on to safety and left his men to face possible death or capture. At that time in the history of our country, Stewart's request for relief merely defined his position in society: as a gentleman, he was concerned only with the judgment of his peers.

On 7 May Jones issued Stewart orders to report to Washington, then proceed to Boston and take command of *Constitution*. Stewart requested Jones's permission to delay his departure. One can assume that the announcement of his departure did not receive a mild reaction from *Constellation*'s officers. As a matter of fact, Jones informed Stewart that subsequent to his request he had received three requests for transfers from junior officers. Jones commented that their position, once enviable, now left them caught by the fortunes of war, and they, too, wanted to quit the ship.[33]

The contents of Stewart's next letter proved controversial and most probably were intended as a cover-up. He wrote Jones only a few days after receiving orders that all the ship's materials were replaced, provisions loaded, and water casks filled, and the ship now put into a state of readiness.[34] Stewart had previously directed the stripping of *Constellation*'s provisions and crew, and in preparation for a siege, he had the ship prepared to ward off attackers. When Capt. Charles Gordon assumed command of *Constellation*, a brawl broke out over her poor condition. Letters of implicated officers reached Jones with their explanations, all implying that Stewart misled Jones before he left the ship. After examining the evidence, the secretary concluded the matter with a mild letter voicing his dissatisfaction with Stewart, who, as late as October 1813, was still hanging around Boston waiting to get *Constitution* past a blockade and to sea; in this way Jones let him off the hook without so much as a public reprimand.[35]

Master Comdt. Joseph Tarbell replaced Stewart and became acting commander of *Constellation*. He originally arrived at the Gosport Navy Yard 30 March and was Capt. John Cassin's son-in-law. He received a promotion to captain in July 1813, following the battle of Craney Island, but eventually Jones appointed Charles Gordon commander of *Constellation*, leaving Tarbell in charge of the gunboats assigned to Norfolk.[36]

In preparation for an attack on Norfolk, the governor of Virginia, James Barbour, placed Brig. Gen. Robert Barraud Taylor, a Norfolk attorney, in charge of the Norfolk military district in January 1813. Taylor left his command in April and did not return until 2 June 1813.[37] This break in command contributed to the slow pace of the militia's preparations for the defense of Norfolk and delayed the planned fortifications on Craney Island. Stewart reported to the Navy Department that an army corps of engineers' work party had begun throwing up a battery on the island, remarking that he feared the delay would be too long. Several days later, as Stewart prepared to leave *Constellation*, he admitted in a final letter to Jones that every sign pointed to an attack on the frigate and Norfolk. Back in London, the admiralty continued to fume over the concentration of Warren's fleet at Hampton Roads even after Admiral

Warren acknowledged that *Constellation*'s position placed her beyond the reach of naval attack.[38]

Locals called Craney Island a barrier island because it consisted of sand cast up for centuries by tides running out of Elizabeth and James Rivers. Underbrush covered its sand, which rose only a few feet above high tide, and except for one tree and a house it was barren. About fifty acres in size and three hundred yards wide, the island, with its western edge hugging the river shore, stretched about nine hundred yards out into the wide mouth of Elizabeth River. Across the river to the east, General Taylor ordered Lambert Point fortified. Between the island and that point flowed the river's principal channel, the one Cockburn never located.

Fortifications planned by the army engineers consisted of a blockhouse which would house three large twenty-four-pound guns and an eighteen-pounder. The engineers, commanded by Lt. Col. Walker Keith Armistead, constructed the battery on the southeast corner of the island opposite Lambert Point. They chose the location because of its position adjacent to the river's main channel. The army never finished the fortification, which, as it turned out, caused no harm because the British attacked the island from the west and north. Of note is the obvious absence of coordination in the army's planning of the fortification in relation to the position of the sunken block ships and a subsequent plan to position the navy's gunboats, a force of far more firepower than the four guns placed nearby on the island, in a line just upriver from the sunken ships and shore battery.

The decision to place gunboats in the channel upriver from the island proved to be an important one that helped turn the battle in favor of the defenders. It probably caused the British to send their second wave of small boats to the west end of Craney Island to avoid the gunboats. Other defensive preparations on the island included trenches and redoubts on the front to the north and west sides of the island, which fronted on the narrow passage called the Thoroughfare, a narrow, shallow passage that separated the island from the mainland to the west.[39]

Charles Stewart's last letter to Jones from Norfolk failed to mention local preparations. He criticized the British for not being risktakers and concluded with the comment that, considering their total force at Hampton Roads, their conduct was disgraceful. Free of *Constellation* and in Washington on 6 June, Stewart met Benjamin Latrobe at a reception. Though he talked openly to him about Elijah Mix's unsuccessful attempts to use torpedoes against British ships at Lynnhaven, he did not volunteer the information that he had quit *Constellation* and that Jones had reassigned him to *Constitution*.[40]

With five hundred troops on Craney Island finally preparing defenses, there rose a concern that a surprise British attack could take the island. An officer from the U.S. Army Quartermaster's Office asked Captain Cassin to supply barges to move the military working party back and forth. Cassin, who exhibited little independent initiative but who devoted much attention to pleasing higher authority, asked Jones for his approval. (Later, when the army asked Cassin to share his whiskey stores, Cassin again sought permission from Jones, remarking that he had just eleven thousand gallons on hand.) As late as 1 June, the commandant of the yard admitted to Jones that he still had not collected materials for the floating battery, but he assured him that it would be built as cheaply as possible. With Tarbell in charge of *Constellation,* Cassin placed Lt. John M. Gardner of the frigate's crew in charge of the gunboat flotilla.[41]

Top British military strategists in London and Admiral Warren agreed that a strike, with supporting land forces, should be conducted against Norfolk and *Constellation.* The secretaries of war still concentrated their strategy on a forceful diversionary action to relieve pressure on British forces along the Canadian border. Warren's interests seemed more personal as he saw Elizabeth River as a source of glory and wealth. Returning to Bermuda in early May with prizes from raids on the upper Chesapeake Bay, he met with Col. Sir Sidney Beckwith, who had recently arrived from Europe with approximately two thousand veterans of the Peninsular War and other miscellaneous forces, including Royal Marines. Planning sessions, with input by Admiral Cockburn at Lynnhaven, delivered to Bermuda by captured Baltimore schooners, resulted in plans for a joint operation, based more on compromise than the clever use of assets. In spite of their unequal rank, Warren and Beckwith shared authority; under the British military system, the concept of a supreme commander did not exist during combined army-navy operations.

Warren and Cockburn pushed for an attack on Craney Island because its guns blocked naval access to the river. A pincer operation by land and sea received Beckwith's approval, and his selection of a landing area to the west of Craney Island was agreed to. Cockburn, though, preferred a landing on Sewell Point and from that point on the east side of Elizabeth River making a direct overland march on Norfolk. The Beckwith plan called for a combined attack by sea and land on Craney Island; when the island was secured, the army units would be freed up for a march on Portsmouth by way of a bridge over the western branch of Elizabeth River, a distance of twelve miles. With a split command and a compromise plan, built on strong individual impressions but also on little knowledge of the local approaches to their objectives once away from the main channels, Admiral Warren reembarked Beckwith's troops and sailed for the Chesapeake, arriving at Lynnhaven 19 June. Additional conferences on arrival failed to alter the plan worked out in Bermuda. Probably because of his continuing objections, Warren replaced Admiral Cockburn as his chief operations officer and substituted Capt. Samuel J. Pechell, commander of his flagship, HMS *San Domingo.* This unusual move gives credence to the suggestion that the principal commanders disagreed on strategy prior to committing their forces to battle. Recalling events in his memoirs, Col. Charles Napier, Beckwith's second, said that as it turned out, too many were involved with planning the Craney Island disaster.[42]

Gen. Robert Taylor returned to his command three weeks before the battle to discover that construction of fortifications had proceeded without a coordinated defensive plan for the island. The principal fortification, a blockhouse located on the island's eastern end adjacent to the river's channel, remained unfinished. Taylor was convinced that if there was an attack, it would be directed at Craney Island from the west and front of the island because a small boat attack up the main channel of the river would prove too risky.[43]

Less than a week before the dawn attack on Craney Island, General Taylor sat down at his writing desk and prepared a report to Secretary of War John Armstrong. A lawyer, Taylor wrote his report in the opaque manner of his trade, tying the past and the future of Craney Island to the then unknown intentions of the British. At the same time, Admiral Warren's gigantic Royal Navy fleet with its contingent of more than two thousand troops and marines began to congregate in front of the town of Hampton in the Roads facing tiny Craney Island, a mere wart in the mouth of Elizabeth River. Taylor wrote 18 June, four days before the battle, that he anticipated no attack on Norfolk.

By indulging himself with this rather hopeful analysis of British strategy, Taylor exposed his real doubts about the outcome of a battle to keep Craney Island out of the hands of the enemy, which he believed was the only immediate objective of the British forces. Taylor anticipated that the island would fall to the overwhelming power of an attack by land and water. He revealed to Secretary of War Armstrong his pessimism concerning the outcome of an attack when he wrote that Craney Island to be useful "with the proposed defense" will require considerable artillery to man and a large additional force to maintain it and that "its [present] situation precludes all succor. . . . If assailed by a larger one [force], the troops should succeed in getting off." Taylor's report to Armstrong concluded with the comment that though he expected Craney Island to fall, it was not important at that time as he did not expect British forces to proceed on to Norfolk, then to Portsmouth, and to attack *Constellation*.[44]

As the United States flotilla of gunboats stood out of Elizabeth River the night of 19 June, Taylor, at his headquarters in Norfolk, surrounded by his staff of six colonels and seven majors, placed a question to the assembled officers: "Under present circumstances is it proper to evacuate the post at Craney Island, if the deposition of the Enemy should indicate an attack on the island or on the Forts on the Harbour of Norfolk?" The thirteen officers present, all of ranks inferior to Taylor's, voted in the affirmative. Lt. Col. Constant Freeman, USA, senior regular officer at Norfolk, voted with the militia officers, but Major Maurice did not record General Taylor's vote.[45] Later that night, two waves of the Norfolk flotilla, under orders issued by Captain Cassin, and led by Joseph Tarbell, *Constellation*'s acting commander, pulled off an exciting but potentially disastrous raid on the British frigate HMS *Junon,* which was anchored and becalmed in Hampton Roads near the mouth of James River. Fifteen gunboats, divided into two waves, and led by Lt. John M. Gardner and Lt. Robert Henley of *Constellation,* moved downriver and into Hampton Roads.

An unfavorable light wind delayed their advance until four o'clock the following morning, when they approached and opened fire on the isolated British ship. The American sailors reported direct hits. A breeze sprang up and *Junon* and other ships nearby got under way, putting the gunboats on the defensive. They escaped back into Elizabeth River with one boat severely damaged and one officer killed. One notable aspect of the raid included the participation by fifty sharpshooters from the Craney Island army garrison, which shows the cooperation among U.S. Navy and Army units at that level. In spite of claims by Tarbell and Cassin in their reports of the skirmish, *Junon* received little damage from the fire of the gunboats.[46]

One presumes that when word of the results of General Taylor's council reached Captain Cassin and Commander Tarbell, who returned with the gunboat flotilla during the morning of 20 June, a second council of war assembled at Taylor's headquarters. Major Maurice recorded as present the six colonels who had attended the prior meeting plus Lt. Col. Walker Keith Armistead, USA, of the army corps of engineers, who was in charge of the construction on Craney Island. The group of officers with majority commissions changed slightly, as a Captain Carr attended and one major dropped out. Also, in a prominent position at the end of the table sat Captains Cassin and Tarbell.

General Taylor requested the officers present to take a vote on the question: "Whether [under] present circumstances it be advisable to withdraw the Forces from Craney Island?" Captain Carr voted no along with all majors in attendance except a Major Lindsay, who voted to evacuate the island or reinforce the contingent already there. Colonels Read and Mason voted aye, that is, for evacuation. The four remaining colonels present, now joined by Colonel Armistead, voted no, indicating that they disapproved of withdrawing from Craney Island. Cassin and Tarbell also voted no.[47]

Information leaked to those outside the meeting attributed the change in the vote to Colonel Armistead's objections, fortified by assurances from Captains Cassin and Tarbell that the navy's gunboats and *Constellation*'s crew would be integrated into the plan for the island's defense. It is difficult to accept what became obvious at the second meeting, that on the eve of the battle of Craney Island, Taylor's plan of defense did not include the navy's assets, as it was less than forty-eight hours later that Colonel Napier's troops disembarked on a beach west of the island. Yet Taylor's papers reveal that only after the two councils of war on 19 and 20 June did the engineer corps with the help of the militia detachments assigned to Craney Island begin to reposition to the west end of the island the great guns already placed in the battery at the east end. Almost simultaneously, navy gunboats moved into position in the main channel of Elizabeth River east of the island.

Artillery pieces on the island consisted of four 6-pounders placed there to guard work parties building the battery and preparing redoubts and hauled there over several weeks prior to the battle. In addition, engineers placed two 24-pounders in the battery on June 20. They mounted these two large pieces on carriages and placed them in such a manner that they could be aimed only in the direction of the river channel east of the island. By the time that the engagement started 22 June, engineers placed two additional pieces, another 24-pounder and an 18-pounder, in the area of the blockhouse at the east end of the island. It was only when the defenders perceived that British troops had landed above the island to the west that soldiers hauled two of the 24-pounders from the battery to the other end of the island to face the approaching British regulars.

These two great guns and the four six-pounders comprised the total American artillery that Major Faulkner's men and *Constellation*'s sailors fired, first on the troops who landed above the island and then on the waves of small craft that proceeded directly to the island. An eyewitness describing the scene wrote that the guns had no platforms and that they lay on the ground without coverings, though a bank was hastily built up in front of them to protect the artillerymen from musketry. The observer noted that the other pieces remained set up in the battery on the east side of the island throughout the battle, along with two additional 24-pounders that arrived during the battle too late to use.[48]

On the evening of 21 June, 150 men from *Constellation* transferred to Craney Island and integrated into the gun crews, or were assigned to strengthen the garrison at its weakest points. Maj. James Faulkner, commander of the artillery units and an intelligent man with only militia experience, did what Warren and Beckwith could not do: he set up under his command a combined army-navy artillery group, a unit that, when the attack began, fired often enough and straight enough to turn the enemy back on two fronts. Thus, on the day of the battle *Constellation*'s total crew of almost 350 officers and men quit the ship to man the gunboats, to handle the island guns, or to perform other chores as they developed. In charge of the *Constellation* units on the island, Lts. Benedict I. Neale, William B. Shubrick, and Acting Lt. James Sanders commanded the ship's crew and Second Lt. Henry B. Breckenridge led the marine unit. Only Sailing Master Benjamin Bryan and twelve crewmen remained on board *Constellation*.[49]

On the morning of 22 June 1813 an awesome show of naval power filled Hampton Roads as the morning mist lifted. In addition to seven transports carrying Beckwith's troop units and one thousand Royal Marines, Warren's impressive fleet totaled more than twenty ships, including six ships of the line, several frigates, gun brigs, and four or five schooners, Chesapeake Bay–built. Facing this immense force, 750 men waited, hunkered down on Craney Island, with two large guns and several smaller ones, almost all fully exposed to the enemy's glasses. However, the hundreds of large guns of this vast armada proved to be useless as the broad shallow flats stretching out into the Roads offshore from Craney Island kept the British fleet at bay.

With their vision limited by the mist hovering over the river, the defenders of Craney Island did not become aware that the British troops had landed until a horseman forded the Thoroughfare shouting the news. The first wave of British troops had landed near Hoffler's Creek at the mouth of Nansemond River, less than two miles west of Craney Island. With the island's available guns now facing west across the shallow Thoroughfare, Major Faulkner's gunners waited for the red-uniformed troops to break clear of the underbrush at water's edge. Once they were visible, the militia and sailors blasted away at close range.

A second wave of Royal Navy small craft loaded with sailors and marines plus a Company of Foreigners, composed of French prisoner volunteers, formed a second wave following the departure of Beckwith's troops. This provided the defenders with the time needed to handle Beckwith's attacking land forces before facing a frontal attack by water. As the Thoroughfare was only waist-deep, it could be forded easily, but when the redcoats broke out of the underbrush, they became fully exposed to the defenders before they got a chance to cross the narrow waterway. Lt. Col. Charles Napier, second in command, quickly ordered his veterans to fall back, signaling the failure of that phase of the attack. A gleeful mix of troops and tars watched the British break off the attack in disorder and retreat out of range of Faulkner's concentrated fire.[50]

The second wave, said to have included a thousand troops, sailors, and marines, approached the island in small craft from the northwest on a course from their ships that took their shallow-draft boats and barges over a bar that extends north from Craney Island some distance into the place where James River tides meet those of Elizabeth River. This approach to the island kept the attackers hidden from the great guns of Armistead's battery on the east side; nor could they be brought under the fire of American gunboats covering the eastern flank of the island.

The course taken by the approaching waves of British small craft met with disaster as the water shoaled long before they reached the island. Once the British were aground, chaos developed as Faulkner's big guns, repositioned to face the approach-

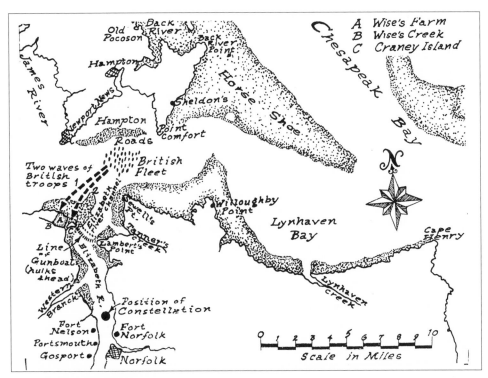

The attack on Elizabeth River, Norfolk, Virginia, and USF *Constellation*, Craney Island, 22 June 1813. *Alan C. Chesley*

ing craft, opened up on the enemy's boats, now piling up on each other like a squeezed accordion. Their guns stuffed with grape and scrap iron, the American gunners quickly disabled two or three boats. Panicked British deserters ran for the island as the wounded drowned. Retreat sounded, this time after the British commander, Capt. J. M. Hanchett of HMS *Diadem*, lay dying. Infantrymen and crewmen from *Constellation* rounded up prisoners. The invasion of Elizabeth River ended, and miraculously, Craney Island's defenders dashed Admiral Warren's chance for rich prizes and a valuable trophy, U.S. Frigate *Constellation*.[51]

Lt. Col. Henry Beatty, who commanded the combined militia, regular army, and navy units on Craney Island, wrote a report of the victory to his superior, Gen. Robert Taylor, who monitored the unexpected outcome of the attack from Norfolk. Beatty shared the amazing victory with all units involved. Captain Cassin, exhibiting a more parochial view and perhaps being somewhat more realistic in view of Taylor's vacillations' gave the sailors under his command credit for the outcome. The Battle of Craney Island had little effect on the conduct of the war and was considered by most as little more than a skirmish. Though the small but famous engagement was over in hours, repercussions from the secretaries of state for war in London were loud and mighty, in light of the incredible British force committed. But, as I have written before, it was that kind of a war.[52]

Having been badly burned, the British never attacked *Constellation* or Norfolk again, which is perhaps a true measure of the importance of the American victory. As Elizabeth River remained open, small baycraft continued an extensive inland trade through the river into Norfolk. Once there, shippers transferred cargo into small barges which passed farther upriver to a canal that connected with Albemarle Sound and ultimately to barrier island ports such as Okracoke Island. These barges returned with the valuable cargoes of privateers and blockade runners discharging in the protected bays behind the islands. As the Royal Navy tightened its grip on the entrance of the bay, cargo continued to flow between the barrier islands and Chesapeake Bay via Norfolk and to rendezvous with blockade runners slipping in and out around the South Atlantic's many barrier islands.[53]

England curtailed its naval occupation of Chesapeake Bay following the failure of a combined army-navy attack on Baltimore 14 September 1814. As a result of his sustained action, Admiral Cockburn's eighteen-month campaign to destroy the region's external trade succeeded. However, after his failure at Baltimore, Vice Adm. Sir Alexander Cochrane, Admiral Warren's replacement, stood down the bay toward New Orleans, drums beating the same mournful notes his predecessor's band had played following the debacle of Craney Island some fifteen months earlier.

The success of the British High Command's plan for a Chesapeake Bay campaign depended on the diversion of American forces from the Canadian front. That strategy failed. America's war strategy, such as it was, followed the pattern of political sectionalism; military problems had to be handled locally. As a result, the War Office learned too late that the "hit and return to ship tactic" used on Chesapeake Bay—even the destructive raid on Washington—had little strategic effect beyond the Tidewater region. British hesitation to make a full commitment in manpower and ships plus the success of American privateers suggested to His Majesty's government that conflict with the United States should be negotiated.

In stark contrast to the Madison administration's feeble conduct of the war, United Sates mariners provided the country with an initial but far-reaching sense of national pride. America's civilian navy, consisting of several hundred letter of marque vessels, mostly schooners, siphoned off the profits of British trade at sea and produced an ever-rising level of marine insurance rates back at Lloyds in London. On the North Atlantic as well as on the Great Lakes facing Canada, America's small federal navy emerged as a heroic force. Being human, its captains survived the war richer and arrogant. Even Captain Stewart, who finally got U.S. Frigate *Constitution* to sea seven idle months after deserting *Constellation*, tasted the sweetness of success, though the great guns of *Constitution* made his victory over two smaller ships, HMS *Cyane* and HMS *Levant*, somewhat tarnished.

After the astounding defeat of British naval and army units at Craney Island, life on board *Constellation*, moored in Elizabeth River, produced eighteen months of boredom, bickering, and a few days of genuine excitement. Capt. Charles Gordon assumed command in the autumn of 1813, replacing her temporary commander, Captain Tarbell. Though Tarbell proved to be somewhat of a loose cannon, he received a share of blame for *Constellation's* deplorable state of disarray following the departure of Stewart and the battle of Craney Island, of which Gordon chose to make an issue when he assumed command.[54]

When the finger pointing stopped, Secretary Jones, well aware of Stewart's role in creating the mess but lacking power or interest, did not pursue the matter.[55] Gordon attacked *Constellation's* unready condition with great vigor, and within a few months he began to request Jones's permission to make a dash for open sea. During 1814, Gordon made several efforts to free *Constellation* from the blockade, but he failed to break out. The frigate survived the embarrassment of her confinement, and because of the victory at Craney Island the navy conceived her to be a lucky ship, with her reputation intact. Jones's decision to place the unlucky Gordon in command of her surely tested this reputation.[56]

Charles Gordon entered the navy with the support of a family with powerful connections. For decades his family maintained itself on the shared power of its many branches. In the young nation's politics and naval service, the Nicholson brothers, Samuel, James, and John, of earlier navy days, gained prominence and position, if not always glory, which in the process made the family nationally prominent among the members of the East Coast social establishment. Gordon's mother was their sister. Congressman Joseph Hopper Nicholson served as chairman of the House Ways and Means Committee. Though his early navy career is without known blemish, Gordon gained a reputation as a social butterfly. As flag captain of U.S. Frigate *Chesapeake*, serving under Commo. James Barron and following the incident with HMS *Leopard* in 1807, Master Commandant Gordon turned to his family and friends in high places to protect him after bungled command decisions placed his career in jeopardy.[57]

To assess the blame for causing the incident that brought the nation close to war, *Chesapeake's* junior officers requested a court of inquiry. Navy Secretary Robert Smith chose Gordon's cousin, Capt. Alexander Murray, senior officer of the Philadelphia Navy Yard, to head up the proceedings. Subsequently, Barron and Gordon with others were ordered to stand court-martial. Smith appointed John Rodgers, a bitter enemy of Barron, senior officer of the court-martial. Smith also ordered Stephen Decatur, who had publicly criticized Barron's behavior, to serve the court along with other officers. Littleton Waller Tazewell, a close friend of Gordon's family, was appointed judge advocate. It was payback time and Gordon was the principal benefactor.

The court-martial convened and Gordon chose to protect his career by throwing himself on the mercy of an already friendly court by agreeing to testify against Commodore Barron. Some observers wrote that the judge advocate prepared his testimony. Commodore Barron concluded his testimony with the statement that his condemnation would come as a result of a pledge of Gordon's acquittal. His prediction proved accurate as he was booted out of the navy for five years and Gordon got only a private reprimand. In the long run, the junior officer got the worst of it: little respect from his contemporaries, a reputation as a flawed officer, and wounds from a duel inflicted by one of Barron's relatives that handicapped his career and ultimately contributed to his early death.[58]

When *Constellation* sailed through the capes of Chesapeake Bay in early May 1815, it seemed almost miraculous that Captain Gordon had his ship ready for duty, though in reality the Gosport Navy Yard had no other ships to keep in repair. John Rodgers said Gordon was a good seaman.[59] The ship's immediate destination was New York, where she would report to Commo. Stephen Decatur (U.S. Frigate *Guerrière*), who would sail shortly for the Mediterranean Sea to bring the dey of Algiers, a raider of American commerce during the recent war, once again under control.

Decatur's contemporaries and biographers agree that his vanity and perhaps a wound to his head overwhelmed his common sense after the loss of U.S. Frigate *President* in early 1814, an embarrassing event for this proud officer. The loss of his ship under conditions normally acceptable for other men Decatur himself deemed unacceptable, a result of his perception of his position in the public's eye. The commodore sailed for the Mediterranean Sea, accompanied by U.S. Frigate *Constellation*, Captain Gordon in command, inside each man a deep passion to square his position in the naval establishment.

Certainly, the records illuminate a commodore bound on a cruise to fight a personal war with his festering ego. Vessels accompanying the two American frigates included the captured *Macedonian* (Capt. Jacob Jones), sloop of war *Ontario* (Jesse D. Elliott, commander), brig *Epervier* (John Downes, commander), brig *Firefly* (George W. Rodgers, commander), brig *Flambeau* (J. B. Nicolson, commander), brig *Spark* (Thomas Gamble, commander), schooner *Spitfire* (A. J. Dallas, commander), and *Torch* (W. Chauncey, commander), a formidable force if one considers that Commodore Bainbridge aboard USS *Independence* set sail for the Mediterranean Sea with a second fleet soon after. But in that postwar period no one questioned such displays of power from America's naval heroes, who enjoyed free run of the American government.[60]

After brief pauses at Cadiz and Tangier, Decatur's squadron, except *Firefly,* which had sprung one of her masts, arrived at Gibraltar 15 June, making a grand sweep of the harbor perhaps more suitable for a victorious Royal Navy fleet. Having learned that the Algerine admiral, Rais Hammida, on board his frigate *Mashouda,* had recently sailed for the Mediterranean Sea, Decatur quickly gathered his flock and flew east in search of his prey. Two days later, *Constellation* sighted *Mashouda* in the vicinity of Capo de Gata on a heading for Algiers under easy sail. Gordon alerted Decatur by signal, but his signal officer missed the commodore's return order to maintain surprise by showing the British flag. As *Constellation* continued to over-haul the Algerine, Gordon hoisted American colors and bore down on the ship, a frigate rated forty-four guns, with a reputation for great speed. Now alerted to pend-ing danger, *Mashouda* crowded on a cloud of sails.[61]

Having reached the long-distance range of her great guns, *Constellation,* on a par-allel course, opened fire on the Algerine frigate with a broadside from her larboard (port) guns. At that time all other ships of Decatur's squadron trailed Gordon's ship and his adversary. Once the action began, Adm. Rais Hammida, wounded by a shot from *Constellation,* ordered the captain to seek haven in a neutral Spanish port. Mashouda's captain wore ship and took a new heading in the direction of Carthegena. The rest of the American squadron, following at least a half mile to the rear of *Constellation,* were now able to close quickly and as they came up, *Guerrière,* Decatur's flagship, poured two broadsides into *Mashouda* at point-blank range.

Sailing together, with their yards almost touching, Algerine musket fire caused several casualties on *Guerrière*'s upper deck, when suddenly one of her great guns on the gun deck exploded, killing and wounding many of the crew. At that point, Flag Capt. Jacob Lewis of *Guerrière* broke off the action, even though the Algerine frigate had not struck. The former Royal Navy brig-sloop *Epervier,* Capt. John Downes, commanding, took a position on *Mashouda*'s quarter, pumping iron into the silent ship until she struck.

Naval historians writing about this action disagree on details as Decatur, the commodore, and already an American hero, received full credit for the victory. Few dared question his actions that day or at any other time during the course of his aggressive cruise that year. It became his successor's job to set straight American affairs in North Africa after Decatur departed. The actual details of the action between the American squadron and the Algerine frigate are obscured by a record that contains little information to balance Decatur's battle report in which he men-tions no ship other than *Guerrière.*[62]

As the battle evolved, *Constellation* engaged *Mashouda* first, then *Guerrière,* and finally, the small guns of the brig *Epervier.* When the guns of *Mashouda* fell silent and the American commanders gathered, Decatur privately lavished praise on

Captain Downes of *Epervier*, which seems almost patronizing, considering the condition of the enemy frigate at the time the brig-sloop positioned herself safely on the Algerine frigate's quarter; at the time, according to observers, the Algerine crew had gone below deck, coolly accepting their inevitable fate.[63]

There seems little foundation to the conclusion of some strategists who write that Decatur snatched a glorious victory away from Captain Gordon, the unlucky captain of *Constellation*. I have uncovered no letters of Gordon's suggesting that Decatur cut him out of the attack, thereby denying him a victory. Assuming that *Mashouda*'s new course put *Guerrière* on a broad reach and a heading that would bring her up on the Algerine frigate, now on course for the Spanish coast, the shift allowed Captain Lewis to bring his ship into battle position before *Constellation*, now trailing *Mashouda* after she altered course. This maneuver forced Gordon's ship to follow her around to the new heading. However, even if Decatur cut between *Constellation* and *Mashouda*, as some have suggested, this privilege belonged to the commodore, particularly as Gordon had already ruined his tactical plan to surprise the Algerine.[64]

Gordon wrote Commo. John Rodgers, now chief of the Navy Board of Commissioners, suggesting to his fellow Marylander that Decatur had irresponsibly overloaded his great guns before the attack, thus causing the explosion. His attitude worsened by his recurring health problems, Gordon also harped to Rodgers about his past situation with *Constellation* at Norfolk, even suggesting to Rodgers that he felt isolated from other navy officers because he never whipped an Englishman; in this way Gordon attempted to patronize the insecure Rodgers, who failed to capture any naval craft larger than a schooner in the war recently ended.[65]

When William Bainbridge replaced Decatur as commodore of the Mediterranean Sea squadron, he ordered Gordon to remain with him. Capt. John Shaw replaced Bainbridge and then Isaac Chauncey replaced Shaw in quick order.[66] During the remainder of this cruise, *Constellation* sailed from port to port running errands for American consuls and their children, dealing in merchandise, and buying Madeira wine and Spanish sherry. Gordon wrote that if he ever displeased the commodore because of this activity, it could be inconvenient to him, as one "who never had the good fortune to whip an Englishman."[67]

A ship in the squadron that composed America's first distant fleet diplomatic service, *Constellation* spent the winter of 1816 at Port Mahon. This fleet represented the first of many overseas missions designed to cruise the seven seas showing the flag and protecting American commercial interests overseas. While a far cry from the excitement of war, it fit the more subdued ambitions of senior American naval officers, most of whom were now beyond middle age. Gordon wrote a friend that he asked Rodgers to send out *Java* or *Guerrière* for him in another effort to use personal relationships rather than merit to advance himself.[68]

With his health deteriorating, Captain Gordon found it increasingly difficult to maintain control over his ship's junior officers. His poor health probably affected his mind, contributing to a rising level of paranoia.[69] Captain Isaac Chauncey, commodore of the Mediterranean Sea Squadron, informed the new navy secretary, Benjamin W. Crowninshield, that Charles Gordon died early in September 1816, stating that while diarrhea killed him, his other complaints contributed to his final illness. Chauncey appointed William M. Crane commander of *Constellation*. The frigate remained in the Mediterranean Sea another year, returning to Norfolk in December 1817 where she was placed in ordinary.[70]

Five

Like Fish Out of Water

$\mathcal{A}$ surge of political support for a powerful and permanent naval peace establishment gripped Washington as the War of 1812 ended. Congressional advocates for a strong navy, at that time riding a wave of public acclaim for its wartime accomplishments, passed several legislative acts to expand the navy into a powerful fleet of ships of the line and heavy frigates. Congress, demonstrating enthusiastic support unique for the young nation, passed a number of bills that materially altered the country's naval strength and the political clout of the service, resulting in significant expansion of the number of ships on its register and the size of its land-based supporting facilities.

Following the War of 1812 the Distant Station Policy unfolded spontaneously. Decatur's Mediterranean Sea cruise of 1815 revealed the prevailing mood of the Madison administration, offering the navy encouragement as its heroes sought to convert from a fighting force into a quasi-diplomatic arm of the executive branch of the federal government. The role, encouraged by America's overseas traders and ship owners, enjoyed the support of President James Monroe and several succeeding administrations. The new mission found the navy in an increasing number of aggressive initiatives related to the nation's overseas traders, a group that in 1817 had begun to decline in number proportionately as the nation's population and domestic wealth climbed dramatically, aided by an increase of investment in industry. Additionally, the country's expanding population had begun to turn away from the rim of the Atlantic Ocean, as people moved westward across untouched mountains and plains.

The squadrons of Commodores Bainbridge, Chauncey, and Smith followed Decatur's manic cruise, and each applied damage control in efforts to limit the harm done by the American hero's bullying tactics. Bainbridge, commanding the battleship

USS *Independence,* a magnificent new floating symbol of America's growing maritime power, arrived at Gibraltar as Decatur prepared to depart. The symbolic importance of powerful squadrons did not escape the navy or Congress as Bainbridge's fleet, followed by Chauncey and then Smith, cruised the beautiful inland Mediterranean Sea, representing a country that enjoyed good relations with most of the people situated around its shores with their ancient civilizations. This remarkable transition in American naval policy from fighting force to diplomatic attendance required the maintenance of expensive ships far from home for relatively long periods. The Distant Station Policy soon expanded to other oceans as a direct result of the goodwill extended to the navy by postwar Washington. The service, seeking positions for its senior captains, worked hard to bolster its political clout.

Senior navy officers—decorated heroes riding the crest of popular acclaim—joined with pronavalists in Congress to support legislation to create the structure of a permanent naval establishment. Soon after the successful launch of the concept of a Distant Station Policy, a friendly Congress authorized several ship construction programs, increased the facilities of the six existing navy yards, added to their number by one, increased the number of navy shore stations around the country and overseas, and authorized hundreds of thousands of dollars to acquire and stockpile timber, particularly live oak.

Navy expansion gained momentum over subsequent decades, a significant period in United States growth, yet minus any serious threat of major military conflict. Due to the efforts of politically active senior officers, strongly supported by pronavalists in most branches of the government, legislation creating a permanent navy was passed over a period of approximately twenty years between 1815 and 1835. In addition to gaining passage of several acts for the construction of ships of the line, frigates, ship-sloops, and small vessels, the navy successfully promoted a policy of retaining older ships in service indefinitely. Furthermore, pronavalists successfully established a third, key goal of the service, almost without resistance and with no specific legislation: the expansion of navy yards to accommodate construction of almost all new navy ships and repairs. Ironically, with the realization of these aspirations, the navy consolidated its political power in the highest level of government, which, in time, affected in important ways how the navy administered its affairs during the decades leading up to mid-century, a period that included significant advances in vessel and ordnance technology. To a noticeable degree, naval technology, forced to follow a parallel course with the life cycles of older senior officers, allowed change to occur slowly, as progress within military establishments is usually effectively controlled by seniority systems. Never since the period that followed the War of 1812 had navy officers exercised such effective control over the service.

For good reasons, Congress created the Navy Board of Commissioners, which, following its formation in 1815, rotated its composition of three senior officers among the post-captains of the country's previous wars with France and England. The duties of the commissioners relieved the secretary of the navy of certain administrative functions, allowing him to operate at a cabinet level. With the reorganization, the commissioners negotiated all contracts for materials and supplies for yards and ships. More specifically, Congress assigned to the commissioners responsibility for ship design, construction, and control over facilities and personnel of navy yards, responsibility for repairs, and the equipping and provisioning of ships.[1]

The Commissioner Act limited the board's authority to administering naval affairs; it did not grant commissioners line or executive authority over operations and personnel. The office of the secretary retained control over the number of ships in commission, vessel operations, officer promotions, and personnel limits. Though commissioners contracted for materials and provisions for the navy, the secretary of the navy and the secretary of the treasury shared responsibility over the accounting for disbursements. The legislation that created the Board of Commissioners separated the board from accounting for special appropriations and budget expenditures. This decision by Congress effectively placed this responsibility for payments of contracts with naval agents, who handled compliance and payments directly with navy accountants in the secretary's office, which, in turn, shared its financial accountabilities with the Department of the Treasury.[2]

Soon after the legislation went into effect, Capt. John Rodgers, the board's first president, posed the question of authority, claiming that the law provided that the Board of Commissioners report directly to the president of the United States. Rodgers's interpretation of the act would extend the commissioners' authority over vessel operations and personnel, placing these executive functions beyond the control of the secretary of the navy. B. W. Crowninshield, the navy secretary who replaced Jones, pointed out to Rodgers that the secretary of the navy, as a cabinet officer, received his powers directly from the president, as chief executive officer and commander in chief, who in turn received the authority to delegate from the Constitution, not Congress. Crowninshield, with the approval of President Madison, retained authority over vessel operations, promotions, and personnel caps, and delegated to the commissioners only those powers he considered appropriate—a sensible ruling for the Republic. For the student, the dispute is remembered as a specific instance in the nation's history when the military, this time the navy's senior officer corps, made a grab for power beyond limits set by the Constitution.[3]

Though the secretary of the navy retained control over navy personnel, promotions, assignments, and the number of ships in commission, the creation of a Board of Commissioners diminished the secretary's authority. The three navy post-captains who sat on the board exerted control over fellow officers by means of the navy's seniority system and also worked independently of the secretary with Congress to gain the navy's expansive goals through new legislation. While the Executive Office kept a tight reign on fleet operations, Congress and the Board of Commissioners cooperated on vessel construction programs, appropriations for repairs, and funds to improve and enlarge the navy's shore-based infrastructure.

A solid alliance between Congress and the commissioners produced long-term funding programs and continuity in administering construction and repair programs as navy secretaries arrived and departed with some frequency. In time, administration of the navy under the shared control of the Board of Commissioners, Congress, and the secretary of the navy became a bureaucratic quagmire as maintenance of a large peacetime navy establishment grew more and more expensive under the commissioners' guidance. Many of the increases in the navy's budget over the years during Rodgers's long period of control over the board resulted from the expansion of navy yards, necessary because of congressional approval of unnecessary new ships, the commissioners' policy of retaining old ships in service, the stockpiling of timber, and the continuance of policy that denied private yards the opportunity to bid on navy construction or repair work.[4]

John Rodgers, the navy's senior officer following the retirement of Alexander Murray on 6 October 1821, sat at the top of the navy's command structure until he retired in 1837, serving nineteen years as president of the Board of Commissioners. Thus, during most of the years of the board's existence, its power rested in his hands, and this, along with his senior position within the service, allowed him to wield great influence in Washington. As senior officer of the navy, he exerted unquestioned authority over fellow naval officers, which gave him de facto control over the officer corps, though the secretary awarded individual promotions and assignments. However, in practice, most navy secretaries exercised these powers only after consultation with Rodgers, particularly concerning officer assignments and promotions. The commodore kept tabs on aspiring officers through his own system of fitness reports.[5]

Usually able to work harmoniously with senators and congressmen, Rodgers placed before them a vision of his navy and the composition of its permanent fleet early in his tenure. When he retired his commission in 1837, he left a navy much like the one he envisioned during the early days of the Board of Commissioners. Always a booster of the navy's sentimental traditions, he played a constantly passionate, patriotic, and often stubborn role to keep the navy's historic and trophy ships in commission. His efforts proved remarkably successful. Congress supported most of his long-term program of repairing and rebuilding ships by continually approving increases in the navy's annual appropriations for shipyards even though costs of the navy's aging sailing fleet continued to rise during his years in Washington, perhaps extending their use into a period when the technology of steam engines and iron ships should have received greater attention.

Pronavalists maintained a firm alliance with Congress for most of two decades. This provided the navy with a steady flow of appropriations for new ships and funds to expand shipyards. They worked together to promote preservation of the navy's historic and trophy ships, providing huge appropriations for repairs and approving large sums to improve and enlarge the navy's infrastructure and for purchase of timber and other materials. I found not a single serious incident of Congress rebelling against the navy's well-publicized policy of retaining its oldest ships in service. To the contrary, once it became established policy that all public ships would be built and repaired in the navy's own yards, many in Congress maintained enthusiastic support for the expansion of public shipyards. Congressmen, enjoying at the polls the direct election-day benefits of these facilities, became avid supporters of John Rodgers's proposed construction or repair budgets, which inevitably produced increased employment at navy yards. Steady expansion of the shore-based portion of the navy in seven states, including Maryland and Virginia, which shared three facilities, empowered their employees at the ballot box. The melding of the goals of the navy and Congress produced legislation that expanded the fleet far in excess of the nation's needs and, at the same time, silenced opponents' questions concerning the commissioners' policy of rebuilding the navy's aging ships.[6]

John Rodgers, a complex and controversial figure in Washington, whose navy service dated back to the first cruise of *Constellation* in 1798, pushed favored policies and missions that fit neatly with the interests of the navy's senior officers. If any characteristic dominated Rodgers's personality, it was loyalty to his clique of officers, be they right or wrong. Joining Rodgers on the first Board of Commissioners were two other senior officers, Capts. David Porter and Isaac Hull. As the board commenced its duties in 1815, its primary thrust centered on converting the nation's spontaneous enthusiasm into plans and legislation for a powerful fleet, a goal that dovetailed harmoniously with the aspirations of every officer in the service.[7]

With the Navy Act of 29 April 1816, Congress authorized nine ships of the line and twelve large frigate-44s, similar in size to Humphreys' *Constitution* class, for the navy's peace establishment.[8] The bill's proponents gave little thought when authorizing these large ships to the fact that, when these large ships were built and ready for sea duty, the costs of operating them would push the navy's annual budget so high as to adversely affect the nation's finances. A study of operating costs, combined with construction costs, maintenance, and repairs over the life of each large ship, makes the legislation appear near to fiscal recklessness. While it is difficult to understand the planning process that guided the navy and Congress in 1816, if such a process existed at the time, it is possible that President Madison's administration, tired but happy to get beyond the war and ready to leave office, could not find a voice to object to this incredible token of gratitude given the navy by Congress. Madison would leave to future administrations elected the job of sorting out the nation's finances, when the funds required to build, operate, and maintain such a vast underutilized fleet would present Congress with a monstrous embarrassment.[9]

Today, though it is impossible to peer into the minds of Rodgers and the group around him, one may conclude with some certainty that the giant ship program, particularly the ships of the line authorized, represented a bounty due America's senior navy officers for lifetimes of service, capped finally by success. These officers worked under limitations in the Continental navy and then the early federal navy when they engaged the young nation's tormentors with vigor and courage but with few victories. Ignored through much of Jefferson's administration, many of the same officers returned to participate in the naval victories of the War of 1812. Rodgers, leader of these men and ships, but with his thinking distorted by memories of his own lost opportunities, sought to create a strong navy composed of ships that were of little use in the post–War of 1812 world. Like so many military men who preceded him, as well as many who would follow him into modern times, Rodgers planned for the next war with the last war's armament. Eventually, the building program of ships authorized under the act of 1816 stretched over decades, but, even so, it survived largely intact as most of Rodgers's great fleet of 1816 were launched, the last frigates commissioned just prior to the start of the Civil War.[10]

The act of 1816, called an Act to Increase the Navy, appropriated $1 million per year for six years for new ships. Congress specified that funds provided under the act could not be used for purposes other than to build the classes of ships named, nine ships of the line and twelve large frigates, rated forty-four guns. No funds could be transferred out of the project. This is important because Congress passed a subsequent act in 1827, titled an Act for Improvement of the Navy, which appropriated money for the purpose of expanding and improving the navy's ship yards and provided funds to accumulate stockpiles of live oak and other timber. Just as Congress restricted the 1816 Act to Increase the Navy to the construction of a specific number and classes of ships, under the terms of the act of 1827, Congress voted money to improve the navy, and the two acts did not overlap; nor did the second act amend the earlier one. Appropriations made under each of these headings—Increase and Improvement—outlined the projects covered by each piece of legislation and specified that funds allocated could not be intermingled.[11] Construction started on one ship of the line and three frigates almost immediately following the passage of legislation, all construction under the act assigned to existing navy yards. In the interest of preserving timber from rot or other damage, the secretary of the navy ordered the commissioners to frame up all ships authorized in the stocks as soon as possible.[12]

Responding to a request by the Senate Committee on Naval Affairs, Commodore Rodgers, reporting for the secretary of the navy, provided an outline of the size and composition of the navy's peace establishment as well as its current disposition— ships in ordinary requiring repairs and ships in commission on the date of the report, January 1819. With numbers of vessels broken down into classes, the commissioners' projections included twelve ships of the line, of which the navy had three in service, plus nine authorized in 1816 and under construction, twenty frigates, including twelve large frigates authorized in 1816, and seven others currently on its register: *United States, Constitution, Constellation,* and *Congress,* built two decades earlier; *Guerrière* and *Java,* contract frigates commissioned in 1815; and *Macedonian,* a trophy ship; the twentieth frigate was authorized in 1813 and burned in the stocks at the Washington Navy Yard. The commissioners' list projected requirements for small vessels including twenty sloops of war and fifteen schooners, most of which were unauthorized and largely unmentioned until Rodgers's report was filed in 1819.[13]

Rodgers's 1819 report made it apparent to everyone in Washington, including Congress, that the commissioners planned to keep all of the navy's historic and trophy ships in service indefinitely. Senior officers promoted three reasons at that time for keeping the navy's older ships in service—the most important being a determination to surround themselves with the monuments and memorials of past naval victories. The ships included U.S. Frigate *Constellation,* the navy's first frigate and Truxtun's ship, in which Rodgers, Porter, and other senior officers served aboard when she successfully fought *l'Insurgente* years earlier; *United States,* Decatur's ship, which beat *Macedonian* and brought her into the U.S. Navy; also *Hornet, Enterprize, John Adams*— the last named for the father of the navy—and, of course, U.S. Frigate *Constitution,* already a national monument in 1820. All of these ships had played important roles in naval history and had been commanded by the navy's senior officers, most of whom still served as constant reminders of their past contributions to the nation.

Tradition, sentiment, and a strong sense of pride of the navy's legendary service played major roles in the creation of the commissioners' policy on repeatedly repairing and rebuilding historic ships. Few decisions would be made between 1820 and 1842, particularly as they related to the retention and repair of the navy's oldest ships and English trophy ships in service, that did not reflect the determination of senior officers, particularly John Rodgers, to perpetuate them indefinitely as memorials of their victorious wartime cruises. One may argue that *Cyane,* Captain Stewart's trophy ship, subject to one major repair, should not have received the second rebuild, but the navy and much of the nation recognized little difference then between marble statues and the nation's wooden hull monuments—*Constellation, Constitution, United States, Hornet,* and the lucky *Enterprize,* as well as *Cyane* and *Macedonian*—all treasures of America's struggle for freedom of the seas.

The commissioners' second reason to keep old ships in service centered on the practical limits of its operational budget. Except for *Constitution, United States, Guerrière,* and *Java,* the navy's older vessels were smaller and of ratings inferior to first-class frigates. *Congress, Constellation, Macedonian, John Adams, Cyane, Hornet, Erie, Ontario,* and *Enterprize* required smaller crews. Because of annual budget limits for the costs of provisions and pay for ships in commission, the service usually did not normally keep more than one ship of the line and two first-class frigates at sea at one time. Budget restrictions also forced the secretary to make the greater proportion of the fleet active in any one year second-class frigates, sloops of war, and smaller vessels such as schooners.[14]

The third reason for Rodgers to favor retention of historic and trophy ships in service—and probably the most practical one under circumstances developing over the years—related to these ships' rising need for major repairs following shorter cycles of service. Frequent periods of great repairs and shorter, more frequent cruises for veteran ships provided the Board of Commissioners the means by which large portions of surplus live oak and other materials collected at the navy's major yards could be reduced before losing it to rot or thieves. Near-panic purchasing of large quantities of live oak and other timber for stockpiling, combined with a limited knowledge of preservation techniques, coincided with shorter and shorter intervals between major repairs required by historic ships, many of which had originally been built with green or inferior wood. The ships' repair schedules provided an opportunity to rotate a significant portion of the yards' aging timber, which had been accumulated in large quantities through special appropriations made by a generous Congress but which, after short periods in the weather, had begun to deteriorate. As years passed and new ships came on line, a fourth and more unfortunate reason developed for keeping old ships on active service. Compared to the new ships, they proved to be better sailers in many instances than ships drafted and built by navy master builders and constructors in the expanded system of public yards.[15]

Legislators' liberal appropriations for the navy tightened some during a national banking crisis in 1819. Fiscal restraint being in order, Congress expressed concern over the size of the annual commitment to the large ship program authorized by the act of 1816, the Act to Increase the Navy. By amendment in 1821, Congress reduced the amount of funds available yearly from $1 million to $500,000 and stretched the building program over an additional six years. The new legislation transformed the navy's large ship program from one of military readiness into a long-term contingency plan. Further changes to these acts in later years kept a number of these ships in the stocks for decades. The stretched-out building program provided navy yards with continuous construction work, a compromise satisfactory to the commissioners, who were aware of budget limits on provisioning and recruiting crews, which caused the navy's largest ships to become virtually surplus. Furthermore, stretching the large ship program over many years did not disturb pronavalists in Congress or the workers employed in navy yards.[16]

Though there is no doubt that the slowing down of the large shipbuilding program in 1821 represented an effort at fiscal conservation during America's first financial crisis, Congress also reduced the size of the yearly appropriation for large ships for other reasons as legislators rethought their initial approval of the vast building program in 1816. The most obvious problem presented by a large fleet of new ships, beyond their initial construction cost, would be the expense of keeping the new giant ships in commission, an insurmountable problem as Congress gained insight into manning costs from experience gained operating the navy's first ships of the line, *Franklin, Washington,* and *Independence.* The considerable expense of maintaining large crews to man ships sailing halfway round the world on two-year cruises for mere ceremonial purposes most certainly created a backlash in Congress.

Legislators faced with the unavoidable results of their prior action realized that larger appropriations would be required to repair the fleet in later years as the navy began to receive in 1821 ships built under the act of 1816. All ships built during the war that survived it—*Washington, Franklin, Independence, Guerrière, Java, Erie, Ontario,* and *Peacock*—lined up in ordinary for major repairs, along with ships built prior to the war. Then, an unexpected pressure on appropriations developed with the shocking realization that USS *Ohio* and other ships built under the act of 1816 had begun to decay even before being commissioned. Finally, the need to fund the construction of schooners and sloops of war outlined in Rodgers's report to Congress in 1819 seemed more plausible in 1821 than the completion of expensive large ships, most destined for long stays in ordinary.[17]

The act of 1816, which increased the number of large ships, and the act of 1821, which amended the earlier act by stretching the major building program over decades, in combination with the commissioners' plan to keep the navy's historic and trophy ships in service, contributed directly to the conversion of the navy from a small wartime naval attack force into a bloated peace establishment. As a result of Board of Commissioners' policies, an increasing number of ships remained in ordinary each year, as budget limitations allowed only a small number of ships in commission and at sea in any year. As a result, an underutilized fleet, consisting of many ships which were inactive and deteriorating, depended on a system of shipyards which in a few years would employ thousands of civilian mechanics and laborers. Under the command of aging senior naval officers with limited administrative experience, the navy's shore facilities already suffered rising levels of inefficiency. Under existing congressional pressure higher construction and repair costs immediately followed the assumption by commissioners of their responsibilities, particularly at larger yards such as Boston, Gosport, and the New York Navy Yard, which handled most repairs.[18]

The navy assigned classes of vessels to sea duty according to the mission. Commodores and senior captains usually commanded large frigates and ships of the line assigned to distant stations. The principal naval missions of the service, however—protecting the sea lanes close to the United States and monitoring the slave trade—dictated the use of sloops of war and schooners. Most important, American commercial shipping faced unstable conditions in the South Atlantic Ocean and Caribbean Sea caused by the breakdown in Spanish authority and increased activity from pirates and rogue privateers in those seas. The navy's deficiency in small vessels existed until it replenished its fleet of schooners, repaired older sloops and corvettes, and in 1825, received funds from Congress to build ten new sloops of war of twenty guns.

The navy sold several older schooners, including *Nonsuch,* and the brigs purchased during the last war, replacing them with a squadron of fast Baltimore-type schooners. Congress, responding to a navy request, passed the new legislation in May 1820 which provided $60,000 to build five schooners of twelve guns each. As a result, the navy added *Alligator, Dolphin, Grampus, Porpoise,* and *Shark* to the fleet. The navy built all of these small vessels at public yards. Two years later, David Porter received authorization to purchase eight small Chesapeake Bay pilot boat schooners, which he formed into a Mosquito Fleet to fight pirates, principally operating in the waters around Cuba and Puerto Rico.[19]

On more distant oceans, the initial success of naval diplomacy in the Mediterranean Sea led to a division of ships at sea into several individual missions or squadrons assigned to different parts of the globe. In this manner, the navy converted the wartime success of single ship engagements against the Royal Navy into a series of quasi-diplomatic missions on behalf of American commercial interests overseas. The navy's wide support in Congress and within the Madison and Monroe administrations made the transition seamless. The missions, while occasionally effective in freeing ships or rescuing seamen in war zones, rarely resulted in meaningful diplomatic success for the United States and, to the contrary, often left foreign leaders angry or frustrated by navy commander-diplomats' inept handling of assignments.

Few of the predominant characteristics of veteran American naval officers prepared them to serve their country as diplomats. On the other hand, the activities of the navy's narrowly focused commanders did not differ greatly from most other members of the nation's upper classes in business or politics. The United States government's foreign policy represented the goals of its influential citizens as expressed in the Monroe Doctrine. Patriots fighting to throw off Spain's grip on South America learned the true nature of United States policy through the activities of these sailor-diplomats—Biddle, Downes, Ridgely, Stewart, and their colleagues. If the new nations of South America judged the behavior of Monroe's sailor-diplomats correctly at the time, they learned early on that U.S. foreign policy supported nonintervention policies only against European nations, not against itself or its citizens. On the level of international politics, the hope for U.S. support died quickly.

Commanders, inexperienced in the flexible nature of diplomatic affairs, often arrogant and concerned for their personal interests, reduced the effectiveness of the Distant Station Policy. However, distant missions often bolstered the service's political standing in Washington, supplementing the more practical and enduring political alliance that the navy developed with Congress. Certainly, in the end, the Distant Station Policy existed primarily to provide employment for the navy's officer corps. As it happened, these missions fit neatly into President James Monroe's foreign policy agenda, particularly in South America, as an age of commercial imperialism succeeded the age of colonial conquest.

Between 1817 and 1824, President Monroe assigned to the navy a number of single-ship or small-squadron cruises to South America for fact-finding and show-the-flag missions. Monroe, concerned with European interference in North and South American affairs, moved the nation into a more active role in international relations. The long voyage of USS *Ontario* (James Biddle commanding) to South America and to the Pacific Northwest, which included stopovers at Rio de Janeiro and Chile, Peru, and Oregon, departed during the fall of 1817 and terminated at Annapolis, Maryland, on 25 April 1819. Biddle's mission provided some substance and consistency to the nation's foreign policy in Chile and Peru, previously handled only by State Department agents on assignment in that unsettled part of South America, which at that time was intent on throwing off entrenched Spanish Royalists control.[20]

Biddle assisted American mariners, international whalers, Chilean and Peruvian patriots, and on at least one occasion, Spanish Royalist merchants. Unfortunately, Captain Biddle's inability to resist financial opportunities seriously jeopardized U.S. neutrality in Peru. While Spanish Royalists, patriots, and various dictators' armies were jockeying for power in Peru and Chile, Spanish Royalists asked Biddle to provide the safety of USS *Ontario* to move specie out of the war zone. When Biddle agreed to provide this service for a commission, his action amounted to a breach in United States neutrality. Under the rules of war, once Biddle allowed Spanish specie placed on board his ship, USS *Ontario* became subject to seizure by the Chilean patriot navy, led at that time by an unpredictable sailor of fortune, Lord Sir Thomas Cochrane.

USS *Ontario* departed Valparaiso for Chesapeake Bay with specie in the amount of $201,000 on board, of which $160,000 belonged to Spanish Royalists who contracted with Biddle in Peru to carry it to Rio de Janeiro. Not only did this decision have repercussions among congressmen at home, who raised the issue of Biddle's personal neutrality, but it opened the larger question concerning whether the navy's senior officer corps understood their obligations, which included controlling the urge to gain personal profit while involved in sensitive diplomatic missions. U.S. Frigate *Macedonian* followed *Ontario* into the war zone, which included the politically unsettled Pacific coastal waters of South America as far north as Mexico.[21]

Navy tradition, if not standing regulations, forbade commanders from taking foreign-owned specie on board a U.S. Navy ship. James Lawrence, commander of USS *Hornet*, received an offer of naval freight (specie) as he prepared for a voyage to Europe in 1811. The specie was Spanish owned. When President Madison learned of the contemplated transaction, he set a precedent with his decision that United States Navy commanders should not carry specie not owned by United States citizens. Madison's decision became a part of navy tradition, and every commanding officer had knowledge of the president's order. Though Biddle was considered one of the more intelligent of the navy's diplomat sailors, he laid down a pattern of behavior that other commanders happily followed, ignoring the danger that their freelancing caused for their ships and United States foreign policy.[22]

President Monroe recalled Capt. Oliver Hazard Perry from duty with the Mediterranean Sea fleet to head a mission that took the war hero to Venezuela for a parley with Simón Bolivar, the liberator of much of South America above the equator. Perry selected U.S. Frigate *Constellation* to fly his pennant. However, *Constellation* had recently returned from a long cruise in the Mediterranean Sea to enter the navy yard at Gosport 3 January 1818 and be placed in ordinary. Repairs to the frigate did not commence until 18 April, and the yard did not have her ready on Captain Perry's scheduled departure date. The hero of Lake Erie switched his flag to USS *John Adams* and added USS *Nonsuch*, the navy's weatherly Baltimore schooner, to carry him the final leg of the journey, three hundred miles up Orinoco River to Bolivar's capital, Angostura. President Monroe ordered Perry to promote America's relations with the Liberator, who at the time had not secured control over Venezuela.[23]

Perry transferred his flag from *John Adams* to *Nonsuch* at the mouth of the great Orinoco River and reached Angostura after fighting strong currents and rampant fever. To his disappointment, he learned Bolivar was absent. Don Antonio Zea, the patriot's vice president, met with Perry and promised that his patriot government would try to restrain their privateers, many of them Baltimore schooners manned by American sailors, and to make restitution for captured American-owned ships. Perry promised goodwill and early recognition of the revolutionists' goals by the United States government. After a final banquet in Perry's honor on 14 August 1819, *Nonsuch* stood down Orinoco River. Perry was now racked by yellow fever. He died six miles before the schooner reached Trinidad.[24]

President Monroe's new secretary of the navy, Smith Thompson, selected Capt. Charles Morris to head the second part of the deceased Perry's diplomatic mission. Morris visited Monroe at his home and received the president's cornerstone diplomatic message, this time for the rebelling government of Argentina at Buenos Aires: The patriots could expect the friendly support of the United States government but to earn it the patriot government of Argentina must rein in its privateers, who were currently attacking American commerce indiscriminately on the high seas.[25]

In early November 1819, *Constellation* and *John Adams,* both over twenty years old, and having completed maintenance repairs at Gosport, were ready for the long cruise. John B. Nicolson received the appointment to flag captain of *Constellation,* and Lewis Warrington retained command of the corvette.[26] Commodore Morris's squadron of two ships (USS *Nonsuch,* Lt. Daniel Turner commanding, joined them at Montevideo), cleared Cape Henry 12 November 1819. After a cruise of sixty-seven days free of incident, Morris's ships dropped anchor off Montevideo. *Nonsuch,* having already arrived, lay at anchor there. Since the depth of the Rio de la Plata off Buenos Aires would not handle *Constellation*'s draft, Morris transferred his flag to *John Adams.* The smaller ship took on a local pilot and sailed upriver to deliver Morris, who would live in Buenos Aires during his stay in Argentina. In spite of these precautions, *John Adams* grounded, and, according to Morris, received some damage. With the ship lightened and with assistance from *Constellation*'s boats and crew, she floated.[27]

Morris recorded in his journal that he stayed in Buenos Aires for one month. Soon after his arrival the government of the Supreme Director Puerreydon was deposed by General Rondeau. Morris completed his presentation to the general, who, pleased with the United States' gesture of goodwill, agreed to license Argentina's armed vessels. However, before Morris left the capital, Rondeau was replaced by the government of Don Manuel Sarratea. Morris noted in his journal that he thought Sarratea was unqualified to control the discordant and restless population. He called for his barge and returned to *John Adams.* Three days later the squadron hoisted anchors and departed for the United States.[28]

Constellation passed abeam of the Island of Lobos 27 February 1820 and dropped anchor at the Island of St. Lucia 6 April, elapsed time thirty-eight days, not a bad passage for the old frigate. During her cruise north she reached a speed of eleven knots on several occasions and sailed frequently in the range of nine and ten knots. In the early morning (6:00 A.M.) of 4 March, in heavy squalls, the ship's main topsail yard carried away and threw Edward Butterfield overboard. Captain Nicolson distinguished himself as he successfully backed the ship's topsails, lowered the stern boat, and plucked Seaman Butterfield from the dark sea. After brief stopovers at Martínique and St. Thomas, *Constellation* departed for Hampton Roads 12 April and passed Cape Henry ten days later, ending Commodore Morris's mission to Argentina. Captain Nicolson provided the Board of Commissioners with a report on *Constellation*'s sailing qualities when he completed this cruise. He wrote that the historic ship sailed much better than *John Adams,* the only ship that he had sailed with on the cruise. He wrote that *Constellation* outsailed the smaller ship on and by the wind and that, as a seaboat, she was as good as any he had ever been on board.[29]

In light of later developments in the Pacific Ocean off Chile and Peru, it seemed a provocative move on the part of President Monroe to assign the ex–Royal Navy trophy ship, U.S. Frigate *Macedonian,* to relieve USS *Ontario.* Lord Cochrane, commander of the Chilean Patriot Navy, was an ex–Royal Navy officer and a British patriot. In the unsettled situation off Chile and Peru, as commander of Chile's navy, he established control over the sea lanes and declared a blockade of west coast ports. Cochrane seized a number of American trading vessels and was continually on the prowl for shipping to loot when *Macedonian* arrived at Valparaiso 28 January 1819. Capt. John Downes commanded the frigate, which, like *Ontario,* cruised on a single-ship mission. John C. Calhoun, Monroe's acting secretary of the navy, cautioned Downes before he left to be discrete. However, by his selection of *Macedonian* and Downes to command her, Calhoun failed completely to anticipate the diplomatic indiscretions that followed, most of which were a result of Downes's behavior.[30]

John Downes served as first lieutenant on board USS *Essex* (David Porter, commander) during her famous cruise to the west coast of South America in 1813. He proved himself a fighter when Porter placed the British prize, *Georgiana,* a ship of 270 tons, under his command. Later, Porter awarded Downes command of the captured British ship *Atlantic,* which Porter took into naval service and renamed USS *Essex Junior.* Downes spent more than a year on the west coast before the Royal Navy captured Porter's squadron at Valparaiso. Following the war, Downes, commanding USS *Epervier,* a British trophy brig, participated in the capture of the Algerine frigate *Mashouda* in 1815 while serving under Commodore Decatur. Both Porter and Decatur issued letters commending Downes's service.[31]

Soon after his arrival on the Pacific West Coast in *Macedonian,* Captain Downes became aware of opportunities to provide safe haven for foreign specie, its owners seeking places to put their wealth stranded by the instability of a war zone. Working with smugglers and others shipping and receiving contraband, the American captain offered his ship as a floating bank for gold and silver, evidently without regard to its origins or owners. The specie was called "naval freight" in line with traditional practice. Downes's orders from the secretary of the navy limited the commander's privilege to the carriage of specie owned by United States citizens at a freight charge of 2.5 percent of the value of the gold or silver delivered to the ship. In a demonstration of the unlimited freedom of commanding officers under the Distant Station Policy, Downes offered his ship to all comers without political restriction. He set rates according to the risk to which the specie's owner was subjected. North Americans in the west coast trade paid 2.5 percent unless their activities involved contraband. Spanish Royalists paid a commission as high as 10 percent. Downes took the practice established by Biddle in the region to a higher level of greed.[32]

More harmful to the United States' foreign policy than Downes's brash display of arrogance was the captain's complete insensitivity to the embarrassing position in which he had placed the United States. Downes had been sent to protect and further the interests of his country. Instead, his financial deals made *Macedonian*, a ship of a neutral nation, subject to seizure by Lord Cochrane under international law for aiding the Royalists and carrying contraband. Even more important, the captain's activities were contrary to the political goals of the patriots of Chile and Peru and to the goals of the Monroe government. Yet Cochrane, having placed Chile's and Peru's coastlines under blockade, failed to exercise his privilege to seize *Macedonian*. No military incidents resulted from Downes's brash behavior, but his indiscretions destroyed the United States government's flimsy facade of diplomatic neutrality. This had a lasting effect on Latin American freedom fighters, who believed that the United States supported their goals, having thrown off Great Britain's yoke a few decades earlier.[33]

Captain Downes outraged the diplomatic communities in Chile and Peru. But the strangest twist to the story of Downes's grab for wealth was that Lord Cochrane, as he invaded Peru to dislodge the Spanish Royalists at Lima, blockaded the port of Callao. As it happened he snared *Macedonian* in port. By that time Downes had stowed as much as a million dollars' worth of specie on board his ship. For reasons never explained, Cochrane allowed *Macedonian* to depart unchallenged from Callao. Downes never detailed his commissions to the secretary of the navy, but they are thought to have exceeded $100,000, a figure roughly eighty times his yearly salary. When *Macedonian* reached the Chilean port of Valparaiso, U.S. Frigate *Constellation* (Charles G. Ridgely, commander), Downes's relief ship, had not yet arrived.[34]

Capt. Charles G. Ridgely assumed command of *Constellation* following her arrival at Hampton Roads after the completion of Commodore Morris's mission to Argentina. The ship received wear and tear repairs at Gosport and sailed from New York for Rio de Janeiro on or about 25 July 1820 after a two-week delay caused by adverse winds at Sandy Hook.[35] In his clichéd style, Ridgely wrote Secretary Thompson that the ship in all respects answered his most sanguine expectations. He wrote that he was particularly pleased with the officers and *Constellation*'s crew seemed as fine a body of men as ever went to sea. When his ship dropped anchor at Rio de Janeiro, Ridgely sang another tune. *Constellation*'s main mast needed replacing, his rapport with his officers had disintegrated, and a huge army of rats had taken over the ship. To his credit, Ridgely never stopped praising the crew nor did he ever lose his admiration for *Constellation*.[36]

Constellation reached Rio 11 November but once carpenters discovered decay at the base of the main mast, more than seven months passed from the date of departure at New York until the ship reached Valparaiso in February 1821. After fourteen days in Rio endeavoring to replace the mast, Ridgely left that port for Rio de la Plata and spent twelve days there looking for a replacement. Failing to obtain a mast at Montevideo, he made the painful decision to return to Rio de Janeiro, where *Constellation* lay for six weeks as her carpenters located and installed the new main mast.[37]

Ridgely wrote in his sea journal 25 January 1821, six months following his departure from New York, that *Constellation* at that hour "attended with heavy gales and tremendous seas which carried the ship as far south as 60 degrees latitude." The captain, in a self-congratulatory manner, wrote that he had not lost a man, and that there had been no accidents to the crew or to the ship, and no scurvy, though the crew had been aboard for twenty months. Ridgely explained that he had put the crew on three watches and paid attention to their clothing and food, requiring them to put on clean frocks and trousers four times a week in warm latitudes and the best woolen clothing in high south latitudes. Besides the usual rations, Ridgely wrote, he gave the crew a half pound of pickles, sour cruel, and raisins in pudding and lemon acid twice a week; he made them drink their grog mixed with water at dinner and a second allowance with supper at 5 P.M. with meat; after, they had music until time for quarters and then, down with hammocks.[38]

Continuing his journal on 28 January, Ridgely wrote that he "carried the press of sail the whole of the day which has placed me around the Horn and as far to the westward as I want to be." Bubbling with pride, he wrote that Captain Porter boasted of having made the passage sooner than any other ship of war ever! Then Ridgely wrote, "O what will he think, then, of the *Constellation* beating him nearly two days and with the exception of the last twenty-four hours and a few hours, every inch of the way against a heavy sea as winds so violent as for me to lay to the quarter parts of two days." According to Ridgely, Porter's passage required thirty-four days from St. Catharine's, while *Constellation*'s was thirty-five days from Rio, farther to the north, bragging that the weather compelled him to go eastward of the Falklands. The historic frigate arrived at Valparaiso 7 March 1821.[39]

There Ridgely had found *Macedonian* waiting to return to the United States. The two frigates parted company and Ridgely sailed for Coquimbo to assist two

American ships, *Chesapeake* of Baltimore and *Warrior* of New York, that Captain Downes had left there in distress following their seizure by Lord Cochrane. Later, in March, Ridgely reported to the secretary of the navy that he had reached *Chesapeake* of Baltimore and that he had found her captain, a Mr. Pauson, dead, and a fortune in bullion missing. The ship *Warrior* of New York lay stranded nearby. His report to the secretary was pointedly critical of Downes, who refused assistance to these ships rather than delay his departure. *Constellation*'s crew repaired *Chesapeake* and Ridgely successfully salvaged the ship and her cargo of copper. Placing a crew from *Constellation* aboard, Ridgely sent her off to Baltimore and no doubt enriched himself handsomely as a result.[40]

Ridgely wrote in his private journal that General San Martín, leader of the patriot forces, hoped to drive all neutral ships, including warships, out of Peru's coastal waters because these ships had participated in removing treasure from the country both before and after the fall of Lima. Ridgely also noted in his personal journal that he refused a second invitation to meet with the patriot general because of the general's refusal to assist neutral ships. The captain followed those comments with a personal note in his journal that read, "I have never taken a dollar on board my ship nor have I opened a registry for the purpose of taking money as freight."[41]

There exists evidence that quite the opposite situation prevailed before the close of Ridgely's cruise, which lasted just one year in west coast waters. On one occasion, operating in cooperation with the Royal Navy's HBMF *Creole* (Capt. Thomas Hardy, commander), Ridgely played a role in moving a large treasure of silver specie and plate out of Peru. He referred to the incident in correspondence with a Spanish contact and with his relief, Charles Stewart (commander, USS *Franklin*). Ridgely's private journal called his venture admiralty property, and confirmed the arrangements with letters, copies of which he placed in his private journal. He received silver bars and plate on board *Constellation* at Callao, Peru, about 20 January 1822. Ridgely, after his failure to resist greed, grew wary even when he wrote in his private journal, though in this instance he informed Stewart concerning the pending admiralty caper, as he continued to try to convince himself that he conformed to navy regulations. A more likely possibility existed that Ridgely had been hoodwinked into aiding the Royal Navy to remove Spanish loot, blinded by the glamorous persona of Capt. Sir Thomas Hardy, famous for his service with Lord Nelson.[42]

Ridgely's efforts to assist his countrymen, mariners caught up in a cruel war, must be praised, particularly when measured against Downes's disgraceful behavior. Many American whaling ships operated in these waters at that time and several, including *Hero* of Nantucket, were raided by pirates or Lord Cochrane's fleet, losing ships and crews, too; some were put off on isolated islands and others were impressed into Cochrane's rebellious, piratical crews. But in view of Ridgely's orders and mission, the good he accomplished could never be balanced with his arrogant and greedy behavior. In spite of his denials, Ridgely enriched himself at the expense of his mission in that period in history. In one instance, he recorded his failure to resist offers of bribes when he received the Royalist Vice King Pezuela aboard *Constellation* and provided his entourage with safe haven for an unspecified amount of money. Ridgely's confederates, Capt. E. Smith and Supercargo Hefferman, eventually made arrangements to transfer the Royalist party and a fortune in specie from the United States warship to the American ship *General Brown* at a remote rendezvous; that ship then departed Peru for Rio de Janeiro. When all was said and done, Ridgely conspired with others to arrange for Royalist administrators to flee Peru under the nose of General San Martín by means of the intervention of a United States Navy frigate. He committed a grave infraction of neutrality, acted against the interests of the revolutionists, and in the process failed to comply with the orders of his superiors.[43]

Ridgely acknowledged the secretary's orders to return in April 1822, and *Constellation* entered New York harbor almost exactly two years following her departure from that port at the end of July 1820. He reported the condition of his ship to the Board of Commissioners, listing a number of specific repairs that would be required before the ship received another two-year assignment. Of particular interest to *Constellation*'s physical history, Ridgely mentioned to the commissioners that the ship leaked in the bow's forward sections in a hard sea at a rate of thirteen to fourteen inches per hour. Previous captains had reported this problem two decades earlier. Ridgely also suggested to the commissioners that ten guns should be removed from her armament because her sea performance would improve noticeably if she carried the number of guns she rated.[44] The commissioners ordered the ship placed in ordinary and Ridgely joined his wife in New York, where he nervously awaited news from Lima concerning his new riches while at the same time arranged a large investment in a cotton mill outside of Baltimore, where he had grown up.[45]

The selection of Charles Stewart as commodore of the first United States Pacific Squadron surprised no one familiar with his record. A man of action, he volunteered for positions that offered opportunities for glory and wealth. Once in command of the ship of the line USS *Franklin*, which replaced *Constellation*, Stewart proceeded to rewrite the manual of greed, elevating previous sailor-diplomats' personal activities to a higher organized level. His subsequent court-martial, called by the secretary of the navy in response to complaints filed by Peru's patriot government, charged Stewart in multiple specifications upon his return to the United States in 1824. The commodore denied that he disobeyed the secretary of the navy's orders during his two-year stay in the Pacific, though he admitted to the court that he operated his own fleet of schooners in trade along Peru's coast and that he accepted specie from foreigners for safekeeping aboard *Franklin*.[46]

Stewart carried foreigners as passengers and protected the activities of American traders accused of smuggling by patriot governments. He admitted to the court that he provided a floating bank and that he assigned USS *Franklin*'s crewmen to the construction and repair of vessels owned by him and others; further, he admitted convoying ships of commercial associates inside Peru's coastal territory. Captains Downes and Ridgely testified in the veteran officer's defense. Capt. James Barron, once the victim of a stacked court-martial, served as senior officer of the court; every other officer serving had less seniority than Stewart. The commodore in presenting his defense argued simply that his activities as presented in the specifications could not be proved. The court agreed and complimented the acquitted officer for his past service to his country. The court did not consider the damage he had done to the foreign policies of the United States.[47]

Policies of the executive branch consistently refused commanders the privilege of carrying specie on navy ships destined for foreign ports; nor could they provide these services to noncitizens. Madison expressed objections to James Lawrence's scheme to carry Spanish specie on USS *Hornet* in 1811. Secretary Crowninshield ordered Capt. Charles Morris, when commanding U.S. Frigate *Congress* in 1817, to refuse to accept as freight Spanish specie or bullion. He warned Morris that Royal Navy practice set no precedent for United States officers.[48] Secretary Thompson instructed John Downes to refrain from any acts that could compromise America's neutral stance. He ordered him to take nothing in the way of men, money, or provisions aboard *Macedonian* for either party—Spanish Royalists or men from Spanish provinces—to anywhere, except specie belonging to U.S. citizens.[49] When Ridgely followed Downes, he hid his illicit activities from the outside world, but his private journal and personal correspondence survive to reveal his deceit.

At the time that Smith Thompson ordered Commodore Stewart to replace Ridgely in *Constellation,* the secretary explained that "the nature of the struggle for freedom that is carrying on in South America, being a struggle on one side for liberty and independence, makes it fit and proper to avoid any collision with them." The secretary ordered Stewart to do nothing that could be construed to favor the Spanish. He specifically instructed the commodore to decline to take on board, for either party engaged in hostilities in Peru or Chile, men, money, provisions, or supplies to anywhere except specie to the United States. The complaints against Stewart originated with Peru's patriot government, which was seriously aggrieved by his behavior.[50]

The dismal record of navy commanders suggests that by 1824, in important areas of national policy, the secretary of the navy had lost effective control over the senior officer corps of the United States Navy. Though Captain Rodgers and less senior captains, by law, remained subject to the civilian control of the secretary and ultimately the president, disobedience to executive orders is clearly documented in the behavior of Captains Biddle, Downes, Ridgely, and Stewart. Yet in many ways the indiscretions of the navy's top officers assigned to diplomatic service reflected the particular qualities that made naval officers good at their vocation: commanding ships at sea. These included such characteristics as being authoritative, arrogant, strong-willed, independent, ambitious, dictatorial, and willing to take risks; and they were the men of that period who typically joined the navy to share in the spoils taken during the course of a cruise.

The navy established the West Indies Squadron in 1821; then, soon after, the government decided to place a squadron of United States Navy ships along the west coast of South America. A Brazilian Station was authorized in 1826 and an East Indies Squadron in 1835. The navy combined the Home Squadron and the West Indies Squadron into a single fleet in 1841 and created an African Group in 1843, the latter organized after Congress reorganized the department's internal structure in 1842. Commodores, with magnificent new ships of the line or frigates, some old, some famous, some new, but most of which had never fired a broadside except as a ceremonial salute, sailed into foreign ports with spectacular displays of pomp and brass. It proved to be an irresistible solution for a navy with a surplus number of ships and senior officers unwilling to retire.

The Navy Board of Commissioners, flush with success as new ships of the line began to hit the water in 1820, turned their attention to other problems inside the navy, as they bolstered its force of smaller ship-sloops and schooners, vessels that all maritime nations needed to protect their coasts and trade routes. It would be an over-simplification to write that the problem was simply an imbalance of warships. The Board of Commissioners faced the nagging problem of personnel restrictions imposed by the executive branch, which limited the employment and promotion opportunities of lower-ranked officers, their ambitions clipped short by budget limitations that allowed no more than a few of the largest ships in commission each year. The commissioners, responding to grumbling by officers who were stuck in rank for years for lack of a command or even a berth, directed their attention to the existing imbalance in the composition and size of the navy. The situation provided Rodgers with ample cause to move forward with the smaller vessel requirements that he outlined to Congress in 1819.

The navy could get only four sloops of war to sea in 1820. These included the old *Hornet*, originally built in 1806 and rebuilt in 1811, and three ships built by contract in 1813–1814—*Erie*, *Ontario*, and *Peacock*, all of which would soon require major repairs after five years of constant postwar service. USS *John Adams* and *Cyane*, corvettes, rounded out the navy's group of ship-sloops that survived the war. Because of the excessive number of ships available in the immediate postwar period, there was no urgent need for a program of great repairs prior to 1820. That situation changed as the combination of an insufficient number of small ships and their unseaworthy condition made the navy's repair requirements an important order of business for the Board of Commissioners in 1820. In the meantime, Congress had begun to consider legislation for the construction of small vessels as outlined in Rodgers's wish list in 1819.

Among the first ships to receive great repairs as the era of expanding repair work opened were the historic ship U.S. Frigate *United States* and the trophy ship USS *Cyane.* Later, the commissioners turned their attention to USS *Erie,* the sloop of war built during the War of 1812 by Thomas Kemp, whose yard at Fells Point built many of the nation's finest privateer schooners. The navy commissioned *Erie* early in 1814, while the war still raged, but in one of the navy's strangest but least-known episodes, her commander, Charles G. Ridgely, requested and received Secretary Jones's permission to deactivate his ship at Baltimore during the War of 1812 rather than attempt to run the Royal Navy blockade at Hampton Roads.[51]

Congress had originally initiated programs of rebuilding navy ships years earlier when it provided legislative approval and funds to rebuild U.S. Frigate *Philadelphia,* which had sunk at Tripoli, but was never rebuilt, and *Adams* and *Constellation* in 1812, which Tingey rebuilt. Congress once again supported the navy's repair and rebuilding policies that the commissioners presented in 1820. This does not infer that Congress did not notice the increasing costs of repairing vessels at the navy's yards or the rising cost of new construction. However, the commitment to a system of public yards, now politically irreversible, made the legislators' concerns academic. Committees of the House and Senate routinely questioned the estimates provided by Commodore Rodgers, but in no important instance did Congress suggest that a ship be scrapped rather than rebuilt, though yards often underestimated the cost of great repairs. Later, Congress, as it had done before the War of 1812, reconfirmed with special legislation the concept of redesigning and rebuilding ships, mentioning by name specific ships to be rebuilt. This procedure became effective after Secretary of the Navy John Branch questioned the rebuilding policy of the commissioners in 1829, specifically noting that year in his annual report that USS *John Adams,* which according to the commissioners had been rebuilt, was to his way of thinking an unauthorized new ship.[52]

William Doughty, the navy constructor at the Washington Navy Yard, prepared drafts for USS *Erie* and her sister ship *Ontario.* He modeled them after the design of the sloop-ship *Hornet,* drafted and built at Fells Point by William Price.[53] These ships incorporated many of the characteristics of Chesapeake Bay pilot schooners, though both of the Kemp-built ships had critics among navy officers.[54] As a result, before *Erie*'s repairs commenced, the commissioners asked Doughty to inspect the sloop and prepare a revised draft for her should the decision be made to rebuild her. Doughty prepared a drawing, which survived. He titled it *Construction Plan of the Sloop of War* Erie, *As Rebuilt* and increased the ship's principal dimensions to 121 feet 11 inches by 32 feet 6 inches by 14 feet 9 inches depth.[55] Constructor Doughty wrote David Porter that should a decision be made to rebuild the ship from the keel up, his new drawing should replace the original draft.[56]

The decision to dismantle *Erie*'s hull and replace it with a new one of slightly larger dimensions made *Erie* the first redesigned and almost completely rebuilt ship so handled under the authority of the Board of Commissioners, though the process would be repeated several times in subsequent years. In 1853 John Lenthall faced a similar situation with the aged U.S. Frigate *Constellation*. Both naval constructors prepared revised drafts that they hoped would eliminate flaws and modernize their ships, scheduled to be rebuilt under similar conditions though thirty years apart.[57]

Erie returned from the Mediterranean Sea after a survey abroad, arriving at the New York Navy Yard in January 1820. There she was placed in ordinary. The commissioners retracted original orders to repair her when they became aware that sufficient uncommitted repair funds would not be immediately available.[58] In 1822, after some delay, the New York Navy Yard commenced rebuilding *Erie* from a new keel upward.[59] Secretary Thompson informed Senator James Pleasant of the Naval Affairs Committee that the navy intended to rebuild *Erie*. Complying with the senator's request, Rodgers supplied him with an estimate of the cost of a new ship of her class, $60,000.[60] The estimated cost of rebuilding *Erie* was $58,000. Her original cost including equipment in 1814 totaled $56,174.36.[61] The cost of rebuilding *Erie* is not known, but her sister ship, *Ontario*, an extensive and expensive rebuild, cost $70,532.[62]

The historic ships of the United States Navy plus those vessels built during the War of 1812 and the navy's trophy ships entered a period during which it became necessary to continually rotate them between cruises and extensive repairs at one of the navy's shipyards. Ships in ordinary waiting repairs in 1822 included the frigates *Java* and *Guerrière*, both of which had entered service in 1815 and now required great repairs, and *Macedonian* and *Constellation*, both of which needed repairs following continuous service at sea since 1819. *Java*'s repairs, estimated to have cost $80,000 when finally completed in 1827, totaled $138,628. An estimate of repairs for *Constellation* amounted to $20,000 in 1822, but the commissioners decided to place the nation's first frigate in ordinary and the actual cost of her repairs, completed in 1825, is unknown. The navy completed repairs to *Macedonian* and *Congress* and returned them to service.[63]

Several years elapsed before Rodgers made his presentations to Congress for a new class of sloops of war. Rodgers admitted in his request for ten ships that putting these small ships in service would make it unnecessary to keep larger-class vessels in commission. Rodgers stressed the point that an additional number of sloop-ships would correct the disproportion between sloops and large ships, which had proved unacceptable. Of course, the existing disproportion to which Rodgers referred resulted from his prior interest in building frigates and battleships, which Congress generously had fulfilled in the act of 1816. But Rodgers seemed worried, too, about discontent among his officers, many of whom remained on the beach or served for years without promotion as the nation's fleet of large ships remained out of commission, without money for crews. The commissioners presented Congress with an estimated cost of $85,000 per sloop of war, and the legislators approved the bill to build the ships in 1825. The commissioners divided the building of the ten ships among several navy yards.[64]

Commodore Rodgers shipped out to the Mediterranean Sea in USS *North Carolina* in 1826. William Bainbridge served as president of the Board of Commissioners during his absence. Bainbridge turned his attention to the problem of poorly prepared ship repair surveys or estimates. One highly visible result of the increasing number of great repairs, which were more frequently required, was a stream of poorly prepared, underpriced estimates. This pattern suggested to Bainbridge that those performing ship surveys were not qualified to perform their tasks, making them embarrassing and inconvenient to the navy. Commodore Bainbridge appointed Samuel Humphreys chief constructor of the United States Navy (he had been constructor at the Philadelphia Navy Yard). Bainbridge instructed Humphreys to ensure that surveys of repairs would be accomplished with more accuracy, to promote greater order at the navy's seven yards (Pensacola's navy yard opened in 1825), and to make repairs with dispatch and economy.[65]

The feisty English emigrant constructor, Josiah Fox, wrote in 1810 that "it should be obvious to every reflecting mind, that persons of Military Character (Naval Officers), were the least fitted for conducting or having in any degree in the direction of building, equipping, or repairing ships of any class of persons whatsoever."[66] Fox directed his poison-dipped words at Capt. Thomas Tingey, formerly his superior at the Washington Navy Yard, who arranged for Secretary Smith to fire Fox in 1809 for reasons never revealed. Tingey took over the responsibility of repairing and rebuilding several ships long out of commission. Chapter 3 covered criticisms of the quality of work performed under Tingey's command. Of particular interest to the *Constellation* story are the bitter comments made about the yard's work as the ship received final preparations for a cruise in January 1813. (Actually, Captain Morris experienced far more grief with USS *John Adams* as a result of the yard's shoddy work.)

Captain Tingey's administration of the Washington Navy Yard came under review once again in 1825. To provide for his return to France following General La Fayette's farewell visit to the United States, the new ship, U.S. Frigate *Brandywine*, lay at anchor off St. Marys' pilot station at the mouth of the Potomac River awaiting the arrival of the hero of the Revolutionary War from Baltimore. The navy named, launched, and equipped the new frigate, according to her captain, Charles Morris, for this special occasion. Captain Tingey, whose men built the ship at the Washington Navy Yard, working with carefully selected officers connected by family to the Revolution, completed the ship as Morris arrived just in advance of her planned sailing date. After final emotional farewells, the large new frigate stood down Chesapeake Bay as the voyage home for General La Fayette began without a hitch on a bright September day in 1825.[67]

Captain Morris wrote coolly in his journal that a few hours after the pilot left and with the ship now in the Atlantic Ocean, it was discovered that *Brandywine* leaked rapidly. In the oblique writing style of the times, Morris describes the crisis as a development that "was not more unexpected than unpleasant." La Fayette was impatient to continue the voyage and Morris, placed in this terrible position as a result of the shoddy work of Tingey's yard, agreed to continue, turning on the ship's pumps and taking whatever steps he could to guarantee the general's safe passage. He commented that the weather and sea caused the ship to roll deeply but as the planks swelled the leak gradually diminished. At the time President John Quincy Adams selected Morris for the mission, he served as a navy commissioner, a position he returned to after an extended visit in Europe. Tingey retained his position at the Washington Navy Yard until his death.[68]

The commissioners assigned little repair work to the Washington yard, but while the yard remained under Tingey's command, the navy continued to have new ships built there. The keel of USS *Columbus* was laid in May 1816, evidently before timber contractors cut trees and molded her live oak frame pieces. According to Rodgers's explanation to Congress, this made it necessary to shape *Columbus*'s frame pieces from promiscuous live oak stockpiled at the yard, substantially running up the cost of labor. For this reason and others never explained, that ship of the line cost appreciably more than others of her class. While one cannot conclude for certain that Tingey made such decisions (John Rodgers lived in a house in full view of the yard), it stands out as an example of poor administration of expenditures at a time when the ship, once launched, had no important use.[69]

Some senior captains made long-term careers as commandants of navy yards. Capt. Alexander Murray, a true hero of the Revolutionary War as sailor and soldier and afterwards handicapped by deafness, stayed in naval service as commandant of the Philadelphia Navy Yard for longer than a decade. That yard built new ships; with Samuel Humphreys serving as constructor and with little repair work, that yard had not grown as rapidly as Gosport. Other examples of long-term commandants included John Cassin, who stayed on at Gosport until 1821. James Barron, whose troubled navy career included a five-year suspension, became commandant at Gosport Navy Yard in 1825 and later transferred to the Philadelphia yard. He proved to be a popular officer when he returned to service (though his career continued to be distorted by his bitter relationship with John Rodgers), but he remained troubled as he continued a passionate fight for a pardon for his role in the *Chesapeake-Leopard* affair. Barron interested himself in developing technology and made several inventions, including one for a floating dry dock. Lewis Warrington replaced Barron at Gosport and remained there several years.[70]

Often commandant positions rotated among senior officers coming off sea duty or terms on the Board of Commissioners. Examples include Bainbridge, Isaac Hull, and Charles Morris, all of whom took commandant assignments for personal reasons. After a review of the records, it seems safe to conclude that experienced captains—veterans of past wars—made no better commandants than they had diplomats. Most senior officers and some younger ones too, placed in positions requiring training in diplomacy and administration, functions vastly different from commanding a ship at sea, failed to make the adjustment. The fact that the navy functioned almost free of civilian oversight during the period the commissioners administered its affairs contributed heavily to the failures of individual officers assigned to administer naval affairs, to handle diplomatic missions, or to manage navy yards.[71]

Preparing repair estimates that realistically calculated the extent of a ship's need for repairs in advance proved more fantasy than fact. If a navy officer prepared a survey, generally he based his conclusions on the need to keep the vessel on station, so his reports often proved tentative and mainly covered obvious flaws. The Board of Commissioners appointed naval constructors or master builders for each yard, their position on yard organizational charts always blurred, particularly their relationship with the commandants. Commissioners depended on naval constructors to prepare ship surveys at each yard. Constructors, most of them trained as naval architects, interacted closely with a yard's master mechanics, each being dependent upon the other. Civilians in a yard who received yearly salaries included, in addition to the constructor or master builder, yard clerks and timber inspectors, totaling only a handful of men. At Gosport Navy Yard, master mechanics worked under a system in which they as well as the lowest-paid laborers, some of them slaves hired out by their masters, assembled each day for check-off with a timekeeper and then were hired on a daily basis. This degrading administrative device lumped all workers together including supervising personnel, separating them administratively and socially from the navy commandant and his uniformed staff, who were on top of the yard's pecking order.[72]

Gosport's labor records reveal poor labor relations existed between navy supervising personnel and civilian master mechanics at the yard. The system squeezed the small salaried civilian group—charged with the duties of handling estimates and drafts, scheduling work, timekeeping, and supervising store clerks—between yard workers, who made up the largest group, and the navy brass. Because neither competition with private yards nor the incentive to be efficient for the benefit of the commandant and his staff existed, salaried civilians, including constructors, handling their duties within a yard, had much in common with the yard's master mechanics and the men who built and repaired the ships. Both groups of civilians, living together and excluded from the navy clique, worked instead in each other's interest.[73] Politics provided an additional bond. National political parties played a role in the appointment of constructors, salaried employees, and master mechanics. As political appointees, the civilian employees became immersed in a spoils system that linked them to each other, to local political organizations, and, ultimately, to their congressmen.[74]

Yard workmen, as they grew in numbers over the years, became the principal beneficiaries of a system in which constructors or master builders, including supervisors like Frances Grice at Gosport Navy Yard, continually underestimated the cost of repair work. Grice and master workmen of the yard worked with full knowledge that a ship in ordinary, once the commissioners received a cost figure, faced one of two fates: repair or removal from the navy register. Commissioners rarely ordered ships abandoned in the marshes. With ample supplies of timber and other materials, all authorized by a friendly Congress, the atmosphere dovetailed happily with the commissioners' ongoing policy of repairing all navy ships regardless of age. Even the poorly constructed frigates built during and after the war continued to receive commissioners' approval for great repairs until finally overtonnage in large ships made *Java* and *Guerrière* of little use to the Navy Department. Obviously surplus in 1841, both were broken up by 1842.[75]

Reviewing the composition of the fleet commissioned in 1825, ten years following the creation of the Board of Commissioners, Secretary Samuel Southward placed ten ships rated sloop of war or superior in sea service. He named USS *North Carolina*, a new ship of the line and Commo. John Rodgers's flagship, to lead the Mediterranean Sea Squadron.[76] The other nine ships commissioned in 1825 were historic or trophy ships or ships built during the previous war. The commissioners ordered three new ships of the line placed in ordinary, bringing the total there to six in 1825.

The composition of the fleet in commission in 1825 revealed the miscalculations made by the first Board of Commissioners when they pushed Congress for passage of the act of 1816, creating a navy top-heavy with large ships that were now too expensive to operate. This blunder, compounded by other decisions made in 1813 and 1816, created a navy of many large ships destined to rot in ordinary. These questionable decisions, first pushed by Charles Stewart and his group of pronavy lobbyists in 1812 and then promoted again by John Rodgers and other senior officers in 1815 and 1816, forced the Navy Department from Crowninshield forward to depend principally upon the smaller, badly built ships of the War of 1812 and historic and trophy ships, all of which would undergo continuous cycles of repair. Though sentiment played an important role in the commissioners' decisions, budget limitations faced by navy secretaries provided an additional important reason why *Constitution, United States, Constellation, Congress, Macedonian, Java, Guerrière, John Adams, Cyane, Hornet, Erie, Ontario,* and *Peacock* remained in commission indefinitely. Even the new sloop-ships, which Rodgers claimed the navy needed for new missions, were in a large measure built to provide billets for officers left on the beach because the navy's large ships stayed moored in ordinary.

As the first ten years of the Board of Commissioners ended, it became more and more apparent that its members, led by John Rodgers, had caused to be built ships the young nation could not afford to operate. No greater failure than this can be charged to Rodgers and the group of senior officers around him. Their woolly headed, self-serving decisions produced in short order a massive system of navy yards. Their size placed them among the largest industrial organizations in the country, but they were also noncompetitive, badly administered, expensive, wasteful, producers of shoddy work, and the primary cause of the eventual downfall of the Navy Board of Commissioners in 1842.

Following *Constellation*'s return from Chile, the navy placed her in ordinary at the New York Navy Yard, where she remained in 1823 and a portion of 1824. She received some minor wear and tear repairs amounting to $9,445, and then was recommissioned. Master Comdt. W. B. Finch received orders to deliver the ship to the Gosport yard, which he did. *Constellation* arrived at Portsmouth in late January 1825. The yard outfitted the frigate for sea, a process that stretched over most of 1825, to ready her for service in the West Indies Squadron. Secretary Southard appointed Capt. M. T. Woolsey her new commander.[77]

Six

1829 Hull Modifications

*C*apt. Lewis Warrington, a protégé of Commo. John Rodgers, left the position of commandant of Gosport Naval Yard and assumed command of the West Indies Squadron in early 1825. Secretary Samuel Southard assigned Capt. Melancthon T. Woolsey as flag captain of U.S. Frigate *Constellation* and Warrington hoisted his broad pennant aboard the historic ship. Following up on Commo. David Porter's years of zealous pursuit of pirates in the region, Warrington reported to Secretary Southard that no piracies had occurred for several months prior to January 1825 and that the situation had remained quiet since his arrival. Commo. Warrington ordered ships of his squadron to cruise the coasts of Cuba, and he kept one or more ships in or near the ports of Matanzas and Havana.[1]

When John Rodgers quit the Board of Commissioners to take command of the Mediterranean Sea Squadron, Secretary Southard made changes in its composition, replacing Rodgers with Commodore Bainbridge as president. Captain Morris served, too, during Rodgers's absence, along with Capt. Jacob Jones. Warrington joined the board in 1827, which allowed the commissioners to continue to administer naval affairs in a manner consistent with Rodgers's policies during the period of the break of his authority from 15 December 1824 to October 1827.[2]

Commodore Warrington relinquished his command of the West Indies Squadron to Charles G. Ridgely, who took over the squadron in February 1827. Almost as soon as Ridgely arrived, the officers of *Constellation* commenced a campaign to force the new commodore to allow the ship to return to Gosport Navy Yard for repairs. They claimed that the accumulation of sea animals on her bottom had grown so heavy that the ship did not respond to her rudder quickly enough for safe navigation. On one occasion *Constellation* went aground on the beach of the Isle of

Pines and remained stranded for a period of time. As a result her bottom became covered with several inches of oysters. Since the ship had not been coppered for several years, the crustaceans quickly attacked the ship's bottom. In their letter of complaint lodged with Captain Woolsey, who passed it along to Commodore Ridgely, the ship's officers claimed that as a result of the mishap "she will neither work nor sail." As a result, they argued, she should not continue on a cruise. In his letter of transmittal to the Board of Commissioners, Commodore Ridgely suggested that Woolsey's officers exaggerated her condition.[3]

By the middle of June Ridgely altered his tune and notified the commissioners that if *Constellation* remained on station for three additional months, she would be unseaworthy and therefore in no condition to return to the United States; with or without orders he intended to send her home. He also admitted that once again *Constellation*'s deep draft had caused her to go aground, this time on a bar across the entrance to Pensacola, where she remained stranded for four hours. The frigate arrived back at Gosport in July 1827, and the commissioners ordered her placed in ordinary. The backup of ships requiring repairs there had reached a rather staggering number.[4] Nevertheless, Captain Warrington, acting for the board, ordered Comdt. James Barron to conduct the usual surveys except to her hull. The commissioners ordered Samuel Humphreys to Norfolk to conduct that survey.[5] Humphreys' report, if he made one at that time, is missing.

Placing a ship in ordinary consisted of more than simply mooring *Constellation* in a designated holding area. The regulations on preparing a ship were explicit and the work required extensive. The commissioners' regulations and instructions of 1819 were updated by the board under Bainbridge in 1825.[6] The rules required crews assigned to ordinary to conduct a rather complex series of procedures which began with the dismantling of all ships' stationary and running rigging and all masts and spars other than the lower masts, which laborers covered with tar and capped. Yard crews cleared the ships of all movable equipment such as furniture, galleys, water casks, hammocks, provisions, and guns and carriages. A crew caulked hulls as needed and then blackened and tarred them with varnish applied to their topsides. Ordinary crews fitted hatch openings and the spar deck with waterproof covering and whitewashed holds and between decks at designated intervals.

Officers in charge of vessels in ordinary placed great emphasis on keeping the ships clean and on stacking ballast and other items on battens, keeping all doors open to allow air to circulate. Carpenters removed planks in the magazine bulkheads to aid circulation. Later, amended instructions ordered the removal of outside planks, ceiling, and bulkheads, allowing increased circulation throughout the ship. Commandants assigned permanent crews to live aboard, sometimes lighting and tending fires to keep a ship dry. And, in a last-ditch attempt to slow the progress of rot, Congress authorized special appropriations for roofs over ships in ordinary. The battle to fight decay never stopped but, on the other hand, it was never properly engaged either, as navy rules forbade the repairing of ships placed in ordinary until they returned to service.[7]

Upon being placed in ordinary on about 1 August 1827, *Constellation* was stripped of her guns, carriages, and casks, as well as her rigging, yards, and spars, as required by regulation. A partial inventory of her equipment held for her in the custody of the officer in charge of ordinary included sails, no value given; spars, $3,866.11; rigging, $11,508; and galley equipment, $1,656; surveyors valued other material removed but not individually listed at $18,848.04, for a grand total of $35,878.15. The stored equipment, after reconditioning, was returned to a ship following repairs or rebuilding. If the commissioners authorized the sale of old equipment, the proceeds reduced the cost of the work subsequently done in the yard. All of these activities were performed under the direction of an officer assigned to care for the ships in ordinary and were outside the jurisdiction of the yard storekeeper.[8]

A few months before *Constellation* entered Gosport, badly in need of repair, and the commissioners ordered her placed into ordinary, Congress debated important and sweeping legislation to improve navy yards. It had become increasingly apparent that the Navy Board of Commissioners, with congressional support, would hold to policies that required that public yards build all new warships and that all future repairs and rebuilding would be assigned to them, eliminating any consideration of competing private yards. In addition, by 1827, the commissioners made clear their determination to maintain a policy of retaining most of the older ships on the navy register indefinitely, forecasting a continued rise in the volume of repairs. Congress believed that the situation required new legislation to bring the navy's yards to a state of development and readiness to handle the projected increase in building, rebuilding, and repairs as the full impact of Rodgers's plans, first revealed in his outline of the navy peace establishment back in 1819, reached full bloom. In short order ships of the line, frigates, and sloops began to line up for repairs along with older ships built before or during the War of 1812.

Legislators moved to strengthen the navy's infrastructure and on 3 March 1827 passed an Act for the Gradual Improvement of the Navy of the United States. The act served as confirmation of the Board of Commissioners' strategy for administering the expanded fleet, including ships already launched and in service or in ordinary, those in stocks, and those still on drafting tables. The act authorized the purchase of large quantities of live oak timber, a move resulting from the fear that live oak timber supplies were finite. By authorizing the expansion of yards and the purchase of new equipment, the board, with the cooperation of Congress, pursued its goals under the assumption that the problems and inefficiencies of navy yards resulted from inadequate equipment, rather than from the nature of the work performed or as a result of men working without incentives or efficient management. As Rodgers's policies fell into place, the yards needed work houses, wharves, bulkheads, timber sheds, and dry docks, all of these facilities authorized by the Act of 1827 to Improve the Navy.[9]

The legislation proved to be one of the most important acts (along with its extension passed in 1833) affecting the navy as it committed the United States government to the board's policy of public yards, eliminating for generations the participation of more efficient private shipyards in navy shipbuilding and repair activities. Practically speaking, by reserving navy shipbuilding and repairs for navy yards, the act of 1827 provided the funds that, in time, made the yards capable of handling their responsibilities, which would increase in volume and complexity in future years. In addition to providing for considerable expansion to existing facilities, the Act to Improve the Navy included the authority and funds for the construction of dry docks at Boston Navy Yard and at Gosport Navy Yard. These giant, expensive facilities, when placed into operation, allowed the navy to repair warships from the keel up, perpetuating the ongoing repair of historic ships almost indefinitely.

The act allocated $500,000 per year for six years to purchase hundreds of thousands of cubic feet of molded live oak framing plus other types of cut lumber. Contractors precut live oak into frame sections for the construction of new ships of several classes, especially ships of the line, large frigate-44s, and sloops of war. Timber and other materials purchased under the act could not be used for repairs. Also, Congress emphasized that though the act of 1827 appropriated funds for timber for new ships, it did not authorize any new ships to be built.[10]

This, then, was the situation at Gosport as *Constellation* lay moored in ordinary waiting for her first major overhaul since Captain Tingey supervised her rebuild back in 1812. All in all, the old frigate had participated in six cruises in the intervening period and had logged thousands and thousands of miles in the Mediterranean Sea, the North Atlantic, the Caribbean Sea, the South Atlantic, and on the Pacific coast of South America. With her relatively small crew of 350 men, *Constellation* proved a reliable and affordable ship, and truly a historic ship. Popular and lucky though she proved herself to be, she would forever remain an unwanted runt frigate, too fast, too hard to manage, and too crank for most of the navy's ambitious senior officers, jockeying for commands. Officers preferred the larger, steadier gun platforms, so once again the navy's oldest frigate, haunted by Truxtun's having tagged her as unstable, stood waiting for another commodore and another shipbuilder to attack her shapely hull.

The commissioners forecast concern over the possibility that there were insufficient repair funds in 1827 to repair the ships requiring attention. They instructed

Table 6.1. Survey of Estimate of Repairs to *Constellation*

Workmanship, incl. carpenters, caulkers, blacksmiths, plumbers, and laborers	$39,500.00
Materials of Wood	12,700.00
Materials of Iron	7,078.00
Materials of Copper	6,801.00
Materials of Lead	300.00
Materials of Oakum, etc.	845.00
SEMI-TOTAL	$67,224.00
Rigging and Cables	18,497.00
Joiners	6,000.00
Spar Making	2,920.00
Gun Carriages	1,000.00
Sails	4,352.00
GRAND TOTAL (CENTS ADDED OR DROPPED)	$99,994.00

Source: Survey, dated 17 November 1827, submitted to Barron on that date and transmitted by Barron to Rodgers with his letter of 22 November 1827, RG45, Entry 220, National Archives.

Comdt. James Barron to estimate the cost of repairing the ships at Gosport. However, on 17 October 1827, the Board of Commissioners altered its original instructions and ordered Barron to survey the hull of *Constellation* and get the results back to Washington as soon as possible. Barron's instructions included an order to supply an estimate of the cost and the time required to thoroughly repair and fit her for service.[11] Barron, a hated enemy of Rodgers and always under pressure from him, reported to the commissioners on 14 November that the estimate would be ready in a few days. He anticipated that the report would show *Constellation* to be "an almost entirely worn out ship."[12]

A team at Gosport consisting of Robert Rose, Francis Grice, James Pooks, W. E. Thompson, Charles Chapell, and H. M. Armistead prepared a survey and estimate of the cost to repair *Constellation* dated 17 November 1827 and submitted it to Barron (see table 6.1). When John Rodgers received the cost figures from Barron, he ordered all work on the ship stopped, though it was not known that the yard had removed *Constellation* from ordinary at the time.[13]

The commissioners had a large problem in 1827: too much repair work scheduled and only $475,000 for repairs in Secretary Southard's estimated budget for 1828. Rodgers, who wanted *John Adams* rebuilt, asked Barron to provide the commissioners with a schedule for repairing the sloop of war, approval to rebuild her having been received from the secretary of navy. On 19 November the commissioners issued orders to Barron to commence *John Adams's* repairs. Then, altering his approach, Rodgers ordered Barron to delay repairs for *Constellation* and have master builder Francis Grice prepare a comparison between repairing the ship and building a new ship of *Constellation's* class. This is much the same route that Rodgers followed in 1821 when the commissioners considered modifying *Erie's* hull and rebuilding her from a new keel up, keeping Congress aware of her costs and their final decision.[14] In the meantime, the trophy frigate *Macedonian* returned from a cruise in the South Atlantic and she, too, required extensive repairs. Once again the commissioners ordered chief constructor Humphreys to Portsmouth to examine *Constellation* and *John Adams*.[15]

On 7 December 1827, Rodgers ordered Barron to slash his yard crews by 265 mechanics and ninety-two laborers, proof that though the yard had much work scheduled, the navy had insufficient funds available to handle the backlog.[16] Ignoring Rodgers's order, Barron proceeded to discharge (strip) *Constellation* immediately as he and Humphreys, who finally had reached Gosport, concluded that the commissioners wanted the chief constructor's report as soon as possible. In the meantime, Barron received master shipbuilder Francis Grice's estimate of repairing *Constellation* compared to the cost of building a new ship of the same class. Grice figured the cost of a new ship (hull only) at $100 per ton burden (*Constellation*, 1,270 tons), for a total estimated cost of $127,000. This is the figure the commandant forwarded to the commissioners for a new hull for a ship of *Constellation's* size.

To calculate the cost of repairing Constellation, Grice used the cost to repair U.S. Frigate *United States* (1,620 tons burden). Grice figured the cost to repair the larger ship worked out to $69.52 per ton. Grice multiplied the smaller ship's tons burden, 1,270, by $69.52, which provided him with a figure of $88,290 to compare with the cost of a new hull, $127,000. Grice's second estimate for repairs for *Constellation*, figured in this manner, totaled $11,000 less than the previous estimate sent to the commissioners.[17] When the Treasury Department finished calculating the actual cost of remodeling and repairing *Constellation* in 1829, the total approached $170,000.[18]

The actual cost of *Constellation's* modifications and repairs, $170,000, exceeded Grice's estimate for a new hull by $43,000. But none of Grice's estimates included the cost of replacing equipment and other gear. Here one gains insight into the problems that dominated the handling of estimates in light of existing repair and accounting procedures. Under the legislation that created it, the Board of

Commissioners could not enter into the settlement of accounts over which the secretary of the navy's office and Treasury Department retained complete control. This meant that the commissioners were isolated from the responsibility for the final costs of any contract. The commissioners' authority ceased with their approval of repairs following the receipt of estimates. The wide deviation between estimates and actual costs was no accident. Civilian employees of the shipyards learned to manipulate the system and payrolls became inflated.

The reports Samuel Humphreys prepared for the commissioners concerning the costs of repairs and modifications to the hulls of *Constellation* and *John Adams* are not located in the records of the commissioners' correspondence or ships' files. Though Rodgers's records suggest that he received no surveys from Humphreys, he infers that his report on *Constellation*'s state and condition was positive as he ordered Barron to proceed with her repairs, but at a pace that included the "most economical number of mechanics." Barron also received an order to delay repairs to *John Adams*.[19]

The process of stripping *Constellation* of her planking and ceiling started on a nonpriority track during the winter of 1828. Captain Barron reported to the commissioners 21 February that repairs on the ship were progressing.[20] It became apparent that as the yard readied *Constellation* for sea during the spring of 1829, someone—the commissioners, Humphreys, Barron, or Grice—ordered the ship's hull significantly, even radically modified before she was cut down and rebuilt. There is a document that places a set of 1829 offsets in the possession of the Baltimore custodians of the ship in 1955, but these offsets disappeared while in the group's custody. Nor have any drafts prepared in 1828 dealing with modifications to the ship's hull been located in naval records at the National Archives. But subsequent measurements by *Constellation*'s officers after recommissioning, along with a drawing prepared in 1839 by Francis Grice, the master shipbuilder in charge of her 1829 rebuild, confirmed that the ship's hull was radically modified under Grice's supervision in 1829.[21]

Repair work on *Constellation* continued at a slow pace throughout 1828. Barron reported using live oak timber purchased under authority of the act of 1827 in *Constellation*'s hull. The commissioners warned him to replace the amount used immediately. When the yard completed work on her hull, Barron forwarded to the commissioners a report of materials used. Whether or not the yard actually replaced timber taken for an unauthorized use or merely reported the requisition to the Treasury Department, which debited repairs and credited the Act to Improve the Navy account, is not clear. Certainly, it became routine, given how easily stored materials could deteriorate, to use for repairs stockpiled timber reserved for new ships. Still in 1828, with the act of 1827 only a year old, records do not show how the commissioners ordered these transfers handled.

The program to build timber sheds began at Gosport, and large quantities of live oak framing timber, purchased by the commissioners, arrived at the yard in 1828. To further confuse matters, Rodgers reported to Secretary Southard that someone purchased three complete frames for frigate-44s, exceeding allowances under the act of 1816 (an Act to Gradually Increase the Navy). He proposed to the secretary to charge this inadvertently issued contract (which had already been delivered) against the act of 1827. One visualizes the growing bureaucratic chaos as commissioners, commandants, naval agents, the secretary's office, and the Treasury Department functioned physically and legally separated from each other, creating an increasingly high level of inefficiency that would, in time, bring down the Board of Commissioners.[22]

Niles Register reported to its readers 11 October 1828 that in the process of repairing *Constellation*, Gosport Navy Yard stepped her lower fore, main, and mizzen masts the week previously. Just two months later constructor Grice reported to Barron that the yard had completed work on the frigate's bottom. By the end of December 1828, he reported the ship so near completion that few carpenters would continue to be required. Barron forwarded Grice's letter to Rodgers in Washington with a question about reducing the number of carpenters employed. Rodgers instructed Barron to commence rebuilding *John Adams,* adding that a draft covering her modifications would be forwarded. In a letter to Secretary Southard sent just prior to the secretary's departure from office, however, Rodgers intimated that at the end of February 1829, *Constellation*'s repairs would continue at Gosport through the winter.[23]

John Branch, President Andrew Jackson's first secretary of the navy, took office in the early spring of 1829. Washington insiders considered the new secretary a country politician with no maritime experience. He quickly established himself as an irritating independent thinker who caused Commodore Rodgers and his Board of Commissioners no end of trouble for the period he remained in Washington. To further complicate Rodgers's previously unquestioned position, President Jackson and his new secretary of the navy were friendly to James Barron, who had been a thorn in Rodgers's side since returning to the navy after the War of 1812. In addition, Barron was senior to all other officers except the admiral, as Rodgers was called behind his back. Branch carried on a correspondence with Barron and Rodgers over the course of the following year, probing Rodgers's management of naval affairs as he attempted to unravel the confused operations of the navy and its shore-based facilities. Branch ordered the commissioners to prepare U.S. Frigate *Constellation* for sea, orders that the commissioners transmitted to Barron 20 May 1829. Barron, who set up back-channel communications with Branch, informed the secretary that though he had been ordered to take over the commandant's billet in Philadelphia, he intended to stay at Gosport until after he finished preparing *Constellation* for service.[24]

In general, the principal modifications or alterations to the shape of U.S. Frigate *Constellation*'s hull included an increase in her maximum beam at the dead flat, accomplished by a corresponding increase of approximately 1 foot, 5 inches in her molded breadth at that location. The modification of her hull resulted in the refairing of her shape above the floors, none of which the shipyard replaced. The yard accomplished the modification of her hull shape by replacing live oak frame pieces from the level of the first futtocks upward to the ship's rail. Other major alterations included a new round stern and rudder assembly and new galleries and captain's quarters. Her increase in breadth made it necessary to replace all of her decks and internal works from the keelson up, including waterways and stanchions. Once again those responsible for redrafting *Constellation*'s hull, presumably with the approval of the Board of Commissioners, modified the ship's hull to improve her stability.[25]

Though it remains unknown whether Francis Grice and Samuel Humphreys drafted the changes in *Constellation*'s design, the paper flow at the time and Humphreys' movements suggest that he had a hand in preparing the modified draft. Commandant Barron ordered *Constellation* stripped of her planking in mid-December 1827 on about the same day as Humphreys' arrival at Gosport Navy Yard. The navy's chief constructor reached Portsmouth after the commissioners received the yard's estimate of repairs in the amount of $99,994 dated 17 November. He also had an opportunity to review Grice's comparison of the cost of a new and a rebuilt ship of *Constellation*'s class before he left Washington for Gosport. Humphreys' report reached Rodgers's desk by 5 January 1828, as on that date the commissioners issued orders to proceed with *Constellation*'s repairs. Because there is no record of drawings redrafting her hull having been sent to Gosport from Washington, it is logical to conclude that Grice and Humphreys worked out *Constellation*'s modifications after they completed an examination of the stripped ship.[26]

Under Francis Grice's supervision, the yard's carpenters and mechanics, working under orders to assign crews only in the most economic numbers, completed the majority of work on *Constellation* in 1828 and January 1829. The yard charged approximately 61,832 days' labor against the ship in 1828–29. Of that total, work performed in 1828 amounted to roughly 40,000 days; work in 1829 totaled about 22,000 days, though the yard records suggest that some work performed in 1828 may have been charged out in 1829. The yard stripped *Constellation* of her interior and exterior planks and ceiling and partially dismantled her frame to the first futtocks. From that point upward, the yard rebuilt the hull almost new, replacing a number of first-futtock pieces in her midbody sections (see table 6.2). A list of materials used and a summary of the principal areas of the ship repaired survive in a single volume containing costs for repairing ships during the Board of Commissioners' tenure, probably compiled at the request of a congressional committee. Semimonthly returns

Constellation

Commenced Repairing at Gosport in the month of Jany - completed July.

1829

Rails. Timbers &c
- Main Rail - Hammocods: and Plank sheer New
- Top timbers & Stantions 213 new
- Third futtocks . . . . . 68 "
- Second - do - - - - - 53
- First - do - - - - - 27
- Plank between Ports - Strings & Wales - - - - - New
- Bottom Plank under the Wales - Nine strakes on each side

Spar Decks
- Beams - - - - - - - - - - - - - 18 New
- do - - - - - - - - - - - - - 2 Scarphed
- Half Beams to Hatch - - - - - - - - - 2 New
- All the Carlings & Ledges except 02 Carlings - - - New
- Waterways - Deck plank - bad heads & Fife rails - - - do
- Trunk & Hook over Bowsprit - Spar deck clamps & 10 Port sills -
- Twenty four lodge & twenty dagger Knees.

Gun deck
- 12 Beams & two half Beams to main Hatch
- 28 Carlings: 84 Ledges: 8 Lodge Knees and 6 Dagger Knees
- Waterways: Deck plank Spirketting: clamps Plank between Ports-New
- All the hatchy: Partners of Masts: Bowsprit bitts; - - - -
- Fore & main Top sail Sheet bitts: Cross bit to after cable bitts } New
- Eight Port Sills - - - -

Birth Deck
- 19 Beams & two half Beams to main Hatch: Waterways
- Carlings: Ledges: Hatches: Deck plank: Spirketting & } New
- Clamps: - 44 lodge & 40 Dagger Knees. - - - - -

Orlop and Hold
- Orlop Deck - - - - - - - -
- Ceiling - Mast Steps: upper piece to Kelson & Dead wood -
- forward & aft with lower piece of Kelson forward & aft - - -
- One Kelson Knee: two Riders aft: two B Hooks & large bilge } New
- pieces abreast the mast & Stantins to all the Beams under deck -
- One Kelson Knee: two riders aft: Magazine: Pump well shot
- and Chain lockers - - - - - - - -

Outside Repairs
- Upper piece of Stem 15 feet long: but water & head Complete
- Port Shutters: Scupper holes: all the Channels and fore and } New
- main Sheet chocks - - - - - - -
- Galleries & taffrail: Stern & Rudder: - - - - - - New
- Bottom retuned old - False Keel: 10 fore hoods near Keel - - - - do
- Recoppered with 32 & 34 g Copper -

Caulking
- Caulked inside & outside;

Cost of Materials Dolls 81117 . 71
Labour   · 86565 · 31
Total . . . Dollars 167683 · 02

See the Appropriate Book for this Ship for the details of the cost. letter C. —

Summary of repairs at the Gosport Navy Yard, 1828–29, by Francis Grice, master ship builder. *National Archives* (RG 19, Entry 5, 1:171)

Table 6.2. Futtocks, Stanchions, and Top Timbers Replaced in 1828

Stanchions	53 each side of ship
Top timbers	53 each side of ship
Third futtocks	34 each side of ship
Second futtocks	26 each side of ship
First futtocks	13 each side of ship
Floors	None replaced

Source: Returns of Repairs to Vessels, RG19, Entry 5, 1:171.

of the work in progress on *Constellation* have survived and are at the National Archives.[27] The sketch of the ship's profile showing the new timbers illustrates the distribution of the new frame pieces (see fig. 6.1). The drawing also shows the location of new frame sections, which enabled Master Builder Grice to alter the ship's dimensions and modify the hull's shape.

Following *Constellation*'s return to service in 1829, three different officers aboard the ship recorded her modified dimensions, which were used to prepare a half-body plan. Franklin Buchanan, who previously served on the frigate under Captain Gordon in 1815 and who served again under Captain Wadsworth in 1829, recorded measurements of the ship's decks in his personal journal (see table 6.3). Lt. William Pearson, acting on Captain Wadsworth's instructions, also measured the frigate's decks and recorded the ship's dimensions for Wadsworth's *Watch, Quarter, and Station Bill* (see table 6.4). Midn. James Miller, who also served on the ship under Captain Wadsworth, recorded *Constellation*'s measurements in his journal (see table 6.5), as did Midn. John W. Mason (see table 6.6).

A half-body midship section was prepared reflecting the modifications to *Constellation*'s hull in 1829, created from the calculations made by Pearson, Buchanan, and Miller, all of whom measured the breadth of *Constellation*'s decks but not necessarily from the same reference points. Normally, using the measurements from three officers would be suspect, but in this instance the new dimensions are proved by the drawing made by Francis Grice of the modifications he did in 1828–29. Figure 6.2 shows the ship's new midsection drafted using the measurements taken by the three officers. Using three sets of dimensions of the ship's decks to prepare *Constellation*'s new midsection drawing required certain assumptions about the location of the correct reference points, which were selected following a series of trial and elimination calculations. Once chosen, the measurements between the surviving reference points matched the dimensions

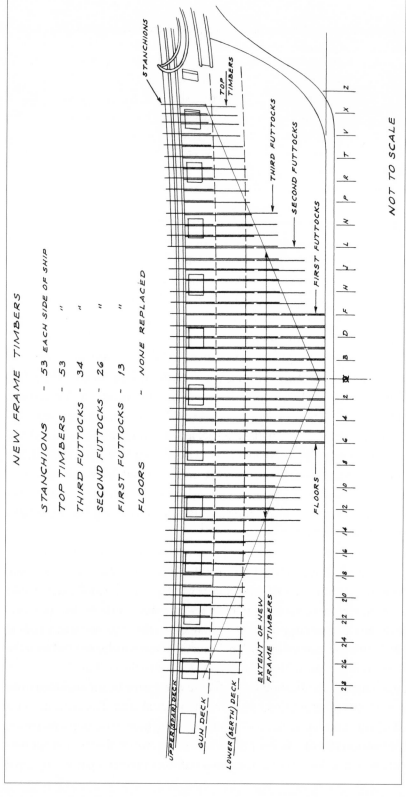

NEW FRAME TIMBERS

STANCHIONS — 53 EACH SIDE OF SHIP
TOP TIMBERS — 53 "
THIRD FUTTOCKS — 34 "
SECOND FUTTOCKS — 26 "
FIRST FUTTOCKS — 13 "
FLOORS — NONE REPLACED

NOT TO SCALE

Figure 6.1. USF *Constellation's* new framing installation, 1829. The extent of framing modifications is drawn in accordance with the frigate's record of repairs, 1828–1829. *William L. Crothers*

Table 6.3. Length and Beam of *Constellation*'s Decks Recorded by Franklin Buchanan, Naples, 9 October 1830

Deck	Length	Beam
Spar Deck	167 ft.	33 ft.
Main Deck	163 ft.	40 ft.
Berth Deck*	156 ft.	33 ft., 8 ins.
Depth from the underside of spar deck to tops of floors at main hatch		26 ft.

Source: Buchanan's Journal No. 6, Special Collections, Nimitz Library, United States Naval Academy.
*Buchanan meant Orlop Deck, not Berth Deck.

taken by each officer. In this manner, the final drawing required only easy fairing of the ship's new lines. The shape of the refaired hull is not known exactly, as offsets, which are known to have once existed, could not be located.[28]

Franklin Buchanan made his measurements to the inside of the ceiling, which provided the maximum clear deck breadth. This is consistent with his manner of measuring the decks following Tingey's rebuild. He measured the orlop deck, which he mistakenly labeled Berth Deck, 33 feet 8 inches, four inches greater than the dimension of this deck contained in Joshua Humphreys' 1795 draft. Pearson's measurements fall exactly on the inboard edge of the waterways of the gun and berth decks when faired with the new orlop deck breadth recorded by Buchanan.

Buchanan measured the new breadth of *Constellation*'s spar deck 33 feet to the inboard edge of plank-sheer, approximately. Pearson's breadth of spar deck is 34 feet 3 inches—the only point that matches this figure was taken at the underside of spar deck plank at the inner face of the top timber. Pearson probably interpreted "molded" as a measure to the extreme edge of the deck planking, where the waterway rises at an angle. Miller's measurement of breadth of beam of 40 feet 8 inches was taken at the height of the maximum breadth line from the center line to the ceiling.

As a result of Grice's modifications, *Constellation*'s extreme beam increased from 42 feet 4 inches in 1812 to approximately 43 feet 9 inches in 1829. The assumption is made that all of Humphreys' structural scantlings were used. The ship's increased beam resulted from an increase in her molded breadth at the midsection to approximately 42 feet 7 inches, more than two and a half feet greater than her original

Table 6.4. Dimensions of U.S. Frigate *Constellation* Recorded by Lt. William Pearson, 1829

Moulded length* of the spar deck at the dead flat	34 ft., 3 ins.
Moulded length of the gun deck at the dead flat	39 ft., 2 ins.
Moulded length of the berth deck at the dead flat	38 ft., 10 ins.
Height from the surface of the gun deck to the underside of the spar deck beam	6 ft.
Length of the spar deck from the after paro of the stem to the forward part of the taffrail	167 ft.
Length of the gun deck from the after side of the apron to the after hood ends	152 ft., 3 ins.
Length of the berth deck from the stemson to the transom	155 ft., 4 ins.
Depth from the upper side of the spar deck beam to the upper side of the floors at the main hatch	26 ft.

Source: U.S. Frigate *Constellation,* Alexander S. Wadsworth, commander, Watch, Quarter and Station Book, prepared by Lt. William Pearson, RG45, Entry 406, National Archives.

*Lieutenant Pearson used the word *length* mistakenly; he meant breadth.

molded breadth when launched in 1797. The word "approximate" must be used because no offsets or drafts prepared in 1828 exist to support these modifications. The change in her shape as the result of refairing the ship's hull was accomplished from measurements recorded by Lieutenants Buchanan and Pearson and Midshipman Miller. These measurements, when converted into the drawing, depict a definite, logical progression in beam, from Humphreys to Tingey to the 1829 rebuild. When drawing the ship's modified midsection (fig. 6.2), the final configuration was the result of fairing *Constellation*'s lines. These findings fit well with the extent of the new timbering indicated by figure 6.1. So it is apparent that Grice and his mechanics made a second modification in *Constellation*'s shape to increase her stability (see fig. 6.3).[29]

Table 6.5. Measurements Taken by James Miller While Serving in *Constellation*, 1832–33

Length of Gun Deck	165 ft., 10 ins.
Length of Berth Deck	155 ft., 10 ins.
Length of Keel	149 ft., 6 ins.
Breadth of Beam	40 ft., 8 ins.

Source: Midn. James Miller's Journal, *Erie/Shark/Constellation*, 1832, Maryland Historical Society.

Table 6.6. Measurements Taken by Midshipman John W. Mason, U.S. Frigate *Constellation*, Circa 1831

Burden	1,100 tons
Length of Keel	136 ft.
Length of Gun Deck	164 ft.
Length of Spar Deck	168 ft., 10 ins.
Length from Knightheads to Taffrail	175 ft., 8 ins.

Source: Midn. John W. Mason's Journal, Misc. vol. 138, G. W. Blunt White Library, Mystic Seaport, Connecticut.

With tentative conclusions reached and a preliminary drawing prepared, I was browsing through old issues of *American Neptune* when I reread Evan Randolph's article, *Fouled Anchors? Foul Blow.* Randolph wrote that he found a transverse section drawing of *Constellation* dated 11 January 1839 among the documents in *Constellation* ship files accumulated by Lloyd A. Olsson, a researcher at the Naval Historical Center working under its director, Rear Adm. Ernest M. Eller. The retrieved drawing turned out to be a photocopy of *Constellation*'s half midsection, rather roughly drawn by master builder Francis Grice to a scale one-quarter inch to a foot and dated 11 January 1839. At that date, Charlestown Navy Yard had started to prepare *Constellation* for her third great repair. After establishing that Gosport remained Grice's place of employment in 1839, a check of the log of the Boston yard revealed that in January 1839 workers had yet to perform any significant repair work on *Constellation* and that she did not enter dry dock until the following month, a schedule dovetailing with the date of Grice's drawing. An assumption was made that in preparation for docking the ship, Comdt. John Downes requested the drawing of the ship's modified extreme beam following her 1829 rebuild in order to ascertain

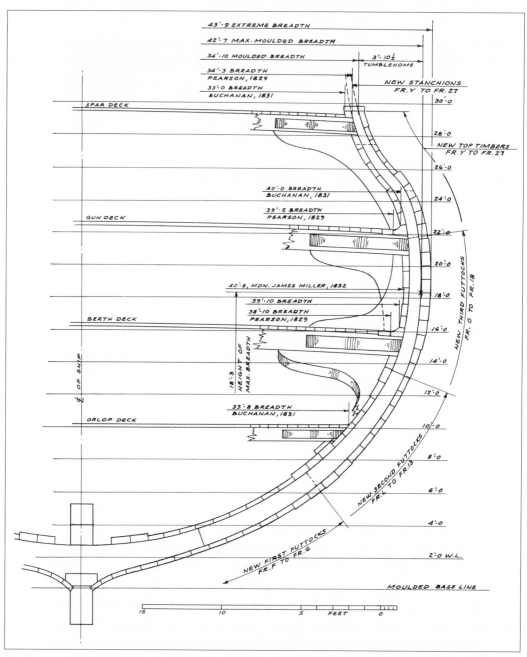

Figure 6.2. USF *Constellation*'s midship section, 1829, reconstructed in accordance with measurements made by Lieutenants Pearson and Buchanan, and Midshipman Miller. *William L. Crothers*

the position of her gun deck beam ends. He needed this information to arrange proper supports for the ship's hull when she was placed in dry dock at Boston for the first time.[30]

While we can only guess at the reason for the existence of the drawing, there is no doubt that Grice's 1839 drawing closely matches figure 6.2. According to the newly acquired Grice drawing, the ship's maximum beam was 43 feet 10 inches, just one inch different from the drawing reconstructed for this book. In addition to the maximum breadth being a virtual match, an overlay of the two drawings showed that the lower body between the keel and the twenty-foot waterline was a near match and that the lower edge of heavy planking was also practically a match. Here, then, were unrelated data that proved the calculations made concerning the radical nature of *Constellation*'s 1828–29 modifications.

According to the records of costs of materials and labor used, prepared after the yard completed *Constellation*'s partial rebuild, modifications and repairs to the ship's hull included the replacement of the frigate's complete stern assembly, including new galleries and taffrails and a new stern and rudder assembly. Contemporary constructors and navy officers called *Constellation*'s newly designed stern and transom a "round stern" because of a spherical-shaped counter or lower transom. Naval architects called the complete new stern assembly elliptical in style. At the time of the changeover from the square-shaped stern assembly with a flat counter or lower transom, navy constructors believed that the round stern, which became popular after 1820, provided both commercial and navy ships with structurally stronger after-sections. Certainly, this was reason enough to convince the navy that the modification of her hull would contribute to the effort to change *Constellation*'s ends—subject of continuous attention since Truxtun first complained about her trim as he readied her for sea back in 1798.[31]

Howard Chapelle studied American navy ships' plans in preparation for his book on the U.S. Navy published in 1949. He wrote that one reason for the rapid acceptance of the round stern design by navies was that the new stern shape allowed guns to be positioned in after cabins 45 degrees off of the ship's center line. American naval commanders, who, after all, controlled ship design during the period of the Board of Commissioners, wanted their ships built with galleries, as the idea of stern guns mounted in the captain's personal quarters proved unpopular. Most larger ships, therefore, retained galleries. Though Chapelle referred to the newly designed sterns of U.S. Navy ships as round and mentions the elliptical stern design separately, he does not provide information on what differences, if any, existed between the round and the elliptical shapes of 1820. Perhaps this is because the differences relate to the location of the two parts of a single assembly rather than to two separately developed designs.[32]

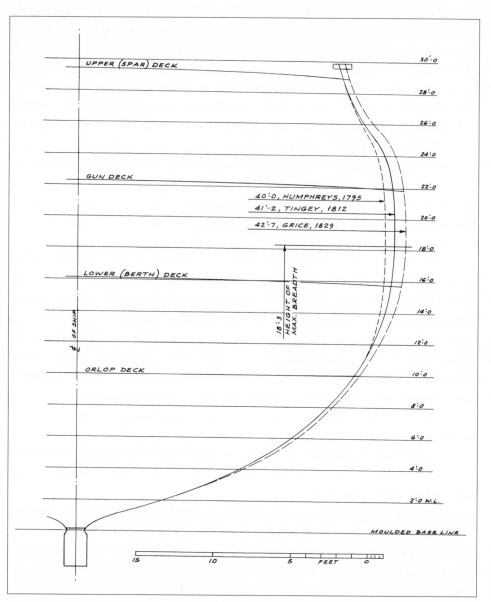

Figure 6.3. USF *Constellation*'s molded midship sections, 1795, 1812, 1829. *William L. Crothers*

With surviving documents, descriptions, and paintings detailing her stern modifications, there seems no question that under master builder Grice's supervision, U.S. Frigate *Constellation* received a new round lower transom or counter and a taffrail and transom rounded at the corners in a style usually termed elliptic (see fig. 6.4). The position of the new galleries in relation to the transom and the counter below it caused the new assembly to appear square when viewing the profile of the ship. Lt. Frederick Fitzgerald DeRoos, R.N., while observing U.S. Frigate *Columbia* under construction at the Washington Navy Yard in 1826, noted in his journal that she had a round stern. He proceeded to explain that "its rake and flatness, combined with the judicious construction of her quarter galleries, gave it [*Columbia*'s stern] quite the appearance of being square."[33]

Constellation's newly designed captain's quarters included the area aft of the mizzen mast on the main or gun deck. To provide the captain with privacy from the run of the deck, a bulkhead, removable in battle, separated his quarters at that point. Forward of the captain's personal cabin, including the galleries, the ship mounted four long 18-pounders, two on each side. When engaged, the bulkhead opened to the gun deck allowing crews clear passage to serve these guns. Normally, with the bulkhead in place, the captain's dining room, which also served as a chart room, shared the space with the guns. To the rear of the dining room was the captain's private cabin, consisting of a circular apartment which served as a parlor with staterooms built on each side. What De Roos viewed as a cleverly built but somewhat disguised round stern, Midn. E. C. Wines, who served aboard *Constellation* under Captain Wadsworth, described in his journal as the commander's private quarters, with the captain's circular-shaped main parlor at the rear of the ship.[34]

Wines wrote that when he first saw *Constellation* moored in the river the beauty of her hull struck him as unequal to anything he had seen afloat; the easy swell and curvature of her sides and the general harmony of her proportions emphasized the differences between the oldest frigates and the newer ones, whose sides rose almost perpendicular with the water.

The new Jackson administration made a last-minute decision to send its ministers to Great Britain and France as passengers on board *Constellation*. To accommodate them, carpenters moved the thwart ship bulkhead that separated the captain's after cabin forward to the after gun carriages. They reconstructed Wadsworth's circular after cabin by placing the fore and aft bulkheads formerly enclosing its two staterooms somewhat more amidships, dividing the cabin into three sections of equal size.[35]

Barron reported to the commissioners that *Constellation*'s new draft measured 20 feet 6 inches aft and 18 feet forward, ship provisioned and ready for sea 1 July 1829. Her draft prior to the rebuild measured 21 feet 6 inches aft and 18 feet 6 inches forward, according to Captain Warrington, aboard the frigate in Caribbean waters in

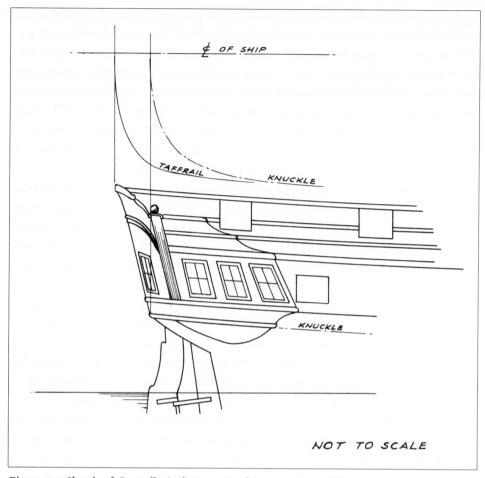

Figure 6.4. Sketch of *Constellation*'s new round (counter) stern, drawn in accordance with the 1829 sketch "Mizzen Mast Survey, *Constellation*, 1840," National Archives (NARA), RG45, Entry 374. *William L. Crothers*

1826. Six inches of the reported reduction overall resulted from the removal of the backing post (referred to by seamen as the prick post) from the lower edge of the stern post and the removal of another similar protrusion from the forefoot. Of the total reduction of 1 foot aft, 6 inches could be attributed to an increase in the ship's buoyancy. While the draft forward fell six inches, Barron attributed all of that reduction to alterations made to the ship's forefoot. Warrington, speaking for the commissioners, seemed satisfied with the reduction.[36]

As the yard made final arrangements to prepare the ship for sea, the commissioners instructed Barron to keep *Constellation*'s armament as before, twenty-eight long 18-pounders and sixteen 32-pound carronades. Midn. E. C. Wines wrote in his famous journal of her cruise that Great Britain had presented these guns to *Constellation* in gratitude for her two victories over French frigates in the Quasi War with France. Evidently, the new rudder assembly caused concern as ship stores included a spare rudder stock and extra pindles.[37] Barron informed the new secretary, John Branch, that the yard would have the ship ready by 1 June, but in the end it would be the readiness of the commander and his officers that determined her final departure date.[38] The secretary's office notified the commissioners on 7 June of Master Comdt. Alexander S. Wadsworth's appointment to command *Constellation*.[39] Finally, after much inclement weather, Barron reported the ship ready 19 June.[40]

The ship stood out Elizabeth River 16 July 1829 for New York to take aboard her passengers. She departed New York 12 August, towed from her mooring at the Battery by the steamer *Benjamin Franklin*. The American ministers Louis McLane and William C. Rives and their entourages were on board, along with Commo. James Biddle, who was under orders to take command of the Mediterranean Sea Squadron. There seems to be no record of special arrangements made to accommodate Biddle, but the yard built additional temporary living quarters on both sides of the half deck, the area of the gun deck forward of the captain's quarters abaft the main mast, also referred to as the officer's promenade and reading room.[41] The ship anchored in the Narrows on 13 and 14 August and on the evening of the fourteenth the wind shifted, allowing the crew to hoist anchor and get under way for England. Wines recorded fair winds until 28 August when the winds rose, forcing the watch to reef topsails and house *Constellation*'s masts. The ship flew along under close-reefed fore and main topsails. On the twenty-ninth she blew out her topsails as wind roared through naked masts, her thousand lines creating noise like thunder, according to Wines. He wrote that the ship rose above mountainous waves to fall forward into their troughs with shattering impact. Rough seas prevailed for the remainder of the passage to England.[42]

Niles' Register reprinted a report from Portsmouth, England, that "*Constellation*, American Frigate of 36 guns, Captain Wadsworth, anchored last night at Cowes, in twenty-three days from New York." Her arrival drew further journalistic attention as Niles wrote another article two weeks later, reporting that *Constellation*'s visit produced some Royal Navy interest, according to a London paper, as she was visited by a number of persons who experienced the most "uniform attention from officers and crew." The London paper continued, according to Niles, with comments about the ship, noting "that though one of the oldest vessels in American service, she is a very fine one and according to nautical men, presently contained many improvements to rigging and internal arrangements which might be introduced with advantage to our navy."[43]

Constellation departed Cowes 20 September and hove-to the next evening off Le Havre just long enough to transfer the American minister and his family to a harbor steamer. The frigate proceeded on to the Mediterranean Sea, which greeted the recently rebuilt ship with a great storm. Approaching Majorca with Mount Toro capped by black clouds, the officer of the watch noted a dark line of them forming ahead which had begun to roll down toward the ship. The gale struck with strong irregular gusts, and as its force increased, the storm drove the ship with it, forcing an order to put the helm hard over and allow *Constellation* to scud before it. Her jib was lost and her jib boom carried away. With sails finally furled, upper yards sent down, and masts housed, the ship was hove-to under storm stay sails.

Above the high-pitched screech of the wind and roar of the sea, which quickly built up heaving masses of water, carrying the ship down and up like a racing horse, the quarterdeck officer of the watch heard the dreaded shout of man overboard. Captain Wadsworth immediately ruled the danger too great to order the crew to man a boat. The officer of the deck stepped forward, transferred his command to another officer, and jumped into a quarter boat. When he sang out for volunteers, the oarsmen's stations in the boat quickly filled, and another lieutenant took a position in her bow. Lowered into the sea and away from the danger of being crushed by *Constellation,* the boat pulled out of sight in the direction where the man was last seen, having disappeared before a life ring could be tossed.

The boat reappeared briefly at the peak of a wave and disappeared downward in unison with the hearts of shipmates gripping the frigate's rail. Wines, relating the incident, noted that it was a beautiful and noble sight to see the generous tars crashing through the pitching sea to rescue a comrade. In about half an hour the boat found and picked up the man. His survival certainly was a miracle. The boat successfully returned to the ship, a second improbable feat. Once the crew lashed the boat close to *Constellation*'s stern, lines were played down to the men in the boat and each one had to be hoisted up onto the ship's deck. At this point, Commodore Biddle appeared from below and grabbed the lieutenant's hand. Wines heard him comment that he would not have allowed the rescue had he been on deck.[44]

So began an idyllic two-year cruise for Midshipman Wines and his shipmates, a tour marred only by duels and disease and occasional storms and lectures to the crew about the evils of sin and drunkenness. For Wines, who had a thoughtful, inquiring mind and a poetic sense of history and architecture, the cruise became an opportunity to fill his journal with accounts of the wonders he had seen. His account would fascinate any young person on a Grand Tour of Europe, a universal experience of the American young and well-to-do, few of whom recorded their adventures into antiquity better than Wines as he traveled on his cruise ship crisscross the inland sea and east and west, visiting the glorious relics of the region's ancient civilizations.

While the midshipman did not bother to record a race between *Constellation* and Henry Eckford's corvette, *United States,* there is a record from another journal describing the challenge and its result. An eyewitness reported that the race was short and

USF *Constellation* departing Port Mahon, 1831. The frigate's new round or elliptical stern is visible. Painting by Nicola Cammillieri. *Naval Historical Foundation*

quick. *Constellation,* two years out of Norfolk, had finished her last run through eastern Mediterranean waters and on 27 July 1831, the day that the ships met, her destination was Port Mahon, the U.S. Navy base. Once there, she was to await orders and mail before sailing for the United States. A handsome new ship of war hailed the historic frigate, and her commander, Capt. George Coleman de Kay, identified his ship as a new one built by the famous American shipbuilder Henry Eckford. Eckford, who served as navy constructor at New York and drafted USS *Ohio,* informed Captain Wadsworth that he had an American crew aboard *United States* to deliver the warship to her owner, the navy of Turkey. According to the captain's brother, James Ellsworth de Kay, the ship's physician, who recorded its outcome, *Constellation*'s officers spoke highly of the sailing properties of their vessel and therefore Captain Wadsworth acceded to *United States*'s wish to test her speed. Doctor de Kay's journal recorded that the race ended in half an hour. He wrote that with sails set, the two ships moved off together, but soon *Constellation* slipped back into *United States*'s wake and the ships parted company to proceed on their previous courses in opposite directions. *Constellation*'s log recorded the meeting of the two ships, but not the race. Between the hours of 7 A.M. and meridian, *Constellation* recorded in her log speeds of nine and ten knots over the four-hour morning watch.[45]

Constellation stood out of Port Mahon 5 October 1831 and passed Gibraltar on the thirteenth. She had a smooth crossing free of headwinds, arriving in Hampton Roads twenty-nine days later on 3 November. Decommissioned, but not placed in ordinary, the well-traveled ship, though tested by several great storms, required only minor repairs. Master builder Grice, after a survey, informed Gosport's new commandant, Capt. Lewis Warrington, that as the ship required only caulking and other minor repairs she would be ready for sea in three weeks.[46]

After thirty-three years of service, *Constellation* had proved herself once again more than just a historic ship. Her size made her a most practical ship in view of the navy's recurring problems with its operating budget, which kept a cap on personnel. Her crew numbered roughly 350 men, significantly less than that of a first-class frigate or ship of the line. *Constellation*'s rebuild in 1828–29 cost about $170,000, and the navy figured she could give ten more years' service without major repairs. As a second-class frigate, *Constellation* cost about $145,000 a year to maintain and pay a crew, compared to a large frigate's cost of about $175,000 for a year at sea. Operating ships of the line consistently had been proved uneconomical and impractical, and they remained, for the most part, in ordinary or in yards as receiving ships.[47]

Constellation, impressive for her famed French victories, large enough to show the United States flag with a commodore's pennant flying, but a command usually avoided by senior officers, immediately returned to service. She was an efficient ship, popular with her crews, officers, and commanders, and evidently still fairly fast. Despite her age, small size, modifications, and an array of past complaints over the years, the navy kept her almost continually in commission. She simply cost less to operate. It seems inconceivable that John Rodgers and the other veteran officers who controlled naval affairs for three decades following the War of 1812 never ordered additional small frigates built, a failure that caused an imbalance in the United States navy peace establishment and was never addressed even though large frigates and larger battleships rotted in ordinary. While no mile-for-mile comparison exists, it is safe to conclude that no frigate or ship of the line provided the same consistent service as *Constellation* did between 1815 and 1845, with the possible exception of *Constitution.* The second-class frigate's service record included no extended period of inactivity prior to her entrance into ordinary at Gosport that year.

Master builder Francis Grice and his mechanics at Gosport replaced a large portion of *Constellation*'s frame above her floors in 1828, most of these live oak sections having been new in 1812. This suggests, or possibly confirms, that the Humphreys-Grice modifications of her hull radically altered its shape and that because of this, increased the cost of repairing the ship, changing the job from a thorough repair to a rebuild. Modifications in design of an older ship cause labor expenses to rise; cutting out and removing old timbers and planks and using new materials to reshape the ship's hull added substantially to repair costs. This accounts for a portion of the difference in Grice's calculation for repairs of $99,994 and the actual total cost of rebuilding the modified ship, which fell somewhere between $167,000 and $181,000.[48]

In the end, the cost of rebuilding *Constellation*'s hull in 1829 totaled $114,000, just $13,000 less than Grice's estimate for a new hull ($127,000). This latter figure, based on a cost of $100 per ton burden, correctly reflected the normal cost of a new hull as one-third of the total cost of a fully equipped new ship. Other more expensive items charged to *Constellation*'s rebuild—new sails, $10,561 and cables, $11,169—represented the cost of replacing old worn-out gear with new equipment.[49]

An important determination made when estimating repairs centered on whether or not an estimate forwarded to the Board of Commissioners by the master builder or naval constructor included repairs only or repairs plus modifications and new equipment, or a completely new hull. Sometimes the added expense resulting from rebuilding and equipping an older ship rather than merely repairing it accounted for the difference between advance estimates for repairs and the final cost. Neither Congress, the executive branch, nor the national press complained of *Constellation*'s costs in 1812, 1829, 1839, or 1853. The navy received efficient, economical service from its oldest ship.[50]

Questions concerning rising costs related to rebuilding older navy ships originated with the executive branch of the government, not Congress, as presidential administrations labored to keep a lid on the overall costs of government. Reaction to the high cost of rebuilding, particularly if the final cost figures exceeded the cost of a new ship of comparable tonnage, caught the eye of John Branch, President Andrew Jackson's first secretary of the navy. Branch, described by some Washington insiders as a country politician without maritime experience, proved himself to be a tough administrator but like most Americans was somewhat deficient in his knowledge of geography and of naval administration under the Board of Commissioners. His critics ignored the real question: Did any previous secretary understand the complexities of naval affairs, accounting, and repair policies and did only Branch have the audacity to question Commodore Rodgers about navy repair policy?[51]

When John Rodgers ordered USS *John Adams* rebuilt in 1827, he ruled the navy and much of the United States government—at least that portion of it that dwelt with the navy. But after Gen. Andrew Jackson took office in March 1829, Rodgers found himself in a political battle that shook the navy's timbers—for a while. Branch's battle to cut navy costs opened against the doughty dictator of naval affairs. Rodgers became the focus of Secretary Branch's official distress when he discovered that USS *John Adams,* designed and built in 1799, was undergoing an expensive rebuild at Gosport without his knowledge or permission.[52]

The complexities of naval accounting and, indeed, of the naval repair policy of rebuilding ships proved beyond Branch, a man whose past required questioning far less subtle concepts. He put it simply: If the navy broke up a ship and built USS *John Adams* in 1829 from the keel up at a cost that exceeded her original cost, the ship, by definition, must be a new one. In this one instance, many of the complexities of tradition, history, and sentimentality, as well as the widest possible array of navy repair policies and concepts, entangled one small, poorly designed ship. With a record of no particular accomplishments, *John Adams* survived into a period when the navy needed additional small ships in service to accommodate its inactive master commandants and captains. It should be noted that Congress played no role in the verbal battle between Branch and Rodgers. Commodore Rodgers endeavored to explain and gain Branch's support for the navy's repair, rebuilding, and construction policies already fairly clearly defined by Congress through the many naval acts passed between 1798 and 1829.[53]

The fact that *John Adams* carried the name of the father of the United States Navy proved over time to make her indestructible in a political and sentimental sense. Certainly she was a controversial ship, as her supporters, led by John Rodgers, kept the much-modified ship in service long after she needed to be condemned and replaced. Nevertheless, the rebuilding of the 1799 ship in 1829, redesigned as she was, did not in any way deviate from the navy's prevailing policies. It applied the same policies uniformly to its other older sloops of war, *Hornet, Erie, Ontario,* and *Cyane.* This group of sloop-ships, like many other navy rebuilds, received modifications that added extra cost to the total cost of rebuilding. Much of the additional difference between the cost of the original ship and the rebuilt one may be attributed to the increasing inefficiency and rising costs incurred at navy yard repair facilities.[54]

Rodgers, writing for the commissioners, ordered *John Adams* rebuilt 2 January 1829, though the yard had previously stripped her hull planks. His instructions included an order to modify her to the same dimensions of hull, masts, and spars as the ten new sloops authorized in 1825. In another communication he informed Gosport that a draft would be sent. Finally, on 2 March 1829, a few days before Jackson's government was sworn in, Rodgers sent Commandant Barron *John Adams*'s draft and supplemental instructions. Branch, while visiting Gosport months after work started on the sloop of war and following an executive order that no new ships would be built, observed what he believed to be a new ship in the final stages of construction. He ordered Barron to stop work, and then he confronted Rodgers, in effect accusing the commissioners of illegally building a new *John Adams.* He charged him with exceeding the intent of Congress or, as *"was admissible by a fair construction of its terms,* have caused to be built a new sloop of war." Branch equated rebuilding with new construction.[55]

156

More than a century before the provenance of U.S. Frigate *Constellation* became a debated issue among naval architects, Branch charged that the navy built a new ship under his nose in the guise of rebuilding an old one. His specific charge, centering on the rebuilding of *John Adams,* claimed that legislation approved by Congress did not allow repair funds to be used for rebuilding a ship, that is, providing a ship with a new hull or something close to it when the old one could not be repaired. By doing so, according to Branch, the commissioners defined the terms "wear and tear" and "repairs for ships in ordinary," which included rebuilding, in such a broad, all-inclusive manner that the practice enabled navy yards to build new ships without congressional or executive approval, a privilege beyond the board's authority as set by Congress. As a result, Branch concluded that lumping repairs and rebuilding under the same appropriation line item, separate from new construction, broke the law, as the commissioners, in the instance of *John Adams,* in real terms authorized the building of a new ship. The secretary took the unusual position of rendering a decision normally addressed by a court or by Congress itself. Unfortunately, the secretary's inexperience allowed him to question the policy of rebuilding which Congress had had the opportunity to consider many times reaching back to ships rebuilt prior to the War of 1812. In an audacious act, prior to consulting the president or Congress, Branch made public his accusation against the Board of Commissioners as he accused it of illegally using repair funds for purposes not contemplated by Congress.[56]

The secretary ordered work stopped on *John Adams* and instructed Rodgers to present him with a complete set of particulars concerning the commissioners' action. In long, rambling letters to Branch, Rodgers defended the navy's policy of rebuilding ships with funds authorized by Congress for repairs and cited several past examples. The secretary would not budge from his reasoning that the commissioners built new vessels of war, substituting them for those unfit for further use. He took his argument with Rodgers to President Jackson. When Branch outlined his case against the commissioners to the president, he pressed home his conclusion that the rebuilt *John Adams* was in fact a newly constructed ship and an illegal use of repair funds.[57]

The president responded to the secretary's plea for support of his position on 2 November 1830. In a landmark decision the chief executive ruled that the commissioners possessed sufficient justification to rebuild *John Adams.* However, after ruling favorably on the practical existence of the concept of rebuilding navy ships, Jackson ordered that in the future Congress must specifically authorize appropriations for rebuilding and that the appropriations should be separated out of funds authorized for general repairs and those designated for new construction. Jackson's order recognized the existence of three categories of ship yard work—repairs, rebuilding, and new construction. In addition, it confirmed a longstanding recognition by Congress that rebuilding existed as an alternative to new construction, not a sub-stitute for it.[58]

For a few years following Jackson's decision to request in advance authority from Congress to rebuild specific ships, bills were passed providing the navy with author-izations and funds to rebuild *Macedonian* and *Congress.* Congress also passed the act of 10 July 1832 to provide funds to rebuild *Java* and *Cyane.* These rebuilding projects were all covered by special acts of Congress and listed as separate line items in the navy's annual appropriations for years following congressional approval, these appropriation acts having no expiration dates. While legally the commissioners could delay or never rebuild the ships approved, passage of the acts authorizing rebuilding of *Macedonian, Congress, Java,* and *Cyane* provided the navy with the legal concurrence of Congress of the policy of rebuilding ships that included the replace-ment of hulls.[59]

Though *Macedonian* received a new live oak frame, a new keel, and in fact, a new hull, her rebuild, representing an almost new ship, must be listed forever as a rebuild under law, since Congress recognized her rebuild by a specific act. The fact that later navy records often listed her as having been built new in 1836 was a matter of conven-ience; that is the year from which the navy dated the age of her hull. The story of the fight between Rodgers and Barron over *Macedonian*'s survival and her special position as a memorial to Decatur's heroic life before his death in a duel with Barron, placed this ship in a political arena far removed from any other historic ship. Nevertheless, as a policy, her case exists as an example of the existence of rebuilding in the wooden ship era for principally sentimental or patriotic reasons, though without doubt *Macedonian*'s rebuild incorporated new technology, particularly her ordnance.[60]

The legal trail that led to the rebuilding of U.S. Frigate *Congress* five years after her original hull rotted out at Gosport to Portsmouth, New Hampshire, the yard in which the navy rebuilt her, is complex. Added to a unique set of legal manipulations is the undeniable fact that the original U.S. Frigate *Congress,* also built at Portsmouth, was rated a second-class frigate, though the frigate on which construction began in 1839 rated forty-four guns according to a new draft prepared under the supervision of Samuel Humphreys, which modified her previous dimensions, model, and rate. Though she was apparently a new ship, Congress in its wisdom never repealed the legislation (act of 30 June 1834) that authorized *Congress*'s rebuild; so when she ulti-mately was rebuilt in 1839, the original authorization, An Act to Provide for Rebuilding the Frigate *Congress,* continued to control, with an appropriation of $181,000 included and dated 1834.[61]

Though the acts concerning the rebuilds of *Macedonian* and *Congress* passed in Congress during the Jackson administration, the commissioners held up work on both ships pending the removal of a cap on increasing the number of ships in the fleet. The Portsmouth Navy Yard received a go-ahead to lay down a new keel for *Congress*-44 in 1839 after the United States posted a general mobilization alert because of disagreements with Great Britain over the border between Maine and Canada. Congress passed new legislation that permitted the navy to complete building or rebuilding any ships previously authorized. Funds to rebuild *Congress*-44 came partially from the act that authorized the ship's rebuild in 1834, with additional funds provided from the navy's 1840 appropriation. This law allowed all prior acts governing the funding of new construction, rebuilding, and repairs, as well as acts authorizing improvements and increases to the navy from 1816 forward, to be combined into a single fund or line item appropriation. The consolidation of these acts allowed funding to be completed for *Congress*; it also authorized the navy to provide her, a rebuild, with a live oak frame despite the fact that prior acts limited the use of live oak to the construction of new ships, not rebuilt ones.[62]

Constellation, with a new commander, Capt. George C. Read, rejoined the Mediterranean Sea Squadron in the spring of 1833, Daniel T. Patterson (*United States*) having relieved Biddle as commodore. Very little of importance happened on this cruise until *Constellation* and *United States* encountered a great storm while returning to Port Mahon from a visit to Turkey. Cruising in the Aegean Sea in mid-December 1833, following their departure from Smyrna (Ismir), the ships sailed on a southerly course that carried them through the Greek islands. The two historic frigates encountered a storm with easterly winds of greater velocity than a West Indies hurricane, according to Commodore Patterson. As their passage carried the ships around many islands during a period of low visibility, with land on every side, the situation produced great anxiety. Patterson reported making the harbor of Milos, where he was reunited with *Constellation.* The French navy experienced bad luck as ship of the line *Superb* beached on the island of Paros, which saved her crew. *Constellation* received heavy damage, losing several yards, topmasts, sails, boats, and other equipment, all swept overboard. The painting illustrating the ship in the storm was commissioned in remembrance of *Constellation*'s safe passage. As a junior officer, Read made no reports directly to the Navy Department, but upon his return to the United States he praised the sailing qualities of his ship. He noted specifically that *Constellation* steered, stayed, and worked well in 1833.[63]

Constellation loaded two statues, one to war and the other to peace, gifts from the city of Naples to Congress. Cholera broke out aboard *Constellation* near the end of the two-year cruise, forcing Captain Read to alter his ship's itinerary following a visit to Toulon where he received orders from Commo. Daniel Patterson covering the final months of his ship's cruise. Read's orders stated that he should not depart for America until he had rendezvoused with Patterson, so he sailed for Port Mahon. Having been told months before to deliver the statues to Washington prior to the

USF *Constellation* in the great storm of December 1833. Painting by Michele Funno. *On loan to Maryland Historical Society. Courtesy of Richard Gamble.*

opening of Congress's next session, he grew increasingly concerned when Patterson's flagship, *United States,* did not appear at Mahon by 1 September 1834, the date set for his departure to the United States. The dreaded epidemic hit *Constellation* while she was anchored at Mahon. Read delayed his departure, remaining at anchor outside of the harbor as *Constellation*'s doctor valiantly treated the sick members of the crew. Six weeks passed.

Finally, on 7 October, Read proceeded west to Gibraltar. The port authorities refused the ship entrance, but Read managed to get supplies aboard. Under the urging of the ship's surgeon, Doctor Morgan, who believed that the Atlantic Ocean air would help his patients, Read, ignoring Patterson's orders, stood out of the Mediterranean for home. Three more men died, but finally, on 1 November, with a fresh northerly, the progress of the disease slowed. *Constellation* entered the Capes in late November and the ship delivered the statues and their sculptor, along with Mrs. Read, to St. Marys, Maryland, at the mouth of the Potomac River. *Constellation* dropped down to Hampton Roads where Read prepared a defense for the secretary of the navy against expected charges of disobedience to Commodore Patterson's orders.[64]

As events unfolded for Captain Read, he found that he would be faced with court-martial, not for disobedience to orders but for charges growing out of his treatment of a young midshipman during the recently completed cruise. While at sea, Read had ordered Midn. John O. Wilson to go aloft. Wilson panicked and refused to climb the ship's rigging. The captain then ordered Wilson bound and hoisted to the masthead. The charges included conduct unbecoming an officer, cruelty, and scandalous conduct. Read was convicted by a court of his peers, including Lewis Warrington, president of the court. A thoughtful, evenhanded court suspended the captain from the navy for one year.[65]

Upon the return of *Constellation* from the Mediterranean Sea in 1834, concern arose about the condition of the ship's bottom and master builder Grice scheduled her for observation and repair in the Gosport dry dock, recently completed. This would be the first time that *Constellation* had returned to dry land since her launching 7 September 1797. The first ship to use the Gosport facility, *Delaware,* had entered the dock 17 June 1833. It had been feared that the new ship of the line had damaged her coppered bottom when first launched, and Grice used the occasion to test the new facility as well as a device he invented to allow a ship to set her keel down on blocks without damage resulting from hogging. Grice called it the Screw Shore. The machine measured the shape of the keel, that is, its arch or hog, before the ship entered the dock, allowing blocks to compensate for its curvature to be placed under the keel before the water around her fell. By this means the keel's shape and the ship's sheer remained unaltered. Norfolk newspapers reported that Grice's machine and the docking of *Delaware* succeeded without accident as the big ship settled on her blocks without even a crack in the pitch of her seams.[66]

Work on the dry dock commenced in 1827 following passage of the Act to Improve the Navy that year. It cost over a million dollars and its enormous reception area, into which a ship entered, consisted of cut and fitted granite slabs. Once its water gates closed, a giant steam pump removed water from the dock, allowing the ship to set down upon carefully placed blocks of varying thickness, the amount calculated by Grice's invention. And so, a year after the Gosport dry dock opened, *Constellation* entered the new dock and Grice took a look at a very hogged ship. Though a pig's hogged back is convex and its belly concave, a ship's keel sags at her ends, the convex curvature of the midbody supported by its greater buoyancy, causing *Constellation*'s keel to droop at her less buoyant ends after thirty-seven years of submersion in water.[67]

A long, sharp-built ship, *Constellation* had a hogged keel that placed her ends under great strain as her hull softened, causing her to take in water through her deck seams. Grice attempted to ease the problem, which previously affected somewhat the sailing qualities of the ship, by working out the planks on her bottom and before replacing them, adding hog streaks or planks to form a false bottom. Then, new hull planks and copper, fastened to the streaks, completed the false bottom on each side of the original keel. Other work performed on the ship included the replacement of rigging, masts, and spars. The yard also replaced the controversial pine wales first used for the ship in 1812 and then again in 1829, much to the displeasure of John Rodgers. After the ship left dry dock in late January 1835, work proceeded on her repairs at a leisurely pace into September 1835, the cost, mostly for labor, amounting to $14,528, with the average labor rate of $1.40 per day.[68]

When commissioned again, Mahlon Dickerson, Jackson's third secretary of the navy, assigned *Constellation* flagship of the West Indies Squadron, Capt. Alexander James Dallas, commander of the ship and commodore of the squadron, by far the largest and most active fleet of the navy in that period. Dallas entered the navy early in the century and served with John Rodgers on U.S. Frigate *President* when he engaged HMS *Little Belt* in 1811. As a lieutenant he commanded USS *Spitfire*, a Baltimore schooner in Stephen Decatur's Mediterranean squadron in 1815.

Dallas's flagship stood out of the Virginia Capes for the Gulf of Mexico 8 October 1835. The squadron initially included frigate *Constellation*, flagship; *Vandalia*, *St. Louis*, and *Falmouth*, sloops of war; and *Grampus* and *Experiment*, schooners. Dallas released USS *Falmouth* soon after arriving on station because the voyage down the coast revealed a previously undetected need of repair. In 1836 the strength of the squadron increased with the addition of *Concord*, *Warren*, *Boston*, and *Natchez*, all sloop-ships. The squadron's missions included supporting the army's war against Florida's Seminole Indians. It also intercepted slave ships moving human cargoes between Cuba and the United States and Texas and protected the foreign commerce and property of U.S. merchants in countries around the rim of the Gulf of Mexico, in the Caribbean Sea, and on islands of the West Indies.[69]

Upon his arrival in the Caribbean Sea, Dallas circled his territory, visiting politically unstable Venezuela, then Trinidad, Curaçao, Havana, several Mexican ports including Tampico, and Vera Cruz. Prior to entering the Navy Base at Pensacola Bay, he made a stopover at Key West. At the Venezuelan port of Puerto Cabello, Dallas notified local military authorities that he did not care what their political beliefs included, it was his duty to protect United States citizens' property previously landed in that port. Under the policy of Manifest Destiny that applied throughout Dallas's territory during that period, the navy interpreted its duty as protecting the property rights of U.S. citizens in foreign countries.

A seaman on board *Constellation*, Ned Myers, whose journal James Fenimore Cooper edited and published, wrote little about his time in *Constellation*'s crew. He noted that when *Constellation* and seven or eight other navy ships entered Vera Cruz, the Mexicans became alarmed as they thought it was an invasion. Myers remained a member of *Constellation*'s crew for the full three years she stayed in the gulf but left few comments because nothing material occurred on the cruise. The duty was hard because the navy used the crew as armed soldiers which, as Myers wrote, "may be all right for some, but bad weather for blue jackets."[70] After completing his initial cruise, Dallas turned his attention to the Indian uprisings in Florida, where troops supported local fishermen fighting to maintain positions in Tampa Bay and Charlotte harbor. The navy squadron proved handicapped by shallow water approaches to Florida's bays, resulting in Dallas's request for smaller vessels. Secretary Dickerson attended to this and eventually several revenue cutters plus three steamboats reinforced Dallas's group.[71] Seamen and marines from *St. Louis* provided relief for an army detachment at Fort Brook in Tampa Bay, some of the naval landing party remaining on the island. Even though Dallas made the decision to keep *Constellation* moored at Pensacola at this time, he had already begun a series of letters to Dickerson complaining of his ship's performance.[72]

Dallas converted *Constellation* from a warship into a combined permanent headquarters station and receiving ship in the spring of 1836. Once this was done, Dallas turned his attention to the subject of the navy's role in transporting specie. In a letter addressed to Master Commandant William Taylor, commander of the *Warren*, Dallas laid down his policy. He suggested that Taylor inform American merchants that navy ships would carry specie into New Orleans. But Dallas did not stop there as he informed Taylor that should there be offers to carry specie into Havana he should deliver it there at a higher commission. Dallas's instructions inferred that if the quantity of specie offered was sufficiently attractive, *Warren* would be diverted to carry the naval freight into a foreign port. As Dallas's mission included policing the slave trade centered in and out of Havana, this offer gave the appearance of profiting from activity Dallas had orders to eliminate.[73]

The war between Mexico and Texas put American merchant ships at risk, particularly from attacks by Texas cruisers and privateers. After the Texan schooner *Invisible* captured the American brig *Packet*, Dallas commenced patrolling the Mexico-Texas coasts and later actually formed convoys to shepherd American vessels between New Orleans and Mexico. Faced with a shortage of officers, Dallas moved *Constellation*'s officers back and forth to fill other ships' requirements. For instance, acting sailing master Raphael Semmes of *Constellation* received a temporary appointment of lieutenant and transferred to USS *Vandalia*, which had only two lieutenants.[74]

The revenue cutter *Jefferson* ran into difficulties at Tampico, a port believed open to U.S. warships by treaty, when Mexican authorities imprisoned the schooner's landing party. When word of this affair reached Dallas, he dispatched the sloop-ship

Warren, providing her commander with authority to land his marines to protect American citizens. Meanwhile, in a letter from Pensacola, Dallas informed Secretary Dickerson that he had decided that it was inadvisable to put to sea with *Constellation.* Though he sounded as though he found fault with the ship, he based his decision on three practical reasons. First, he had insufficient crew because his men served on other vessels. Second, he could receive dispatches quicker if he remained at strategically placed Pensacola. Finally, he would be available to attend to Indian affairs and the Mexico-Texas war from a central location.[75] The squadron's need for crewmen became so critical that Captain Rousseau sailed *St. Louis* into Havana and Cuban outports in search of men. He recruited twenty-nine on one sweep, one with scurvy and the rest with symptoms of the disease.[76]

A not unusual argument broke out between the navy and the army when Dallas threatened to remove marines originally sent to reinforce troops under siege at Fort Brook in Tampa Bay and kept there indefinitely by the army. Commander Mix of *Concord* notified the army he intended to pick up the marines. A refusal from the officer in charge of the fort created an interservice war of words.[77] By July 1836, with revenue cutters reinforcing Dallas's squadron, these small craft allowed the navy to enter Florida bays previously not navigable by Dallas's vessels. The navy's three steamboats, *General Dade, American,* and *Izard,* transported troops in a stepped-up effort to subdue or wipe out Florida's Indians. Captain Rudolph of the cutter *Dexter* received a reprimand for allowing the escape of Indian prisoners held aboard his ship and for leaving Indian Key's inhabitants unprotected. In the meantime, a report reached Dallas that a large force of Seminole Indians in canoes had reestablished themselves on islands of the Everglades. The sloop-ship *Boston* arrived at Pensacola from Boston at the end of August with sixty-two supernumeraries for the squadron, somewhat relieving crew problems that Dallas had wrestled with since he arrived.[78]

On 31 August 1836 Dallas fired off a letter to Acting Secretary Boyle in which the last sentence summarized his observations concerning the situation in Florida: "The truth is, I see no one, hear no one, but the officers and seamen who are in any manner actively engaged." Another letter to Boyle written at this time, accompanied by a report from the captain of the steamboat *American,* under Dallas's command, stated that one of his boats captured a canoe loaded with animal skins near the mouth of the Suwanee and that Indians showed little interest in killing white men.

Dallas ordered the cutter *Dallas* and the ship-sloop *St. Louis* to convoy American merchant vessels between Belize and Mexican ports and assigned *Concord* to cruise the length of the Mexican coastline. The potential problem there resulted from increased activity by privateers flying the flag of Texas. To increase his active force, Dallas allowed *Vandalia* to return to duty, commanded by an officer from the *Warren* and using sails from *Warren* and *Constellation.*[79]

Commodore Dallas, once he arrived on station at Pensacola in January 1836, initiated a series of letters to the Navy Department criticizing the performance of the U.S. Frigate *Constellation*. Concerned with appearances, he wrote Dickerson in October 1836 that should a visit to Cuba be necessary in view of troubles in Spain, he would not be able to visit Havana with an imposing force because officers and men from *Constellation* served on other vessels of his squadron including the steamers and the revenue cutters. The frigate was so deficient in both officers and crew that the ship could not leave Pensacola. Dallas removed his flag from *Constellation* in favor of the sloop-ship *Concord* and assigned Master Commandant Mix to temporary command of the idled frigate.[80]

The ship's log revealed that *Constellation* seldom left her mooring over the following two years. On one short cruise in May 1837, Dallas sailed his flagship to Matamoras, at the Mexican-Texas border near Brownsville. From that Mexican port he sailed to Vera Cruz, arriving there on 26 June 1837. *Constellation* remained there five days, returning to Pensacola on 15 July. The log provides no reason for the cruise, but it is recorded that the historic ship's speed reached six knots and, rarely, seven knots during this run down the Mexican coast. Almost twelve months passed before Dallas stood out of Pensacola Bay again. A short cruise took *Constellation* to the port of Tampico, Mexico. While she was anchored there, a sloop owned by the British consul came alongside and the American frigate received eighty-four packages of bullion and specie from her. The following day, *Constellation* stood out of the Mexican port and on 21 June 1838 the frigate's crew kedged her over Pensacola's bar. The reason for this quick run was specie, which resulted in a commission for Dallas.[81]

Though a French blockade of Mexican ports added to the many complications of Commodore Dallas's missions—the Indian war, slave trade, the fighting between Mexico and Texas, as well as continuing privateer activity—the squadron continued to experience difficulty holding on to officers and crewmen for its ships, a problem traced to boredom as the ships were isolated from American life and continuously cruising, which produced only marginal results in three years. The navy found few potential opponents to challenge. Dallas expected the arrival of USS *Levant,* and asked Secretary Paulding to place 150 to 200 extra men on her. In 1838, ships under Dallas's command, in addition to *Constellation,* moored at Pensacola, included sloops of war *Vandalia, Natchez, Erie, Ontario,* and *Concord,* plus other small vessels and steamboats.[82]

Dallas notified the secretary that *Constellation* required extensive repairs in letters dated August and September 1838, and the old frigate, under command of Lieutenant McIntosh, parted company with her disenchanted commodore, arriving at Boston 24 October 1838. Dallas, with his flag now aboard *Vandalia,* made calls at Tampico and Vera Cruz in October and November. He found the Mexican government

165

fighting a revolution at Tampico when a French fleet arrived at Vera Cruz and threatened to invade Mexico unless the embattled government accepted its demands. Dallas, in his reports to the Navy Department, failed to provide details of the French conditions for peace. After discussions with the French, the contents of which Dallas did not reveal, *Vandalia* returned to Tampico to pick up a consignment of specie. Dallas notified Paulding of the shipment of specie that he placed in charge of *Vandalia*'s purser at Belize, then chartered a steamboat and sent the officer into New Orleans with it. The commodore also mentioned that he missed an opportunity to load a large quantity of specie seized by the government of Mexico before it reached Tampico to keep it out of the hands of revolutionaries. These incidents at Tampico are additional examples of how the transportation of foreign specie, an accommodation that benefited only United States Navy commanders, reduced the effectiveness of the navy's police action and the quality of the information reported to Washington. In this instance, a lust for specie seemed to determine the destinations of Dallas's ships, some of which evidently were diverted from official duties to haul navy freight.[83]

Seven

1839: Modifying Prior Modifications

During the early winter of 1836, shortly after his arrival on station, Commo. Alexander J. Dallas in his flagship U.S. Frigate *Constellation* made a grand tour of the expansive, diverse region over which the United States government charged the West Indies Squadron to cruise, and at that time in a state of tumultuous transformation. Almost immediately, Dallas commenced writing a series of letters to the secretary of the navy complaining about the sailing qualities of his flagship. The negative statements continued over the next three years, as the commodore mixed his complaints about *Constellation* with a dialogue reflecting a keen sense of his own unrecognized immensity, as evidenced by the importance of his command.

An analysis of Dallas's correspondence suggests that the principal reason for his dissatisfaction with the historic frigate lay with her rate, not her poor performance as a sailer, though in time that became a problem, too. In his first critical report, the only one with any specificity, the commodore complained to Secretary Dickerson that *Constellation* proved to be "so bad a sailer and worker that under no circumstances could I avoid or overtake any vessel of moderate speed."[1]

Dallas claimed that his ship failed to make good headway to windward sailing on a reach or tacking, a complaint that suggested that the underlying cause of the problem levied by *Constellation*'s first detractor in a generation resulted from the work done under supervision of Gosport's master builder, Francis Grice, when the ship was placed in Gosport's new dry dock in 1834. Grice ordered carpenters to fill the curvature in the ship's bottom (he called it a hollow in her floor) caused by the hog of the thirty-year-old keel which totaled about one foot. If Dallas's complaint had merit, it meant that Gosport's carpenters, after building *Constellation*'s false bottom, finished repairing the ship without adding a cap or extension to the ship's false keel to compensate for the portion of keel covered by the build-up of the false bottom. The portion of the keel protruding below the bottom provides ships with lateral resistance to maintain headway. Without that resisting force, the frigate would tend to increase its deviation or slippage to leeward. Though working under more flexible conditions provided by the dry dock just completed, Grice's mechanics, having never faced the challenge before, evidently did not attempt to correct the problem, faced as they were with a seemingly impossible task of fitting *Constellation* with a keel extension while the ship's keel sat on blocks of various heights measured to compensate for the sagging (hogged) ends of the ship.[2]

In later complaints, Dallas usually compromised his criticism as he suggested to the secretary that a ship of larger capacity such as *United States* or *Raritan* would "place him at ease under all circumstances." Was Dallas protesting *Constellation*'s performance or did he exhibit the usual scorn of an American senior captain for the navy's second-class frigates, a pattern that stretched back over the nation's naval history to the time when Thomas Truxtun left *Constellation* to take command of the larger frigate, USF *President*? In reality, Dallas was concerned with both, since his complaints about Grice's recent work on *Constellation*'s bottom were evidently legitimate. Still, by suggesting to the secretary that a positive response to his requests would resound to the honor of the country and be a credit to him, the commander made himself subject to criticism. Dallas made himself look particularly ridiculous since Pensacola was his base of operations; the bar at the entrance of the harbor kept ships larger than *Constellation* from entering there. Dallas allowed *Constellation* to remain moored at Pensacola until her decks rotted and her bottom became covered by a thick layer of sea growth, which eventually made her unseaworthy.

Constellation with her deep draft often grounded on the bar that crossed the entrance to Pensacola Bay. The circumstances suggested to the Navy Department that Dallas exaggerated the negative side of *Constellation*'s sailing qualities while promoting an impossible wish to have a more auspicious warship from which to command his squadron. Because her only possible replacements at that time were *Macedonian,* undergoing rebuilding, or *Congress,* then moored at Gosport on Rotten Row, the question of *Constellation*'s sailing problems went unattended. The commodore's concerns cannot be rejected outright; an examination of *Constellation*'s log tends to support his complaints about her slow speed, though her long periods of idleness in the harbor at Pensacola allowed oysters to accumulate on her bottom quickly.[3]

When Dallas completed his initial swing around the cruising grounds of his squadron's assigned territory, which took his ships to Venezuela, Cuba, other West Indies islands, and into the Gulf of Mexico along the Mexican and Texas coastline, he informed Dickerson that he would moor *Constellation* permanently in the harbor of Pensacola because he did not believe it advisable to put to sea in her. Later, he admitted to the secretary that because of a shortage of men he found it necessary to reassign one-third of his flagship's company to other ships, further distorting the basis of his complaints concerning *Constellation*'s sailing qualities. Dallas completed this communication with the information that due to convenience of the location he expected to keep the frigate at Pensacola until the Indian War in Florida and the war between Mexico and Texas ended.[4]

After remaining on board *Constellation,* moored at Pensacola, for several months in 1836, Dallas returned once again to his problems with the frigate, writing to the secretary that he would be pleased if Dickerson assigned a flagship he could depend on since that was not the case with *Constellation.* He wrote Dickerson that the historic ship would make a fine sloop of war if cut down, but as a frigate "she is, in fact, good for nothing." He reversed his former decision to remain at Pensacola, reporting that his strategy made it necessary to command a frigate more certain and active as he might need to be in the Gulf of Mexico during winter months. He closed this letter begging Dickerson to let him know if he could expect to be gratified.[5] Several months later he tried again, informing the secretary of a rumor according to which the navy planned to replace *Constellation* with the larger 44-gun frigate *Columbia.*

Dallas criticized his flagship brutally. In pleas for a different ship, Dallas requested replacements of seamen and officers to fill out the complements of crews of the ships in his squadron, including *Constellation.* As the commodore could not sail from Pensacola under the circumstances he outlined, his requests, no doubt, seemed disingenuous to the Navy Department. His failure to realize that *Columbia*'s draft made her useless at Pensacola caused him to look foolish.[6]

Constellation remained Commodore Dallas's flagship moored at Pensacola and Dickerson retained his cabinet post through 1837, one year into the term of Jackson's successor, Martin van Buren. James K. Paulding, more experienced in naval affairs, replaced Dickerson in the spring of 1838, and in August Dallas informed the new secretary that *Constellation* had to be repaired up north because the work could not be performed at Pensacola. He meekly suggested that *Constellation* should be returned to him if that was the wish of the government. He wrote that in the meantime he would hoist his flag on one of the sloops of war and "be as actively employed as if *Constellation* was there."[7] Paulding forwarded Dallas's letter to Isaac Chauncey, then president of the Board of Commissioners, John Rodgers having retired. The new secretary suggested that the ship should be ordered to New York Navy Yard, but the Gosport dry dock was fully booked. The Boston dock was available to handle *Constellation,* and that's where she ended up.[8]

Dallas agreed that, in his opinion, *Constellation,* with her bottom in a foul state, required entering dry dock for thorough repairs. He added that the ship needed new decks and probably a survey to determine the full extent of her repairs. The commodore

169

sent *Constellation* north under command of Lt. James M. McIntosh, almost exactly three years after her departure to the gulf from Norfolk. She left Pensacola 3 October 1838, five days following USS *Concord*'s departure for Boston. Both ships arrived 24 October, *Constellation* in twenty-one days and *Concord* in twenty-six. The ship hit a top speed of eight knots, but most of the time sailed at a slower pace.[9]

At about the same time that *Constellation* reached Boston, the Board of Commissioners issued a circular dated 1 October 1838 notifying commanders of all navy ships of the board's decision to assign an identification number to each navy vessel. U.S. Frigates *United States* and *Constitution* received numbers two and three, as to be expected. Rather than honor *Constellation* with number one—designating her as the first ship commissioned in the federal navy—the commissioners gave that number to USS *Virginia* and the second-class frigate received the identification number nine. Just another small insult directed at the navy's first frigate.[10]

Secretary of the Navy Dickerson's appointment of Capt. John Downes as commandant of the Charlestown Navy Yard dated from 28 February 1835. Downes, a native of Boston, claimed that he served more time at sea than any other active officer prior to his appointment. He had no specific training or personal characteristics that made him different from several other senior officers who served as commandants during that period of navy administration under the Board of Commissioners. Historians writing about the Boston yard suggest that Commandant Downes endeavored to work with the yard's unruly workforce, at that time a rebellious group that ranged between 250 and 450 mechanics and laborers. If true, his efforts proved unsuccessful. The Board of Commissioners instructed Downes that upon arrival in Boston harbor *Constellation* should be placed temporarily in ordinary as the board wanted U.S. Frigate *United States* taken into dry dock ahead of her after the yard completed work coppering USS *Concord*'s bottom. Downes scheduled both ships to precede *Constellation* into the dock because the yard expected her to tie it up for an extensive period of time.[11]

Upon his arrival in Boston harbor, Lieutenant McIntosh anchored *Constellation* about a half-mile below the navy yard. On 3 November the ship *Columbus* was hauled off the upper wharf and *Constellation* took her place. Laborers from the yard took her masts out and returned her to an anchorage. On 6 November a crew from the yard's ordinary hauled the historic frigate into the lower yard and began to strip her of equipment as *Concord* entered dry dock, where she remained until the twenty-seventh. The commissioners instructed Downes to have the necessary examinations and surveys made on *Constellation*. The commandant worried about getting both *Concord* and *United States* out of dry dock and *Constellation* in before ice set in Boston harbor.[12]

Captain Downes forwarded *Constellation*'s survey and estimate of cost of repairs to the commissioners attached to a letter dated 11 December 1838. The detailed report, probably prepared under the supervision of Josiah Barker, navy constructor at the

Boston yard, is undated and unsigned and no original copy of it remains attached to Downes's letter of transmittal. A copy of the survey reveals that Barker prepared a detailed document with far greater specificity and with it a careful estimate of cost in far greater detail than Francis Grice's or Samuel Humphreys' reports at Gosport in 1827 and 1828. Barker's survey—the basis of what became a partial rebuild of *Constellation*—initiated another great repair just eleven years following the 1797 ship's rebuild at Gosport, that expensive repair followed by two additional visits to the yard for repairs in 1832 and 1834–35. *Constellation,* forty years of age in 1838 and called the Yankee Race Horse, labored like a Belgian work horse between 1815 and 1838, and her last cruise under Dallas had been difficult on ship and commodore.[13]

The progress of widespread deterioration of *Constellation*'s hull had taken a toll on the wooden ship, affecting its integrity and strength. Irreversible structural weaknesses combined with obsolescence would, in a few years, bring *Constellation*'s usefulness as a frigate to an end. Her hull, though repaired extensively in 1812 and 1829, when faced now with the forces of wind and sea rebounded not as a strong unit as she was designed to do, but as weakened sections consisting of a patched upper body on a sound bottom attached to a suspect keel. The partial tear-down-and-build-up-again repair process, the work of frequently disgruntled navy mechanics who were unhappy with navy pay scales and navy hiring policies over a long period of declining labor relations, had, by 1838, made *Constellation* the victim of shoddy work. As the quality of work declined, costs rose, particularly to repair the navy's oldest ships.

The declining level of performance by the navy yards' workforce shortened the period of sea service of the navy's vessels and the cost of more frequent repairs increased. Cost curves of repair cycles grew in height as vessel age squeezed them closer and closer together. It is the nature of wooden warships that older ones require a high level of efficient, skilled care. Records reveal that as the era of wooden ships and canvas sails reached a final run in the United States Navy, the artisans who traditionally cared for them sensed inevitable change. The opportunity for older navy ships to receive thorough repairs deceased as their chances of long-term survival declined. Such are the effects of technological revolutions.

Passing time and new developments in naval ordnance made the frigate class obsolete. Like the aged salts in charge of the Board of Commissioners, obsolescence meant that U.S. Frigate *Constellation* had just a few more years of active service left, her life extendable only a few years by modification. And then, only after the navy decided to rebuild the ship from keel up would she be able to be kept on the active register as the navy's oldest ship. That did not happen in 1839–40. So the partial rebuild in Boston, spread over most of two years, would serve the purpose of a holding action of the old guard, though certainly not as much of a sentimental gesture as the expensive addition of U.S. Frigate *Congress,* a new frigate-44, to the fleet in

1841, a project just getting under way in 1839 to the northeast of Boston at the Portsmouth Navy Yard.

Constellation's Boston survey, "An Estimate of the State and Condition of the Hull of the Frigate *Constellation* and the probable Time and Expense to Fit her for Sea— (Sea Stores Excepted)," opened with a prognosis of the ship's bow including her apron, which naval constructor Josiah Barker found to be rotten. From this point, the survey proceeded directly to the replacement of about one-third of *Constellation*'s first, second, and third futtocks, which were defective, according to the survey, and therefore had to be replaced. About one-third of the futtocks of *Constellation*'s frame consist of approximately twenty-four of the total number of first, second, and third futtocks on each side of the hull from the floor up. All of the frame pieces Barker designated as defective in 1839 Gosport Navy Yard had installed new into her frame just ten years earlier in 1828–29. At the time of this survey the yard had not yet stripped off planks and opened her up. When the report was prepared, *Constellation* lay alongside a wharf or moored offshore, making it unclear how Barker and his carpenters pinpointed such specific defects in *Constellation*'s frame and the exact position and number of futtocks to be replaced in advance. The importance of a modification of this nature, taken before Barker's workforce removed the ship's outer planks, suggests that a prior decision to remove the futtocks could be related to plans previously advanced to alter the shape of *Constellation*'s hull a third time.[14]

There exists no correspondence to and from the Board of Commissioners relating to modifications of *Constellation*'s hull in 1838. There is no information in the yard's two journals or in Downes's correspondence to the board about redrafting *Constellation*'s hull. Nor is there a record of discussions between constructor Barker and chief constructor Humphreys concerning modifications of *Constellation*'s hull. And there is nothing in Barker's correspondence with Commandant Downes suggesting that plans to redraft her originated at the Boston yard; further, there are no records of any transmittals of drawings, orders, or other data passing between Commandant Downes and the secretary of the navy, Barker, or Congress on the subject of redrafting the shape of *Constellation*'s hull, which would be substantial. The absence of documentation duplicated the disappearance of records in 1828–29, including the transmittal of drafts, specifications, instructions, or descriptions of *Constellation*'s modifications ten years earlier at Gosport Navy Yard.

Though the Boston yard's journal details the progress of the work relating to the installation of the new futtocks, there is no mention in the yard journal, as the hull work progressed, of any plans or instructions to modify the frigate's hull or that the work in progress would produce any need for drawings such as the Transverse Section Drawing that shows the modifications made. Yet in fact the redrafting of *Constellation*'s hull at Boston is the third on record of extensive modifications to the ship, and included those made in Washington in 1812 and in Gosport in 1829. All three, because of missing documentation, are presumed to have been ordered on the initiative of a commandant—which is probably absurd. A much more logical explanation is that given the pattern of missing documents relating to *Constellation*'s physical history, the number of lost documents far exceeds the number of forgeries uncovered by previous researchers.

It is startling to confront the fact that no records of drafts or of correspondence sent to the Boston Navy Yard authorizing modifications survive in the otherwise complete record of Board of Commissioners correspondence; nor are there any orders or drafts specifically relating to advance plans for the ship or pertinent correspondence and instructions for any of *Constellation*'s modifications prior to 1853 in navy archival records. This void in *Constellation*'s ship files verifies, at least in part, the claim made by one researcher, referred to in this book's preface, who declared that no documents supporting claims that the navy rebuilt *Constellation* in 1853 exist in the naval archives of any institution. Fortunately, that void, like the black hole in space, had yet to be completely investigated.

Strong circumstantial evidence gleaned from the Boston survey of 1838 suggests that the Charlestown Navy Yard received orders to alter *Constellation*'s maximum molded beam once again and to refair her hull. The survey's recommendation to replace one-third of the ship's first, second, and third futtocks and bulwarks, most of which Gosport Navy Yard installed new ten years earlier, is fairly conclusive evidence that Barker carried out the modifications to replace the radical alterations made to *Constellation*'s breadth at the Norfolk yard during her previous partial rebuild under the supervision of master builder Francis Grice. Also there is the drawing that Grice forwarded to Barker from Gosport of *Constellation*'s dead flat section in January 1839, prior to the beginning of her repairs at Boston, which provided constructor Barker with a sketch drawn to scale of the modification of the ship's midsection Grice supervised at Norfolk ten years earlier. The original of this critically important document is now missing, but there is a copy in the ship's record section of the Naval Historical Center.

Grice prepared and forwarded the original drawing to Boston to assist the yard during dry docking of *Constellation* or to provide Barker with her revised breadth to guide the Boston constructor's preparation of offsets or take-offs for the modifications made to the shape of her hull. A drawing prepared at the Boston yard survives in the National Archives' ship plans collection at College Park, indexed as Drawing No. 107-13-4B and titled Transverse Sections of Frigate *Constellation*. It is one of a group of four drawings prepared under Barker's supervision at Boston in 1839–40. Added to the original titles of the three drawings of her hull by the Boston draftsman are several words including, "Norfolk, then either January or Feb. 1853," along with other reference marks added by John Lenthall, the chief constructor, who redrafted the frigate that year. The original set of three plans, drawn to scale, plus the one developed to illustrate the load plan of *Constellation*'s orlop desk, may be traced to a draftsman at the Boston yard by comparing the distinctive handwriting repeated in the title of each of the four drawings, verified by the proof that the load plan was prepared there. *Constellation*'s load plan, a copy of which is reproduced in this chapter, was located in the records of the Boston Navy Yard at National Archives at Waltham. The drawing of her bow (No. 107-13-4), her keel (No. 107-13-4A), and the previously mentioned drawing, Transverse Sections of Frigate Constellation, reference number above, all prepared at Boston in 1839 or 1840, are held in the collection of the Ship Plans Section of the National Archives at College Park, Maryland.[15]

Barker's survey of *Constellation* concluded that those sections at the bow and stern including the keelson as well as the ceiling below the berth deck needed work. Though berth deck beams and knees passed inspection, the surveyor determined that waterways and planking were worn or defective. The survey reported the ceiling between the berth and gun deck in good condition, gun deck beams and knees, good, except for six or eight knees, the condition of deck beams and knees above the berth deck still good but not the planking. The section of the survey that estimated costs allocated $37,508 for carpenter work, of which $14,900 was allocated for labor and $22,608 to the cost of wood materials including live oak timber pieces for the futtocks scheduled for replacement. The next largest cost reflected by the estimate was allocated to the joiner department, $3,574 for materials and $11,888 for labor. The estimated work assigned the blacksmith department totaled $8,060 for materials and $6,400 for labor. The estimated cost of *Constellation*'s repairs totaled $103,704.

Barker's estimate of the cost of carpenters working on the ship's hull may have been flawed. The amount of the projected labor cost totaled just $14,900, an amount far less than necessary since the survey estimated that the cost of wood materials required for the repairs would be $22,608. Normally, when estimating hull repairs in older ships, the surveyor's estimates for labor costs exceeded the cost of wood materials by substantial amounts.[16]

The Charlestown Navy Yard clerk's daily journal of the activities of the yard principally centered on the employment of mechanics and laborers and recorded the workforce checked off each day as individual workers received their assignments in the yard. The journal logged a total of 231 civilians working 24 October 1838, prior to the startup of *Constellation*'s repairs. The yard's labor force increased to 454 civilian workers in December 1838, up substantially over previous months, though the main repairs on *Constellation* did not commence until February 1839. Storekeeper clerks kept another log covering the progress of work on each ship's repairs recorded at bimonthly intervals and set up in a manner that enabled those in authority to monitor work completed and the work yet to be scheduled. When storekeepers opened a ship log for *Constellation,* the clerk recorded the beginning of repairs in January 1839 and the schedule of work assigned to each master mechanic's department or shop in the yard. The log estimated that the frigate's hull repairs, inside and out, would require carpenters, joiners, and plumbers to work a total of 24,112 days. With an average wage of $1.60 per day, the estimated total for labor employed on her hull, including hewing and installing the new futtocks, totaled $38,579. This figure for estimated labor costs for repairs to *Constellation*'s hull, rather than the survey, is judged to be more realistic. The difference may lie in yard procedures because much of the cost of the work on her hull related to modifications, not repairs.[17]

During the months of November and December 1838, *Constellation* remained in ordinary where she was stripped of her masts, equipment, and ballast in preparation for dry docking. The only regular laborers working on the frigate prior to moving her into the dry dock were coopers working to remove old casks and build new ones. Their work continued throughout the month of January 1839 up to 16 February, when *Constellation* entered the dock. The *Army and Navy Chronicle,* quoting an article from a Boston paper, wrote that the ship's bottom was entirely encrusted with oysters, which were of a size that sold locally for one-half cent each. Her draft measured 17 feet 8 inches aft and 12 feet 7 inches forward. These measurements may be compared to her original draft at the time of her launch at Stodder's yard in the late summer of 1797 into the warm water of Patapsco River, when Truxtun measured Constellation's draft as 13 feet 3 inches forward and 18 feet 6 inches aft.[18]

During the first two weeks of the ship's period in dry dock, carpenters and laborers stripped the frigate's defective outer planking, decks, and futtocks. As the constructor planned to reduce *Constellation*'s molded breadth and refair her hull, he ordered the Transverse Sections Drawing previously mentioned to be prepared showing the shape of the ship following modifications, or, perhaps, a preliminary version of it, from which carpenters prepared molds and cut out new futtock pieces in accordance with new offsets (see fig. 7.1). Laborers removed old copper, collected it, and sent the scrap to Washington Navy Yard for reprocessing. Old timbers were carted away from the ship along with waste materials from the area of the dock, which would later be burned or auctioned.

Carpenters hewed the replacement futtocks in their shed and bolted them into the ship's frame. The work of replacing one-third of the frame's futtocks required about one month between 15 March and 15 April, according to *Constellation*'s yard log, though carpenters probably commenced work on the frames even before *Constellation* entered dry dock. Once completed, measurements were taken off before carpenters covered over the frame with planks and ceiling. Barker's

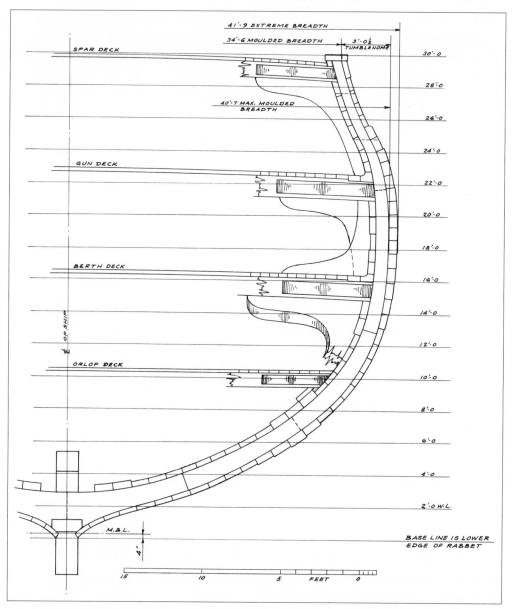

Figure 7.1. Midship section of USF *Constellation*, 1839–1840. The drawing is based on half breadths recorded in Transverse Sections Plan, 1839, NARA 107-13-4B. *William L. Crothers*

draftsman, before preparing the final version of the Transverse Section Drawing, took off the frigate's new measurements.

Major work on the ship's frame and hull continued through the middle of April. The yard assigned carpenters to *Constellation* varying in numbers from 70 to 107, during the period when they hewed new live oak timbers and bolted the new futtocks into the frame. Modification of the frigate's hull shape, the third since she was built in 1797, reduced *Constellation*'s maximum molded breadth from 42 feet 7 inches, as discussed in chapter 6, to a new maximum molded breadth of 40 feet 7 inches. Her extreme beam, formerly 43 feet 9 inches, according to the Pearson, Buchanan, and Miller's measurements, Barker reduced to 41 feet 9 inches, greater than her maximum breadth in 1797 but less beam than after her rebuilt hull measured in 1812 and 1829.[19]

The Board of Commissioners initiated a new program of purchasing live oak promiscuous timber pieces with funds from the navy's annual appropriations for repairs in 1838. Previously, the board purchased most live oak framing with funds under appropriations to Increase the Navy or to Improve the Navy. Timber stockpiled under those appropriations could not be withdrawn for repairing ships. The commissioners notified Commandant Downes that ten thousand cubic feet of promiscuous timber would be delivered under contracts let and that the contract included five thousand feet of timber for repairs made under the navy's annual appropriation for its Wear and Tear account. Though these purchases specified only pieces cut for large frigates, sloops, and schooners, the yard possessed authority to use this timber for replacement of *Constellation*'s defective futtocks, as the Board of Commissioners did not purchase live oak timber cut specifically for frames of second-class frigates for repairs, or, for that matter, for new construction either.

Should storekeepers deliver out of stockpile live oak timber or other materials purchased for new construction but used for repairs, they made appropriate adjustments to their inventories, debiting repair stocks and crediting timber to stockpiles held under the Act to Increase or the Act to Improve the Navy. If timber requisitioned for repairs could not be replaced from repair stocks on hand, then the storekeeper through the commandant notified the Bureau of Construction, Equipment, and Repair, which would then debit the navy's repair Wear and Tear account and credit the appropriate new construction appropriation.

As a result of political tension with Great Britain, Congress passed the War Powers Act of 3 March 1839, which authorized the navy to complete new ships in stocks as well as ships that Congress previously authorized rebuilding but kept on hold during the Jackson administration. The following year, 1840, Congress passed a bill allowing the navy to combine all existing appropriations under a single heading, whether it had been previously voted and funded for new construction,

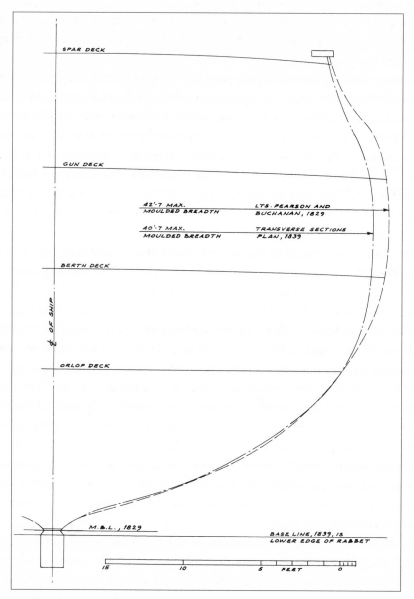

SPAR DECK

GUN DECK

42'-7 MAX.
MOULDED BREADTH

LTS. PEARSON AND
BUCHANAN, 1829

40'-7 MAX.
MOULDED BREADTH

TRANSVERSE SECTIONS
PLAN, 1839

BERTH DECK

℄ OF SHIP

ORLOP DECK

M.B.L., 1829

BASE LINE, 1839, IS
LOWER EDGE OF RABBET

15   10   5   FEET   0

Figure 7.2. This drawing of the molded midship sections of USF *Constellation* in 1829 and 1839 was made in accordance with the measurements taken by Lieutenants Pearson and Buchanan in 1829 and with Transverse Sections Plan, 1839. *William L. Crothers*

improvement of the navy (timber and materials), or for repairs. Because of the flexibility gained by this act, live oak timbers required for *Constellation*'s repairs could be taken from stockpiles previously reserved for new ships, then molded and cut down to fit her smaller frame. However, the Boston yard completed her hull repairs before the 1840 act passed.[20]

As the commissioners never purchased live oak frames or frame sections molded specifically for frames of second-class frigates, this produced a significant elevation in the cost of labor. The extra labor required to hew timber frame pieces into sizes to fit molds cut in accordance with a second-class frigate's dimensions and specifications meant higher costs. This forced ship carpenters at Boston, and at all navy yards, to requisition frame pieces or promiscuous timber pieces cut specifically for other classes of ships and to rework them to fit molds of *Constellation*'s frames. Higher than normal labor costs affected the cost of her repairs every time carpenters modified the second-class frigate's hull.

This raises a question concerning the amount of waste produced when carpenters in Boston in 1839 recut promiscuous live oak timber pieces into futtocks of a size to fit *Constellation*'s smaller frame from a stockpile of timber molded and cut for other classes of ships, that is, ships of the line, frigates, and sloops. For example, when USF *Guerrière*'s white-oak frame was replaced with one of live oak, it required thirty-six thousand cubic feet of live oak timber to make a frame for a ship of approximately sixteen hundred tons burden. *Guerrière*'s new frame, when complete, consisted of about twenty-two thousand cubic feet of molded timber. Thus, in the course of building a new frame for *Guerrière*, carpenters lost as waste 39 percent of the total timber drawn out of stockpile measured in cubic feet when hewing promiscuous live oak timber into frame pieces. Normally, in this process, according to contemporary experts, about 25 percent of the total quantity drawn out of stockpile had to be set aside because of damage or dry rot from weather and water after years in open storage. An additional quantity was lost cutting large timbers down to fit *Guerrière*'s offsets.

In addition to the loss of timber due to wind, weather, and water damage, the unavailability of molded timber for *Constellation* on each occasion she was rebuilt caused labor costs to skyrocket as carpenters worked thousands of additional days to laboriously prepare stone-hard promiscuous live oak timber to fill the ship's replacement requirements, a process repeated during all four of the extensive modifications to her hull in 1812, 1829, 1839, and in 1853–54. In fact, it is a matter of record that *Constellation*'s original cost ballooned between 1795 and 1797, partially because of the increased number of carpenters required to cut her frame pieces from promiscuous timbers or from frame pieces hewn to the specifications of the larger frigate-44, which had originally been scheduled to be delivered elsewhere.[21]

Capt. Charles Morris, who became president of the Board of Commissioners upon the death of Isaac Chauncey, notified Downes that the board ordered the Washington Navy Yard to fabricate fifty iron tanks for *Constellation,* an indication that the commissioners believed that the second-class frigate would be on the navy's register for years to come. Downes sent specifications for the new tanks to Washington with the comment that *Constellation,* "being so sharp, I think it doubtful whether tanks made in conformity with these models would suit any other frigate." Downes referred to the ship's deadrise and finely shaped ends, particularly her after-sections, originally built sharp by David Stodder's Fells Point shipwrights, a condition that caused so many conservative commanders to be uncomfortable sailing in her. Storage of these tanks below the orlop deck required additional work in the ship's lower hold.[22]

Work continued on *Constellation* at Boston throughout the summer months as carpenters worked on the ship's orlop deck, fore and aft (fig. 7.3), and replaced the apron and rebuilt her lower stem assembly. Because of extensive work performed in *Constellation*'s bow area, the yard's draftsman prepared the drawing of its shape, distorted by the ship's hogged keel, which pulled the ship down at its ends and after time produced a sag or droop to her bow section.[23]

All departments of the yard continued repairing the ship during the summer of 1839, though the number of men working tapered off significantly until, finally, the Board of Commissioners ordered all work stopped because the navy had exhausted its current year's appropriation for repairs. Before closing down the work site, Downes sent Captain Morris a drawing of *Constellation*'s hogged keel, prepared after she entered dry dock. The commandant reported to the commissioners that dock workers managed to place blocks under her so that her keel did not straighten as the water drained from under it. Though the original could not be located, copies may be found at various locations including the National Archives at College Park.[24]

Gosport Navy Yard built a new stern assembly for *Constellation* in 1828. After it had been surveyed and found rotten, the Boston yard replaced major components of the stern including galleries and the rudder assembly. Grice sent a copy of a drawing illustrating the round stern assembly as built at Gosport which the Boston yard used to guide carpenters reconstructing her stern. A copy of this drawing marked "*Constellation,* 1840," the year that work was completed at Boston, can be found in the book, *The* Constellation *Question*. The original of this drawing is missing, but copies survive at several collections. (See the sketch of *Constellation*'s elliptical stern in chapter 6.)[25]

With new lines and dimensions, a result of the recent modifications to her hull, *Constellation,* when moored once again in Boston harbor, looked more like the ship drafted by Joshua Humphreys in 1794, though Barker altered her hull dimensions enough to make it necessary to refair her lines yet again. Her new dimensions gave

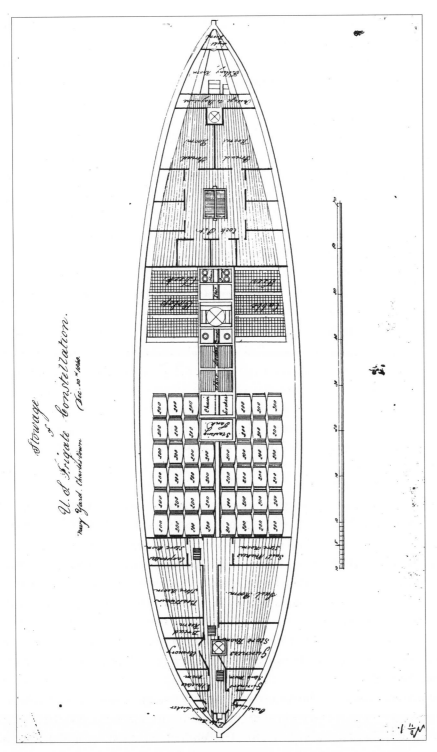

Figure 7.3. The orlop deck plan and stowage of wooden casks in the hold of USF *Constellation,* Boston, 1839–1840. *National Archives, Waltham, Mass.*

her slightly greater breadth than Humphreys' original plan, but she lacked by five inches her beam following John Lenthall's modifications in 1853.

The drawing of Transverse Sections of Frigate *Constellation* (107-13-4B), prepared by the Boston yard's draftsman, gives the dimensions and shape of nine sections of the ship following her rebuild at Boston in 1839–40. The draftsman who prepared this drawing selected an external reference line, then measured from that line to the center line of the ship, and by that means calculated her molded breadth through nine sections. When the yard's draftsman completed the Transverse Sections Drawing and the keel and the bow drawings, he drafted the shape of *Constellation*'s hull as rebuilt at Boston. These drawings together provide the first-ever drafts of the ship-frigate as built. Moreover, the Boston draftsman's base line for the three drawings in the series is the same as John Lenthall's base line in his drafts of *Constellation* in 1853—the lower edge of the keel rabbet.[26]

The administration of Charlestown Navy Yard had not been an easy command for Capt. John Downes, who was faced with a disgruntled civilian workforce that became militant after the commissioners ordered all work stopped in autumn of 1839, when repair appropriations dried up. Downes had returned to the city of his birth in 1835, weary of life at sea after twenty-five years. As commandant, he settled down in that great city with his family, insulated by the wealth he had brought home from Peru two decades earlier. Four years later, in October 1839, Downes received a letter from Secretary Paulding which he felt deeply as the rudest of all possible cuts. The secretary notified the commandant to hold himself ready for sea duty.

Downes responded, first claiming poor health, then reminding Paulding of his long service at sea, but finally admitting that he did not wish to go. The secretary let the commandant dangle for eleven months before he directed another shocker, ordering Downes to sail to the Orient on U.S. Frigate *Constellation* after he got her ready for recommissioning. Downes recoiled from that assignment with a display of irrational anger, thrashing back at Paulding like a man sentenced to long-term incarceration.[27]

Commandant Downes's reactions to Paulding's unsettling orders, included in a letter to the secretary in which he objected to the selection of *Constellation* for this round-the-world mission, suggested that USS *Independence* would be a more suitable choice for a commodore in view of the importance of the mission. The incident reached a bizarre level when Downes fell victim to an old navy game: He reacted in an official manner to a rumor directed at the affairs of a senior officer. The yard's purser informed the commandant that information spreading in Washington at the time implied that President Van Buren was dispatching Downes to the Orient for marching in a Bunker Hill Day parade organized by the opposing Whig Party. Upon hearing this, Downes foolishly confronted Paulding, a move that provided the secretary with an opportunity to lecture the captain on the inference of his statements, that such serious matters of public interest could be affected by petty private activities. Nevertheless, Paulding canceled Downes's orders and gave Capt. Lawrence Kearny the assignment to command the East Indies Squadron, though *Constellation* remained the navy's choice as the flagship for the important diplomatic mission. There seemed to have been no further discussion concerned with the suitability of the historic frigate for the cruise. As Kearny served at that time as flag captain of Commodore Ridgely's ship, *Potomac,* assigned to the Brazilian Squadron, Paulding issued orders to Capt. George W. Storer to deliver *Constellation* to Kearny at Rio de Janeiro and once there to switch his command to the frigate *Potomac.*[28]

Work resumed on *Constellation* during the spring of 1840. Workmen handled the loading and stowage of the ship's new iron tanks and began loading ballast. Riggers stepped the ship's masts and proceeded to rig her in the summer months of 1840, following the long period of inactivity when the yard laid off most of its labor force, forcing the unemployment of this group of skilled mechanics for nine months. In August Downes received instructions from the commissioners to have *Constellation* prepared for a three-year cruise to the East Indies and China. By the time George W. Storer reported aboard to take temporary command of the ship, New England's trees had turned color once again with the autumn weather, two years having passed since the arrival of the frigate at Boston. Almost immediately, a highly irritated Storer initiated a flood of complaints concerned with *Constellation*'s condition, which he directed at Downes. The results of Storer's shipboard surveys reached the commandant as the cold New England winter settled in. *Constellation*'s temporary captain kept up a steady flow of surveys that pointed to the poor condition of the historic ship and her armament. The flow continued long after the ship set sail for Rio.[29]

Partial List of Items Stowed in Hold

792 pigs: 130 in spirit room; 662 in main hold—total wt. 160,048 lbs.

50 iron water tanks—67,779 lbs. containing 23,534 gallons

1 filling tank—1,360 lbs. containing 265 gals.

42 200-gal. water casks containing 8,400 gals.

Weight of gunners outfits—277,489 lbs.

Weight of gunners stores—24,740 lbs.

Weight of boatswain stores—127,211 lbs.

Mast and spars except lower mast and bow sprit: 658,627 lbs.

100 bbls. of pork—starboard side, fore and aft.

125 bbls. of beef—larboard side, fore and aft.

Spare caps, forward of cable tier, starboard side; tar midships, forward under fore hatch; spare gun carriages against the bulkhead forward each side; trunks and beds in starboard tier; sheets, cables, hawsers, towlines & messenger in the tiers on each side, chain cable of 120 fathoms in starboard locker; chain cable of 105 fathoms. larboard locker; and about 5 or 6 fathoms with a swivel intended to be placed on the larboard cable, 15 fathoms from the anchor; round shot wads; lumber, etc. stowed away as usual; 500 18 lb. grape, 400 32 lb. grape, 300 32 lb. canisters & 300 18 lb. canister shot stowed in a locker near the main mast and in the bay rack bins.

Source: Constellation's Stowage Plan and draft computations, Daily Yard Journal, RG181, NARA, Waltham.

Constellation's Draft of Water [under] Various Conditions

March 27, 1840—Ballast stowed, no mast or anything else—aft 17' 10"—13' 6"

April 8—With water tanks stowed & all masts stepped—18' 3"—14' 9"

May 25—Water tanks & casks filled, provisions, ship rigged, gun batteries on board, cables, sprit room casks, and waist anchors stowed—20' 3"—17' 5"

Oct. 27—Crew on board—20' 5" —18' 9"

Dec. 9—When under way for sea—21' 6"—20' 2"

Source: Constellation's Stowage Plan and draft computations, Daily Yard Journal, RG181, NARA, Waltham.

At the end of the year confrontations between Storer and Downes concerning the condition of *Constellation,* which he originally reported ready for sea in November 1840, followed a torrent of complaints and surveys of the work done at the yard on the sloop of war USS *Concord* and U.S. Frigate *United States,* repairs to both ships having preceded those to *Constellation.* The commissioners asked Downes to explain why his yard had neither caulked nor surveyed *Concord's* hull during her stay there in late 1838. Downes wrote that he did not believe it any more necessary to examine the soundness of the hull of *Concord* than to examine the hull of *Constellation.* He continued that he had no doubt, however, that after boring test holes into *Constellation's* hull throughout, some defective part might be uncovered. On the defensive, Downes claimed that it appeared that all vessels leaving the Boston yard destined for New York or Norfolk, after being repaired and fitted at Boston, received a survey that resulted in their condemnation. The commandant suggested that the commissioners consider convening a board consisting of navy constructors to survey ships before and after receiving repairs.[30]

Repair of *United States,* which preceded work on *Constellation,* produced an uproar in the Navy Department and much criticism of the Boston yard's work, far exceeding the crescendo when *Concord* returned to service. Though officials directed criticism at Downes, they also sensed that the situation in Boston was beyond his control. The problems resulted from the navy's hated labor policies and administrative ineptness, which caused labor conditions to deteriorate, a situation that gained momentum there and at other yards as the navy's wooden sailing ship navy grew old and required greater repairs more frequently.

Advance surveys proved inadequate and the political spoils system awarded inferior workmen key jobs in navy yards. As the costs of construction and repair work climbed, the relations between navy supervisors and the yards' civilian workforce declined. The daily check-off system robbed skilled mechanics of their pride and dignity. Morale dropped and the quality of work fell, problems that peaked for Downes and the navy between 1838 and 1840, when the commissioners forced the yards to close down for months. Labor conditions grew increasingly bitter, a situation that had become blatantly obvious in 1839 when *Concord, United States,* and finally, *Constellation* returned to service in unseaworthy condition.

Downes, commenting on the surveys made after *United States* left Boston, noted that the reports stated that her frame was much cut by boring during previous repairs. Numerous thorough repair cycles, frequent hull modifications, and partial rebuilding of ships above the waterline made necessary the replacement of live oak frame pieces, which were not normally affected by decay or wear once installed. Boring new holes and test holes and reusing old bolt holes in the navy ships' live oak frames caused the fastening to loosen in rough seas, which gradually weakened the frames.

The civilian workforce of navy yards, eager to extend periods of employment under the check-off system, disgruntled or not, voiced no objections to the Board of Commissioners' system of retaining old ships in service. The increasingly frequent repairs to historic ships such as *United States, Constellation,* and *Constitution,* plus the increased frequency of repairs required by newer ships like *Concord,* undermined the system that the Board of Commissioners created, having worked so closely with Congress over four decades, eliminating all competition for new construction and repairs to the navy's fleet.[31]

The board ordered the frigate *United States* into Gosport Navy Yard in March 1840 for what developed into another extensive repair. A survey prepared under Captain Kearny's supervision on the condition of *United States* after the ship departed Boston became a sweeping condemnation of the quality of work performed at Charlestown Navy Yard. It reported a rotten transom, a rotten apron, a partially rotten stern post, and a rotten stemson, all uncovered after a thorough repair under Downes's supervision. Downes's position became particularly embarrassing that year as in a few months Captain Storer's complaints about the condition of *Constellation* began to circulate.[32]

Storer found himself enmeshed in an array of problems. It fell to him to oversee preparations for *Constellation*'s long, difficult cruise to the Orient, which, as it turned out, included circumnavigation of the world's seas. As he would serve as commander of *Constellation* only as far as Rio de Janeiro, he could have ignored her condition, but to his credit he did not. The difficulty of recruiting plagued the ship, as, in addition to Storer's problems with her condition, it proved difficult to sign on a good crew; no doubt, this problem was made somewhat more troublesome by Secretary Paulding's order limiting the number of men of color on board navy ships to 5 percent. The navy agent at Boston approved Storer's request for $50,000 against the purser's requisitions, only to discover after spending $31,000 that the Navy Department limited the purchase of purser's supplies to $5,000. After that, Storer became deeply mired in numerous new surveys that pinpointed additional shabby work that the yard performed on *Constellation,* the burden falling upon Commandant Downes to explain yet again how it could be so.[33]

Before Storer made his departure, he had *Constellation* hauled down below the yard to an anchorage in Boston harbor. There he continued to inspect his ship, sending back to Downes his officers' survey reports, complaining about the conditions onboard the ship as they uncovered them one by one. Surveys claimed that the air ports were not sealed securely, that the galley leaked, and that much of the officers' furniture remained unfinished. They mentioned careless oversights such as the lack of a protecting box for the fresh water pump. Surveys objected bitterly to the condition of many of the ship's guns as well as the small arms provided her. Storer thought the main mast was stepped in a faulty manner and leaked at the base and that the condition of the ship's standing rigging, including shrouds, left *Constellation* poorly rigged and her crew at risk.[34]

Downes responded by appointing boards of locally assigned naval officers to survey the ship. The Boston-based surveyors, led by Capt. Joseph Smith, overruled Storer in most instances, which enabled Downes to inform the commissioners that these survey reports allowed them to understand the "character of the complaints made by Storer." Unfortunately for Downes, the matter did not die at that point. When *Constellation* reached Rio de Janeiro, Captain Kearny, who recently had faulted Downes for the condition of *United States,* began a series of surveys that established the legitimacy of Storer's complaints, if not then, certainly by the time *Constellation* completed the second leg of her cruise between Rio and Capetown. Though Kearny delayed his departure from Rio, supervising further surveys and repairs on *Constellation,* the fury of his criticisms of Boston's work increased under his command after her passage from Rio to Capetown. Fifteen months later, Captain Warrington, the last president of the Board of Commissioners, continued to pursue the matter of *Constellation*'s repairs with Downes.

Constellation departed Boston 9 December 1840. USS *Boston,* the other ship under Kearny's command, sailed several days earlier from New York for Rio de Janeiro. A last-minute report from Commander Abbot, Commandant Downes's assistant, stated that as the result of still another survey of *Constellation* conducted by Lt. A. E. Downes, he could confirm that the ship's rudder was covered by a hood or coat, a device designed to divert water away from the ship's stern ports. Of course, the report, like the others, proved false, as water entered the ward room and at the berth deck level, forcing the ship's officers and crew to keep the area bailed of water.[35]

Storer reported to the secretary of the navy on arrival of his ship at Rio 24 January 1841. He found matters in upheaval there as Captain Kearny, in U.S. Frigate *Potomac,* had been run aground by a pilot on Rio de la Plata in mid-December and the ship had not yet returned to Rio. Kearny reported that by stripping his ship of guns and other weight, the ship's crew freed her without damage to her bottom. Charles G. Ridgely, commodore of the Brazilian Squadron, absolved Kearny of responsibility for the pilot's error.

Potomac returned to Rio 1 February, which allowed Kearny to take command of *Constellation* and *Boston* on 4 February, Storer transferring his flag to *Potomac.* Kearny ordered Cdr. J. C. Long, in Boston, to sail for Capetown and wait for him there. *Constellation*'s new captain and the East Indies Squadron's new commodore then set to work examining his ship and reviewing a new set of surveys made by *Constellation*'s officers for Captain Storer during the passage from Boston down to Rio. Shorer reported that a second survey of the ship's guns found many of them potentially dangerous to the crew. Kearny condemned several. Before departing, Kearny wrote a letter to the commissioners enclosing a preliminary summation of *Constellation*'s condition as he found her; he reported that it would be necessary to overhaul and refit her sails. Further, the hull needed recaulking outside from stem to stern; the galley had to be moved from berth deck to gun deck to avoid fire hazard to deck beams; water entered through rudder ports into the wardroom and berth deck; there were no guns for boats and no cradles; the ship was deficient in her battery, shot, and small arms; and many of the ship's guns were in dangerous condition. On 6 March 1841, Kearny departed Rio de Janeiro.[36]

Kearny reported *Constellation*'s arrival 5 April at Table Bay, near Capetown, twenty-eight days out of Rio. The ship logged 3,485 miles in twenty-eight days—an average speed of just over five knots. The long run across the southern ocean provided Kearny with opportunities to drill his ship and crew under most sailing situations and to test *Constellation*'s old guns and the seaworthiness of her patched hull. Though the crew won his immediate praise, Kearny found many problems with the ship. Not only had the ship yard's riggers and sailmakers failed to provide the ship with well-fitted sails and reliable running rigging, Kearny criticized *Constellation*'s standing rigging, so necessary to keep *Constellation*'s intricate system of masts and yards in place; some of the spars were more than 150 feet above the deck, where safety is vital. Lieutenant Claibourne wrote home describing their plight after a surveying team, consisting of officers from *Boston* and *Constellation,* condemned the rigging in toto, noting that the ship's standing rigging was "indispensably necessary to the safety of the ship and crew."[37]

A loose rudder caused it to fail survey and many of the ship's guns proved to be in such bad condition that Kearny had them stowed in the ship's hold. Kearny confirmed the accuracy of the complaints Storer levied against the yard's work, completely undermining the whitewashed reports of the officers Downes assigned. Kearny attended with particular concern to the rigging, most of that work having been done during and after the commissioners ordered the work stoppage in the fall and winter of 1839–40. Though faced with evidence presented first by Storer in Boston and confirmed by surveys made after the ship's departure, and then reconfirmed by Kearny's additional reports, Commandant Downes refused to accept that the poor quality of work originated in his yard. A year later, long after Kearny's Capetown reports reached Washington in 1842, the commandant continued to cry foul play as he claimed that negative surveys prepared onboard *Constellation* originated with officers who wanted off the ship.

The principal need of *Constellation*'s officers was a dry wardroom to replace the one that leaked badly, the rudder having no cover though two surveys by Downes's officers claimed otherwise. After a few days at Table Bay, an anchorage considered unsafe by Kearny, *Constellation* and *Boston* sailed to Saldanha Bay, where work parties picked from crews of both ships repaired *Constellation*'s faulty gear and equipment. After the work was completed in late July, *Constellation* backtracked to Capetown, where Kearny drew $16,000 in bills of exchange on Baring Brothers for purchases. Finally, *Constellation* stood out of Table Bay 30 July, heading east into the morning sun.[38]

The sloop of war *Boston* and frigate *Constellation* sailed across the vast open reaches of the oceans of the Southern Hemisphere, touching at Johanna, Quallah Battoo, and Pinang, and finally reaching Singapore on 4 November 1841. Kearny held the ships two months at Singapore, reporting to the secretary that he delayed his departure for China hoping that news would reach him on the subject of the United States' relations with Great Britain. Evidently satisfied that America was not at war once again with the Royal Navy, *Constellation* left Singapore 5 February 1842, arriving at Macao, China, on 22 March 1842.[39]

Constellation and *Boston* anchored in the harbor of Macao at the mouth of the Canton River 23 March 1842. The Opium War between Great Britain and China had moved into its final phase in northern China. A British expeditionary force pressed forward with its great superiority in armament, slaughtering large numbers of Chinese and at the same time pushing forward a harsh set of treaty terms. The British had attacked in 1839 after Lin Tse-su, director of the Board of War, on orders of the emperor, came to Canton, the center of commercial activity with the outside world, to stop the great flow of opium into China. He ordered the local administrators to shut down the activities of British and American merchants, seized many of them, and ordered all opium confiscated. After authorities collected and burned twenty thousand chests of opium, the Chinese government released the British and Americans. Fleeing the mainland, foreigners regrouped on the islands of Macao and Hong Kong at the mouth of the Canton River. This tense period escalated into open warfare when the Chinese refused any further contact with the opium traders and cut off supplies and even water. The local British naval commander, Captain Elliott, ordered Royal Navy ships under his command to attack. A large Royal Navy expeditionary squadron eventually reached China and reinforced Captain Elliott's forces.[40]

Word of the war in Canton reached Washington before Kearny left and the United States government provided its naval diplomat with relatively simple and straightforward instructions considering the unusual nature of the principal source of the problem: a group of British and American merchant smugglers conducting tremendously profitable trade in opium, a drug outlawed in China. Opium was brought to the country and stored in floating warehouses out of reach of Chinese authorities. Distribution depended on a system of bribery of Chinese officials. Concurrent with the illegal narcotics trade, foreign merchants, principally British and Americans, carried on legitimate trade with hong merchants in tea and other Chinese products. Kearny's orders were to assist American traders but at the same time to pay due respect to the laws of China. His government instructed Kearny to impress upon the Chinese people and government the friendly disposition of the United States, a government that encouraged only trade sanctioned by China. Amazingly, considering the period in history, the United States ordered the commodore to prevent the smuggling of opium into China by Americans or others under the cover of American flag vessels, that is, in ships registered in the United States of America but owned by one of its citizens in residence overseas or by foreigners, in China, often a practice followed by English smugglers. The mission required the attention of a diplomat with great patience and intelligence, an almost unknown combination of characteristics of naval officers on previous diplomatic missions.[41]

Though Kearny's instructions seemed straightforward concerning the opium trade, a solution to the question of how American interests were to be protected proved complicated. The commodore became aware that American firms operating legitimately in Chinese commerce, say, the tea trade, were the same firms that managed or operated opium clippers cooperatively with British dealers or independently of them. The U.S. Department of State complicated matters by selecting private commercial agents on assignment in foreign ports as consular officers, a system long practiced by the U.S. government. A similar practice in China reached back over decades to John P. Cushing, consul at Whampoa who was also an official of Pickering Brothers, principals in the first large American opium operation in China. That organization eventually became Russell & Company, still the largest American opium dealers when Kearny arrived in 1842. A different set of company officials of that firm served the Department of State as consular or commercial agents when *Constellation* dropped anchor there. It was this self-serving group that awaited the arrival of Commodore Kearny to serve him as advisers. Warren Delano, Franklin Delano Roosevelt's grandfather, held the post of vice-consul at Canton at the time Kearny arrived on the scene in *Constellation* in March while the war between China and Great Britain still raged in the north. Delano, a principal in Russell & Company, also represented the disposed British interests along the Canton River. He was an experienced trader who had grown very rich over the years in China.[42]

James P. Sturgis, United States vice consul at Macao, Edward King, consular agent at Macao, and P. W. Snow, consul, all principals in Russell & Company, sold or transported opium and traded in tea and other Chinese products. Under Chinese law, foreigners could not reside inside China unless they represented a foreign government; therefore, representing the United States in an official capacity proved vital to their company's narcotics operations as well as to their companies' other activities. The American government unknowingly provided an additional assist to American opium traders by allowing commercial and consular appointees living abroad to own American ships, an exception in the country's navigation acts regulating federal registration of ships. Profits from sales of opium were enormous, but the trade was important, too, because it supplied American merchants and ship owners with specie to purchase Chinese products like tea or other products in world markets. Isaac McKim, Baltimore's world-famous merchant of an earlier period, purchased opium in Turkey and sold it to China shippers at Valparaiso for specie, which he used to purchase Chilean and Mexican copper for his factories in Baltimore. Opium, like specie, became a medium of exchange in international trade.[43]

Commodore Kearny, patient and endowed with the demeanor of a trained diplomat, bolstered by intelligence and courtesy when in negotiation, demonstrated qualities not normally characteristic of senior naval officers of the period. He absorbed all the information and advice he could gather. As the war moved toward a British military victory, which, of course, would create great loss of face for the emperor's administrators, Kearny honed his line of communication, bypassing the traditional hong merchants to deal directly with a Chinese admiral and the emperor's chief representatives in the region, Lin Tse-su, and the governor of Canton.

Kearny notified ship owners in Chinese waters that he would seize American ships caught with cargoes of opium. He dealt patiently with the inflated demands of

American merchants against the Chinese, as in the case of Augustine Heard & Company, which sustained losses when mobs destroyed foreign warehouses and offices. As the victorious British admiral pushed harsh treaty terms on the Chinese government, the American commodore assured the Chinese that the United States remained China's friend, and gently but firmly asked them to include in their negotiating position with the British the proposition that conditions of the new Commercial Treaty would not favor Great Britain's merchants exclusively.

Kearny directed the attention of the governor of Canton to the importance of the commercial trade of the United States with the hope that this trade "will receive consideration, and their citizens on that matter be placed upon the same footing as the merchants of the nation most favored." His courteous approach to the Chinese, free of hyperbole and urgency but reinforced with assurances of American friendship and cooperation, seemed effective, particularly in contrast to the British position on opium that placed the smuggling problem on the Chinese government as an internal crisis inside that country. Finally, in response to Kearny's diplomacy, the Chinese recognized the importance of America's friendship during the recent war and informed the commander that American merchants in China would not be excluded from trading by any treaty with Great Britain. As of 1 January 1843 the situation still awaited final settlement, so Kearny postponed his scheduled departure from China.[44]

Lawrence Kearny's private and public declarations placing the United States government in opposition to the participation of American citizens and ships in the opium trade, along with the commodore's special facility for representing America's position to Chinese officials as they considered their options following the Opium War, eventually resulted in the extension of the British trade concessions to American merchants as well as those of other nations trading in China. Perhaps at that point, Kearny should have departed for home, but several American merchants, having experienced losses to boats, offices, and warehouses as a result of Chinese mob activity during the war, urged Kearny to delay his departure and to press for collection of their claims against the Chinese government. Because the losses to the American firms occurred as a result of mob violence or from damage incurred during the Opium War with Great Britain and had nothing to do with American opium activities, Kearny felt obligated by his orders to assist his countrymen in collecting their legitimate claims. He delayed his departure.[45]

The process of gaining knowledge of the affairs of Russell & Company, Augustine Heard & Company, and others enabled Kearny to present their claims to the Chinese. From exposure to their activities Kearny discovered the extent of their operations, which allowed him to move beyond the curtain of secrecy under which the companies operated and revealed to him the conflicts of interest that obviously compromised America's diplomatic position. Their opium activities made their official status as consular and commercial agents of the United States government hypocritical and counterproductive.[46] Kearny lay before Daniel Webster, secretary of state, his analysis of the corrupt system of American business interests handling consular affairs, used all over the world by the State Department to oversee the nation's affairs. Kearny pointed out that it existed as a system designed to spend the least government money possible.[47]

Once Great Britain's military force defeated the poorly armed Chinese, American opium dealers, with the drug originating in the British colony of India and in Turkey, resumed an important role in the trade's revival. Even as they pushed Commodore Kearny to handle their war loses and claims against Chinese mobs, American firms dispatched American-registered schooners and brigs to India for cargoes of the illegal drug or sold their vessels to Englishmen who operated them under federal register and flying the American flag.

Kearny notified local American captains that he would seize their vessels and void American registry documents if he caught any ship with opium aboard. But opium was a flood that could not be contained. Even as Augustine Heard & Company pushed Kearny to collect its claims, seeing new opportunities for Americans in the opium trade, the firm instructed its home office in Boston to have two fast vessels built at Fells Point, the clipper brig *Frolic* and the fast Baltimore schooner *Dart*. Both of the company's new American opium clippers arrived in China in 1844, after Kearny's departure.[48]

Kearny, in the meantime, having pushed his countrymen's claims as far as he could, watered his ship at Amoy and finally departed Chinese waters on 22 May 1843, sailing east once again, this time across the broad Pacific Ocean, his destination the Sandwich Islands, now the state of Hawaii. China did not make the commitment to a most-favored nation clause in the treaty with Great Britain, extending their gains to all foreigners, until 1 August, more than two months following *Constellation*'s departure. Nevertheless, Congress awarded Commodore Kearny credit for nurturing this important diplomatic event into existence. Before departing, Kearny shot one final verbal blast across the bow of one of the American vessels, caught loaded with opium. Informed that Englishmen owned the U.S.–registered schooner *Ariel*, Kearny seized her and took her register, which he invalidated, turning the schooner's papers over to the American vice consul, himself an opium trader. Then, the commodore forced *Ariel*'s master to relinquish his cargo of opium to Chinese authorities.[49]

Some weeks before his departure, Kearny wrote from Canton to his children of his satisfaction "that all of the objects of his cruise to China were now achieved and that he neither expected to be hanged or shot by sentence of Court Martial." He continued to josh them, stating that it could be possible that he would be tried as a wizard for finding his way home after sending him out in a ship unfit for service anywhere. Though Kearny made light of his problems with *Constellation*, which included the ship's troublesome rigging and an advanced leaking condition caused as caulk worked its way from between topside planks, a process that continued beyond Capetown, his ship covered the distance, 6,409 miles between Amoy and Honolulu, in forty-seven days, an average speed of 5.68 knots per hour.[50]

Upon arrival at Oahu, Kearny found one of Her Majesty's Royal Navy captains urging King Kamehameha III to cede his island kingdom to Great Britain. The serious nature of British intent fell to the level of diplomatic farce when the king incarcerated several of *Constellation*'s seamen for "horse racing through the streets of Honolulu." With the British flag then flying above the island fort, Kearny protested that Kamehameha had lost his right to imprison an American citizen as long as his kingdom remained under British control. Kamehameha notified the American commander that the British captain, Right Honorable Lord George Paulet, had pressured him to cede the islands to him, but he, the king, did it only as he felt confident that he would get them back. However, realizing the serious nature of his act, the king notified Kearny that because of abrogation of local laws, he had, in effect changed his mind about ceding his islands to Lord Paulet.[51]

Constellation departed the Sandwich Islands 22 August for Monterey, California, at that time Mexican territory. The historic ship covered the distance between Hawaii and Monterey in eighteen days, averaging 6.25 knots. Then, on the long leg between Monterey and Valparaiso (8,007 nautical miles) *Constellation* covered the distance in sixty-one days, averaging a speed of five and a half knots. After a brief stopover for water and supplies at Rio de Janeiro, the tired ship and crew dropped anchor in Hampton Roads 9 May 1844, after about three years at sea, including more than a year in Chinese waters. Commodore Kearny informed the secretary of the navy that he chose to end the cruise at Norfolk because of unfavorable winds and a bad set of sails.[52]

Constellation, under tow of steamers *Star* and *Engineer*, came up to Gosport Navy Yard on 10 May and moored abreast of Ship House B. Between 12 and 17 May, Kearny's crew stripped the ship of stores, rigging, and provisions and on 18 May 1844 Commodore Kearny relinquished command of *Constellation* to Commandant Wilkinson of the Gosport Navy Yard. On 22 May the yard removed an anchor (6,820 pounds) from the ship while she was moored at Ship House B. Laborers removed various sea rations and provisions from the ship 25 May and on 28 May, another anchor (3,800 pounds) as well as landing two guns, an 18-pounder and one 12-pounder, both English-made. The work removing *Constellation*'s anchors continued through 30 May. On 1 June, laborers landed some of the ship's furniture and placed it in the South Wing of Ship House B. Two days later the yard hauled her off the Ship House B Wharf and moored the ship near St. Helena's Island. A yard crew landed two bower anchors, a stream anchor, and four kedge anchors from *Constellation* on 17 June, and two days later her extra spars were landed and sent over to the yard. On 4 July 1844, the sixty-eighth year of independence, *Constellation* saluted the occasion with seventeen guns. Between 18 May 1844 and 8 July 1845, *Constellation* served as a receiving ship.[53]

A call for reorganization of naval affairs and the end of labor problems that plagued navy yards placed the navy in the public eye in 1845. There were questions about the need for public yards and questions concerning the ability of the United States Navy to fight the next war, given the state of ship design and the quality and cost of new construction. What kinds of new ships should be built, what should be done with old ships, the rising costs of both, and the competence of senior officers to solve these problems—these controversies rose to a boiling point during the years *Constellation* circumnavigated the globe, but were still on the table to be resolved. Actually, following *Constellation*'s departure for the Far East in December 1840, she became part of the controversy in an article that criticized the Board of Commissioners for selecting the aged vessel as the flagship of the East Indies Squadron.[54]

Following several years of debate devoted to the condition of the United States Navy and its ability to fight a war against the Royal Navy—always the measure of naval strength—the forces of reform gained an upper hand, though progress advanced slowly. Problems in the yards—exclusion of senior officers from naval administration, the need to reform Navy Rules and Regulations to guarantee the rights of seamen, and the planned changeover from sail to steam—gained increased attention. The navy began to take into serious consideration the future of its three historic frigates. *Constellation,* a ship badly prepared for her recently completed, remarkable cruise, played an important role in changes that by 1845 advanced beyond the discussion stage.

Without doubt, the decision of Congress in 1842 to dump the Board of Commissioners in favor of a system of bureaus headed by individuals represented the most important effort to reform navy administration. The move restored direct vertical control of the navy establishment to the secretary of the navy. In addition, it replaced a faceless board with individually accountable bureau chiefs who reported directly to the secretary of the navy. Unfortunately secretaries came and left frequently, and many served with neither experience in naval affairs nor the time to analyze the traditional baggage the navy carried. The drive to create a leaner organization rose like waves hitting a beach, only to fall back again.[55]

Reform relinquished its position to the expediency of mobilization as a result of several minor foreign affairs matters blown up by politicians and the press.

Diverting attention from navy reforms, the government became preoccupied with a spat with France over war claims from the previous century, squabbles with Great Britain over the country's eastern and western boundaries with Canada, and an embarrassing conflict with Mexico. These pumped-up issues allowed the federal government to push through Congress a number of emergency programs that delayed for another decade many of the reforms that once seemed at hand.

Blocks of legislators in Congress resisted radical changes in the navy establishment, particularly the nation's policy of building and repairing ships in public navy yards. Legislators from Atlantic and Gulf states, voting as a unit on maritime and naval affairs, remained solidly enthroned as guardians of the untouchable position of the navy's public yards. As a result of their benevolence, established by legislative acts passed earlier in the century, pronavalists, linked together by common interests, voted their opposition to reform. Nevertheless, heard more often as time passed, reformists called for better balance between the old and largely obsolescent navy and new technology as voiced by a bright group of engineers, inventors, and scientists whose vision of the next war already existed on their drafting tables.

Even as the old navy finished, equipped, and launched new sail-powered ships that sat for twenty years or more in stocks and repaired even older ones, the number of steamships authorized increased in numbers. Congress, though partially immobilized by its split, could not resist voting out appropriations for new ships. But, in a state of constant denial, Congress refused to increase the size of the navy fleet in commission and the number of men in uniform. In no better manner could the current situation in Washington be expressed than by the act of 17 June 1844 which limited the "whole number of petty officers & seamen, ordinary seamen, lands men, and boys, in the naval service" to seventy-five hundred.[56]

The fact that after 1844 the navy took all ships of the line out of commission may be considered reform. The navy commissioned the newly designed frigate-44 *Congress* and launched four other large frigates, these taken out of stocks after almost three decades: U.S. Frigates *Raritan, Cumberland, Savannah,* and *St. Lawrence.* Though obsolete, all were launched and equipped under political pressure for mobilization. On the other hand, the navy condemned and broke up sloop of war *Natchez,* frigates *Guerrière, Java,* and *Hudson,* and ship of the line *Washington,* upping the score of reformists. Congress authorized appropriations for several steam-powered warships: *Missouri, Mississippi, Princeton, Union,* and *Allegheny.*

Responding to objections from its shipyard constituents, Congress turned its back on a movement within its chambers that would have allowed the construction of public vessels in private yards. To further ease the flow of public funds between new construction and repairs (and to avoid shutdowns at yards such as the one that affected *Constellation* in 1839), Congress reverted to a privilege granted the executive branch in 1840 and retracted in 1842 when in 1844 it authorized once again consolidation of appropriated funds for new construction and repairs. The legislators also rejected Harry Bluff's (M. F. Maury's) suggestion that the navy turn away from its dependence on live oak, substituting a policy of using less expensive materials such as white oak to construct new ships which were intended to last only a few years. Finally, and of great importance to the physical history of USF *Constellation*, Congress retracted the executive order issued by President Jackson and restored to the navy authority to rebuild ships without seeking congressional approval.[57]

The navy continued to construct new sail-only vessels after 1840, including sloop of war *Saratoga* and brigs *Bainbridge, Truxtun,* and *Somers.* Legislators passed legislation for the last all-sail ships built for the United States Navy in 1843, authorizing six large first-class sloops of war. The navy, as it had under Rodgers, ordered one ship built at each navy yard and six drafts prepared by six naval constructors. All constructors drew their designs from older models; American naval constructors ignored advances in warship design currently favored by the Royal Navy, particularly the Symmonds Plans, which produced fast sloops of war like HMS *Rover*, featuring increased breadth and lighter draft. USS *Germantown*, drafted by John Lenthall at Philadelphia Navy Yard, measured 150 feet between perpendiculars with a breadth of 36 feet. *Rover's* dimensions were 115 feet between perpendiculars with a breadth only one-half foot less than *Germantown.* The other five ships built under the last legislation for sailing ships were USS *Portsmouth, Plymouth, Albany, St. Marys,* and *Jamestown.*[58]

Germantown, authorized in 1843 and built in 1846, had the distinction of being the last new sailing ship designed, built, and commissioned for the United States Navy. John Lenthall, her constructor, made this declaration, so important to the reconstruction of the story of USS *Constellation,* in the navy annual report of 1854, at the time he supervised the conversion of that historic ship from frigate to sloop of war.[59]

Following service as a receiving ship, which lasted until 8 July 1845, the navy took *Constellation* out of active service and began to prepare the ship for ordinary pending a decision on the fate of the navy's first frigates: *Constellation, United States,* and *Constitution.*[60] Once *Constellation* was placed under jurisdiction of navy personnel assigned to ordinary, the yard commenced to remove all the ship's provisions and equipment. An ordinary crew assigned to the ship hauled her over to the yard's main shears, where laborers took out her iron tanks and wooden casks and placed them in the yard's tank house. Laborers landed her chain cables and unstepped her three masts, placing them on the wharf pending removal to the mast shed. On 22 July, according to the yard's log, *Constellation* finished landing ballast. The crew hauled her off the wharf and secured the ship to moorings.[61]

Baltimore newspapers, alert for news of *Constellation,* became aware of the navy's plans to convert the ship from sail to steam power, though when the news first broke no such order existed.[62] *Niles Register* picked up on the story and proceeded to lecture the navy on the achievements of America's favorite frigate that "were never eclipsed, even by the subsequent achievements of 'Old Ironsides' herself." Quoting the *National Intelligencer,* Baltimore's famous weekly journal, Niles pointed out that if the project (providing her with steam engines) failed, the American people would not readily excuse any act which sheared from *Constellation* the laurels she so gallantly earned in the early days of our glorious navy. Niles reminded the government of the strong emotional attachment of the country to its first frigates, *United States, Constitution,* and *Constellation,* which served as living links to the early days of a young nation attacked on all sides by the maritime empires of Europe. The navy received a strong indication that *Constellation* had become a national shrine.[63]

On instructions from George Bancroft, secretary of the navy, Capt. Robert F. Stockton received orders from the Bureau of Construction, Equipment, and Repairs to estimate the cost of manufacturing and fitting *Constellation* with engines, boilers, and a propeller. The secretary also ordered Samuel Humphreys, still chief naval constructor, to Norfolk to survey the condition of the ship and estimate the cost of alterations to accommodate the new steam-generating equipment. Only at that time did the yard air her hull out and place the ship in ordinary. Humphreys arrived in mid-July 1845 and with Foster Rhodes, the naval constructor assigned to Gosport, conducted a survey.[64]

Humphreys' report concluded that *Constellation*'s obsolescence made her conversion particularly expensive. Moreover, she would require lengthening sixty feet, rather than twenty-seven feet as suggested by Stockton, in order to accommodate an engine room and space for coal. These additions added substantially to the weight of the converted ship. While not recommending against the conversion of the sailing ship to steam power, Humphreys, an experienced bureaucrat, suggested it would cost far less to razee her as a sloop of war. The cost of Stockton's project, including completely rebuilding the ship, could have reached an amount in excess of $400,000 based on Humphreys' and Stockton's estimates. The project died, but Humphreys' suggestion that perhaps the best and most economical way to save the historic ship would be to modify her into a sloop of war, fitted out with the navy's most modern cannons, began to take on a life of its own.[65]

Prior to the rush of activity in July 1845 to determine if *Constellation* should be given engines and a propeller, yard crews had not begun stripping her hull according to navy rules for preparing ships placed in ordinary. It was not until a year later that labor assigned to ships in ordinary stripped *Constellation* of planks, ceiling, masts, and bulkheads. After scrapping her topsides, navy officers assigned to ordinary examined her timbers for rot. That report has not survived.[66]

Charles Skinner, chief of the Bureau of Construction, Equipment, and Repair, demonstrated that he did not completely share the sentimental feelings of the nation for its historic ships when he floated the idea in the navy's annual report for 1850 that U.S. Frigates *United States, Constitution,* and *Constellation* should no longer be fitted for sea service. He suggested that the first two be replaced by *Sabine* and *Santee* and that the old frigates, including *Constellation,* should be returned to the port where they were first built.[67]

Skinner followed up that recommendation in the annual report with a letter to Secretary Graham dated 25 February 1851 in which he changed his strategy, pointing out that *Constitution* could be returned to sea for a trivial cost but *United States* and *Constellation* required thorough repairs to fit them for service. Rather than spending large sums on *United States,* Skinner recommended to the secretary that the money be used to modernize, equip, and launch *Santee,* which had been in stocks for longer than two decades. He made no further recommendation concerning *Constellation* in that letter. Graham did not act on Skinner's recommendation, but the letter became another step in a progression of recommendations and reports that preceded the selection of a course of action that determined the futures of the three original frigates. *Constitution* returned to sea duty in 1852, *United States* and *Constellation* remained in ordinary, and Congress failed to appropriate funds to modify *Santee* and *Sabine* for several more years.[68]

Another proposal to convert the navy's sailing frigates to steam, though not directly concerning *Constellation,* originated with Francis Grice in 1851. The naval constructor was then stationed at the Philadelphia Navy Yard. John Lenthall, having replaced Samuel Humphreys as chief constructor, advised against Grice's proposal, which dealt specifically with the conversion of the first-class frigates *Santee* and *Sabine* to steam-powered frigates; Humphreys believed that the conversion could fail. Grice did not let go of his project and submitted a model of his modified frigate to Captain Skinner, who continued as chief of the Bureau of Construction, Equipment, and Repair through 1851.[69]

Skinner presented Grice's proposal to a board of senior officers consisting of Charles Morris, Lewis Warrington, and Joseph Smith, who rejected outright the proposed conversions, commenting that "although steam propellers may be advantageously combined with sails for vessels, it can only be well done in vessels built expressly for such a combination." The board's rejection of Grice's suggestion meant that, after decades, the fate of first-class frigates *Santee* and *Sabine,* in stocks with hulls complete, but in many aspects, already obsolete, had yet to be determined.

With attention now directed on them in the annual report of 1851, the future of those two frigates became linked to the fate of *Constellation* and the other historic frigates. Old laws still limited the number of navy ships of each class, and Congress had recently passed legislation limiting navy personnel to seventy-five hundred men.[70]

Yet another proposal came to the secretary's attention. Capt. Silas H. Stringham, commandant of Gosport Navy Yard, proposed a new scheme for converting *Constellation,* this time lengthening her from about 164 feet to 240 feet overall. Bureau Chief Skinner forwarded the proposal to John Lenthall, who responded in a letter dated 18 December 1851 and frequently quoted since. Lenthall pointed out to Skinner that to rebuild *Constellation* according to Captain Stringham's suggestions, in addition to extending her length to 240 feet, the second-class frigate's other new dimensions would have to be changed to 58 feet in breadth and 41 feet in depth. After providing a summary of *Constellation*'s previous repairs, Lenthall suggested, as his predecessor had, that "if the ancient renown of this ship makes it desirable to retain her, the plan heretofore under consideration of the Bureau seems well adapted to carrying it out." After once again pointing out the ship's reputation for instability, Lenthall recommended that "with a light spar deck and heavy armament on the gun deck, from an inferior ship of a higher class, she will become the first of a lower class and always be a formidable vessel."[71]

The navy rejected Captain Stringham's proposal as it had all previous ones to convert sailing ships to steam power. The bureaucratic process by which the fate of the nation's first frigates would be settled gradually came into focus. When Bureau Chief Skinner passed Lenthall's suggestions to Secretary Graham, they were accompanied by his recommendation that "if the *Constitution* [*sic, Constellation*] is worthy of repair, the first disposition would be to convert her into a sloop of war with a battery of heavy guns." With Lenthall's recommendations attached, Skinner's letter to Graham established within the naval establishment the foundation of a policy concerning the future of *Constellation*. From December 1851 forward no official documents deviated from the position that the Bureau of Construction, Equipment, and Repair put forward 19 December 1851. During the period between that date and November 1852 when *Constellation* left ordinary, the recommendation passed through the executive branch and Congress.[72]

By the middle of the nineteenth century, the United States Navy stood committed to steam. Older sailing ships were broken up or sold rather than repaired in many cases. Ships of the line were no longer in commission, and razeed vessels replaced obsolete ships to accommodate the new shell guns. Expensive rebuilding of older sailing vessels became rarer, though the rebuilding of USS *Vandalia* proved to be a noticeable exception. She is important to *Constellation*'s story because, without fanfare, then or later, this ship was redrafted and her length increased thirteen feet at the dead flat. No one ever called *Vandalia* a new ship following the modifications, which were drafted by Samuel Hart at Gosport in 1849. This was accomplished just four years before the rebuild of *Constellation* at the same navy yard. Though the records of her rebuild are more clearly documented than similar work done to ships such as *Vandalia*,[73] it remains a disturbing fact that *Constellation*'s rebuild became the subject of controversy.

Eight

FROM FRIGATE TO RAZEE-SLOOP OF WAR

ollowing the commissioning of the navy's last new sailing ship, USS *Germantown,* in 1846, the Navy Department began to consider proposals to modernize its aged sailing fleet. Several plans came before the department to modify frigates, including *Constellation,* to steam power in order to prolong their usefulness. As a result of this attention, preliminary proposals emerged concerning the future of the service's three historic ships. *Constitution,* though she required still another rebuild in 1858–60, would be retained in service on limited duty as a school ship, a decision not publicly debated before 1852. *United States,* evidently having lost the strong political backing of the Decatur-Rodgers clique, deteriorated in ordinary, out of sight and soon beyond repair, a situation that became irreversible after *Santee* took her place on the navy's register. In the end, the navy modernized only *Constellation.*[1]

The order to repair *Constellation* came following policy discussions that took place early in 1852, before Secretary of the Navy John Pendleton Kennedy replaced William A. Graham. A proposal by Capt. Charles W. Skinner, chief of the Bureau of Construction, Equipment, and Repair, to Secretary Graham suggested that the best solution for *Constellation*'s current plight, if she were to be retained, would be to modernize her and reduce her in rate to a sloop of war. Skinner, acting on advice received from chief constructor John Lenthall, informed the secretary that if *Constellation* "is worthy of repair, the first disposition would be to convert her into a sloop of war with a battery of heavy guns."[2]

Skinner followed up his December 1851 letter to Graham with another a month later in which he detailed the bureau's recommendations for *Constellation* in more specific terms. He referred Graham to his comments in the navy's annual report of 1850, where he suggested that U.S. Frigates *United States, Constitution,* and *Constellation,* all built in 1797, no longer be fitted for sea because the aging ships frequently needed extensive repairs. In his January 1852 letter Skinner moved beyond that suggestion, pointing out that a recent survey on *United States,* which had been repaired in 1841 and 1846, estimated the cost of new repairs at $152,000; since she had not been opened up, Skinner added, that figure would prove conservative. *Constitution's* repairs totaled $198,617 in 1848 and at the end of her current cruise another extensive overhaul would be required.[3]

In reference to *Constellation,* Skinner informed Graham that to prepare her for service as a frigate would require large outlays. In view of existing circumstances, the bureau recommended that the frigates *Sabine* at New York and *Santee* at Portsmouth, New Hampshire, which had been on stocks since 1822 and 1820, respectively, be completed to take the place of *United States* and *Constellation.* He recommended that *Constellation,* "being a small frigate mounting 18-pounders, may be razeed and made as an efficient sloop of war." Skinner reminded Graham "that the entire number of sloops of war belonging to [authorized for] the Navy are now employed with one exception and that one [*Fairfield*] could be prepared for service at an expense equal perhaps to a new ship." Skinner devoted the remainder of his letter to recommendations for new ships, steam and sail, although Congress never authorized new sailing warships again. This letter became the foundation of the policy under which the new secretary, John P. Kennedy, and the newly appointed chief of the Bureau of Construction, Equipment, and Repair, Capt. W. Bradford Shubrick, issued orders to the commandant of Gosport Navy Yard in November 1852 to take *Constellation* out of ordinary and commence repairs.[4]

Between January 1852, when Skinner promulgated his bureau's policy on *Constellation's* future, and 3 November 1852, when Gosport Navy Yard took the ship out of ordinary, the Navy Department received another proposal on the subject of converting *Constellation* to steam power. Though the issue seemed settled when a congressman forwarded Gosport Iron Works' inquiry to Kennedy, the new secretary asked Captain Shubrick to outline the navy's position on converting *Constellation* or any other sailing vessel to steam. Shubrick informed Kennedy in a letter dated 18 August 1852 that the department, after considerable deliberation, had concluded that it would prove no costlier to build new vessels than to alter *Constellation* or any other sailing warships by installing steam engines.[5]

John Pendleton Kennedy of Maryland held the cabinet post of secretary of the navy between 26 July 1852 and 3 March 1853, the final months of President Millard Fillmore's administration. He replaced Graham, who resigned to run for vice president of the United States on the Whig ticket with Gen. Winfield Scott. Kennedy, a native of Baltimore, though trained as a lawyer, adapted to the broader life of an intellectual. He became a nationally admired author, friend of the high and mighty, congressman, and speaker of the Maryland House of Delegates, and was described by his admirers as a friendly man of worldly interests. Once appointed secretary, he gave constant and thoughtful attention to the navy's disarray and low morale, so obvious to outsiders in 1852.[6]

Because of the brief period he held his office, Kennedy's 1852 annual report is the major document by which he provided the government with a blueprint for the navy's future and the principal record of his abbreviated term. His sparse official correspondence never mentioned the U.S. Frigate *Constellation*, and yet her name appears in his only annual report several times. No orders concerning her removal from ordinary survive, yet she was removed on his watch. Because the process that led to *Constellation*'s repairs began under Kennedy's leadership, something about this intelligent Marylander may be learned from a letter to his wife. He wrote the following sentence in the free-flowing style of a man of letters: "I like it. I like the stir and command and importance of things, to be handling frigates like toys, and disposing of men and guns, as if I had them in my hand."[7]

In the sparse records relating to Kennedy's accomplishments during the short period he handled naval affairs, one set of related documents survive which link this prominent Marylander to the fate of the historic Fells Point–built ship, *Constellation*. Kennedy's role, along with that played by his chief of the Bureau of Construction, Equipment, and Repair, Captain Shubrick, is documented in an exchange of letters between them and in correspondence between the U.S. Senate and President Fillmore's administration relating to Navy Department appropriations. These documents, supplemented by Kennedy's annual report of 1852, outline in a definitive manner the course of action taken by the Navy Department that year and the role played by the two men as they initiated the process that led to *Constellation*'s removal from ordinary for repair. There are no surviving orders issued to the commandant at Gosport to start repairs. Shubrick's orders to John Lenthall to make the drafts to modernize, modify, and rebuild are no longer in the bureau's records. However, proof that Kennedy initiated the action that saved the ship that was so highly revered by the navy, the American public, and obviously, by Kennedy's Maryland neighbors, is clearly documented.[8]

The Senate passed and dispatched to President Fillmore on 26 August 1852 a resolution that requested the president "to cause to be laid before the Senate at the commencement of the next session, with the Annual Reports of the Heads of the Departments and the accompanying reports of the Chiefs of Bureau, an abstract or compendium, also, of said last named reports." A second paragraph of the resolution asked for a similar compendium of the reports of the secretary of the treasury on Finances and Commerce and Navigation, together with Treasury's full report, these to facilitate the preparation of a compendium of annual reports. By this resolution, the Senate informed the Fillmore administration of its determination to gain advance knowledge of the principal new projects of all executive department bureaus so that legislators could calculate the financial effect of these new projects on the government's finances by comparing their estimated costs against projected increases in revenues, most of which the government generated from taxes on foreign commerce.[9]

On 19 October 1852 President Fillmore, through his secretary of state, transmitted a copy of the Senate resolution of 26 August 1852 to Kennedy, directing him "to cause to be laid before the Senate at the next session of Congress, abstracts of the chiefs of Navy bureaus as ordered by the resolution."[10] Kennedy prepared his annual report, dated 4 December 1852, signed it, and shortly thereafter distributed it throughout the executive department, to Congress, and through the press to the American people. In his only annual report, Kennedy did not cover repairs planned for individual ships in his State of the Navy summary except to suggest that the frigates *Santee* and *Sabine* should be modernized and launched.[11] Rather, he deferred those details to the report of the chief of the Bureau of Construction, Equipment, and Repair, Captain Shubrick, who dealt specifically with the navy's recommendations for *Constellation* and other matters as well as with the compendium ordered by the Senate resolution of 26 August.[12]

In this manner, Kennedy directed Congress's attention to the bureau's report, in which Captain Shubrick included in budget estimates for fiscal 1853–54 a request for an unspecified amount to fund the repair of *Constellation* (and *Franklin*). Specific references to *Constellation* appeared in Shubrick's report on page 350 as an index or abstract. They appeared again on page 351 and a third time on page 630, where the report presented the abstracts or compendia of the chiefs of the bureaus' requests for increases in funding, as required by the Senate resolution of of 26 August 1852. In the abstract prepared for his bureau, Shubrick specifically requested an increase in funds for fiscal 1853 for repairs to *Constellation*.[13]

After Captain Shubrick directed Congress's attention to the abstract or compendium by means of the index in his report, he added on page 351 his general proposals to modernize obsolete ships. He proposed that it would be sound economy to discontinue the use of some of the navy's oldest ships, and introduce others in their stead by launching the two frigates, *Santee* and *Sabine,* following modernization. He explained that these frigates were now inferior and progress in the technology of steam power and modern armament made them of little value in their present condition. Shubrick stated that "provision has been made in the estimate [of expenditures for fiscal 1853–54] for repairing *Franklin,* 74, reducing her to a razee of fifty guns, and *Constellation,* frigate of thirty-six guns, reducing her to a sloop of war, by which two valuable cruising vessels would be made available."

Here, then, are the contents of Shubrick's report containing the navy's specific request for funds to repair *Constellation.* Though Shubrick did not compare *Santee* and *Sabine* to *Constellation,* the armament of all three ships made them equally inferior, as in addition to their unseaworthy state of repair, obsolescence made all three useless as warships. At this time the fates of *Constellation, Santee,* and *Sabine* became interwoven, not only through the strategy of replacing *United States* and *Constellation* on the navy's roster of frigates with *Santee* and *Sabine,* but as a result of the similar manner in which chief constructor and later bureau chief John Lenthall modernized the hull of each ship to make them useful as warships. Or, to put it another way, Lenthall adapted the principal modifications used to modernize *Constellation* in making the changes in length and other alterations he drafted for *Santee* and *Sabine.*

Shubrick's report recommended that Congress authorize six new steam warships rather than three steam and three sailing ships as the navy proposed in the 1851 annual report. Thus, regarding new ships for the navy, Kennedy's Navy Department fully committed the service to steam-powered warships in 1852, months before repairs on *Constellation* commenced.[14]

Under the heading of Document No. 16 on page 630 of Kennedy's annual report, the abstracts or compendia of three bureau chiefs as required by the resolution of 26 August appeared, including that of the chief of the Bureau of Construction, Equipment, and Repair. Shubrick's report referred to the employment of petty officers and seamen, the estimate for which is the same as for the year preceding, and to the estimate for wear and tear of vessels, which had been increased and assigned reasons for the increase; it also recommended an increase in the number of ships, as well as "the repairing of the *Franklin*-74 and *Constellation,* frigate."[15] Of course, it is possible that a change in policy at a later date superseded Kennedy's recommendations in the annual report for 1852, or that subsequent orders countermanded Kennedy's, initiating repairs to *Constellation.* As a matter of fact, the navy never issued orders to razee *Franklin,* as the navy broke her up and built a new *Franklin,* one of six steamships which Shubrick requested in Kennedy's 1852 report and which Congress authorized in 1854. But the important aspect of Kennedy's advance notification to Congress concerning the navy's intention to repair *Constellation* is that no charge of secrecy as to its plans can be levied against the department.[16]

The circumstances surrounding the removal of *Constellation* from ordinary in late 1852 on verbal orders originating with Secretary Kennedy and passed to Gosport Navy Yard by Captain Shubrick progressed in a succession of publicized events. By the time Kennedy's recommendations to repair *Constellation* appeared in his report in early December 1852, Gosport Navy Yard had already removed the ship from ordinary and commenced taking out ballast and her iron tanks in preparation for hauling her out. On 23 February 1853, the date that yard workers hauled out *Constellation,* Kennedy still held office at the Navy Department.

Plans to repair *Constellation* could have changed over the winter of 1853 as work dismantling her did not commence until after Kennedy turned over his office to his successor, James C. Dobbin, in early March 1853. However, there is nothing in the well-documented progression of events that followed to suggest any change in policy by the new administration. To the contrary, Secretary Dobbin's first annual report, issued nine months later at the end of 1853, confirmed a continuance of *Constellation*'s repairs at Gosport Navy Yard.

Samuel Hartt, the first civilian chief of the Bureau of Construction, Equipment, and Repair, in his section of Secretary Dobbin's annual report for 1853, published 6 December 1853, seven months after repairs on *Constellation* commenced, stated that "the frigates *Macedonian* and the *Constellation* have been razeed to first-class sloops of war, and will be found arranged under that head. The former has been completed, and joined the squadron in the China seas; the latter is still in progress of repairs at the navy yard at Gosport."[17]

Though the facts leading up to the repair of *Constellation* are well documented, some historians have argued that the navy had a secret substitute ship policy and that the navy built a new *Constellation* in 1853–54. Contemporaneous navy documents furnish no support for the existence of a secret navy agenda. Rather, the navy's specific intent was to modernize the historic *Constellation,* incorporating in her design certain modifications of her hull to make her a valuable cruising ship and to repair her unseaworthy condition. Simply put, there is no documentary evidence allowing the conclusion that Kennedy and Shubrick, followed by Dobbin and Hartt, shared a secret agenda to destroy *Constellation* and build a new ship. Any action taken other than that reported to Congress in the navy's 1852 annual report, six months before the yard began to dismantle *Constellation,* is not supported by the official record.

Moreover, since the navy had already laid before the Senate its plans for *Constellation* and had requested the funds to repair her, any claim that the navy asked to divert repair funds to build a new sailing ship is unsound and illogical. The navy already had decided to build no more new sailing vessels, recognizing that steam power had proven essential for modern warships. Further, building a new *Constellation* conflicted with the representations contained in Kennedy's report, which neither Congress nor the navy ever reversed. Those with an interest in or knowledge of *Constellation* from 1852 forward believed that she should and would be repaired. Any hypothesis to the contrary is not supported by contemporary press accounts. Once the ship was modernized, the Navy Department satisfied two sets of constituents: traditionalists who viewed *Constellation* as one of the country's sacred shrines and technocrats who pushed to modernize and equip the navy's old ships with modern ordnance to make them useful warships, if only on a stop-gap basis.[18]

The navy, under the direction of Secretaries Kennedy and Dobbin, faced the problem of the historic ship's future after previous administrations spent years considering alternatives which usually were limited to either converting her to steam or modifying the ship in order for her to carry heavy armament. Building new sailing warships in 1852 never became a part of the equation and the argument that the navy requested repair funds for *Constellation* for the purpose of building a new sailing ship is not supported by events after Kennedy took office. Whether or not *Constellation* should be replaced with a new sailing ship was never the subject of debate. The navy moved forward from sail to steam power rather quickly after the bureau system replaced the Board of Commissioners, so Congress never authorized any new sail-on warships after 1843. Sentimental concern for saving the historic ship *Constellation* formed the foundation of the course of action upon which the navy made decisions in 1852 and acted on the following year.

From the end of 1852 into January 1853, laborers at Gosport Navy Yard unloaded ballast and tanks from *Constellation,* transporting her equipment to storage sheds. One method of determining if the navy repaired or destroyed the ship is related to the manner in which the naval officer in charge of ordinary or the yard's storekeepers disposed of equipment removed from a ship in ordinary. It is also related to the manner in which the Bureau of Construction, Equipment, and Repair, responsible for all ship equipment, handled equipment held in storage in the ship's name. After the commandant of Gosport Navy Yard placed *Constellation* in ordinary in 1846, some of the equipment removed from her remained under the control of the naval unit in charge of the ordinary; other equipment, such as iron tanks, anchors, chain cables, cordage and ballast, the yard stored with the facility or shop responsible for special equipment. When the yard hauled out the ship for repair, items of equipment such as furniture, sails, rigging, spars, boats, and casks passed from control of the officer in ordinary to the mechanics responsible for repairing and reconditioning it.

As in the case of *Constellation,* other reusable equipment—such as iron tanks and spars, property of the ship—would be taken out of storerooms and delivered to the shop charged with reconditioning or repairing it. If equipment did not pass survey, condemned materials would be turned over to the yard's storekeeper for salvage or auction and the ship's account credited for the value of the material. In this manner, the navy reduced the total cost of repairing the ship. As will be seen, *Constellation*'s equipment was returned to the ship directly from the shop servicing it and not through the storekeeper's inventory, as was new equipment from general stores. These procedures applied when a yard repaired a ship. New ships received new equipment.[19]

Gosport's clerk recorded in the log 17 January 1853 that the yard worked on *Constellation* that day, placing bilge ways under her in preparation for hauling the ship up the North Slip. Bilge ways were the lengthwise members of a cradle over which bilge blocks were hauled when yard workers winched the ship up the inclined ways onto the stone slip. A week later, Capt. Samuel Breese, commandant of Gosport Navy Yard, addressed a letter to Captain Shubrick at the Bureau of Construction, Equipment, and Repair in which he reported on the current situation concerning *Constellation* and enclosed with the letter "a drawing respecting *Constellation*."[20]

Correspondence received by the bureau from Gosport for the years 1853, 1854, and 1855, the years the yard repaired *Constellation,* is not at the National Archives, but summaries of the bureau's inbound letters survive. This log of inbound correspondence noted that the bureau received a drawing of *Constellation*'s keel 26 January 1853 from Gosport Navy Yard. Though there is disagreement concerning who prepared the drawing and what year it was made, there is a consensus that the drawing sent by Commandant Breese to Washington is the keel drawing identified in the holdings of the National Archives as Drawing No. 107-13-4A. Commandant Downes of the Boston Navy Yard ordered it prepared by the draftsman attached to that yard in 1839–40.[21] In the summary of another letter received at the Navy Department, Breese informed Capt. Joseph Smith, chief of the Bureau of Yards and Docks, that mechanics had yet to place crabs obtained from Washington in position to draw *Constellation* from the water.[22]

The *Portsmouth Daily Transcript* of 2 February 1853, in an article about *Constellation,* reported that the navy at one time proposed to add an auxiliary propeller to her, but objections by the general public overruled changes in the character of the ship given her historical connections. The article went on to say that *Constellation* had been on "rotten row" in ordinary for several years—where she might have stayed had not the present needs of the service compelled the department to have her repaired.[23] In the meantime, navy constructor E. H. Delano received a second drawing at Norfolk. This one, titled "Transverse Sections of the Frigate *Constellation* (107-13-4B)," provided master ship carpenters with up-to-date information concerning the historic ship's prior hull modifications. With drawings providing *Constellation*'s breadth and the hogged keel and the rebuilt bow, constructor Delano had the information carpenters required to build bridge ways and blocks to haul the ship out.[24]

After using the drawings of *Constellation*'s sections and take-offs in preparation for hauling the ship, Commandant Breese sent the transverse sections and bow drawings to the bureau for transmittal to John Lenthall, who as chief constructor drafted *Constellation*'s proposed modifications. Though the summary of the letter, sent to bureau chief Shubrick, does not specifically identify the drawings enclosed, it describes them as "showing the shape of *Constellation*."[25] Yard labor spent another week positioning the anchors for hauling out the ship.[26] On 22 February, sailing master Young noted in the Gosport log that eight overseers and 169 laborers made preparations to haul out the historic ship, as the yard used great care with this phase of the operation. That same day, the steamer *Engineer* towed *Constellation* from the wharf where she had previously discharged her tanks and ballast to the North Slip. The yard shut down at sunset.[27]

Constructor Edward Delano supervised the yard's workforce and carefully prepared to haul out the ship. The following day, eight overseers directing 153 laborers, and with all mechanics from different departments of the yard, working with the aid of capstans, hauled up *Constellation* on ways at the North Slip. Sail Master Young wrote in the yard's log that the operation was completed without incident at one o'clock in the afternoon and that Captain Breese gave everyone involved the rest of the day off. To expend this effort and expense on the dangerous and hard work of hauling the ship, only to destroy her, is not logical and contradicts the underlying reason for this operation. If the navy wanted a ship destroyed, breaking up the hull would have taken place on Rotten Row. And then there followed the unusual gesture of Commandant Breese giving those participating a half-day off. In a time of hard-nosed labor relations, such a spontaneous expression of gratitude could only be the result of a successful effort to save, not to destroy *Constellation*.[28]

In April, carpenters began to dismantle *Constellation*'s hull, first landing the last of her equipment, which consisted of the remainder of her ballast, a single iron tank, the ship's bell, and scrap metal taken from her hull. The storekeeper took the ballast into his stores and probably sent the iron tank to Washington Navy Yard for repair, both items remaining the property of the ship. Scrap taken into stores would be accumulated and a storekeeper would arrange transportation to the Washington Navy Yard, where it would be refined. Only the Bureau of Construction, Equipment, and Repair had authority over the disposal of the ballast, bell, and the iron tank, as this equipment remained the property of the ship even as the storekeeper took possession. If the equipment was surveyed and disposed of, storekeepers credited the value received, plus the value of all scrap recovered, for the ship's account.[29]

The *Portsmouth Daily Transcript* carried the story of successfully hauling *Constellation* the following day in its lead column, which read in part:

> Yesterday, the time-honored ship was hauled up on one of the slips in the Navy yard. She is to be razeed and converted into a first class sloop-of-war, and will be otherwise thoroughly and extensively repaired. The *Constellation* is a second-class frigate of thirty-six guns, and was launched at Baltimore in the year 1797, more than half a century ago. Her

timbers are very rotten, and for the most part will have to be replaced with new; and her model will no doubt, require some alteration to confirm somewhat with ships of more recent construction.[30]

The community of Portsmouth, home of Gosport Navy Yard, at that time employer of more than one thousand men, had other matters to ponder as March approached. President Fillmore's Whigs were about to be replaced by the new Democratic Party president, Franklin Pierce. Everyone at the yard anticipated a clean sweep of Whigs out of office, yard clerks' and master mechanics' jobs being part of a national political spoils system. In Washington, James C. Dobbin immediately replaced Kennedy as secretary of the navy as the new party began to work down the pecking order, ultimately reaching the shipyard's storekeeper. Dobbin appointed Robert M. Boykin to that job on 25 April, a couple of days after appointing John L. Porter master shipwright in the yard. Constructor Edward H. Delano placed Porter in charge of rebuilding *Constellation*'s hull. The fallout resulting from the replacement of the yard's civilian mechanics, as well as a delay in receiving Lenthall's drafts, postponed the start of repairs and hauling of timber out of the yard's stockpiles.[31]

Following Secretary Dobbin's swearing-in ceremony, the chief of the Bureau of Construction, Equipment, and Repair, Captain Shubrick, offered his resignation. His subsequent removal came as a result of new legislation by Congress, the legislators having acted on a long-dormant recommendation of Lt. Matthew Maury (and others) which required civilian navy constructors rather than naval officers to head the Bureau of Construction, Equipment, and Repair. The process of replacing Captain Shubrick took several months, and the president did not appoint Samuel Hartt, the first civilian chief of the bureau, until 1 July 1853.[32]

Captain Shubrick arrived at Gosport 25 April and visited the yard two days.[33] By then, expenditures charged to *Constellation* for taking her out of ordinary, removing the remaining equipment on board, preparing the ship's hull for dismantling, and hauling her out 23 February totaled $20,328.47.[34]

At about the same time that the navy made preparations to dismantle *Constellation*, Gosport Navy Yard broke up the condemned sloop of war, USS *Fairfield*. As the cost to repair *Fairfield* would have equaled the cost of a new ship, Secretary Kennedy advised the president to break her up. As an effect of this action, there would be room for *Constellation* on the roster of sloops of war. When *Fairfield* did not sell at auction for the minimum price set, the navy dismantled her, salvaging some materials and condemning for auction the items surveyed as unsuitable. Navy regulations covered each phase of the condemnation procedure, including publicizing the ship's auction and obtaining the final grant of authority to dispose of a navy ship, which by law, only the president of the United States could issue.

Constructor Delano notified Commandant Breese on 19 March 1853 of *Fairfield*'s demise, with a final tabulation of the cost of breaking her up and the proceeds gained from the sale and salvage of scrap and other items. If the navy had decided to destroy *Constellation,* too, and remove her from the navy register, such a decision, as provided for by Congress under section 5 of the act of 21 April 1806, would have required a written request from the secretary of the navy and written authorization signed by the president. Neither Kennedy nor Dobbin requested this authority, nor did Presidents Fillmore or Pierce ever sign such an order. Further, if that scenario did exist, the navy would follow procedures similar to those taken when the service condemned *Fairfield* and took her off the navy register of ships, including publicizing the sale of *Constellation.* This never happened.[35]

Workers proceeded to dismantle *Constellation*'s hull. No change of policy affecting *Constellation*'s future emerged under the new Pierce administration. Plank by plank, futtock by futtock, and floor by floor, carpenters stripped her rotten, hogged, and twisted hull, dismantling her plank, beams, and frame sections piece by piece. Carpenters reclaimed live oak floors and frame sections not weakened by borings made by old fastenings, setting aside sound timbers for reuse in the rebuilt hull. The master shipbuilder surveyed the salvaged timber, making the final decision as to which could be reused in *Constellation*'s hull. Laborers accumulated oak planks, yellow pine beams, and discarded timber not suitable for use in the ship, turning into the storekeeper materials surveyed and found unsuitable for reuse. The storekeeper accumulated the old timber after carpenters retrieved old iron and copper fastenings. Storekeepers received salvaged metal and arranged to transport it to the Washington Navy Yard for refining.[36] Laborers burned trash wood.[37]

Budget reductions to the bureau's Wear and Tear account for the two fiscal years falling between 1852 and 1854 as well as navy repair procedures required naval constructors to reuse sound timbers and other materials to repair ships, including *Constellation.* That this actually happened will be demonstrated later in this chapter. Because Lenthall did not materially alter the shape of *Constellation*'s midbody sections when he drafted her lines, workers reused sound floor and futtock pieces after some reshaping in the process of rebuilding her hull. The navy's chief constructor predicted in 1851 that if the navy made a decision to rebuild the ship, her floors would prove to be sound. He probably did not know then, having worked only in Philadelphia, that so many of *Constellation*'s futtocks had been replaced in 1814, 1829, and 1839.

Carpenters, as they worked on *Constellation*'s frame, reshaped old futtocks to molds cut to Lenthall's table of offsets. By these procedures the bureau gained the economies it sought in two ways: lower charges against the bureau's Wear and Tear account, and a savings in labor costs as carpenters shaped fewer molded pieces of

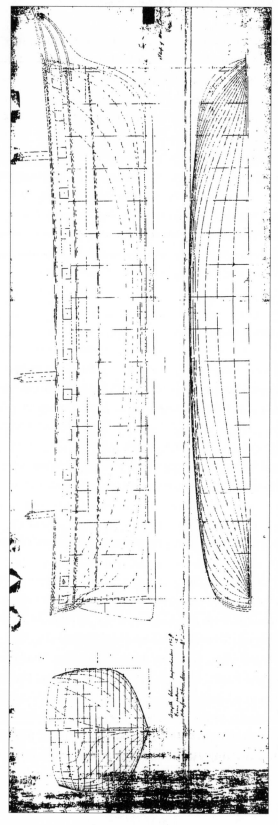

Figure 8.1. Sloop of war *Constellation* as redrafted by John Lenthall, June 1853 (original scale: five feet equals one inch). *National Archives*

promiscuous and framing timber out of the stockpile, most all of it originally cut for larger 44-gun frigates and ships of the line. Moreover, by spreading the fabrication of *Constellation*'s frame over seven months, the yard controlled the number of carpenters working on *Constellation*'s hull.[38] In addition to reusing floor pieces from her bottom, carpenters reshaped an unknown number of the old futtocks and other live oak pieces, many pieces new as recently as 1839.[39]

Once the iron-hard live oak timber was cut and delivered, the principal damage to it occured after installation, when carpenters replaced beams, planks, or other parts of a hull, a process that required backing out old fastenings from floor and futtocks. After repeated replacement of old fastenings, bolt holes enlarged and increased in number, weaking the joints in sections of the frame and creating serious structural defects, such as those Captain Kearny experienced when movement of *Constellation*'s frame and other structural members worked against her planked topsides in heavy seas, which caused the caulking between planks to work loose and the ship to leak.[40]

Chief Navy Constructor Lenthall requested the presence of Gosport's constructor, E. H. Delano, in Washington to assist with the preparation of building instructions for the modified ship. According to Young's log, yard labor commenced hauling out timber for *Constellation* 24 May 1853, coincidentally the same day that the ex-secretary, John P. Kennedy, visited the yard.[41] On 1 June, Delano left for Washington to assist Lenthall with the preparation of drafts for *Constellation*. The following day, the new secretary, James C. Dobbin, visited Gosport.

Using the shorthand language of the yard, Constructor Delano, back on the job 11 June, wrote the commandant of Gosport Navy Yard, Captain Breese, outlining the number of carpenters assigned to the "old" and "new" *Constellation*. During conversations and in informal yard communications and records, yard clerks, storekeepers, reporters, and others used various inexact expressions, such as "old" and "new" or "frigate" and "sloop of war" indiscriminately and frequently incorrectly as they worked or wrote about the ship and the repairs in progress at two locations.[42] Hauling out of live oak timber resumed 8 June and continued on and off through 15 June. Capt. Joseph Smith, chief of the Bureau of Yards and Docks, arrived 21 June. According to Young's log, the yard laid the "frigate" *Constellation*'s new keel 25 June 1853.[43]

An article in the *Norfolk Daily Southern Argus* 23 July described the timber used for *Constellation*'s keel and frame. The reporter pointed out that timber for the keel consisted of nine pieces of white oak logs, "all making about 176 feet in length, say 30 inches deep and siding size about 18 inches." The article mentioned that carpenters building the live oak frame described the characteristics of this timber as hard as iron and as curly and twisting as a bull's forehead. Gosport workers reportedly told the reporter that the live oak drawn out of stockpile for use in rebuilding *Constellation* had been seasoned in the yard's ponds and sheds more than twenty years, the white oak eighteen, and that the timber remained as fresh and sound as when the timber arrived in the yard.[44]

Documentary evidence cited to date confirms that the navy took *Constellation* out of ordinary to be repaired, and that after fifty-five years, much of that time spent at sea, Gosport's carpenters rebuilt the ship from the keel up. Replacing *Constellation*'s keel became necessary because her original keel was badly hogged and materially affected her sailing qualities during her last two major cruises. It became obvious to commanders of the ship as well as to navy constructors who surveyed her that age and a series of partial rebuilds had compromised the strength of the ship. The overall structural integrity of *Constellation*'s hull, consisting of floors and futtocks that constituted the frame of the ship, as well as other components such as keel and keelson, stanchions, waterways, beams, and ceiling, no longer functioned as a structural unit. Each major component of a ship's hull is designed to strengthen and reinforce other components of the structure; as a unit, along with the hull's outer skin, they provided strength and resistance when subjected to the extreme pressure of weather and sea.

With funds limited to an amount available from the navy's Wear and Tear account for repairs, and no special authorization of funds from Congress to rebuild the ship, nor any legislation to build or fund a new ship named *Constellation,* the conclusion is inescapable that the Navy Department, backed by two administrations, ordered Gosport Navy Yard to rebuild *Constellation*'s hull starting with a new keel.[45]

Internal procedures in Gosport Navy Yard that controlled the flow of materials for the repair of a ship as well as the assigned duties of the yard's navy and civilian personnel responsible for regulating yard activity and personnel are governed by Navy Department rules and regulations promulgated by the secretary of the navy after approval by Congress. Procedures in place for rebuilding *Constellation*'s hull consisted of those regulations and financial controls applicable under the heading of "Repairs," an entirely different set of procedures and rules than would control the yard's activities if Congress had authorized a new ship.

When Congress passed legislation authorizing new construction and provided the funding for one or more ships, the navy yards and the navy agents concerned, working under a set of rules set by the Bureau of Construction, Equipment, and Repair, charged expenditures to the special appropriation provided by that legislation. Moreover, a yard never charged the expenses of new ships to general account, "Increase, Repairs &c." but rather to the special appropriation for the new ship. On the other hand, in the case of *Constellation,* storekeepers charged materials and equipment as well as the cost of reconditioning and repairing equipment for

214

Constellation as deductions to the navy's "Increase, Repairs &c." account, adjusted by funds credited to it from the bureau's wear and tear appropriation, funded by Congress specifically for repairs. In this manner, the Navy and Treasury Departments' procedures, controlled by navy rules and regulations, separated new construction from repairs.[46]

In the case of *Constellation* in 1853, from a regulatory and organizational perspective, the yard made repairs to the ship, neither destroying an old one nor building a new one. As the yard was charged with repairing *Constellation,* when carpenters found sound materials suitable for reuse, they freely transferred reusable timber pieces to Ship House B from the site at North Slip as they dismantled the old hull. The transfer of salvaged frame pieces and other components between the two facilities, which constructor Delano complained about because of the distance between the locations, became unavoidable since the replacement of her keel made it necessary to rebuild her from the bottom up inside a ship house.

If Porter's men dismantled and rebuilt the hull at one location as normally took place when a ship is repaired, the claim that carpenters transferred no reusable materials between *Constellation*'s two sites would never have arisen. That is not to suggest that workers moved most or even a majority of old floors, futtocks, and beams to the rebuilding location, though evidence confirms the transfer of some pieces, and calculations of the amount and types of timber taken from stocks strongly support a conclusion that carpenters reused a significant percentage of the ship's old live oak timber pieces in *Constellation*'s rebuilt frame.[47] In an article dated 28 August 1854, the *Portsmouth Daily Transcript* reported that carpenters transferred live oak floors and futtocks directly from the old hull. They did so, according to the article, so that "some portion of the old ship [the hull] might remain in the new, four floor timbers, vis: M, O P, Q and four third futtock, vis: 9 and 10, S and P [which were molded from floors] were reserved, and now compose a small portion of her frame; they are perfectly sound and good."[48]

The article supports important aspects of *Constellation*'s rebuild. First, sound floor and futtock pieces were reused and transferred directly to the hull in the process of rebuilding the ship at Ship House B, thus fulfilling constructor Lenthall's prediction. Second, since Robert Boykin, the yard's chief storekeeper, did not record receiving wood materials from *Constellation*'s old hull and did not sign off any used timber pieces identified as coming from *Constellation,* the article confirms that materials moved freely between the two locations without intervention by the storekeeper's department. The article confirms that the yard's procedures governing repairs were not affected by two working locations; yard workers were logged in each day through the yard clerk's office, then assigned to repair a single ship: *Constellation.* After check-off and assignment, workers as well as materials for

Constellation moved freely between the old hull on North Slip and Ship House B. The logic of the two locations rests with the need to rebuild the ship on keel blocks from the bottom up. The commandant assigned the rebuilding to a covered shed as he planned to extend her repairs over the winter months.[49]

When building a wooden ship in the nineteenth century, navy and private shipyards normally followed a traditional construction and erection sequence. As one gang of ship carpenters sawed, cut scarfs, and bolted keel pieces on blocks, preparing the keel to support the frame and other components of the hull, carpenters began the process of selecting timber for the stern post assembly, the ship's stem, and her frame. The master shipwright announced the day he completed the keel and the yard clerk recorded that important date in his log. In the case of *Constellation*'s rebuild, an entry in the Gosport log noted that the yard laid her keel on 25 June 1853 in Ship House B.

Construction continued in a normal sequence and Gosport's chief clerk, sailing master Young, recorded that at 2:00 P.M., 29 August 1853, yard labor assigned to *Constellation* raised her stern post, and at 3:20 P.M. got it in place. Eight days passed. On 6 September he wrote that carpenters raised *Constellation*'s stem. No further information related to an erection sequence of the ship appears in the Gosport log until the entry marking her launch date, 26 August 1854.[50]

If carpenters followed the normal sequence, after raising *Constellation*'s stem, they proceeded to raise, support, and bolt her amidship square frames, followed by half frames, cant frames, transoms and stern assembly, hawse pieces and stem assembly, keelsons, beam ends and beams, knees, hull planking, deck planking, and lesser structures—in that order. This did not happen.[51]

An analysis of the Gosport storekeeper records confirms that carpenters assigned to *Constellation* did not make withdrawals from the yard's stockpile of live oak timber in advance of the time workers started to dismantle her hull. Floor and futtock pieces were neither shaped nor bolted into frames prior to the date carpenters commenced work preparing the new keel on blocks. Construction of her frame apparently progressed on a schedule related to the selection of live oak timber either from a stockpile or from the ship's old hull; the timber was then worked into floors and futtocks hewn to measurements in Lenthall's new table of offsets. The sequential order that master shipwright John Porter followed as he requisitioned materials for the new frame may be conceptualized by examining the apparent haphazard withdrawals of new live oak timber and other materials out of stores. The situation in Ship House B is inexplicable until one understands that Porter abandoned the normal building sequence, substituting an alternate set of procedures to comply with the requirements of the Bureau of Construction, Equipment, and Repair's building instructions.

Two primary considerations shaped the procedures adapted for the rebuilding of *Constellation*'s hull in 1853. The navy wanted to maintain public confidence that its plans to modernize and modify the ship did not disrupt or distort her historic heritage. Additionally, the chief constructor worked under orders from the Bureau of Construction, Equipment, and Repair that stressed the need to maintain economy, a result of a reduction of the navy's budget for fiscal 1853–54.[52]

On the other hand, had Lenthall striven only for economy, his instructions for her rebuild would have included a new, completely prefabricated frame for *Constellation,* and by this decision, he would wipe out the ship's material links to her historic origin. Gosport stockpiled no precut live oak frame pieces molded to her offsets, and the Bureau of Construction, Equipment, and Repair ordered no complete precut frame for *Constellation.*[53]

Carpenters, upon delivery of a ship's frame purchased in toto from timber contractors, assembled sections into individual frames without the need for extensive shaping of floor and futtock pieces. Then they hoisted the prefabricated frames into position on the keel, supported them, and bolted the complete construction into place with only a minimum amount of labor expense. A complete ship's frame could be raised in a matter of a few weeks. Though the initial cost of the complete frame exceeded the cost of unshaped promiscuous pieces, the elimination of waste wood and thousands of days of labor shaping individual floor and futtock pieces to the frame's offsets reduced the cost of labor of a complete prefabricated frame and of the total overall cost of finishing and erecting it.[54]

Almost every new ship built by the United States Navy following the War of 1812, as well as the rebuilt *Macedonian* and *Congress,* received new frames precut in advance by timber contractors. Time was not a factor for rebuilding *Constellation* so constructor Edward Delano could order a new frame and wait for delivery. If he had done so, he would have reduced the total cost of the hull. But, in compliance with instructions, carpenters built her frame, consisting of old and new timbers, over a period of seven months. This decision added thousands of days of labor as carpenters hewed old and new individual pieces of timber to Lenthall's offsets, increasing overall labor costs significantly. Moreover, the chief constructor of the Bureau of Construction, Equipment, and Repair made these decisions in 1853–54 following a four-year period during which by Lenthall's own estimates labor rates in navy yards increased 25 percent in four years. Though constructor Delano's men at Gosport worked under constraints in numbers employed daily repairing *Constellation* and in that manner controlled labor expenditures, the determining criterion for repairing the ship was the navy's determination to rebuild her hull with as many sound timber pieces as possible from the old frame. Otherwise the use of large quantities of promiscuous timber and framing pieces, almost all originally precut for ships of the line and 44-gun frigates,

Table 8.1. Live Oak Timber Drawn from Stockpile for Ships of the Line (74s)

Month (1853)	Promiscuous Timber Pieces	Framing Pieces
July (June)*	1,968 cu. ft.	1,398 cu. ft.
August	1,297 cu. ft.	none
September	1,802 cu. ft.	none
October	741 cu. ft.	none
November	2,022 cu. ft.	none
December	877 cu. ft.	none

Source: Gosport Storekeeper Returns, 1853–54, vol. 175, RG19, Entry 320, National Archives.

*Storekeeper recorded requisitions after a month's delay.

Table 8.2. Live Oak Timber Drawn from Stockpile for Large Frigates (44s)

Month (1853)	Promiscuous Timber Pieces	Framing Timber
July (June)	none	821 cu. ft.
August	1,016 cu. ft.	995 cu. ft.
September	1,791 cu. ft.	498 cu. ft.
October	1,622 cu. ft.	1,048 cu. ft.
November	3,034 cu. ft.	601 cu. ft.
December	999 cu. ft.	none

Source: Gosport Storekeeper Returns, 1853–54, vol. 175, RG19, Entry 320, National Archives.

Note: Only small quantities withdrawn in 1854; also 488 cubic feet in July 1853 molded but not further identified; and 622 cubic feet of promiscuous timber in August 1853, but not otherwise identified. In addition to the above, 304 cubic feet of framing timber for sloops was withdrawn and 116 cubic feet for steamships.

and all in need of extensive reworking, would make no sense in light of the navy's budget problems and its determination to rebuild the historic ship.[55]

Examining the sequence of withdrawals of timber requisitioned by master shipwright Porter helps to explain what took place in Ship House B as carpenters dismantled the old hull nearby and proceeded to build the hull's slightly larger frame (see tables 8.1, 8.2, and 8.3). Shipwright John Porter withdrew a total of 25,027 cubic feet of live oak timber suitable for *Constellation*'s frame out of Gosport's timber stockpiles. By far the largest portion of the live oak requisitioned consisted of pieces of promiscuous timber, 17,812 cubic feet in all, the total almost equally divided

Table 8.3. Schedule of Scrap Taken from Dismantled Hull

Month (1853)	Material
April	990 lbs. copper scrap
May	None
June	6,490 lbs. old bolt copper
July	None
August	1,161 lbs. hull copper composition
September	350 lbs. old composition metal
	2,700 lbs. wrought iron
	1,412 old bolt copper
October	3,570 lbs. old cast iron
November	None
December	400 lbs. old copper

Source: Gosport Storekeeper Returns, 1853–54, vol. 175, RG19, Entry 320, National Archives.

between timber originally cut for ships of the line and for first-class frigates. Carpenters also drew from the stockpile about 6,500 cubic feet of timber, molded and precut ship framing, about two-thirds for large frigates and the smaller quantity precut for ships of the line.[56]

Before arriving at a figure representing the portion of the total cubic feet of live oak timbers available for hewing into frame pieces or floors, the gross total drawn out of stockpile, 25,027 cubic feet, must be adjusted to compensate for three circumstances that diminished the quantity available for *Constellation*'s frames and other purposes. Deductions to the grand total included the amount of promiscuous timber drawn and used by carpenters in the hull for purposes other than the frame; the percentage of timber rejected because of splitting, rents, or dry rot; and most important, the percentage of the total taken out of stockpile lost as carpenters hewed large pieces originally cut for 74s and 44s down to the size of molds of *Constellation*'s modified offsets.

Because so little information has survived concerning *Constellation*'s great repair, it is not possible to provide supportable estimates of the quantities of live oak timber withdrawn from stores that shipwright Porter's carpenters used for structural purposes other than her frame. Further, any attempt to estimate such quantities runs up against another unknown, that is, the amount of live oak structural material transferred from the old hull for uses other than for the frame. U.S. Navy ships used live oak timber for keelsons, knees, beam clamps, waterways, stanchions, bow timbers such as stemson, deadwood, apron, top timbers, hatches, and for the stern assembly, including transoms and deadwood—in the case of frigates, 7,000 cubic feet altogether.

The quantity of live oak used for purposes other than the frame in *Constellation*'s rebuilt hull taken out of stockpile or salvaged from the old hull is unknowable. Moreover, an accurate estimate of the quantity or percentage of new live oak timber, in terms of numbers of floors and futtocks used in the ship, is unknowable, too.

Constellation's modified dimensions in 1853—176 feet between perpendiculars by 41 feet molded breadth and 21 feet 1³/₄ inches depth of hold—determined the quantity of live oak timber in her completed frame. Her hull, with slightly more beam and an additional 12 feet in length, increased the quantity of live oak in her completed frame from the 16,500 cubic feet required for a second-class frigate to approximately 19,000 cubic feet, complete and erected according to Lenthall's plans. Though admittedly it would be impossible to estimate the number of new and old timbers in the rebuilt frame, a realistic estimate of the percentage of the total quantity, 25,027 cubic feet drawn out of stockpile that carpenters used in the construction of the hull including the frame, may be calculated.

Following Lt. M. F. Maury's exposé of the management of navy yards a decade earlier, navy timber programs had come under continuous scrutiny. The denseness that made live oak strong and highly resistant to rot also made it vulnerable to changes in weather once cut and stored in ponds or open sheds. Cut timbers cracked like concrete or marble when under attack by water, wind, temperature, and ice. Timber pieces, cut out of trees in twisted shapes considered ideal for navy ships' frames or knees, cracked open or warped into shapes that were useless for ship construction. Upon close examination carpenters judged a significant portion of the timber worthless because of the effects of weather and dry rot.

These conditions particularly affected individual pieces of promiscuous and framing timber purchased for repairing ships and not previously set up as complete frames under cover. The navy under the Board of Commissioners accumulated stockpiles twenty years or so prior to the time shipwright Porter began to requisition timber for *Constellation*. Matthew Maury concluded that carpenters set aside one out of four pieces taken out of storage as unusable for ship construction. Based on his thesis, which gained wide acceptance, 25 percent of the live oak timbers—miscellaneous pieces stocked for repairs—withdrawn by Porter found their way into the scrap pile. This reduced the usable quantity taken from stockpile for *Constellation*'s hull by an estimated 6,257 cubic feet, leaving 18,770 cubic feet that was usable for framing or other purposes in the ship's reconstructed hull. That figure, 18,770 cubic feet, is less than the quantity of live oak in *Constellation*'s modified frame. An additional large quantity of timber, also estimated to be at least 25 percent of the total quantity available, represented the waste from cutting down large timbers to the smaller size of *Constellation*'s frame timbers and other components and, therefore, must be taken into account.[57]

When the Bureau of Construction, Equipment, and Repair authorized use of promiscuous timber for *Constellation*'s rebuild, supplemented by some framing timber, most cut to specifications of ships of the line and frigates first class, her situation may be compared to that of USF *Guerrière,* built during the War of 1812. The navy replaced her frame of white oak with one of live oak, evidently most of it promiscuous timber out of stockpile. Capt. Charles Stewart, in a letter to Secretary Woodbury commenting on the amount of live oak timber required to construct *Guerrière*'s new frame, wrote that the yard requisitioned 36,000 cubic feet of live oak to construct a frame that when complete consisted of a total of 22,000 cubic feet. These figures illustrate a situation repeated when *Constellation*'s frames were rebuilt of timber not purchased already molded to the ship's modified offsets. In the case of *Guerrière,* shipwrights rejected or wasted 14,000 cubic feet of the timber, which amounted to 36 percent of the total requisitioned.[58]

Using the figure of 39 percent to estimate the portion lost of the 25,027 cubic feet of live oak timber drawn from the stockpile for *Constellation,* the net quantity used in the frame is 15,266 cubic feet after subtracting damaged timber and waste amounting to 9,761 cubic feet. As *Constellation*'s rebuilt frame consisted of about 19,000 cubic feet, the shortfall amounted to more than 4,000 cubic feet, plus the quantity of live oak used for purposes other than the frame. To conclude, a conservative estimate of the quantity of timber retrieved from the dismantled hull was about 4,000 cubic feet or about 25 percent of the total quantity required for the frame. Carpenters probably salvaged an additional 2,000 or 3,000 cubic feet for other structural components.

To illustrate the point made concerning the percentage of waste produced when carpenters hewed timbers originally stockpiled for larger ships into sizes for *Constellation*'s frame timbers, figure 8.2 provides a visual comparison of the size of uncut promiscuous pieces and *Constellation*'s square frame timbers. Promiscuous timber pieces cut and stored for repairs to ships of the line and 44-gun frigates averaged between 15 and 22 feet in length, and when originally cut, sided from 14 inches to 20 inches, and measured 24 inches in width or more.[59]

Framing timber, precut for ships of the line and first-class frigates by lumber dealers, measured on the average between 11 and 16 feet in length. Contractors sided framing for 74s from 14 inches for floors down to 11 inches for stanchions. Floors for frigates were purchased sided 12½ inches and top timbers, 10½ inches.[60]

My efforts to locate John Lenthall's specifications for *Constellation*'s rebuilt hull and frame proved unsuccessful, another great void in the records of this ship. The

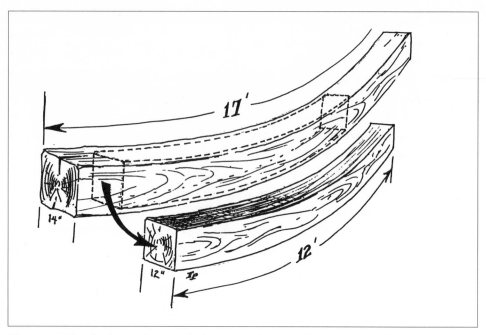

Figure 8.2. Sketch of promiscuous timber rough-hewn to the measurements specified for ships of the line compared to a futtock cut to Lenthall's offsets for USS *Constellation*. *Thomas Price*

information on siding of frame timbers, the lengths of floors and futtocks, bevels, and scantlings of the timber Lenthall specified is missing. However, the ship is moored in Baltimore and when the Constellation Foundation restored her recently, carpenters examined and measured many of her hull timbers. Carpenters removed no floors or first futtocks during the course of the most recent rebuild, but most of the upper frame futtocks had to be replaced and laminated frame sections substituted for live oak frame pieces removed from the ship.

Clerks in the foundation's repair crew recorded the measurements of futtocks and top timbers removed and replaced. Humphreys' original specifications for the ship-frigate called for frame sections about 15 feet in length including scarfs through which carpenters drilled holes for through fittings. Two sister frames were snugged up and bolted to eliminate shear, the frames fastened through connecting scarfs, a method that made the original ship-frigates strong and fair. But the futtock pieces uncovered and replaced in 1997 in *Constellation*'s frame, which the Gosport Navy Yard installed in 1853, measured just 10 to 12 feet in length. Not only were they short, but instead of scarfed ends for securing one futtock to the next the frame pieces taken out during the 1997 restoration had cut-off or butted ends. Carpenters in 1853 secured the ends of the short futtock pieces by cutting mortise holes or slits into sawed-off ends and then driving loose tenons into connecting ends to keep the frame sections from shearing. Shipwright Porter's carpenters removed the old futtocks intended for reuse by sawing the old frame pieces at the tip of the scarfs, which allowed them to be removed without incurring great labor costs and with less chance of damage when dismantling the old hull. When sawed at the tip of the scarf, the salvaged floors and futtocks averaged 10 to 12 feet in length.

Lenthall's lost specifications for rebuilding the 1853 frame, which included the short futtocks removed from the old hull, were part of his plan to use a large portion of the old frame timbers and a minimum amount of new live oak timber out of storage. Sawing them off reduced substantially the cost of recovering the old frame timbers in a reusable form and condition. The rebuilt square frames consisting of futtocks and floor pieces fastened at the ends with mortise holes and tenons secured two frame sections together at the desired molded angle of the butted ends. Tenons kept futtocks from shearing and sistered frame pieces were secured to each other by bolts passing through the frames along their sides.

This important discovery confirms that John Lenthall made specific design compromises that enabled *Constellation*'s rebuild to reuse as many old timbers as possible, having designed a system that made them cheaper to recover. Moreover, the shorter futtocks molded new out of stockpile for *Constellation* in 1853 increased the percentage of waste live oak as the large pieces of promiscuous timber cut mostly for ships of the line and first-class frigates required hewing to the mold sizes of these small frame pieces, many of which were less than 12 feet in length. The resulting waste exceeded 50 percent for each large piece of promiscuous timber used. This information, added to the other evidence, clearly shows that the percentage lost of the total of 25,027 cubic feet of large pieces of promiscuous live oak timber taken from stockpile exceeded previous estimates, as the individual frames are much smaller than the rough timbers from which they were hewn.[61]

The bureau's budget problems as they related to *Constellation*'s rebuild placed great emphasis on monitoring costs. This required a tight clamp on labor costs—the number of workers assigned to the hull and the total number of days worked—particularly on her modified frame. Though Delano's ability to control labor costs depended, in a large measure, on the cost of *Constellation*'s frame, the bureau seemed to have eliminated many opportunities to control those costs when it allowed the constructor to use promiscuous timber for the frame, supplemented by framing timber, all stockpiled for ships of larger dimensions and supplemented by timber pieces from the old frame, that required labor to reshape each piece to *Constellation*'s modified offsets. But since the navy ordered no complete frame or individual frame pieces precut to offsets, constructor Delano and shipwright Porter had the choice of comparing the cost of shaping timber stockpiled for ships of larger dimensions than *Constellation* with the cost of retrieving, reshaping, and bolting floor and futtock pieces from the dismantled frame. Since either choice—old timber or large promiscuous pieces—still entailed labor costs greater than installing a precut and shaped complete new frame, the only justifiable reason for such an obvious conflict in purpose in view of the bureau's drive for economy was the navy's determination to return a significant portion of old timbers to *Constellation*'s frame and in that manner maintain the provenance of the ship.[62]

Porter began requisitioning keel timbers and live oak pieces suitable for frames during the last days of May 1853. The last pieces of new framing or promiscuous timber of any appreciable quantity requisitioned from stockpile appeared in storekeeper returns for December 1853. This withdrawal consisted of 1,876 cubic feet of promiscuous live oak pieces cut and sided for 74s and 44s plus 300 cubic feet stockpiled for repairing sloops of war of the *Jamestown* class.[63]

Storekeepers recorded the last batch of scrap metal recovered from *Constellation*'s dismantled hull the same month, December 1853. The fact that Porter requisitioned the final batch of live oak suitable for her frame from stockpile at the same time his carpenters completed dismantling the old hull sets up a unique parallel—two frames—one in the process of being dismantled and the second in the process of being built to the ship's new offsets. This is but another aspect of a body of circumstantial evidence pointing to the conclusion that *Constellation*'s rebuilt hull contained floor and futtock pieces from the old frame, reworked and bolted into her rebuilt frame together with new timber pieces out of stockpile, all molded and hewn to her new offsets. The only possible reason for dismantling *Constellation*'s old hull and frame at the same pace that carpenters hewed, shaped, and bolted sections of her rebuilt frame related to the incorporation of used timbers into the rebuilt hull and frame as it progressed.[64]

Assuming that storekeepers' records of requisitions remained consistently one month in arrears from the date the master ship carpenter commenced drawing materials out of stores, storekeeper Boykin's records serve as a schedule for building and erecting *Constellation*'s frame and the remainder of her hull. By tracing the record of timber withdrawals from May to December, the months that shipwright Porter requisitioned live oak timber suitable to rework for *Constellation*'s frame, the unique construction sequence of the ship's rebuild may be isolated and outlined.[65]

Both of Porter's two sources of live oak timber for the frame proved imperfect. Slowly, from April through December 1853, an unusually long interval of time, carpenters dismantled the old hull. This suggests that the availability of salvaged sound frame timbers determined the rebuilding schedule of the reconstructed frame. Certainly, economy in the number of carpenters assigned to the ship became the dominant reason for the interval of time taken, but a more compelling aspect of the long erection schedule of her frame is the evidence that the storekeeper's withdrawals of live oak timber suitable for framing continued over the exact period that carpenters dismantled the old hull several hundred feet away. As a choice of timbers, new and old, became available, this choice of timbers, plus the comparative cost to shape or rework them, determined the sequence to which Porter's carpenters adhered. Over the seven-month period that they dismantled the old hull or took promiscuous pieces out of stockpile, carpenters built her reconstructed frame, reusing an unknown percentage of frame sections, floors, and futtocks, or shaping new framing pieces hewn from promiscuous and framing timber taken out of stockpile.

With a unique set of circumstances controlling the rebuilding of *Constellation*, in view of her historic significance, the selection of materials determined the yard's erection sequence. Porter included with his first requisitions in June 1853 materials not normally drawn out of stores until the frame and hull reached later stages of construction: keelson pieces, knees, oakum, and cotton battens in June and July 1853. The withdrawal of these materials at the same time as the keel pieces suggests that Porter's carpenters reconstructed the hull's stern assembly after raising her stern post in August. Keelson pieces, once in place and fastened, form a structural unit consisting of cant frames, keelson pieces, deadwood, counter pieces, and the other components of the ship's stern assembly. Galleries and outside planking completed the stern, and then—and only then—would cotton battens and oakum be worked into planks by caulkers. A sequence of reconstruction determined by availability of reusable material is the only logical explanation for requisitioning these specific materials out of normal sequence. As it happened, Boston Navy Yard replaced much of *Constellation*'s stern assembly in 1839, just fourteen years earlier.[66]

During the months of December 1853 and January and February 1854, Porter's carpenters installed deck beams and inside ceiling, bottom planking, topsides, and deck planks to *Constellation*'s frame. After completing the majority of this work on the hull, inside and out, in February, Porter requisitioned in March, April, and May 1854 additional framing pieces, curved live oak plank stock, knees, beams, round iron, and a white oak keel piece measuring 41 cubic feet, a bowsprit piece, and thousands of additional feet of white oak planking suitable for outside planking of the hull. This combination of materials provides additional circumstantial evidence that constructor Delano, after laying the keel, rebuilt the ship's stern assembly, then moved his carpenters forward from the stern, rebuilding her frame and midbody, and finally, *Constellation*'s bow assembly. This progression, if accurate, adds further credence to a theory that, as Delano rebuilt her hull, he started with her stern assembly and proceeded from stern to bow, constructing the frame and hull, leaving the new bow extension he drafted to the end of the construction and erection sequence. Certainly, Porter's requisitions support this conclusion.[67]

The aged and hogged condition of the ship's keel gave Delano and Porter no choice other than to begin construction with a new keel. However, this provided the yard with additional flexibility in selecting appropriate live oak timber frame and hull pieces, guided principally by the specific requirements of each section of the hull and the availability of sound timbers from the old hull. Since Gosport Navy Yard stockpiles contained no live oak timbers precut to Lenthall's table of offsets, Porter's carpenters had the benefit of matching available salvaged timbers with uncut timber taken out of inventory. Though comparative cost remained one controlling factor, the ability to choose old or new timber pieces allowed carpenters to adhere to the navy's instructions to preserve the ship's provenance.[68]

In the course of normal yard ship construction or repair operations, particularly as related to the calculation of costs, the United States Navy separated a wooden sailing warship into five components. First, the hull or floating gun platform allowed the vessel to take position on the surface of the sea beyond the protective range of the country's land forts. Second, to harness wind power to move the platform, the navy masted, sparred, and rigged warships with sails of cloth on masts and yards of wood held in position by rigging—running and stationary. Third, a ship contained all kinds of equipment, outfits, or shops and stores to make her functional. Fourth, the power of her ordnance and the number of guns determined a ship's class or rating. Lastly, the crew and its provisions made a ship operational.

When estimating the cost of repairing a new ship, the navy separated out of the total calculations the cost of the hull, which, under normal circumstances, had the life expectancy of sixteen years or annual depreciation of approximately 6 percent. In line with normal estimation methods, a new hull's cost amounted to about one-third of the total cost of the five components listed above. A ship's new equipment figured to be about 25 percent of the new ship's total cost. Constructors calculated the percentage cost of sails, masts, spars, cordage, and standing and running rigging at approximately 10 percent of the ship's cost and ordnance at about another 10 percent of its total cost. The cost of the crew and its provisions for the first six months— normally the period for which a calculation was made—added the final 25 percent to the total estimated cost of a navy vessel.

The leeway in this calculation provided the constructor with about 3 percent variance in the cost of components used in an estimate. Items manufactured of metal added substantially to the cost of equipment of a nineteenth-century ship of war; iron such as chains, anchors, ballast, and the iron tanks especially fabricated for *Constellation* are examples of expensive metal products aboard an equipped sailing ship. While the value of old live oak timbers transferred from the dismantled hull to the rebuilding site may represent a small portion of the value of the rebuilt ship, the reuse of many items of equipment substantially affected the final cost of rebuilding *Constellation.*

The first part of this chapter dealt with the controlling legislation and principal administrative orders and regulations that formed the United States Navy's construction, repair, and rebuilding policies for wooden vessels insofar as they affected *Constellation* in 1853. This information is supplemented by a summary of the navy's rebuilding procedures developed in detail through all previous chapters except the first.

The middle of this chapter contained a summary of surviving data relating to the principal construction period of *Constellation* from May 1853 to the completion of the rebuilding of her frame and hull approximately one year later in June 1854. Presentation of congressional legislation and resolutions, navy regulations governing the operation of yards, and supporting archival documents provided proof that, legally, the navy instituted procedures to save *Constellation* but at the same time to modify an obsolete ship. Moreover, the record presented reflected strong circumstantial evidence that Gosport Navy Yard accomplished her modification and repairs in a manner that preserved the historic ship's material provenance.

This part of the chapter will consider the question whether Gosport Navy Yard rebuilt *Constellation* in a manner that complied with the laws of the United States and the regulations and traditions of the nineteenth-century wooden sailing-ship navy. This element of the complicated history of the rebuild of *Constellation,* in view of the modifications made and the nature of repairs required to make her seaworthy, will cover whether Gosport Navy Yard rebuilt her under the traditional requirements of navy rebuilding procedures in view of the fact that Congress passed no legislation ordering this ship rebuilt, nor did it supply specific funding for the rebuild beyond appropriations to the navy's Wear and Tear account in the fiscal years in which the navy repaired the ship.

To answer this question, an analysis of the percentage of *Constellation*'s original equipment transferred from the dismantled ship in the course of her repairs to the rebuilt ship plus the value of old timber reused in her hull will be completed and compared to figures of the published cost of her complete rebuild. Starting in the early nineteenth century, the navy rebuilt wooden ships, such as *Macedonian* and *Congress,* as rebuilds authorized by specific acts of Congress. In each of these instances, records of the rebuilt ships suggest that neither ship contained sufficient quantities of old materials and equipment, recovered from dismantled predecessors, to enable the navy to claim that in the course of these rebuilds, the service kept intact, according to traditional definitions and conditions, their material provenance.

The rebuilt and recommissioned *Macedonian* had little material and documentary connection to the original Royal Navy ship, other than a name and a sentimental connection through the successful capture of the British ship of that name by Capt. Stephen Decatur, a ship later lost to Rotten Row. The navy rebuilt *Congress,* the sister ship of *Constellation,* by authority of an act of Congress in 1834, but after Congress consolidated several appropriations acts under a single line item in 1840, including authority to rebuild the second-class frigate, the navy used the opportunity to set aside its original plan to rebuild the smaller frigate that had sunk in Rotten Row at Gosport. Built as a new, larger, 44-gun frigate and launched in 1841 at Portsmouth, New Hampshire, *Congress* took her place on the Navy Register. Though by act of Congress, as with *Macedonian,* the navy rebuilt her, it is difficult to support claims that her provenance remained unbroken.[69]

Historians are prone to overlook the underlying structure of the navy and dwell on the service's heroes and victories, seldom concentrating attention on the Rules and Regulations which make it function. Historiography concerned with the navy in the first fifty years of the nineteenth century, in the main, does not cover the study of the inadequate administration and civilian oversight of the service. Prior to the reorganization of the Navy Department into bureaus in 1842, the service functioned primarily for the good of its senior officers. Congress disbanded the Board of Commissioners to focus attention on administration and the accountability of senior officers and civilians through a set of Rules and Regulations governing the service. These Rules and Regulations not only controlled the rights and discipline of seamen, but instituted regulations and rules for administration of the navy yards and the manner in which the Bureau of Construction, Equipment, and Repair, and, principally, the Bureau of Yards and Docks, dispersed funds appropriated by Congress for the construction and repair of ships and the yards. Though the system remained imperfect in 1853, one can state with confidence that the reign of the senior officer corps had ended and the navy functioned in a fairly consistent manner under the rule of law.

It followed naturally that as the Bureau of Construction, Equipment, and Repair instructed the commandant of Gosport and constructor Edward Delano to rebuild *Constellation* with repair funds from the bureau's Wear and Tear Account, administrative rules and procedures covering the repairs to ships controlled the transfer of all reusable materials and equipment to the rebuilt hull. Having followed specific procedures in force covering the repair of ships, when the yard completed repairing *Constellation,* her provenance would be certain and easily defended. The administration of her rebuild with supporting documents and cost figures not only complements the documentation covering the legal and political verification of *Constellation*'s unbroken lineage but, taken together, enhances it.

The navy built no new sailing ships equal or close to *Constellation* in size after launching *Congress* in 1841. The new frigate measured 179 feet in length, between perpendiculars, about 3 feet more than the rebuilt *Constellation*. *Congress*'s breadth exceeded the sloop of war's by 5^1/$_2$ feet and her burden by 467 tons.[70] The only other sailing ships built (and the last new sailing ones built for the service) in the decade between 1842 and 1852 were sloops of war of the Portsmouth-Germantown class, several feet less in all dimensions than *Constellation*. When rebuilt, *Constellation* was the navy's only ship, frigate and sloop, of her tonnage in commission. As a result of these factors, plus the loss of the bureau's vessel repair returns and the loss of Gosport's construction records during the Civil War, there survive only storekeepers' lists of materials drawn out of stores for her rebuild, the sequence in which the shipbuilder made his requisitions, and a record of the unusually long period of time taken to dismantle the old hull and rebuild it to reconstruct the procedures in effect when *Gosport* rebuilt *Constellation*. Supplementing those records is the yard's log kept by sailing master Young and a few archival documents.[71]

In the tradition of navy constructors, figures generated below to estimate construction costs of *Congress* will be compared with the cost to build and to rebuild *Constellation*, based on dollar cost per tons-burden of the two ships compared. *Congress*, built entirely of new materials, measured 1,867 tons and cost $421,592.[72] Her hull, including a complete precut-to-size frame, cost $209,577. As was the case with all large United States Navy frigates following the War of 1812, timber contractors cut frame components to molds of offsets calculated in advance and delivered frame components to stockpile. As a result of these savings, the cost of materials for *Congress*'s hull exceeded labor costs, $132,400 to $77,172. What may surprise the reader is that the cost of her hull, $209,577, totaled almost 50 percent of the total cost of the ship, whereas traditionally the hull's cost accounted for one-third of the total cost of a new ship fully equipped for sea. However, in this instance, *Congress*'s costs did not include crew supplies and provisions for her maiden cruise, as was normal when figuring the total cost of a new ship. If these additional costs had been included, they would have raised *Congress*'s initial cost to approximately $500,000.

More than a decade passed between the years the navy built the frigate *Congress* and rebuilt *Constellation* in 1853–55. In that decade costs rose significantly at navy yards. Also, the differences in the dimensions and tonnages of the two ships make comparisons of costs less accurate. *Congress*, a larger ship, measured 467 tons-burden more than the rebuilt sloop of war, *Constellation*. The latter ship's tonnage was 1,400, an increase of 130 tons after Lenthall's new drafts reflected his modifications.

To determine the estimated cost of a hypothetical "new" *Constellation* of 1,400 tons by using navy constructors' normal practice, one divides the cost of the ship *Congress* in 1841 by her tons-burden, 1,867, to obtain a figure representing the cost per ton of the larger frigate, or $225.81. When this figure per ton is multiplied by 1,400, the tons-burden of the "new" sloop of war *Constellation,* the estimated cost of the "new" *Constellation* in 1841 is $316,134, or approximately 25 percent less than *Congress.*[73]

That estimate requires an additional component representing the rise in the cost of labor and materials at Gosport Navy Yard between 1841 and 1854. Lenthall, appointed chief of the Bureau of Construction, Equipment, and Repair in late 1853, warned Secretary Dobbin that the cost of labor and materials at navy shipyards increased 25 percent in a very short span of years.[74] The constructor-turned-administrator worried about his bureau's budget shortfall in fiscal 1853, and may have exaggerated the increase of construction and repair costs as he presented his departmental needs to Secretary Dobbin for the next fiscal year, pushing the secretary for a significantly higher budget. The actual labor cost at Gosport, across all levels of unskilled and skilled labor, reached $1.71 per diem in 1854, up from $1.44 in 1850, an increase of 19 percent.[75]

Constellation's significantly smaller tonnage (25 percent) compared to that of *Congress* required smaller scantlings of lower cost and cheaper promiscuous timber for her frame. To balance these variables, the frame for the "new" sloop would cost more for labor but less for materials in proportion to *Congress* because the navy did not stockpile precut framing for ships of her size. Taking these adjustments into consideration, the cost of a "new" ship of *Constellation*'s tonnage, the increase in labor costs over the decade at Gosport, 19 percent, is entered into the estimate to produce a conservative estimate of the cost in 1854 to build a "new" *Constellation* of $376,199.[76]

A report by John Lenthall, chief of the Bureau of Construction, Equipment, and Repair, to Congress in response to a Senate resolution dated 27 May 1858 states that the cost to modify, repair, and rebuild *Constellation* totaled $277,116.18.[77]

The difference in the estimated cost of building a "new" *Constellation* compared to the actual cost of a rebuilt *Constellation* amounted to $99,083. This figure or balance represents the value of original equipment and materials incorporated into the rebuilt *Constellation,* which, as the figures show, amounted to more than one-third of the total cost of repairs and modifications ($277,116.18) or 26 percent of the cost of a new ship. These calculations may be verified against returns kept by Gosport's storekeepers relating to new equipment issued, or rather, the lack of new equipment issued in the course of repairing and equipping *Constellation.* Moreover, further verification may be obtained by following the trail of materials and equipment taken from the ship in ordinary before the yard dismantled her hull and later returned to the ship during or after the yard rebuilt the hull. These data are supplemented by records of *Constellation*'s equipment held in storerooms and shops, the movement of equipment to and from Washington Navy Yard for repair, and the special characteristics of *Constellation*'s equipment, such as her iron tanks.[78]

The crew of *Constellation,* upon her arrival at Gosport in May 1844 following her cruise around the world under Captain Kearny, stripped the ship of provisions, warrant officer outfits, rigging, and other equipment in accordance with the Rules and Regulations for a ship entering port for repair. Following a period of service as a receiving ship in 1844 and decommissioning, the yard placed *Constellation*'s remaining gear and equipment into storerooms assigned to the ship. Once moored in ordinary, a crew under the command of the officer in charge of ships in ordinary delivered other equipment such as masts, sails, and rigging to the shop or department specifically concerned with repair, reconditioning, and storage of each item of equipment. Under navy yard regulations, these repair shops assumed responsibility for keeping an inventory for each category of ship's equipment assigned to it while the ship remained in ordinary or under repair. A traffic manager in the storekeeper's department forwarded other equipment to Washington Navy Yard, usually equipment made of metal, wooden rigging blocks, and other manufactured items. Laborers discharged the ship's wardroom and captain's furniture, thirty chairs, on 1 June 1844. An officer assigned to ordinary surveyed the ship's furniture and put a value on it before placing it in a storeroom assigned to *Constellation.*[79]

New warrant officer outfits or stores charged to frigate *Congress* cost about $50,000. In compliance with navy regulations, Captain Kearny's crew, charged with stripping the ship on arrival, sent *Constellation*'s warrant officer outfits or stores ashore in May 1844. Following a survey, this equipment became the responsibility of the shop or department in the yard concerned—that is, masters, pursers, boatswain, ordnance, carpenters, sailmakers, armorers, coopers, clothing, or surgeons' department, whichever shop was responsible for reconditioning the outfits. Later, when returned to the rebuilt ship, each department reported the cost of repairing, reconditioning, or replenishing the warrant officer outfits to storekeepers. They, in turn, applied the cost-added segment for repairs or reconditioning of the outfits to the ship's account, kept current by the storekeeper's department for the commandant. In the case of *Constellation* at Gosport in 1853–54, compliance with these procedures may be verified in the storekeeper's records as his office charged *Constellation* for no new warrant officer outfits.[80]

Gosport's masting shop requisitioned fore and main masts, a bowsprit piece, and one spruce stick from the storekeeper. The storekeeper charged these items against his inventory and then added them to *Constellation*'s returns for repairs under the heading "Increase, Repairs &c." When stripping the ship of its equipment including spars and masts in 1846, the officer in charge of ordinary noted in his report that a survey of *Constellation* spars was incomplete. Laborers removed the ship's masts and spars and placed them on the wharf near the shears (lifting rig). Under yard rules and procedures, from there the frigate's masts and spars moved directly to the masting shed for inventory and storage in *Constellation*'s name, bypassing the storekeeper. The storekeeper's inventory confirms that the masting shop charged the ship's account for a mainmast, foremast, the bowsprit piece, and the spruce stick only. After the masting shop reconditioned the mizzenmast and yards taken out of *Constellation,* it forwarded charges for labor to the storekeeper, who added the reconditioning and labor costs and the cost of the previously mentioned newly requisitioned masting materials to *Constellation*'s returns, at the same time deducting the masts and spars from his store's inventory under the designated heading "Increase, Repairs &c." The storekeeper forwarded his returns to the commandant, who sent *Constellation*'s returns, consisting of labor costs for repairing old equipment and for new equipment charged in the inventory under the account, "Increase, Repairs &c." to the Bureau of Construction, Equipment, and Repair, which charged the ship's repair returns to the annual Wear and Tear appropriation.[81]

Sails from *Constellation*'s sail locker, valued at $4,812, originally held in ordinary storerooms, passed to the control of the Bureau of Construction, Equipment, and Repair when the ship was taken out of ordinary for repairs. As ship's equipment, this inventory of old sails came under the custody of the yard's sail loft, which charged for reconditioning old sails and for making additional new sails to complete the ship's requirements prescribed by navy regulations. Masts, spars, rigging, and sails for the modified *Constellation,* for the most part, matched the ones on the ship, which had previously been rated a second-class frigate. The approximate value of her complete sail inventory totaled $15,000, including the old sails surveyed and retained, valued at $4,812. The difference between the two figures is the amount added to *Constellation*'s returns for repairs to her inventory of sails. The yard carried out the same procedures as with the masts and spars and charged *Constellation* returns to reflect the cost of labor to repair old sails, to make new sails, and for the cost of the sailcloth. The returns reached the bureau in Washington, which debited its Wear and Tear account and credited Gosport's charges for its labor costs and its inventory account, "Increase, Repairs &c. for new sailcloth taken from the storekeeper's inventory."[82]

Other items of equipment repaired and returned to the repaired ship included her pumps and the hull's air ports, both carried to Washington Navy Yard shops and later returned to the ship. That yard recorded mechanics' time charged for repairing several items of equipment, including iron tanks, pumps, deck rings, air ports, and scupper stops, all received at Washington and later returned to *Constellation.* As in the case of repairs to equipment at Gosport, storekeepers received the returns for the cost of repairing or reconditioning the equipment from Washington Navy Yard, which they included in the ship's returns for repairs. Navy regulations for the management of shipyards required that the commandant account for each ship's repair returns from records of his storekeepers and that he pass these returns to the Bureau of Construction, Equipment, and Repair so that the yard concerned could be credited for work performed and materials taken from inventory.

The amount credited Washington Navy Yard's returns for labor performed, along with the costs of rebuilding the hull as well as reconditioning and repair of equipment, as accumulated by Gosport's storekeeper, was reported to the bureau each month. Upon receipt of Gosport storekeeper's monthly returns, the bureau entered the accumulated costs against *Constellation*'s repair account, including an amount credited the Washington Navy Yard's current account. The Bureau of Construction, Equipment, and Repair, having accumulated the costs of replacement, reconditioning, and repair of *Constellation*'s hull, equipment, masts and rigging, warrant officer outfits, and so forth, reduced the bureau's current Wear and Tear appropriation by the accumulated amount charged against *Constellation* for repairs during a fiscal year.[83]

Captain Kearny's crew, responsible under navy regulations for disassembling *Constellation*'s rigging, stripped the ship's masts and yards between 12 and 17 May 1844. The crew placed her rigging in special storerooms assigned to the ship by the commandant.[84] So long as a warship remained in ordinary, her running and standing rigging remained in special storehouses under the jurisdiction of the officer in charge of the ship in ordinary. Regulations required the ordinary officer to keep a tally of *Constellation*'s rigging and to maintain it in good order.[85] When the yard took *Constellation* out of ordinary to start repairs, in accordance with yard procedures, Gosport's rigging department arranged to take the ship's old rigging out of the assigned storerooms and to receive it into its shop for survey and repair.

Boston Navy Yard replaced *Constellation*'s running and standing rigging in 1841, and the riggers' work became the source of many problems for Captain Kearny during *Constellation*'s cruise to China, which included circumnavigation of the globe. Under normal conditions the navy calculated that ship's rigging would last eight years. During the course of *Constellation*'s 1853 repairs, Boston Navy Yard supplied the ship with 67,228 pounds of cordage, valued at $8,737.20, replacing most of her old cordage, the amount charged estimated to be half the total cost of reconditioning the ship's running and standing rigging, including labor expenses.

Upon receiving the new cordage from Boston, Gosport's riggers, reusing some of the ship's old blocks and new ones manufactured at Washington Navy Yard, made her rigging. The ship was rigged in the fall of 1854. Once again storekeepers at Gosport compiled the costs run up by the three yards for cordage and blocks as well as rigging costs at Gosport, subtracted the value of the portion of the rigging salvaged, and forwarded the returns to the bureau. Repeating the process, the bureau credited Boston and Washington for labor and material charges, and debited those costs and the cost of rigging the ship at Gosport to *Constellation*'s returns and to the Wear and Tear appropriation.[86]

Laborers hauled out *Constellation*'s casks and some of her iron tanks, built new at Boston in 1840, prior to the time the ship was placed in ordinary and put them in storerooms at Gosport. The yard arranged for additional tanks to be discharged during the period the yard made preparations to haul out the ship. Storekeepers received the final two tanks after carpenters commenced dismantling her. The store-keeper's traffic manager arranged to transport some, if not all, of *Constellation*'s iron tanks to Washington Navy Yard for repair and reconditioning. That yard originally fabricated the iron tanks of special size and shape to accommodate *Constellation*'s sharply rising bottom.

As Lenthall did not modify *Constellation*'s deadrise, the expensive tanks, forty-eight in all, were returned to the ship. The resulting savings represented a significant percentage of the value of used equipment transferred to the modified ship. The yard's log noted that schooner *Mary Jane* arrived at Gosport from Washington 5 September 1854 with the iron water tanks which *Constellation* took on board the fol-lowing month. Additionally, Gosport laborers hauled wooden casks, including thirty-eight held in storerooms supervised by navy personnel, to the ship and com-menced reloading them 29 December 1854. The Gosport storekeeper charged none of these tanks against inventory as new equipment.[87]

Before entering ordinary, the naval officer in charge arranged the discharge of *Constellation*'s anchors and cables as navy personnel prepared the ship for moorings in Rotten Row. The yard arranged to transport the anchors and chain cables requir-ing repair to Washington Navy Yard. Other anchors and cable taken out of the ship under supervision of an ordinary officer, after passing survey, were placed in store-rooms with other gear and equipment belonging to *Constellation*. After her launch in August 1854, the Bureau of Construction, Equipment, and Repair ordered Washington Navy Yard to deliver her repaired anchors and cables to Gosport. Sail master Young's log recorded the return of two anchors and 150 fathoms of chain cable for *Constellation* on the steamer *Engineer*. Laborers put anchors, cables, and hawsers aboard the ship on several occasions during the fall and winter of 1854–55. During the same period laborers cleaned and weighed her ballast and loaded it on board. Storekeepers charged none of this equipment, all property of *Constellation*, against inventory; they charged only costs for repairs and for labor to reload the equipment on board.[88]

Table 8.4 compares the estimated cost of a new sloop of war of 1,400 tons with the actual cost to repair and modify *Constellation*, also 1,400 tons after modifica-tions.[89] John Lenthall informed Congress that the cost to razee, modernize, and rebuild USS *Constellation*'s totaled $277,116, which was $99,083 less than the esti-

Table 8.4. Cost of a New vs. Rebuilt *Constellation*

Estimated cost of a	
new ship of 1,400 T, 1854	$376,199.00
Less credit for scrap turned in	(a)
Less credit for timber recovered	(b)
Less credit for ship's boats	3,398.00 –
Less credit for iron tanks & casks	18,137.00 –
Less credit for old sails	4,812.00 –
Less credit for furniture	348.00 –
Less credit for anchors & cables	13,500.00 –
Less credit for old rigging repaired	(c)
Less credit for ballast	2,100.00 –
Less credit for old spars and masts	(c)
Less credit for *Constellation*'s tools	482.00 –
Cost *Constellation* after	
credits of equipment	$333,422.00
Salvaged rigging, spars, timbers reused,	
& scrap, etc., Amount credited (a) (b) (c)	56,306.00 –
Total cost of *Constellation*'s repairs/modifications	**$277,116.00**

(a) Metal scrap, valuable because of the high cost to extract ores and to manufacture metal products, consisted of 1,000 lbs. lead, 350 lbs. composition metal, 2,700 lbs. wrought iron, 3,570 lbs. cast iron, and 16,623 lbs. copper.

(b) The quantity and value of timber salvaged from the old hull and reused are unknown.

(c) The rigging shop received the ship's running and standing rigging, new at Boston in 1840, to repair or replace. Neither the value added nor the salvage value of old rigging is noted. Likewise, when an ordinary officer surveyed *Constellation*'s equipment, he failed to place a value on her masts and spars already in storage at the time of his report.

mated cost of a new ship of her dimensions. As it turns out, however, the figure Lenthall reported does not represent the true cost of repairing the ship. It does not include the cost to take *Constellation* out of ordinary and hauling her out, $20,328. It also does not include the unknown extra labor cost incurred dismantling the ship's old hull over a six-month period in a manner that preserved reusable timber. Both of these amounts are included in *Constellation*'s repair wear and tear returns, and they would inflate the final cost to rebuild the ship.[90]

Lenthall's figure also did not include the expense of provisioning a crew for six months. In the years between 1852 and 1858, the year Lenthall prepared his report for Congress, the navy modified, along with *Constellation,* the frigates *Macedonian,*

Cumberland, and *Savannah.* The navy razeed each of these frigates to fit them with newly developed heavy-shell guns. The navy also rebuilt *Santee* and *Sabine,* lengthening them 20 feet, 15 feet forward and approximately 5 feet aft, to accommodate new bows and sterns, modifications similar to those made to *Constellation* when Gosport Navy Yard rebuilt her three years earlier. In each instance, the navy's intent remained constant: to modify, rebuild, or repair obsolete ships. John Lenthall, as chief of the Bureau of Construction, Equipment, and Repair in 1858, reported the progress of the program to Congress that year in just those terms.

Fort McHenry lives today as a national shrine celebrating that famous night of 13–14 September 1814 when the Water Battery's French guns intimidated the British invaders and saved Baltimore. During the long period that Fort McHenry remained under military control, however, army engineers continually improved the fort's armaments, and over time they did away with structures that had been part of the fort that night, including those guns. The original bunkers, replaced by new redoubts, support Rodman guns of a later vintage. Yet the fort remains a national shrine, its provenance unchallenged by twentieth-century engineers, architects, or historians.[91]

Constellation has not received the same treatment. Revisionists claim that the ship lost her status as a national shrine when the navy redrafted her rotten, twisted hull, then dismantled and rebuilt it. They would strip from the record the ship's historic past as well as her position in the larger picture of the nation's early struggles for international recognition, the period in which the navy and particularly *Constellation* played a crucial role establishing freedom on the seas for the nation's merchant ships. They would reduce history to a comparison of ships' plans and would require that shrines conform to original architectural drawings and structures.[92]

Decisions made in 1851 seem, well, naval in character. U.S. Frigate *United States* would continue to rot in ordinary. *Constitution* would be partially modified, reduced in rate to a sloop of war, and refitted as a school ship. *Constellation* would be saved from Rotten Row and converted into a modern sloop of war. Lenthall's modifications made *Constellation*'s conversion difficult for later generations to comprehend. Though he changed her hull in important ways, his plans and instructions linked the frigate's past and future material structures. His contemporaries praised him for his genius, but by the year 1991, even in navy circles, it had become expedient to deny his intent and his accomplishments.[93]

As mentioned earlier, Lenthall received at least three drawings from the commandant of Gosport Navy Yard. They included a keel drawing of *Constellation,* the Transverse Sections Drawing of Frigate *Constellation,* and a drawing of her bow, all prepared by a draftsman at the Boston Navy Yard between 1839 and 1841. The availability of these drawings at the National Archives, the only known surviving drawings prepared from take-offs of *Constellation*'s hull prior to 1855, made them the subject of many interpretations, particularly by *Constellation* revisionists, most of whom spin theories about the drawings' origins and their relation to the ship in 1853 without citing sources. In this manner, supporters of the undocumented and therefore unproved claim that the navy built *Constellation* new in 1853 attempt to keep out of focus the direct link between these drawings, particularly the Transverse Sections Drawing, and the drafts Lenthall made for his modifications to *Constellation* during the spring of 1853.

The Boston drawings can be linked directly to Lenthall. The darker handwriting below the three drawings' titles, consisting of the word "Norfolk" and a month and year, is written in the chief constructor's distinctive handwriting and may be compared to his letters. Prior to July 1853, the administrative organization chart of the Navy Department limited the chief constructor, a staff position, to the role of adviser and to redrafting *Constellation* according to decisions made by the Bureau of Construction, Equipment, and Repair. Prior to the start of repairs, Lenthall prepared, with the assistance of constructor Delano, instructions and specifications for rebuilding the ship. For him to accomplish the task without consulting drawings that provided him with "the shape of her hull," as the record reads, would be an act of gross negligence by a chief constructor who was not only trained in navy procedures and accustomed to carrying out orders relating to the drafting of naval vessels, but who was also considered the best-trained and most experienced naval architect of his era. The Transverse Sections Drawing with take-offs is the only plan of *Constellation*'s hull "as shaped" or "as built" known to exist, fifty-six years following her launch. To suggest it did not serve as the basis for Lenthall's modifications is unrealistic and false.

The selection of materials for repairing ships and matters concerning procedures, labor, and scheduling rebuilding of *Constellation,* including selection of timber, reused from the old hull or from stockpile, and the reconditioning of the ship's original equipment, fell under the jurisdiction of the Gosport Navy Yard commandant, Capt. Samuel Breese. The commandant of Gosport Navy Yard received his orders concerning navy yard construction or repairs to specific ships from the chief of Construction, Equipment, and Repair, Capt. W. Bradford Shubrick, in 1852 and 1853. Samuel Hartt succeeded Shubrick in July 1853. John Lenthall did not assume control of the Bureau of Construction, Equipment, and Repair until after constructor Delano and master shipwright Porter completed *Constellation*'s reconstructed frame in late 1853. Neither the bureau's instructions to Commandant Breese nor chief constructor Lenthall's building instructions to constructor Delano survive.

The Transverse Sections Drawing of *Constellation* provided Lenthall with the shape and dimensions of the hull that the navy had ordered him to modify. For his

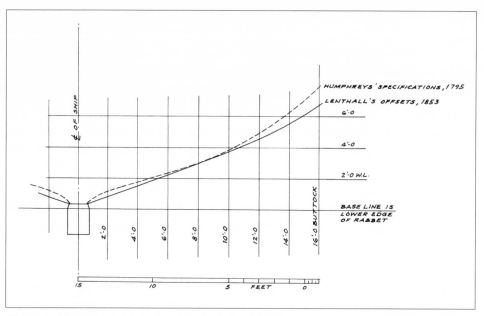

Figure 8.3. A comparison of *Constellation*'s deadrise, drawn in accordance with Humphreys' specifications, 1795, and Lenthall's Table of Offsets, 1853. *William L. Crothers*

own drawings and offsets, Lenthall adapted the base line from the Transverse Sections Drawing prepared at Boston in 1839. The new base line, set at the lower edge of the keel rabbet outside the planks, makes the two sets of drawings interchangeable. Lenthall and the Boston draftsman discarded the previous base line used by other draftsmen before 1839.[94]

Lenthall's modifications to *Constellation*'s hull are attributable to the bureau's decision to modernize the ship's hull and in the process downrate the ship from second-class frigate to a razeed sloop of war. Lenthall drafted alterations extending the length of *Constellation*'s rebuilt hull, mostly at the forward end, adding a new bow and aft, a steamship stern assembly. To razee the ship, Lenthall redrafted the hull's upper decks, raising the gun deck 9 inches and lowering the spar deck 1 inch, a net change of 8 inches. *Constellation*'s new main battery of twenty guns would be supplemented with two pivot guns fore and aft on her open spar deck. In his drafts of the modernized hull, he accounted for each of these modifications as a clearly defined alteration of her 1839 hull shape.

Lenthall's more modest alterations included eliminating the cyma curve in the rise of her bottom, a feature of her design by Joshua Humphreys and no longer in vogue in 1853. The cyma curve is a hollow in the rise of the bilge (see fig. 8.3). The hull's deadrise did not change between 1797 and 1839, and Lenthall did not modify it when he drew up *Constellation*'s drafts and offsets in 1853. The line denoting dead-rise, shown in figure 8.3, redrawn from Lenthall's offsets, rises from the keel in a straight line through its full height above the base line to the curve of the bilge. Though straight compared to Humphreys' original line, the position of the two lines shows that the value of deadrise remained virtually unchanged after reconstruction of the hull.

Deadrise is usually measured in inches above a horizontal base line at a point that intersects a vertical line drawn at a predetermined distance from the midsection centerline. As illustrated in figure 8.3, the amount of *Constellation*'s deadrise, measured in accordance with Humphreys' specifications and adjusted to conform to Lenthall's base line, measured 2 feet 11$\frac{1}{2}$ inches. The amount of deadrise following rebuilding of the hull, according to Lenthall's revised offsets, measured 2 feet 10$\frac{3}{4}$ inches. The angle of the raise of the bottom of the original hull amounted to 21.5 degrees and deadrise after reconstruction of *Constellation*'s hull measured approximately 21 degrees. These variations are considered insignificant by naval architects. What is important to naval architecture is that Lenthall left unmodified the shape of *Constellation*'s lower midbody sections. By doing so, he left undisturbed an important determinant of vessel design.[95]

Figure 8.4 is drawn in accordance with Lenthall's offsets and drafts. The draftsman who prepared this drawing of *Constellation*'s half-body midsection could not use Lenthall's specifications, which are lost. Some of the specifications for scantlings of frames and dimensions of planks and beams are measurements taken from the ship by her current restoration and maintenance staff, from the Gosport storekeeper's returns in 1853, or are based on general structural practice. This drawing of the hull's beautifully proportioned half-body midsection by John Lenthall shows the manner by which he adapted her original much-admired shape as he introduced his ideas to modernize her hull and to razee her upper decks.

Comparing this drawing with her midsection in 1839 as drawn in figure 7.1, readers will observe that Lenthall's draft retained not only the value of *Constellation*'s original deadrise but also her lower hull shape, which remains basically the same as its shape in 1839. The major changes that did occur as the result of a Lenthall modification and made clear by this drawing are alterations to the upper decks, including their height above the berth deck and the reshaping of the upper portion of the hull by eliminating tumble home and drafting a more perfectly proportional convex shape to the upper portion of her hull.

Surveyors conducting inspections of *Constellation* prior to the start of her restoration in 1997 determined that the ship-sloop's hull below the level of the second futtocks was sound and of original construction dating back to 1853. During a previous restoration a repair yard replaced some upper live oak futtocks with white oak and

239

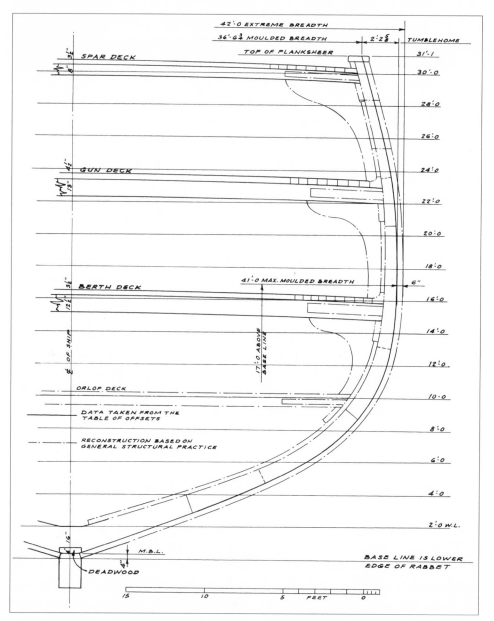

Figure 8.4. USS *Constellation*'s midship section in 1855, drawn in accordance with the Table of Offsets, NARA 142-1-7, and sloop *Constellation*, 1853, Lines and Body Plan, NARA 28-3-5. *William L. Crothers*

exterior planks above the waterline with red oak. The latter had decayed. The restoration crew ripped out most of the upper frame timbers of live oak as prior replacement of the ship's outer planks resulted in deterioration of the hull's upper frame, leaving it in a weakened condition. Moreover, carpenters replaced beams and deck planks above the berth deck and most of her hull planks other than planks covering the ship's bottom. When the Constellation Foundation, her managers at Baltimore, placed the ship in dry dock to inspect her bottom and dismantle her upper decks and frame, workers took measurements of many of the ship's structural components before stripping the portions of the ship scheduled to be replaced. For instance, measurements recorded included the ship's keel, new in 1853, sided 18 inches over its full length. Her original keel sided 18 inches at midship and tapered to 17 inches at the ends.

The floors of the sloop ship are sided 12½ inches, the same as in Joshua Humphreys' original specifications. On the other hand, Humphreys' specifications called for throats of these floors to measure 21 inches, cut out for 6-inch deadwood. Lenthall's offsets specified floors that measured 16 inches at the throat, confirming that if carpenters reused any of the square frame floor timbers in 1853, they had to rework them extensively or to reshape them into futtocks.

Data gathered during the most recent restoration of *Constellation* reveal that Lenthall's building instructions, now lost, specified that frame pieces for the hull in 1853 should be sawed off at the ends and butted flush at the proper angle to the adjoining futtock. Carpenters then attached the ends of the futtocks by wedging loose tenons into the mortised ends of the frame sections, which as a replacement for scarfs, secured the frame against shearing. Futtocks forming the 1853 frame measured only from 10 to 12 feet in length. This method of construction of the 1853 frame allowed carpenters to retrieve old frame sections for reuse by sawing them out of the dismantled hull at the tip of the scarfs rather than laboriously extracting fastenings driven through the sistered frames at the point where the scarfs of one frame overlapped another. In this manner, old futtocks, originally 15 feet in length, including scarfs, could be retrieved and reused at the lowest possible labor cost.[96]

The knowledge that carpenters rebuilding *Constellation* in 1853 attached futtock sections to the succeeding one with tenons rather than bolting them through scarfs is significant as it provides further supporting evidence that carpenters reused timber pieces from the ship's old frame. This knowledge about construction of the 1853 frame solves the riddle of how the yard was able to recover frame pieces from the dismantled hull at a reasonable cost for reuse comparable to or less than the cost of hewing promiscuous pieces into short frame sections. Only by such a method of recovery of live oak frame sections could Lenthall have justified their reuse economically, and it provides solid evidence that Lenthall's original specifications allowed for maximum use of *Constellation*'s old frame timbers.

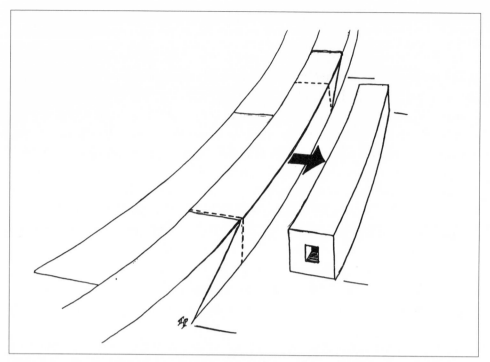

Figure 8.5. This sketch shows the method of recovering futtocks from USF *Constellation*'s dismantled hull. Frames from the original hull are on the left; dotted lines mark the location of an old frame piece sawed out at the tip of the scarfs. The frame section to the right represents the old frame section butted with a mortise hole in preparation for installation in the rebuilt frame. *Thomas Price*

Moreover, readers will observe in figure 8.4 that Lenthall lowered the height of the ship's maximum molded breadth line from 18 feet 3 inches to 17 feet and at that height above the base line at the dead flat section, *Constellation*'s maximum molded breadth measured 41 feet, an approximate 5-inch increase over her molded breadth in 1839. In the drawing, the ship's outer planks are 6 inches thick from keel to planksheer but there is no confirming this information nor whether she had wales in 1855 because of lost documentation. Because shipwright Porter requisitioned in excess of 20,000 feet of 6- to 7-inch white oak planks from the Gosport storekeeper during the course of her rebuild in 1853, however, it is probable that the drawing above is reconstructed correctly.

When USS *Constellation* arrived at Baltimore in the 1950s her hull planking was 4^1/$_2$ inches thick from garboard to the top of the planksheer, according to current records compiled by the ship's managers. This suggests that her outside planking was

Figure 8.6. USS *Constellation*, 1853. The sketch shows the method of attaching futtocks at their butted ends by using mortise holes and tenons. *Thomas Price*

replaced some time ago. If original planking measured 6 inches in thickness, this agrees with Lenthall's dimensions for her maximum beam—42 feet.[97]

Comparing figure 7.1, *Constellation*'s midsection in 1839, with figure 8.4, one observes again that Lenthall did not significantly modify the shape of the lower midbody sections of the ship. Nor did he alter the height of the orlop or berth decks when he relocated *Constellation*'s upper decks, which raised them a combined 8 inches. Variations in the heights of decks in this drawing appear at the ends because of the difference in sheer line above the base line before and after modifications, the result of extending her hull at the bow and removing keel drag, a part of Lenthall's modernization plan. Lenthall's plans, which preserved the integrity of *Constellation*'s midbody, are shown in detail in the drawings that follow.

Figure 8.7 shows the sheer plan of USS *Constellation* following reconstruction of her hull in 1853–54. It is included to illustrate Lenthall's principal modifications to the ship's hull. Her length between perpendiculars is now 176 feet. In his 1794 specifications, Joshua Humphreys did not calculate length between perpendiculars,

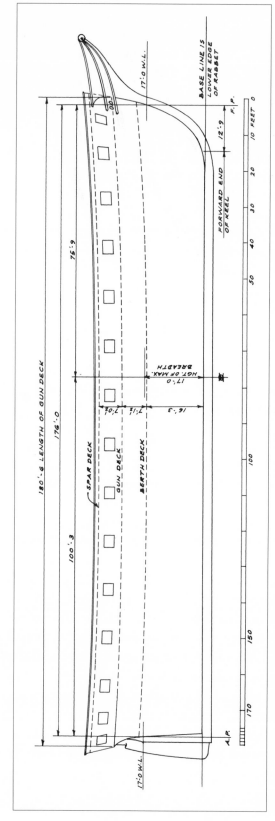

Figure 8.7. The sheer plan of USS *Constellation* in 1855, drawn in accordance with John Lenthall's Table of Offsets and his Lines and Body Plan, 1853. *William L. Crothers*

specifying only that *Constellation*'s length on her gun deck was to be 163 feet, 7 inches, and that he designed her keel 136 feet in length, straight rabbet for tonnage. However, *Constellation,* during prior rebuilds, received replacement rudder assemblies, a new stern, a new bow, and other modifications, which make comparisons of length risky. Lenthall's drawings provide her length on the gun deck of 180 feet 6 inches overall in 1855, a difference of 16 feet 11 inches from her original length recorded by Captain Truxtun.

Many naval architect-historians conclude that Lenthall extended *Constellation*'s length approximately 12 feet based on length between perpendiculars of 164 feet, 12 feet less than in 1855, but without Lenthall's specifications there is no way to determine how he calculated her length between perpendiculars nor the ship's length of keel for tonnage, which would be specified in his missing specifications. Newspapers and drawings from the period of Lenthall's rebuild give the ship's length between perpendiculars of 176 feet and the ship's burden of 1,400 tons.

Figure 8.7 shows the twelve usable gun ports on her gun deck. When armed in 1855, she received sixteen 8-inch shell guns and four 32-pounders on her gun deck. Above this deck, Lenthall's open spar deck eliminated gun ports. *Constellation* carried two large 100-pound pivot guns on this deck during her initial cruise in 1856. Because they were unstable, her commander, Capt. Charles H. Bell, ordered them removed.

Though Gosport Navy Yard replaced *Constellation*'s square stern with one of elliptical shape (sometimes referred to as round because of its spherical counter) in 1829, Lenthall, in the process of redrafting the ship's after-sections, redesigned her stern once again in 1853. His plan for modernization of the ship aft included a steamship stern with fuller quarter sections and a longer run below the waterline. Architects and builders considered the modern stern with circular shape stronger. It provided greater comfort for the ship's officers and crew billeted on lower decks. Lenthall's plan to modernize the ship's bow, which the Boston yard rebuilt fourteen years earlier, included extending it about 10 feet, provided him with an opportunity to redraft *Constellation*'s bow shape above and below the waterline.

Many refer to *Constellation*'s new bow as one of clipper design, though experts of the clipper ship era agree that while Lenthall drafted her new entrance less bluff than Humphreys, it would be inappropriate for a navy sailing ship to have one of clipper design. He did redesign *Constellation*'s convex Baltimore schooner–shaped bow with its raked entrance in favor of a sharper concave entrance below her fourteen-foot waterline. Above that line Lenthall's bow flared into a full convex shape, providing the navy ship with needed buoyancy in the forward part of the hull.

In answer to the question, did John Lenthall protect the integrity of Joshua Humphreys' original design, previously modified three times, one may approach a correct answer by examining his drafts and recalling that since *Constellation* received a new keel, this required that her hull to be completely reconstructed. This necessitated the preparation of completely new drafts, yet the separate circumstances of each of Lenthall's modifications may be isolated.[98]

Figure 8.8 is a composite of the sheer plans of *Constellation* before and after Gosport Navy Yard rebuilt or reconstructed her hull in 1853–54. The data used to prepare this overlay are "as built" take-offs and offsets, all data originated with the Transverse Sections Drawing of *Constellation,* prepared at Boston in 1839 and from John Lenthall's revised offsets, 1855. As these two sources used the same base line, set at the lower edge of the keel rabbet, the drawings are overlaid horizontally on that line. Vertically, the two sheer plans are overlaid at their respective dead flat frame. Once overlaid as a composite drawing, several observations and conclusions will demonstrate John Lenthall's ideas as he introduced his principal modifications to *Constellation*'s revised drafts in 1853.

The specificity of purpose of each principal modification introduced by Lenthall as he redrafted *Constellation* makes it possible to relate them to distinct parts of her hull. In order to razee the ship he redrafted her gun and spar decks. The modifications that lengthened the ship at her bow and stern are discussed in upcoming paragraphs. Lenthall's other modifications are seen as less important in substance.

The Navy Department in 1853 wanted *Constellation*'s upper decks redesigned to accommodate new shell guns as reflected in her change in rate from frigate to sloop of war. Gosport carpenters raised the gun deck approximately 9 inches above its former height relative to the berth deck and reduced the height of the spar deck above the new gun deck by one inch. The ship required fewer gun ports because she would carry fewer guns. The newly designed gun deck, with greater distance between guns, incorporated features that demonstrated a heightened awareness in the Navy Department of crew comfort and accommodation, particularly seamen and gunners, who were increasingly difficult to recruit.

Moreover, by raising *Constellation*'s gun deck and ports, Lenthall directed his attention to an old complaint concerning her original design: that as a ship-frigate, with great draft of water matching that of the heavy frigate *United States,* she sat so low in the water that her broadside could not be brought to bear on an enemy's hull when overtaking an enemy on the weather gage, a situation Truxtun complained of during his battle with *l'Insurgente* in 1799. Though open to the weather, her new spar deck was completely decked over, and as a sloop designed to carry two large pivot guns fore and aft.

The initial impact of overlaying the sheer plans of *Constellation* before and after 1853–54 is an awareness of the limits or constraints of each of Lenthall's modifications. Obviously, he altered the spar and gun decks, raising both in relation to the ship's berth deck and then modernized them in accordance with the navy's instructions.

But, perhaps, of greater note, is the manner by which Lenthall extends the ship's length to the bow and stern of the original hull. The composite drawing delineates the small addition to the hull's length aft end to accommodate fuller sections above the load waterline and a steamship stern. More important, the overlay brings into focus the extension of the bow as pertinent to Lenthall's multiple naval architectural purposes for extending the ship's hull at the bow about 10 feet.

Seen in this perspective, it may be observed, that, like the alterations to the ship's upper decks, the extension in her length is a modification to Constellation's hull which Lenthall limited to the areas he redesigned—the bow and stern. Once his modifications are accepted as localized in content, it is easy to take the next step and conclude that his drafts did not represent a new design for a new ship. What is new, as the result of the bow extension, is the relocation of Constellation's dead flat frame and the profound effects this modification had on the ship's buoyancy, stability, trim, and sheer, producing important naval architectural changes in the ship's performance.[99]

Many have pondered the reasons why Lenthall added approximately 12 feet to Constellation's length. Few have considered the possibility that Lenthall added most of her new length at the forward end of the ship. Most suggest that he extended her overall length to provide more working area between guns of her main broadside. Others suggest that Lenthall provided increased length forward to add a modern quasi-clipper bow and to a lesser extension aft to accommodate Constellation's new steamship stern. In view of the type of bow and stern assembly that replaced the ones installed in 1839, Lenthall could have easily redrafted Constellation with modified bow and stern assemblies without lengthening the ship 12 feet. Macedonian when razeed and modernized had been lengthened just 18 inches.

Increasing the hull's length forward enabled Lenthall to reposition the location of the ship's dead flat frame aft by the amount of the extension of the forward part of the hull. Relocation of Constellation's midship section, supplemented by a redesigned bow with greater flare and fullness above the waterline but less rake below the fourteen-foot waterline, reduced strain in the forward sections of the hull as a result of increased buoyancy and decreased wave resistance. Moreover, the added length to her forward sections shifted Constellation's complete midbody aft by an equal amount. This allowed Lenthall to reposition Constellation's masts in addition to relocating her midship frame. These clever modifications of Humphreys' old hull design effectively altered the architectural characteristics of USS Constellation's hull. Lenthall sought to redistribute hull buoyancy throughout the length of the ship. He altered her sheer and trim as a result of shifting the midsection aft by the amount of her bow extension.

Figure 8.8 shows that Lenthall lowered the ship's center of gravity and redistributed the hull's buoyancy by shifting the ship's midsection aft, eliminating drag,

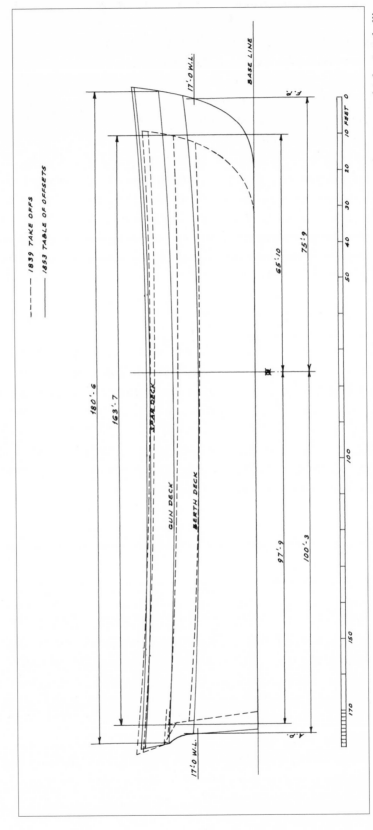

Figure 8.8. Composite sheer plan of the ship *Constellation* in 1839 and 1855, drawn in accordance with Transverse Sections Plan, 1839, and John Lenthall's design, 1855. *William L. Crothers*

lowering the height of her maximum molded breath to 17 feet above the base line an equal amount from stem to stern, lightening the spar, and removing some of the deck guns. In addition to reducing the deck strain forward, his alterations improved sailing performance by reducing wave resistance, particulary in heavy weather, and draft of water; he also made *Constellation* a better gun platform by raising her main battery. Lenthall took a ship modeled on eighteenth-century design and modified her using nineteenth-century naval architectural advances to perform as a contemporary ship.

The importance of the conclusion here—that with the exception of the elimination of the cyma curve and small modifications to the fullness of her bilge and breadth, Lenthall retained the dimensions and shape of *Constellation*'s midbody between her ends below the twenty-foot line—cannot be marginalized. It separates those who believe that Lenthall modified *Constellation* from those who claim that the navy ordered a new ship designed and built in 1853. And though it may be observed in figure 8.8 that the level of the berth deck above the base line differs in the original hull plan from the Lenthall version at the ends, this variation in the comparative height is attributable to the original hull's drag aft, much of which Lenthall eliminated. By this clever plan of modernization he established his reputation as a fine naval architect.[100]

Figure 8.9, drawn to scale, highlights the similarities and differences in the shape of *Constellation*'s midbody section as rebuilt in 1839 compared with Lenthall's modifications to her midsection after Gosport Navy Yard rebuilt her in 1853–54. The data originate with the Transverse Sections Drawing's take-offs and from Lenthall's revised Table of Offsets, dated 1855, prepared after the yard relaunched the ship. This comparison of half midbody sections at the dead flat, as built, provides dimensions of *Constellation*'s maximum molded breadth before and after her rebuild in 1853 and illustrates the modification of the hollow in the shape of her bottom as well as those above the twenty-foot waterline, a result of the navy's decision to razee the frigate. Once again, it is of particular interest to point out the similarities of the two midsections below the twenty-foot line, which as shown in this drawing, complement the overlay of the profile drawings of the hulls in figure 8.8.[101]

Modifications of architectural significance of the rebuilt hull observed in this drawing relate to changes in the level of the gun and spar decks, and modernization of the hull by replacing its traditional shape with a uniform convex shape above the twenty-foot waterline to the top of the planksheer. Moreover, Lenthall's decision to relocate the height of maximum molded breadth line to the seventeen-foot waterline, end to end, placed the hull's maximum molded breadth lower in the ship, which he expected would improve stability.

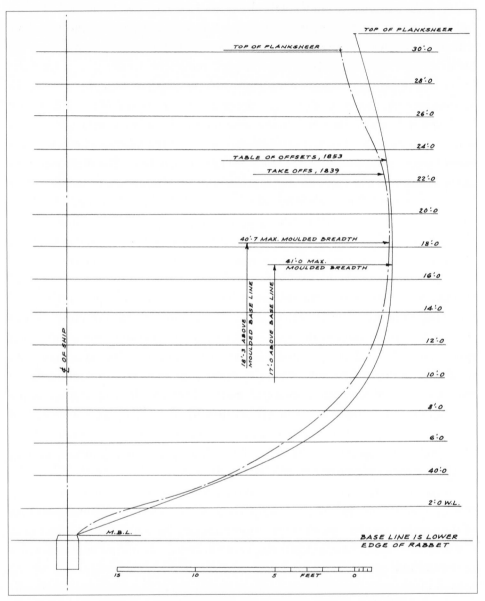

TOP OF PLANKSHEER

TOP OF PLANKSHEER

30'·0

28'·0

26'·0

24'·0

TABLE OF OFFSETS, 1853

TAKE OFFS, 1839

22'·0

20'·0

40'·7 MAX. MOULDED BREADTH

18'·0

41'·0 MAX.
MOULDED BREADTH

16'·0

14'·0

12'·0

18'·3 ABOVE MOULDED BASE LINE

17'·0 ABOVE BASE LINE

10'·0

℄ OF SHIP

8'·0

6'·0

40'·0

2'·0 W.L.

M.B.L.

BASE LINE IS LOWER
EDGE OF RABBET

15   10   5   FEET   0

Figure 8.9. *Constellation*'s molded midship sections in 1839 and 1855, drawn in
accordance with Transverse Sections Plan, 1839, and John Lenthall's Table of Offsets,
1853. *William L. Crothers*

Small modifications in the midship section below the twenty-foot waterline are attributed to straightening the line of the rise of her bottom, previously discussed, and as a result of refairing of the hull's lines, necessary because of alterations in the hull's shape, principally above the level of her berth deck. Refairing is the process by which the designer or draftsman smoothes out a hull's high and low spots caused by the modifications introduced in the drafting process.

Refairing of *Constellation*'s hull lines necessarily followed the drafting of Lenthall's modifications that relocated the height of the maximum molded breadth line from 18 feet 3 inches down to the seventeen-foot waterline, relocation of the ship's upper decks, a reduction of tumble home in favor of the upper hull's uniform convex shape, and removal of the hollow in the ship's bottom. The slight rounding of the rebuilt hull's bilges, smoothing the curve of the hull upward at the turn of the bilges and the small increase (5 inches) of the hull's maximum molded breadth at the seventeen-foot waterline are the result of refairing the hull to accommodate the modifications of the hull's molded line, caused principally by its new convex shape above the level of the relocated upper decks to the top of the planksheer.

Those who conclude that John Lenthall drafted an entirely new ship in 1853 claim that the small variations in the shape of Lenthall's 1855 half-body plan at the curve of the bilge and in 5-inch dimension of the midsection of the rebuilt ship are proof that the navy built *Constellation* new in 1853–54. They reject the naval architectural premise that the small increase in fullness at the curve of the bilge and in maximum molded breadth are the result of refairing and are too slight to represent deliberate efforts on Lenthall's part to redesign her midbody sections. They do not accept the limited aspect of Lenthall's modifications when they present arguments focused on a comparison of the midsections presented above, and they ignore modifications of her hull during previous rebuilds as well as the documented history of the ship that led up to her conversion in 1853.[102]

As the navy ordered *Constellation* razeed and reduced in rate from frigate to sloop of war, an important modification drafted by Lenthall raised the spar and gun decks of the razeed ship. This modification is depicted by the higher level of the top of *Constellation*'s planksheer in figure 8.9. Lenthall's other significant modification to the rebuilt hull of 1855, adding to her length, principally at the forward end, related to his understanding of the deficiencies and limitations of *Constellation*'s eighteenth-century design, which the talented naval architect endeavored to correct to keep the 1797 ship, once modernized, in service.

Figure 8.10 illustrates the shape of *Constellation*'s sections two through eight in 1839 and compares them with the same sections redrawn from Lenthall's Table of Offsets. The drawings of these sections do not include her bow and stern sections, one and nine. Though sections two and eight—forward and aft—respectively, are included in

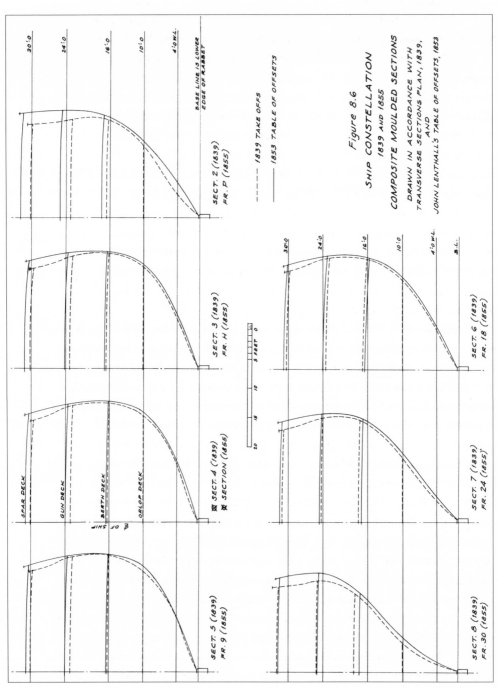

Figure 8.10. Composite molded sections of the ship *Constellation* in 1839 and 1855, drawn in accordance with Transverse Sections Plan, 1839, and John Lenthall's Table of Offsets, 1853. *William L. Crothers*

the drawing, they are not sections normally considered part of the midbody as they show the beginnings of the modifications Lenthall introduced when he extended the length of the hull to accommodate his alterations to the ship's redesigned ends.

The overlay of these sections provides another visual confirmation that Lenthall did not modify *Constellation*'s midbody in any significant manner other than to remove the hollow, concave cyma curve and modify *Constellation*'s traditional concave tumble home. Sections three through six, inclusive, consist of an overlay of *Constellation*'s midbody sections. A comparison of the similarities of these sections before and after her rebuild in 1853 again highlights the isolated extent of Lenthall's modifications.

Beginning with section two, however, Lenthall's modifications relate to the bow extension. The drawing of the overlaid section clearly illustrates the increased fullness of her forward end above the fourteen-foot waterline beginning with this section. In a similar manner, Lenthall redrafted the ship's stern sections, providing increased fullness abaft of section seven at section eight and section nine (not shown in the drawing). Also observed is the relative insignificance of the cyma curve in relationship to the ship's deadrise and the small increase in her maximum molded breadth to her midbody shape.

By showing the sections of the ship in sequence, Lenthall's modifications above the twenty-foot waterline may be viewed as modifications for specific purposes. Finally, the sections of the ship as copied from the data in Lenthall's Table of Offsets, sections two through eight, as shown in figure 8.10, illustrate the ship's new sheer line and the fullness of *Constellation*'s ends above the fourteen-foot waterline.

Supporters of a two-*Constellation* dogma argue that the navy built USS *Constellation* new in 1853–54 and deny that significant modifications took place in the shape of *Constellation*'s hull before 1853. However, when the modifications made in 1853 are compared to those made by Captain Tingey in 1814, Francis Grice in 1829, and constructor Barker in 1839, it can be seen that all strove for the results made apparent by Lenthall's modifications. These earlier efforts represented attempts by previous navy constructors to correct *Constellation*'s perceived reputation for instability under certain conditions and to make her a more dependable gun platform. The only exceptions are Barker's modifications in 1839, which represent an attempt to return her hull to one that more closely resembled Humphreys' original draft.

Lenthall accepted the argument, put forward by several of her commanders, that *Constellation*'s reputation for being crank was inherent in Humphreys' original design, rather than the result of the weight of extra guns. Only Captains Truxtun and Ridgely addressed *Constellation*'s problem of excessive armament. Truxtun reduced her main battery from 24-pounders to 18-pounders and removed 12-pounders on her spar deck, replacing them with carronades. Upon his return from a South

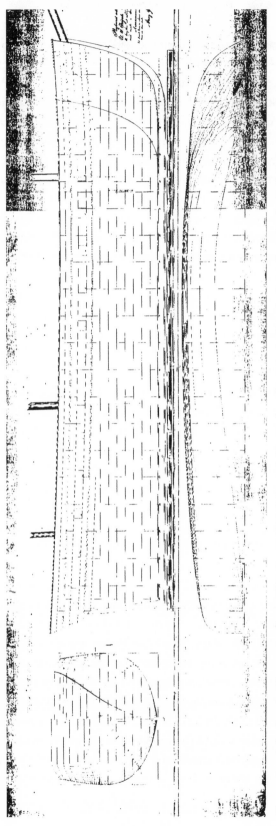

Figure 8.11. John Lenthall's proposed modification to U.S. Frigate *Sabine* to lengthen the hull at the bow. Drawing by B. F. Delano, master carpenter, New York Navy Yard, 26 April 1854. *National Archives*

American cruise in 1822, Captain Ridgely suggested to the Board of Commissioners that *Constellation*'s performance under sail would improve if it ordered the removal of several guns from the spar deck of the ship.[103]

In response to a request by Captain Skinner in December 1851, Lenthall, at that time chief constructor, recommended that if *Constellation* was to be rebuilt she should have a "light spar deck and a heavy armament on the gun deck." Lenthall merely referred to the obvious, that all United States Navy ships of the line and frigates had become obsolete by 1851. As a convert to steam power, he knew that ships retained on active duty, sail or steam, should be rebuilt to mount modern shell guns. He also pointed out to Skinner then that *Constellation*'s hull was beyond repair and required rebuilding. As chief of the Bureau of Construction, Equipment, and Repair, Lenthall wrote in the Navy Annual Report of 1854, several months after Gosport Navy Yard relaunched *Constellation,* that he accomplished that recommendation and rebuilt the frigate "as a spar deck sloop and [she] will be fully equal to the razee sloops of other nations."[104]

The navy ordered *Macedonian* rebuilt as a razee-sloop ahead of *Constellation*. Her modifications included lengthening her keel 18 inches, and after being razeed, reducing her main deck battery to sixteen 8-inch guns. The classic definition of razee is a warship reduced in armament by one deck; thus, the reduction in rate of a ship of the line to razee-frigate and frigates including second-class frigates like *Macedonian* and *Constellation* to sloops of war, or more exactly, to razee-sloops. Though traditionally sloops of war carried their guns on a single deck, navy commanders, always lusting to overarm sailing warships, placed two large-caliber shell guns on the two razee-sloops' spar decks following their conversion. *Macedonian,* which gained a reputation as a dull sailer following her rebuild in 1834, established a new reputation for improved sailing performance.[105]

Eventually, as with *Macedonian* and *Constellation,* the navy converted first-class frigates *Cumberland* and *Savannah* to razee-sloops. No one suggested that the navy built any of these conversions new except *Constellation*. Following the return of *Constellation* to the fleet in 1855, John Lenthall turned his attention to the 44-gun frigates, *Santee* and *Sabine,* in stocks since the early 1820s and in 1855, with hulls complete but deteriorating under sheds, both obsolescent white elephants. These first-class frigates, along with the navy's ships of the line, had become embarrassing reminders of John Rodgers's overbuilt, underutilized navy. When operative and useful as warships, *Santee* and *Sabine* became the last sailing warships redrafted, rebuilt, and launched by the United States Navy. When work commenced on their modified hulls, like *Constellation,* each received a new bow and stern that increased their length approximately 20 feet. And, as ordered by John Lenthall, both ships kept their midbodies intact.[106] The similarity of these modifications to *Constellation*'s rebuild in

1853 is apparent, as with *Santee* and *Sabine,* Lenthall attempted to partially prepare the United States Navy for its next war with ships already obsolete, though modernized as an interim measure.

A legal question rose concerning reclassification of *Macedonian* from frigate to sloop of war. The question, argued by a navy warrant officer, the ship's purser, whose pay dropped with the ship's rate, centered on whether or not the navy possessed authority to reduce preexisting frigates to sloops. A ruling by the attorney general affected *Macedonian* and *Constellation* because in 1854 when the claim was lodged, the navy had razeed these two frigates, reducing their rates to ship-sloops. The navy snafu related to the indisputable fact that, like all frigates, both ships still carried guns on two decks. Of even greater importance, the nation's legal officer pondered whether the navy could reclassify an existing ship without legislation. As a result, *Constellation*'s reclassification remained in limbo until the attorney general of the United States ruled officially that *Macedonian* (and *Constellation*), still rated ship-frigates in 1857, could not be reclassified to sloop of war without the approval of Congress. Therefore, *Constellation* (and *Macedonian*) remained frigates until Congress passed new legislation in 1858 allowing the Navy Department to reduce them in rate. The ruling by Attorney General Cushing, followed by new United States Navy Rules and Regulations of 1858, survives as additional legal proof that U.S. Frigate *Constellation* survived her 1853–54 rebuild and that she survived as a frigate until Congress legislated new regulations that allowed the navy to reclassify her in 1858.[107]

Nine

The Constellation Preserved

$\mathcal{T}$he United States Navy commissioned the razeed frigate, USS *Constellation*, in 1855. Commanded by Capt. Charles H. Bell, she joined the Mediterranean Sea Squadron, an assignment befitting a traditional vessel of the old sailing navy; such two- and three-year cruises were normally beyond the range of the navy's new steamships. During this cruise, one of the last "show the flag" grand tours by these almost obsolete sailing ships, *Constellation* cruised tens of thousands of miles, returning to New York 5 June 1858.

As modern as a wooden sailing ship could be in that time of transition, *Constellation* remained in active service. In a separate decision taken in 1855, the navy retired USS *Constitution* from active service. She received an expensive repair which included modifying her from frigate to sloop of war, after which the navy assigned her to Annapolis as a training ship for midshipmen. With classrooms and other alterations, plus a main battery of modern guns, she served the United States Naval Academy as a school ship. Joshua Humphreys' other surviving frigate, U.S. Frigate *United States*, the navy's oldest frigate, lay rotting in Philadelphia. Thirty-eight other wooden sailing vessels, including four ships of the line that were never launched, focused attention on the United States Navy's untenable position as the Civil War opened in 1861. Only then could the navy break the grip of obsolescence that in 1858 held it frozen in the past.

For decades the Royal Navy struggled to eradicate slave vessels on the high seas using fast schooners and brigs. The U.S. Navy ordered the huge square-rigged ship, USS *Constellation*, to the coast of Africa in 1859 to intercept fast small schooners and brigantines of the slave trade. Under command of Commo. William Inman, in addition to his flagship USS *Constellation* (John S. Nicholas, flag captain), the West

USS *Constellation* at Naples, 1856. Painting by Tomaso de Simone. *Naval Historical Foundation*

African Squadron consisted of two smaller ships, sloops of war USS *Portsmouth* and *Saratoga,* plus four steamships, USS *San Jacinto, Mohican, Mystic,* and *Sumter,* and the supply vessel USS *Relief.* Not only had navy schooners and brigs, which were similar to the vessels they chased, handled the assignment at less expense but, with their greater speed and light draft, more efficiently.

By assigning *Constellation* duty to the coast of Africa, the navy exposed her large crew of about 307 men, plus hundreds more in the other vessels, to the sickly conditions that prevailed there. As it had many times previously in the nineteenth century, the Navy Department clung to its decades-old peace establishment policies of 1820 that offered senior officers foreign assignments without regard for the high provisioning and maintenance costs of large sailing vessels and coal-burning steamships. *Constellation* served as flagship for the West African Squadron's commodore for more than two years. Crews in the squadron's small craft captured three vessels, one of which carried about seven hundred men, women, and children heading into a life of slavery.

Constellation returned to the northern navy yard at Portsmouth, New Hampshire, in September 1861 after the Civil War began. If there had been any questions about the role of sailing vessels in future wars, the Civil War answered them quickly. When the Norfolk Navy Yard burned, fire destroyed the historic ship U.S. Frigate *United States*. The disastrous Battle of Hampton Roads followed with the ramming and loss of the Union frigates USS *Cumberland* and USS *Congress* to the Confederate iron-clad *Virginia*, an engagement that left the Union navy reeling. A makeshift crew let go *Constitution*'s lines at Annapolis as a tow boat stood by to haul the historic ship to Newport, Rhode Island, where the U.S. Naval Academy, much diminished in size by defections, reopened.

After maintenance repairs and without fanfare, the navy issued orders that sent *Constellation* to the Mediterranean Sea once again. Through the bloody years of the Civil War, she sailed port to port like a ship without a country as the Navy Department kept her out of harm's way. She became a receiving ship at the end of the war and then joined *Constitution* at Annapolis in 1871 as a training ship. Both ships served as school ships for the Naval Academy for the rest of the nineteenth century except for occasional celebrations. Among *Constellation*'s special assignments, the federal government selected the ship to carry the United States exhibit to Le Havre for the Paris Exposition of 1878. Ten years later she lifted relief supplies to Ireland.

During the last decades of the nineteenth century the department carried USS *Constellation* on its records and on the Navy Register correctly as a sloop of war. However, on orders from Assistant Secretary of the Navy Franklin Delano Roosevelt, prior to the centennial celebration of the War of 1812, the navy issued instructions to repair the ship for the upcoming celebration; included in the specifications for her repairs were orders to restore her with the deck and profile plan of the ship when rated a frigate, with batteries on her gun and spar decks. The New York Navy Yard made the modifications, and one could argue that the controversy concerning the ship's origins began in 1914, the year of the celebration.

The U.S. Navy's knowledge of and enthusiasm for its surviving historic wooden ships diminished during the years following World War I, but a growing constituency consisting of maritime and navy buffs, historians, politicians, and an infant tourist trade began to agitate for restoration of *Constitution* and, to a certain extent, *Constellation*. As public support in Boston grew to restore *Constitution* to a state of acceptable preservation, *Constellation*, without a similar body of enthusiastic supporters, lay neglected with other historic relics the navy held, though even then there were Marylanders seeking to bring the ship to Baltimore.

The ship remained in the custody of a reluctant navy until President Franklin D. Roosevelt ordered her commissioned in World War II as a land-based headquarters ship. After the war, eager Baltimore organizations pushed the federal government and Congress to allow the ship to berth at Baltimore as a tourist attraction. On 5 January 1954, the Office of Chief of Naval Operations notified all Naval Districts that the Navy Department approved proposals in a bill pending in Congress which would authorize the Bureau of Ships to scrap USS *Constellation*. Moreover, the letter instructed all commandants that if any group wanted to restore *Constellation*, the logical course would be to rebuild her as the frigate of 1797.

The legislation that would have provided the navy with the authority to scrap the ship failed to pass Congress. Following this attempt to get rid of *Constellation* and while embroiled in a nasty controversy in the national press with Howard I. Chapelle, a popular maritime historian, over the ship's age and rate, the Naval Sea Systems Command, confused by its own inaccurate record of the ship's history, designated rate, ordnance, or origin, released *Constellation* to the custody of the city of Baltimore in 1955 under the Navy Donation Program. She arrived in Baltimore harbor laid out in a floating dry dock in unseaworthy condition. Photographs taken at the time of her arrival show a hulk resembling a decaying body on a stretcher about to be received at a morgue. Then, in accordance with navy instructions to restore *Constellation* as she appeared in 1797, a private foundation struggled to

USS *Constellation*, Cork Harbor, Ireland, 1880. Originally published in *Frank Leslie's Illustrated Newspaper*, 29 May 1880. *Naval Historical Foundation*

rebuild the sloop of war as a frigate for decades in compliance with this understanding, while at the same time endeavoring to raise funds in an atmosphere poisoned by controversies that raged on between Baltimoreans and the navy with Chapelle and his supporters.

Caught in a situation that pitted various Baltimore organizations trying to restore the ship against Chapelle and his disciples, the controversy concerning her age, origin, and rate raged on for thirty years as the ship's fortunes rose and fell. Despite her identity problems and badly conceived restorations, once moored in Baltimore's brilliantly refurbished Inner Harbor, *Constellation* became a star attraction. Numbers of visitors to the ship grew dramatically, but admission receipts and state and city grants failed to cover mounting repair costs as maintenance problems due to bad management and low-quality restoration work overwhelmed her budgets. The ship's political support wavered as controversy over her age and provenance continued. With the navy never able or willing to step forward to settle her historical identity problems, funding fell to a drip. By 1992, her very survival was in doubt.

Fearing that her masts would fall or her hull would crack athwartships as her keel hog increased, navy surveyors ordered her closed to the public. This was the situation the city faced when the mayor of Baltimore took *Constellation*'s future under consideration. Still, several more years passed as fate continued to plot a troubled course for the beleaguered ship, her final disposition in the hard hands of a navy that had tried to scrap her. Yet, despite being almost a hulk once again, so advanced had her deterioration progressed, *Constellation,* even without masts, had become such a popular attraction that Baltimore's political leaders realized they could not ignore her. The ship's stature in the Inner Harbor forced her administrators to step up and save her. Originally, neither Maryland's governor nor Congress was expected to provide financial assistance, but as it developed, after surviving forty years of insecurity, the battered ship occupied such a prominent position in Baltimore that Maryland's governor, its legislature, and the U.S. Congress joined in the campaign to save the ship.

So, after years of procrastination, elected Maryland and Baltimore legislators voted public funds to restore *Constellation.* It seemed that at this point in time a new era for the ship had begun. As the Constellation Foundation opened serious contract negotiations with Guy Peter Boudreau to manage restoration of the ship, the project swerved off course as new navy interference brought consideration of his restoration plan to an impasse. A serious new diversionary move by the navy endangered the ship's chances of survival. As the result of the positive efforts of a Maryland congressman endeavoring to assist *Constellation*'s financial plight, a supplemental navy appropriation moved successfully through Congress in 1994. The legislation provided $750,000 to cover the costs of dry-docking the ship, preparing surveys and engineering studies, and researching and publishing archival and official documentation of the historic ship, including its physical and documentary relationship to the frigate *Constellation*.

But the navy declined to disperse the funds as specified by the legislation. Instead, the navy authorized a report, costing $250,000, titled "The Feasibility of the Rehabilitation of the 'Sloop of War' *Constellation*," which the Naval Historical Center Detachment (USS *Constitution* Maintenance and Repair Facility) at Boston prepared and presented to Congress. The report concluded that to restore *Constellation* using traditional construction and materials, the only method of restoration studied and recommended, would cost $35,501,753. As broken down, the *Constitution* group estimated the rehab would require a total of 79,861 man-days, at $250 per day, with labor costs totaling $19,965,250. The *Constitution* group set the cost of materials at $15,536,503.

A report that estimated the cost of repairs of an artifact by such an expensive course of rehabilitation, predictably, had but one purpose: to present Congress with the astronomical appropriation request developed by the study. Several people close to the situation suggested that, once again, the navy's real purpose in making this impractical presentation was to get Congress to reject the request and scrap *Constellation*.

Little surprise greeted the Constellation Foundation's press releases supporting another navy-sponsored report, *Fouled Anchors, The Constellation Question Answered*, which concluded that *Constellation* was indeed a sloop of war and that the navy built her new in 1853. Even though disagreement existed inside the navy, archival records clearly show that the ship *Constellation* had been listed in the Navy Register as a rebuilt sloop of war after 1855. The 1991 report ridiculed the frigate position previously held by the Naval Historical Center, though it argued correctly that the ship in Baltimore was not designed as a frigate but rather a sloop of war. *Fouled Anchors* touted the old Chapelle claim that the navy destroyed U.S. Frigate *Constellation* in 1853 and in her place built a new ship named USS *Constellation* that same year.

With this new interpertation of *Constellation*'s provenance, which gained the immediate support of the Washington-based Naval historical Center, *Fouled Anchors* apparently closed the long, controversial period in *Constellation*'s history that Chapelle had opened in 1945. The 1991 report undoubtedly influenced the navy's decision to prepare the 1994 feasibility study for Congress. The navy officially designated the ship in Baltimore a sloop of war and accepted the position that, in fact, it had built and commissioned a second *Constellation* in 1855.

Funding beyond the initial large sums of taxpayer money given the Constellation Foundation did not come easily. At first, even city and state legislators seemed hesitant to vote for legislation if arguments about *Constellation*'s origins and design continued. To quiet those historians who traced the ship's provenance to the

U.S. Frigate *Constellation*, the Constellation Foundation accepted the navy's new reading of history, including Howard Chapelle's argument that the navy built a second USS *Constellation* in 1853–54 and destroyed the 1797 frigate at that time. These developments silenced old controversies as they faded from local newspapers and journals. Legislators approved necessary funding for the ship's restoration. Private funds, however, lagged somewhat because many Marylanders still believed or wanted to believe that the ship being restored could be traced back to the frigate built in Baltimore in 1797. The two hundredth anniversary of the launching of U.S. Frigate *Constellation* passed unnoticed as Peter Boudreau prepared to dismantle the sloop of war's wasted hull.

The Constellation Foundation's strategy was to press the navy to consider and approve shipwright Boudreau's plan with its estimated price tag of $9 million. The navy withheld approval of the alternate plan nearly two years as the old ship's pumps vibrated through the hull twenty-four hours a day. And even after that, through the course of USS *Constellation*'s restoration, the United States Navy offered only oversight, not financial or engineering assistance. Nor did *Constellation* receive the unallocated portion of the congressional appropriation, $500,000.

Naval architects, like engineers, work with opposing forces: they design new vessels and plan restorations of ancient ones. Among those forces are the high cost of traditional preservation placed in opposition to the availability of funds. For reasons never revealed to the outside world, the navy prepared the immensely comprehensive and expensive report for the reconstruction of *Constellation* by traditional methods without concern for cost. Peter Boudreau pursued a different course. He concluded that Baltimore could expect to lose *Constellation* if the expensive navy plan had no alternative for consideration.

Boudreau's proposal presented the Constellation Foundation with a basically simple yet visionary plan to restore *Constellation*'s structural strength and do it within the limits of the amount of money raised. Surround her frame with a strong wooden epoxy shell and hog would disappear as her original shape returned. Retain as much of her historic fabric as possible and visitors will come. Present the gracious form and basic beauty of the artifact and she will survive. And the price was right. Presented as an intelligent, explainable plan by people with well-honed skills and a realistic understanding of the need for practicality, the plan eventually blew navy opposition out of the water. A review of *Constellation*'s most recent restoration, the first phase of which shipbuilder Boudreau completed in July 1999, leaves no doubt that limited funding drove its course in several directions. Compromises determined important decisions, some of which cannot be fairly judged for years.

Boudreau certainly played a key role as the ship's restoration started, following the Naval Sea Systems Command's approval of his plan. Andrew Davis, naval architect, and others contributed consistently with naval architectural and engineering studies after *Constellation* went into dry dock in the Locust Point section of Baltimore. Working with software that his office developed, Davis's crew supplied design and engineering technical support for the project. Expert in computer applications for ship design, they measured and documented the ship's hull shape and prepared a structural strength analysis report. Previously, Davis assisted Boudreau in preparing the final basic Hull Repair Plan for the sloop of war USS *Constellation.*

An underwater survey conducted while *Constellation* remained in her Inner Harbor berth confirmed that her hull hogged 38 inches. Less noticeable to the eye but potentially more dangerous, a loss of transverse strength caused her midbody to bulge below the rim of her top timbers like a long-abused belly. Once the ship was stripped, Boudreau confirmed that a significant portion of her extreme hog resulted from emasculation of her upper hull strength, causing structural failure, this condition resulting from badly conceived prior restorations during which carpenters removed her full-length spar deck. This, plus general softening of the frame, deck beams, and other structural members, including deck and exterior planking from rot and poor maintenance, affected the ship's transverse and longitudinal strength throughout her hull.

These serious conditions threatened the ship, causing seams to open below the waterline, and kept pumps operating continuously with a custodian in close attendance. Boudreau concluded initially that the complete hull including its bottom required rebuilding or replacing. Just as elevated human body temperature is a symptom of disease and not a disease itself, so keel hog is a warning that perhaps everything is not well with a wooden ship. And like a human, a wooden ship is subject to all sorts of attacks from inside and outside, including the devastating effects of misuse, malpractice, fungi, organisms, and the ravages of old age.

Keel hog is defined as a concave curvature of a keel upward at the center of the hull, resulting in a compensating sag or droop at its ends. It is usually measured in inches above the horizontal of the keel. Well designed and built new vessels should have little or no hog. Old ships, like USS *Constellation,* are museum pieces and they interest most visitors just as other antiquities such as Egyptian mummies or old houses do. But most artifacts do not float on water and this makes an ancient ship very different. In response to the demand in this age of museums, vessel restoration is an industry that employs a growing number of traditional artisans, learned preservationists, and clever naval architects. Keeping aging wooden waterborne vessels free of rot, revealed by its usual symptom, keel hog, is considered impossible.

A vessel that is hogged has an array of probable sources of structural weakness. Locating and uncovering them is the first step. In naval architectural circles, there are three ways in which hog is revealed. There is longitudinal curvature, which has as its source an uneven distribution of vessel weight and buoyancy. Over time as a hull softens, hydrostatic pressure forces the hull to bend longitudinally, forcing the keel to curve upward at its center point. Second, distortion of a hull's bottom due to lack of lateral rigidity such as athwartship bulkheads produces hog as hydrostatic force pushes the bottom upward like pressure applied on an empty tin can. And third, hog results from transverse bulging of the hull structure including the frame, causing decks to draw closer together, the result of which contributes to curvature of a keel. Replacing or shoring up the components that form a ship's interlocking load-bearing structure is the foundation of correct restoration. Only by eliminating these failures may the causes of keel hog be removed.

Final determination of the sound condition of *Constellation*'s lower frame and bottom, made after the ship rested in dry dock and was dismantled, caused an important change in the ship's restoration plan. Original plans called for a complete cold-molded outer shell that would replace exterior planks from her gun port sills, 24 inches above the gun deck, to the keel, end to end. Now the foundation amended it in favor of a cold-molded shell that replaced traditional planking from port sills to a line approximately 7 feet above the keel base line at the midship section and rising in a curve to a point $14^1/_2$ feet above the base line on the stem and $15^1/_2$ feet on the stern post. *Constellation*, once restored, would have a hull with its exterior partly covered with a multilayered wooden epoxy shell consisting of four layers of Douglas fir planks and part-ancient fabric of white oak planks that many thought were original in 1853. The revised plan had no precedent.

Failing strength of a wooden ship's hull is directly related to the softening or rotting of its load-bearing structure, deterioration of fastenings, and hull creep due to a number of material-related conditions, including shrinkage of old timbers. Measuring residual strength is inaccurate, so hog is the practical as well as emotional manner in which the loss of stiffness is calculated. For this reason Boudreau's team ignored the residual strength of *Constellation*'s hull and calculated the combined load-bearing strength of her rebuilt upper frame, the reinforced new gun deck, and the outer wooden epoxy shell. Realization of the restoration's goal of restoring transverse and longitudinal strength to *Constellation*'s hull depended principally on the newly rebuilt upper structure of the hull to provide sufficient rigidity to stop longitudinal bending of the hull, commonly referred to as hogging. As stated previously, keel hog is the result of uneven distribution of vessel weight and buoyancy. Boudreau necessarily placed great emphasis on the load-bearing capacities of the hull structure scheduled to be built new and to its ability to provide sufficient strength to withstand indefinitely the still-water forces the ship would encounter in Baltimore harbor. What he constructed, which in the main consisted of a newly built gun deck made of three layers of epoxy-glued planks fastened to an external multilayer epoxy shell, formed a stiff bridgelike structure, strong enough to hold the ship's designed shape and, when finished, was once again a pleasing sight as one peers down her spar deck from bow to stern.

As the principal components of original fabric retained are located in the lower part of the hull below the gun deck, ship carpenters necessarily built a new gun deck of the strongest appropriate materials. The beams, 13 by 16 inches, are manufactured of laminated Douglas fir. Carlings, clamps to support beams, waterways, ledges, and stanchions are solid Douglas fir. Ceiling timbers from the berth deck to the spar deck are 5-inch Douglas fir planks. The gun deck, as stated, consists of three layers. The lower layer is 1^1/$_2$-inch Douglas fir tongue-and-groove planks laid fore and aft, edges beveled with V-grooves on the exposed underside to appear to be authentic decking. An inch-thick plywood sheath is sandwiched between the upper and lower planks and glued with epoxy on both sides. The top planks are of 2-inch Douglas fir, laid fore and aft with a simulated traditional caulking seam and laid down like traditional planking with proper placement of butts.

Consistently, as restoration progressed, the plan kept faith with the philosophy that, where possible, the historic fabric of the ship would be saved. So, while no longer load bearing, the beautiful, naturally formed knees of the live oak tree are preserved and returned to their locations under the gun deck beams, but their former function of providing a rigid connection between the deck structure and the frame is transferred to the exterior hull shell. Even without knees to provide their load-bearing capacity to the gun deck structure, surveyors estimate that the hull's overall load-bearing strength, with its cold-molded wooden deck and exterior multilayer wooden epoxy hull, is 30 percent greater than at the time the navy rebuilt the ship in 1853.

There is no doubt that cold-molded shell application in lieu of traditional planks created the greatest stir among many different and widely separated groups commenting on *Constellation*'s recent restoration. Though it required two years for the Naval Sea Systems Command to approve the plan, the delay did not concern the reliability of the epoxy-glued shell. The navy pioneered this shipbuilding technique for its wooden mine countermeasure ships over the last half of the twentieth century. Officially, the navy claimed its concern for proper preservation of a historic vessel caused the delayed approval. It wanted assurance the process could be reversed. As *Constellation* is on the National Register of Historic Vessels, the Constellation Foundation sought permission to apply the multilayer shell from that agency of the United Sates government. No problems emerged as the National Register's preservation guidelines do not consider outside planks of a vessel part of its historic fabric.

The former U.S. Navy sailing ship *Constellation,* restored by Maryland marine artisans, a time-tested resource of Chesapeake Bay, has returned to her prominent position on Baltimore's sparkling waterfront. Despite the ravages of time, controversy, and prior inept management, shipwrights completed an imaginative rebuild that combined a significant percentage of the historic fabric of USS *Constellation* with a technically profound naval architectural plan for the reconstruction of her hull and other structural components. So thoughtfully are her twenty-first-century longitudinal and transverse strengthening members hidden or blended with the ship's traditional interior that visitors will marvel at the miracle unfolding before their eyes as they walk her majestic decks. Her sixteen Paixhans 8-inch shell guns, cast in fiberglass and placed on her main deck during the summer of 2001, are a welcome addition to the continuously developing plan to present the ship as a mid–nineteenth-century U.S. Navy sloop of war, designed and equipped to illustrate the final period of wooden sailing warships. Her battery of guns, seated on carriages built in the ship's new Fells Point shop, blend well with other replicas that skillfully supplement *Constellation*'s significant display of historic fabric.

On the brink of disaster and almost beyond hope of economically feasible restoration, *Constellation*'s poor condition made the recently completed rebuild a daunting task. Certainly, armed with a plan that challenged traditional thought, the Constellation Foundation planned her rehabilitation well and made some daring decisions that produced, in the end, the structural and visual success desired. Those traditionalists who fret about the purity of ship preservation should consider that today a knowledgeable human race demands only partial re-creations of its pre-industrial past. Almost all restorations are rebuilt on surviving ruins, archival images, documents, and plans that help preservationists to re-create ancient structures that, realistically, are irreplaceable.

Claims of vessel preservation accomplished solely with traditional materials and woodworking methods are closer to fantasy than to real life. That is not to imply that preservation is a frivolous business; it is merely an admission that funding and common sense usually control restorations of large wooden sailing ships. Even *Constitution* weaves into her fabric an increasing amount of laminated wood and other high-tech materials simply because time and labor costs for ships in dry dock and for turning beautiful protected forests into frame sections and other hull components are too expensive even for her liberal budget to cover.

There are hard-core traditionalists who position themselves as critics of Guy Peter Boudreau, master shipbuilder, who deserves much of the credit for bringing this major phase of *Constellation*'s restoration in at projected cost. Few realists challenge the accomplishment. Once the Constellation Foundation received Navy Department approval, Boudreau and a crew of ship artificers carried it to conclusion in the main. It consisted of a combination of bold ideas for application of a selection of laminated materials in concert with fine wood, metal, and cordage-working skills. Motivated by strong allegiance to the essence of their traditional trades, the planners included reten-

USS *Constellation,* circa 1901. Photograph by J. S. Johnston. *Mustin Collection, Naval Historical Foundation.*

tion of the hull's sound live oak frame timbers and other components of her original fabric in keeping with the ship's role as a museum. Today, *Constellation*'s rebuilt and still-handsome hull functions as a receptacle or vessel for displaying the ship's design and its beautiful structural parts—massive gnarled knees, beautifully shaped breast hooks, and other original structural components, presented as effectively as a beautiful golden frame sets off a priceless painting.

When USS *Constellation* returned to her dock in Baltimore's Inner Harbor in July 1999, Peter Boudreau reported that he detected no keel hog. Using a laser device, he found no change in her sheer after two years in the water.

With the completion of *Constellation*'s major restoration, the mayor of Baltimore disbanded the Constellation Foundation and gave the Living Classroom Foundation, an organization that provides training for disadvantaged youths, the task of assembling a museum and a staff of teachers, artisans, and volunteers to carry out the ship's continuing programs.

Though Maryland shipwrights did not modify her rate, design, or dimensions during the recently completed restoration, the wide use of modern materials incorporated into the ship is faithful to the traditional definition of the navy's nineteenth-century rebuilding practices. They rebuilt *Constellation* for the fifth time. The recent modifications to her hull and decks are no less critical for her survival into the twenty-first century than the modernization and alterations to the frigate *Constellation* in 1853–54 which, as demonstrated in the previous chapters, guaranteed her survival in the nineteenth century through to the end of the twentieth century.

NOTES

CHAPTER 1. MR. HUMPHREYS' FRIGATES

1. Letter, Thomas Jefferson, Paris, to John Adams, London, 11 July 1786, in Knox, ed., *Naval Documents Related to the United States Wars with Barbary Powers,* 1:10 (hereafter abbreviated BW).

2. Letter, John Adams to Thomas Jefferson, 31 July 1786, in BW 1:11.

3. Report of Secretary of State Jefferson on the Mediterranean Sea Trade to the House of Representatives, 30 December 1790, and to the Senate, 3 January 1791, in BW 1:22–23.

4. Message of President George Washington responding to the Senate Resolution Relative to the Ransom of Prisoners, 22 February 1791, BW 1:26, 27.

5. Letter, James Simpson to the secretary of state, 25 November 1793, BW 1:55.

6. Ferguson, *Truxtun,* 101, 108, 122, 123. Also, from *United States Statutes at Large,* 3d Congress, 1st sess., 27 March 1794, *An Act to Provide a Naval Armament:* authorizes four 44-gun ships and two 36-gun ships; or, to purchase ships over thirty-two guns.

7. Letter, Joshua Humphreys to Robert Morris, 6 January 1794 (incorrectly dated 1793), Joshua Humphreys Papers, Letter Book, vol. 1 (1793–97), Historical Society of Pennsylvania, Philadelphia (HSP).

8. Recommendations of the Naval Committee, Thomas Fitzsimmons, chairman, to the House of Representatives, 20 January 1794, BW 1:60–61.

9. Secretary of War Henry Knox met with several Philadelphia shipbuilders (John Wharton, Thomas Penrose, John Powers, and Colonel Marsh) between 1 and 15 April to consider Joshua Humphreys' draft for the 44-gun ship and to make suggestions. Also, Martin, "USS *Constitution:* A Design Confirmed," 258.

10. Mr. Humphreys' frigates measured in tons burden as follows: the 44-gun ship, approximately 1,550, and the 36-gun, approximately 1,250 tons. Cooledge, *Ships of the Royal Navy,* 13. Armament for fourth-rate Royal Navy frigates called for 24-pound guns for their main broadside, the same as *Constellation* during her engagement with *l'Insurgente.* Following that battle they were reduced to 18-pounders. It was no accident that Humphreys' frigates cannot be compared with Royal Navy frigates in 1798. Their fifth-rate ship-frigates of that era were smaller than the *Constitution* class when commissioned and evidently, in 1798, the Royal Navy had none larger. The *Constellation* class was larger, too, than British frigates in 1798. Only after Truxtun reduced *Constellation*'s main battery to 18-pound guns did Royal Navy frigates compare in firepower.

11. A body of commissioners appointed by the Maryland legislature governed Fells Point and Baltimore, which were separate villages prior to January 1797. When the legislature created the city of Baltimore that year, Fells Point was absorbed into the new city. *Constellation* was built east of the boundary of Fells Point in Baltimore County; however, all of the artisans and laborers working on the ship resided in Fells Point.

12. *An Act to Provide a Naval Armament,* 27 March 1794, *United States Statutes at Large,* 3d Congress, 2d sess.; letters, Henry Knox, secretary of war, to Alexander Hamilton, secretary of the treasury, 21 April 1794, BW 1:71–74; Knox to Captains Barry, Nicolson, Talbot, Barney, Dale, and Truxtun, 5 June 1794, BW 1:75; Knox to Joshua Humphreys, 28 June 1794, BW 1:75; War Office to captains/superintendents, 7 August 1794, BW 1:79; Knox to the House of Representatives, 29 December 1794, BW 1:90–92; Knox to Josiah Fox, 16 July 1794, BW 1:76.

13. David Stodder, 1748–1806: Brugger et al., *Maryland: A Middle Temperament,* 165; List of Members, First Presbyterian Church, *Maryland Historical Magazine* (hereafter abbreviated MHM) 35:260; Maryland Tax Records, 1783; Vertical Files, Maryland Historical Society (hereafter abbreviated MHS); Baltimore *Federal Gazette,* 1 October 1806; various issues of *Baltimore American* and *Federal Register* and *Federal Gazette and Baltimore Advertizer* (runaway slave notices); writ by justices of Baltimore County Court, 22 July 1786; *Maryland Journal,* 21 March 1788. Stodder held a commission of major in the Maryland militia; he was one of the largest slave owners in Fells Point and evidently a harsh master as there are many runaway notices in various papers with rewards for the return of slaves. There was a warrant issued for his arrest in 1786 for stealing lumber off another man's property; in 1788, Peter Donnelly was executed for assaulting Stodder. The shipbuilder died 30 September 1806. He had property in Massachusetts which he willed to his mother; he left his tools and blacksmith shop to his slave, Lewis. His wife's name was Marcia Stodder; she received the rest of his property.

14. Letter, Secretary Knox to David Stodder, 22 July 1794, Navy Correspondence from the War Office, 1791–98, RG45, MF-739, National Archives and Records Administration (hereafter cited as NARA). Knox's appointment of Stodder was contingent on his agreement to devote his time exclusively to building *Constellation.*

15. Geoffrey M. Footner, *Tidewater Triumph,* 66–75.

16. Semmes, *Baltimore as Seen by Visitors,* 12, 13, 35.

17. Dudley W. Knox, *Register of Officer Personnel, United States Navy and Marine Corps and Ships' Data, 1801–1807* (Washington, D.C.: Government Printing Office, 1945), 70, 71. The figures were USF *Constellation,* $314,212; USF *Constitution,* $302,719.

18. William J. Kelly, "Shipbuilders on the Patapsco River, 1662–1961," unpublished manuscript, MS 2264, MHS.

19. Pre-Federal and Federal Vessel Registers, Baltimore, RG36–41, NARA; Owens, *Baltimore on the Chesapeake,* 146; Brewington, *Shipbuilding in Maryland,* 343.

20. Hulbert Footner, *Sailor of Fortune,* 173–89, 189–90.

21. Brewington, "The Designs of Our First Frigates," 11–25 and plates; Dudley W. Knox's research into David Stodder's activities in Virginia during the Revolutionary War, RG 45, Entry 464, Box 675, NARA.

22. Letters of Alexander Hamilton to Benjamin Lincoln, 21 January 1791, to Otho H. Williams, 22 January and 13 June 1791, and to George Wray, 23 January 1791, in Syrett, ed., *Papers of Alexander Hamilton,* 7:446–47. Revenue cutters *Virginia,* built at Hampton Roads, and *Active,* built by Stodder at Fells Point, are believed have been similar in dimensions. Virginia measured 52 feet 6 inches by 17 feet 6 inches by 6 feet 6 inches and 54^{93}/$_{95}$ tons burden.

23. *Maryland Journal,* 12 April 1791.

24. *Baltimore Federal Register,* RG36–41, NARA. Jeremiah Yellott and others purchased the new schooner *Active,* 170 tons, from Stodder in August 1794. *Active* made five successful voyages to Jacquimel in eighteen months. Richard Johns registered the new schooner *Vulpes,* built by Stodder in July 1795. Stodder registered the schooner *Punch,* ninety-seven tons, in 1797, and he built *Active* 11 in 1798 and *Greyhound* in 1799. All schooners built by Stodder after 1794 were of the pilot boat model. Readers should note the confusing contemporary use of the terms pilot boat, pilot schooner, pilot boat schooner, and schooner, pilot-boat built. The term "pilot boat" applied primarily to a boat used by pilots to meet incoming ships at the mouth of Chesapeake Bay. It became common practice during the Revolutionary War to call the baycraft used by the Virginia and Maryland navies pilot boats or simply, boats. Schooners and sloops competed for cargo inside Chesapeake Bay. Normally referred to as baycraft, when schooners, they had the same design as the boats of the state navies. These craft usually measured less than thirty tons. The expression "topsail schooner" was not commonly used. When shipwrights began to construct offshore versions of the baycraft pilot schooners for trading to the West Indies, their builders referred to them in the early years as schooners, pilot-boat built. Later, they were called Baltimore schooners. Never did any builder call them Baltimore clippers. This is an English expression of speed, which Royal Navy commanders applied to the schooners in disgust as their ships dropped astern in a Baltimore schooner's fading wake. The term Baltimore clipper schooner or brig seems to have been popularized by the *Baltimore Sun* following the founding of that newspaper in 1839.

25. Letter, Knox to Captain Truxtun, 8 August 1794, War Department Correspondence, 1791–98, RG45, MF-739, NARA. Also, Ferguson, *Truxtun,* 117–18, 197–98.

26. Orders, War Office to Commanders, 7 August 1794, RG45, MF-739, NARA.

27. Letter, War Office to Samuel and Joseph Sterett, 18 February 1795, RG45, MF-739, NARA.

28. Steiner, *Life and Correspondence of James McHenry:* letter, Truxtun to James McHenry, secretary of war, 20 May 1798.

29. Letter, War Office to Truxtun, with instructions for superintendence of *Constellation,* 7 August 1794, RG45, MF-739, NARA.

30. *Naval Affairs* in *American State Papers: Documents, Legislative and Executive,* 1:6–8 (hereafter abbreviated ASP); letter, Knox to Joshua Humphreys, 28 June 1794, BW 1:75. Brewington, "The Designs of Our First Frigates," 11–25.

31. Letter, Joshua Humphreys to Robert Morris, 6 January 1794 (incorrectly dated 1793), Joshua Humphreys Letter Books, 1793–98, HSP.

32. Records of the Adjutant General's Office, 1780–1917, Returns and Receipts of Naval Stores, 1794–1796, Baltimore Navy Yard, RG94, Entry 19, Box 101, NARA.

33. Letter, Knox to Fox, 16 July 1794, BW 1:76.

34. Stanton, "Builder of the First American Navy," 101–11; Westlake, "The American Sailing Navy," 21–41; letters, Joshua Humphreys to Samuel Humphreys, 20, 27 August 1827, Joshua Humphreys Letter Book, HSP.

35. Letter, Knox to John Wharton, 12 May 1794, RG45, MF-739, NARA.

36. Letter, Joshua Humphreys to his son, Samuel, 27 August, 1827, Joshua Humphreys Letter Book, HSP.

37. Col. Henry Humphreys, "Who Built the First United States Navy?," 400–402, containing the letters of Joshua Humphreys to Secretary of War Timothy Pickering, 5 June 1795, and Humphreys to his son, Samuel, 20 August 1827. Joshua Humphreys' letter to Secretary of War Pickering, who replaced General Knox and who knew little about the period during which the planning of the frigates took place in Philadelphia in the spring and summer of 1794, objects to the contents of his letters to Fox (Pickering to Fox, 12 May 1795 [2 letters]), Josiah Fox Papers, Peabody Essex Museum (PEM), Salem, Massachusetts, in which the new secretary lauded Fox for "preparing the draughts and molds of the frigates now building in the United States." Humphreys related to Pickering an early skirmish with Fox describing how he gave him (Fox) directions for the alterations of the frigate draughts to conform to the modifications agreed upon earlier by the committee working under Knox's direction. After he gave Fox instructions concerning the committee's changes to the original draught of the 44-gun ships, he realized that Fox did not conform to his directions for the draughts. He took the work away from him as that "induced me immediately to set about drawing myself; and I produced those [draughts] the frigates are to be built by without Mr. Fox's advice or assistance, but in conformity to the directions I had received." Letter, Josiah Fox to John Fox, 24 May 1794, Fox Papers, PEM. Josiah wrote his brother John, two months before Knox hired him as a clerk in the War Department at $500 a year, bragging that the state employed him and that "[I] am to have the drawing of six Frigates." Chapelle, *History of the American Sailing Navy,* 120–26. After blowing up the importance of Fox's contributions in the drafting of Humphreys' frigates, Chapelle, at the end of this section on Fox (126), admits that the Englishman's contributions were limited to the preparation of building plans of the 44s. Deviations from documented history reduce the value of Chapelle's book as a text on American naval history to a book of vessel plans in which he lovingly re-creates with great skill dozens of U.S. Navy sailing ships. Chapellites, curiously eager to accept his departures from documented history without questioning his failure to use supporting citations, do not question frequently enough the contradictions to documented history that proliferate in this book.

38. Letters, Knox to Fox, 16 July, and Knox to Humphreys, 24 July 1794, RG45, MF-739, NARA; Humphreys to Pickering, 5 June 1795, *Pennsylvania Magazine of History and*

Biography 40, no. 4, 401–2; Humphreys to Fox, 4 October 1794, Fox Papers, PEM; John T. Morgan to Humphreys, 21 October, 1794, quoted in Wood, *Live Oaking;* War Office to Trench Coxe, 14 November 1794, RG45, MF-739, NARA.

39. Letters, Thomas Truxtun to Joshua Humphreys, 5 November 1794, Joshua Humphreys Correspondence (JHC), Letter Book, vol. 2, HSP; Secretary of War Timothy Pickering to naval agents at Baltimore, 18 February 1795, RG45, MF-739, NARA. The package contained William Doughty's draft of *Congress* and *Constellation* (36 guns) signed by him.

40. Report of Secretary of War Concerning Construction of Frigates under the Act of 27 March 1794, 27 December 1794, BW 1:91; Returns, Navy Yard, Baltimore, RG94, Entry 19, Box 101, NARA.

41. Letters, Joshua Humphreys to War Office, 31 December 1794; Secretary of War Knox to Trench Coxe, 14 November 1794; Secretary Pickering to Trench Francis, 17 January 1795; Circular, War Office to All Naval Agents, 15 February, 1795, RG45, MF-739, NARA.

42. Returns Navy Yard, Baltimore, RG 94, Entry 19, Box 101, 21 and 28 February, 2, 3, 20, 24, and 31 March. Also, Circular from War Office to Naval Agents, 6 March 1795, RG45, MF-739, NARA.

43. Report of Joshua Humphreys, Progress of Building Frigates, 23 December 1794, ASP 1:8. In this report, Humphreys refers to the relationship between his frigate design and French razeed ships of the line.

44. Geoffrey M. Footner, *Tidewater Triumph,* 33–42.

45. Ibid., 44–62.

46. Ibid., 62–79.

47. Letters to dey of Algiers from Richard O'Brien, 4 December, and other Department of State Reports, BW 1:223, 232, 233, 253. Joshua Humphreys' association with the brigantine *Hassan Bashaw* is confirmed by his correspondence; see letters, Humphreys to Secretary of State Pickering, 19 July, 11 August, and 25 September; to Richard O'Brien, 2 September; to Trench Francis, 25 September; and to Thomas Truxtun, 6 September 1797, JHC, 1793–97, HSP. Chapelle, *History of the American Sailing Navy,* 136, 138, 140. *Hassan Bashaw*'s principal dimensions were 93 feet 2 inches length overall 27 feet beam, and 11 feet 6 inches, depth of hold; her keel measured 75 feet. Joshua Humphreys, according to this correspondence, supervised the building of the brigantine.

48. Pratt, *Navy,* 85.

49. Letter, William M. P. Dunne to the author, 13 April 1993. Actually the Chesapeake Bay pilot boat can be traced in records to the third decade of the eighteenth century.

50. Ibid.

51. Dunne, "The Frigate *Constellation,*" 78, 79.

52. Letter, Knox to John Wharton, 12 May 1794, War Office, 1793–98, RG45, MF-739, NARA.

53. Ibid. Also, letter, Fox to William Pennock, naval agent, Norfolk, 7 April 1797, Fox Papers, PEM. Fox wrote that he expected that ships the government built in the future would

be conformable in their dimensions to ships of the same class in the British navy, and not large overgrown unhandy ships such as those of Humphreys' draft.

54. Letter, Knox to Wharton, 12 May 1794, RG45, MF-739, NARA. These original dimensions for the 44-gun ship did not survive in Humphreys' final draft, and *Constellation*'s final draft contained the same relative proportions.

55. Ibid.; and Josiah Fox Papers, Letter Book, vol. 1, 7, PEM. Fox measured *Constellation* at the Washington Navy Yard after the ship returned from duty in the Barbary Wars.

56. See figure 8.3, chapter 8, drawing of *Constellation*'s deadrise in 1795 and 1853.

57. Letter, John Lenthall, chief constructor, to Charles W. Skinner, chief of the Bureau of Construction, Equipment, and Repair, 18 December 1851, Bureau Letters, RG45, MF-518, Nimitz Library, U.S. Naval Academy (USNA). Lenthall wrote concerning *Constellation*'s speed and instability: "That this ship, though built upon the plan of *Constitution*, should have been found inferior to that vessel is susceptible to an easy explanation; and it may not be out of place here to remark that it is no new discovery in naval architecture—that large dimensions with small displacement give brilliant qualities to ships—though speed is highly desirable it is not the only quality required in ships of war."

58. Federal Vessel Registers, Baltimore, RG36–41, NARA.

59. I remind my readers that no claim is made that the drafts of either *Hassan Bashaw* or *Constellation* were based on a draft of the pilot schooner. What is stressed in this part of the text is that when Joshua or Samuel Humphreys sought to compromise the hulls of their drafts of gun platforms to gain speed for these vessels under certain conditions, their influence originated with the region's pilot schooners.

60. Letter, J. Humphreys to Samuel Humphreys, 27 August 1827, JHC, HSP.

61. Letter, War Office to William Pennock, naval agent, Norfolk, 14 May 1795, BW 1:97–98.

62. Letters (2), Fox to Truxtun, 2 April 1795, Fox Papers, PEM.

63. Letters, War Office to Stodder, 7 April, and to Truxtun, 17 April, in response to Truxtun's letter of 6 April 1795, War Office Letters, 1793–98, RG45, MF-739, NARA.

64. Letters, Fox to Pickering, 9 June 1795, Fox Papers, PEM; Humphreys to Pickering, probably 5 June 1795 (this letter is undated but located in Humphreys' Letter Book between two other ones dated 5 June), Joshua Humphreys correspondence, HSP.

65. Isaac Garretson's Returns and Monthly Reports, including Stodder's Requisitions, Returns, Navy Yard, Baltimore, RG94, Entry 19, NARA; letters, Truxtun to Humphreys, 26 June 1795, JHC, HSP; War Office to Trench Francis, 29 June 1795; War Office to James Hackett, 4 November 1795, RG45, MF-739, NARA. Chapelle and Polland, *Constellation Question*, 25, 26; letter, War Office to Morgan, 20 October 1795, RG45, MF-739, NARA. Chapelle was wrong when he wrote that by May 1795 Stodder had shaped and dressed *Constellation*'s keel and frame timbers. Actually, as of 20 May, Stodder had not begun to shape the three logs he would saw, lay down, scarf, and bolt for the keel on the foundation he built; nor had he dressed more than a minor portion (208 pieces) of the total live oak frame sections required. Whereas the position is not taken here that Stodder

deliberately altered Humphreys' draft, it is logical to assume that because of the disorganization in Philadelphia and haphazard cutting and delivery of materials, particularly from the live oak forests of Georgia, Stodder had many opportunities to accidentally affect the final shape of *Constellation*'s frame and hull.

66. Garretson's Returns for the Month of October and November, 1795, Returns, Navy Yard, Baltimore, RG94, Entry 19; letter, War Office to Truxtun, 12 September 1795, RG45, MF-739, NARA; report to Congress by Timothy Pickering, 18 December 1795; treaty with Algiers, dated 5 September 1795, with covering letter of dey of Algiers, *Hassan Bashaw*, dated 4 January 1796, BW 1:107–26.

67. Letter, Truxtun to Fox, 4 January 1796, Fox Papers, PEM; letter, Truxtun to Tench Francis, 16 October 1796, Truxtun-Hare Papers, HSP; Federal Vessel Registers, RG36–41, NARA; William Patterson's Papers, MS 904 and 1,084, MHS.

68. Letter, George Washington to Congress, 15 March 1796, ASP 1:25; act of 20 April 1796, U.S. Congress; letter, Truxtun to Fox, 16 March 1796, Fox Correspondence, PEM; Garretson's Navy Yard Returns, RG94, Entry 19, NARA; letter, War Office to naval agents at New York, 20 April 1796, RG45, MF-739, NARA; letter, Stodder to War Department (Fox), 15 July 1796, Fox Papers, PEM.

69. Letters, War Office to naval agents at Norfolk and New York, 11 June, RG45, MF-739; Truxtun to Fox, 20 June and 15 July, Fox Papers, PEM; War Office to Fox, 7 July, War Office to Humphreys, 5 and 6 September, RG45, MF-739; Truxtun to War Office, 9 September, Fox Papers, PEM; War Office to Truxtun, 25 October 1795, RG45, MF-739, NARA.

70. Letter, War Office to Truxtun, 10 May 1796, RG45, MF-739, NARA; Garretson's returns, Monthly Summaries and Records of Requisitions, RG94, Entry 19, NARA.

71. Ferguson, *Truxtun*, 142; letters, War Office to Fox, 7 July; Truxtun to Fox, 20 June and 15 July 1796, Fox Papers, PEM; War Office to John Blagee, 8 August; War Office to Truxtun, 25 October 1796; James McHenry to Truxtun, 5 December 1796, RG45, MF-739, NARA; ASP 1:14.

72. Steiner, *Life and Correspondence of James McHenry*, 250–51; letter, Truxtun to McHenry, 3 March 1797, RG45, MF-739; Garretson's Returns and Record of Requisitions, RG94, Entry 19; McHenry's Report to Congress, 11 January 1797, RG45, MF-739, NARA. McHenry reported that *Constellation*'s whole frame raised, proof that Stodder's carpenters, having finally received all of the live oak framing timbers in the fall of 1796, which allowed him to complete the frame and moved forward on the construction of the hull. McHenry predicted the 36-gun ship would be launched in May. Congressman Parker's Report to the House of Representatives, 25 January 1797, ASP 1, 7.

73. Letters, McHenry to Stodder, 17 April, Stodder to McHenry (War Office), 20 April 1797, RG45, MF-739, NARA.

74. Steiner, *Life and Correspondence of James McHenry:* letter, Truxtun to McHenry, 3 March 1797.

75. Letters, War Office to Stodder, 11 and 17 July, RG45, MF-739; McHenry to Humphreys, 25 July 1797, JHC, HSP; McHenry to Congress, ASP 1:28; McHenry to Capt. Staats Morris, Fort Whetstone, 27 July 1797, RG45, MF-739, NARA.

76. *Telegraphie,* Fells Point, 29 August 1797.
77. Semmes, *Baltimore as Seen by Visitors,* 10–11.
78. *Baltimore Federal Gazette,* 9 August 1797.
79. Ferguson, *Truxtun,* 135–36; *Baltimore Federal Gazette,* 7 September 1797.
80. *Baltimore Federal Gazette,* 7 September, 1797.

CHAPTER 2. A WARSHIP OF A DIFFERENT MODEL

1. Knox, *Register of Officer Personnel and Ship's Data,* 1801–7, 70–71, 78–79.
2. Letters, War Office to David Stodder, 6 October 1797, RG45, MF-739, NARA; Stodder, Thomas Truxtun, Isaac Garretson, and Henry Smyth to McHenry, 7 December 1797, ASP 1:50.
3. Report of James McHenry to Congress, 26 December 1797, ASP 1:52; McHenry reported *Constellation* launched 7 September and as of the date of that report, ready to leave Patapsco River.
4. Report on Naval Expenditures and Disposition of Materials, James McHenry to Edward Livingston, chairman, Committee on Naval Affairs, House of Representatives, 22 March 1798, ASP 1:39.
5. Letter, McHenry to Truxtun, 16 March 1798, in Knox, ed., *Naval Documents Related to the Quasi War between the United States and France,* 1:42 (hereafter cited as QW).
6. Steiner, *Life and Correspondence of James McHenry,* 254–56: letter, Truxtun to McHenry, 20 May 1798. The reader should consider, as he judges Truxtun, that though the commander/superintendent absented himself from the navy yard frequently, he maintained his private commercial affairs throughout four years at the yard which included owning the snow *John and Joseph* jointly with the same naval agents he criticized. In the first part of the letter, Truxtun writes of the indolence of artificers at Fells Point, then later writes that the ones he arranged for were good workmen. His final reference to local shipwrights related to the charge that Fells Point had been the wrong place to build a large ship, although the Chesapeake Bay turned out the finest shaped and fastest small vessels built in America.
7. Palmer, *Stoddert's War,* 7–10, 14–16.
8. Thomas Truxtun's journal, 26 June and 2 July 1798, HSP; instructions, President John Adams to all commanders, 30 May; orders, War Office to Truxtun, 25 and 30 May 1798, RG45, MF-149, Nimitz Library, USNA.
9. Letters (2), Truxtun to McHenry, 23 June 1798, Truxtun's Letter Book, HSP; QW 1:132, 133.
10. Orders, Navy Department to Truxtun, 26 June 1798, RG45, MF-149, Nimitz Library, USNA.
11. Truxtun's journal, 3, 4, and 5 July 1798, HSP; letters, McHenry to Truxtun, 5 December 1796, RG45, MF-739, NARA; Humphreys to Benjamin Stoddert, 25 August 1798, JHC, HSP.
12. Letter, Truxtun to McHenry, 16 July 1798, Truxtun Letter Book, AM6795, HSP.
13. Letter, Secretary Benjamin Stoddert to Truxtun, 14 July 1798, QW 1:206.

14. Truxtun's journal, 15 August 1798, HSP.

15. Letters, Truxtun to Lt. Simon Gross, 18 September 1797, QW 1:12–16; Truxtun to McHenry, 23 June 1798, QW 1:132; see also U.S. Frigate *Constellation* Orders, Muster Rolls, Stores, & Etc., Thomas Truxtun, 1797–1798, AM679, HSP: Principal Dimensions of the United States Frigate *Constellation:* length of keel straight rabbet, 136 feet; molded breadth of beam, 40 feet; depth of hold, 13 feet; depth between decks, 6 feet; depth between gun and upper deck, 6 feet and three-quarters of an inch; length of gun deck, 163 feet 7 inches; length of upper deck, 171 feet. Draft of this frigate when launched 7 September 1797 was 18 feet 6 inches aft and 13 feet 3 inches forward; the difference in draft between fore and aft was 5 feet 3 inches; letter, Alexander Murray to Acting Secretary of the Navy Gen. Samuel Smith, 26 April 1801, QW 7:205; letter, John Barry, commander, USF *United States* to Stoddert, 8 August 1798, QW 1:280. John Brussels piloted *United States* from Philadelphia to Cape Henlopen; she drew 22 feet 6 inches.

16. Letter, Truxtun to Stoddert, 16 August 1798, Truxtun Letter Book, AM 6795, HSP. Letter, Stoddert to Samuel Sewell, 2 July 1798, QW 1:160. The secretary pointed out that frigates in English service measured on an average 940 tons. *Constellation* was built to carry 38 guns and measured up to 1,300 tons. "It is still to be determined whether a ship carrying same number of guns is better for being so much larger than the size adopted by Britain."

17. Letter, Truxtun to Stoddert, 16 August 1798, Truxtun Letter Book, AM6795, HSP.

18. Letter, James Buchanan to Pickering, 5 September 1799, QW 1:159–60.

19. Dunne, "The Frigate *Constellation*," 79–82.

20. Letter, Stoddert to Secretary of State Pickering, 16 October 1798, QW 1:538–39; Ships of War in the Quasi War with France, QW 7:364–71. At full strength, Stoddert's navy consisted of fourteen frigates, eleven ships, two sloops of war, four gun brigs, eight revenue cutters, and three schooners. This total included the French frigate placed under the American flag, *Insurgent,* which was later lost at sea, and the Baltimore schooner USS *Retaliation,* a captured French privateer, recaptured by a French force that included *l'Insurgente.*

21. Letter, Truxtun to Stoddert, 1 November 1798, Truxtun Letter Book, AM6795, HSP.

22. Letter, Stoddert to President Adams, 25 August 1798, QW 1:336; orders, Stoddert to Truxtun, 10 (2 letters) and 31 August 1798, RG45, MF-149, Nimitz Library, USNA; letter, Truxtun to masters of fifteen ships in convoy, 26 August 1798; letter, Truxtun to Stoddert, 4 September, 27 October 1798, Truxtun Letter Book, HSP; journal of James Pity, USF *Constitution,* 14 October 1798, QW 1:532; Truxtun's journal, 24 October 1798, HSP.

23. Letters, Truxtun to Stoddert, 27 October, Truxtun's Letter Book, HSP; Stoddert to Truxtun, 3 November, 10 December 1798 and 16 January 1799, RG45, MF-149, Nimitz Library, USNA; also, Truxtun's journal, 18 January 1799, HSP.

24. Letter, Truxtun to Stoddert, 10 February 1799, QW 2:326–27; instructions for Captain Barreaut, commander of the frigate *l'Insurgente* from General Desfourneaux and

Barreaut's battle report to Desfourneaux, undated translations, RG45, Entry 464, Box 42, NARA; *extract des Services de Michel Pierre Barreaut,* and battle report of Michel Pierre Barreaut commander, *l'Insurgente* to Gen. Etienne Desfourneaux, agent, directoire, Pointe a Pitre, Guadeloupe, 22 March 1799, Marine Archives, Château de Vincennes, Paris; also, Truxtun's journal, 9 and 10 February, HSP.

25. Letters, Stoddert to Truxtun, 11 January 1799, Letters of Secretary of the Navy to Officers, 18 June 1798–28 August 1800, RG45, MF-209, Nimitz Library, USNA.

26. Truxtun's journal, 9 and 10 February 1799, AM680, HSP.

27. Desfourneaux's orders to Barreaut, undated translation; Barreaut's battle report; Desfourneaux's summary of the reports of *l'Insurgente*'s officers concerning Captain Barreaut's behavior during *l'Insurgente*'s battle with *Constellation,* Marine Archives, Vincennes.

28. Ibid.

29. Geoffrey M. Footner, *Tidewater Triumph,* 75.

30. Letter, Stoddert to Alexander Murray, 26 September 1798, RG45, MF-209, Nimitz Library, USNA.

31. Ibid.; Lt. John Rodgers's battle report to Stoddert, 15 February 1799, reprinted in Claypoole's *American Daily Advertizer,* Philadelphia, 13 March 1799; Truxtun's journal, 10 February 1799, HSP; letters, Truxtun to Stoddert, 10 February, 7 March 1799, Truxtun Letter Book, HSP; orders, Stoddert to Truxtun, 8 December 1798, RG45, MF-209, Nimitz Library, USNA; letter, Thomas Williams, commander, U.S. Brig *Norfolk,* to Stoddert, 11 February 1799, reprinted in *Claypoole's American Daily Advertiser,* 11 March 1799; Hulbert Footner, *Sailor of Fortune,* 204–22.

32. Hulbert Footner, *Sailor of Fortune,* 204–22.

33. Ibid., 215–22.

34. Ibid., 224.

35. Letter, Truxtun to Stoddert, 7 March 1799, Truxtun Letter Book, HSP. Truxtun wrote that it was singular that she was the first taken.

36. Letters, Truxtun to an unknown friend, 17 February 1799, reprinted in *Claypoole's American Daily Advertiser,* 13 March 1799; Stoddert to Truxtun, 10 December 1798, RG45, MF-209, Nimitz Library.

37. Ferguson, *Truxtun,* 175–77.

38. Letter, Truxtun to *Constellation*'s officers, 9 August 1799, Truxtun-Hare Papers, HSP. Truxtun quit the navy in protest 1 August 1799 when Stoddert and President Adams refused his demand to revise the navy's seniority list and allow the now-popular captain to leapfrog over Silas Talbot, a political ally of John Adams. While in this instance Truxtun picked the right man to pass over, his ego blinded him to the fact that Talbot owed his original seniority status to Adams's earlier intervention that resulted in Captain Barney's decision to decline George Washington's appointment.

39. Jean Boudriot and Herbert Berti, *La frégate, étude historique, 1650–1850* (Paris: Edite par Aucre, 1992), 115; plan of *Immortalite,* National Maritime Museum, Greenwich, England; dimensions of *Insurgent,* RG45, Entry 464, Box 42, NARA.

40. Boudriot and Berti, *La frégate,* 111; Ferguson, *Truxtun,* 175–76; letters, Truxtun to Stoddert, 10 February 1799, QW 2:326–27; Truxtun to Jeremiah Yellott, 16 February 1799,

Truxtun Letter Book, AM6795, HSP; Loller Cocke to William Pennock, 11 February 1799, reprinted in *Claypoole's American Daily Advertiser,* 12 March 1799.

41. Captain Barreaut's battle report to General Desfourneaux; Rodgers's battle report to Secretary Stoddert, 15 February 1799; Truxtun's battle report to Stoddert, 10 February 1799.

42. Rodgers's battle report to Secretary Stoddert, 15 February 1799; Truxtun's battle report to Stoddert, 10 February 1799; also, *Claypoole's American Daily Advertiser,* 26 March 1799.

43. Ferguson, *Truxtun,* 164, 168, see also preliminary decision to court-martial Barreaut; court's decision to acquit Barreaut; testimony of *l'Insurgente*'s junior officers against Captain Barreaut; Captain's Barreaut's service record, Marine Archives, Vincennes; pension case of William Brown, QW 2:337–38.

44. Letters, Stoddert to Truxtun, 13 March, 15 April 1799, RG45, MF-149, NARA; Truxtun to Rodgers, 11 May 1799, Truxtun Letter Book, HSP; Ferguson, *Truxtun,* 176, 178–87.

45. Letters, Truxtun to Charles Biddle, 17 October 1799, Truxtun-Biddle Papers, HSP; Stoddert to Truxtun, 11 November 1799, QW 4:377–80; Truxtun's journal, 31 January 1800, HSP.

46. Truxtun's journal, 1 and 2 February 1800, HSP; Capt. F. M. Pitot's battle report, 1 and 2 February 1800, QW 5:166–69.

47. Battle report of Capt. F. M. Pitot, *La Vengeance* (a translation of his report to the Ministry of Marine), undated, QW 5:166–69.

48. Ibid.; Captain Truxtun's journal, 1, 2 February 1800, HSP.

49. Truxton's journal, 1, 2 February 1800, HSP.

50. Battle report of Capt. F. M. Pitot, *La Vengeance* (a translation of his report to the Ministry of Marine), undated, QW 5:166–69.

51. Truxtun's journal, 2 February 1800, HSP.

52. Letters, Truxtun to Stoddert, 3 February 1800, QW 5:159; Isaac Henry to Hugh Henry, 3 February 1800, QW 5:162.

53. Letters, Stoddert to the Speaker of the House of Representatives, 20 March 1800, QW 5:332–33; consul Phillips to Secretary of State John Marshall, 9 February and 22 March 1800, QW 5:204, 342; Geoffrey M. Footner, "Glory Denied: The Story of Henry Geddes' Frustrations in USS *Patapsco* at Curaçao," an unpublished article on the subject of the defense of Curaçao by Captain Geddes against French invasion, 23 July 1800.

54. Captain Pitot and his officers' report of battle with HMS *Seine,* 20 and 21 August 1800, Ministry of Marine, translated for Allen J. Crosby, RG45, Entry 464, NARA; Cooledge, *Ships of the Royal Navy,* 365.

55. Cooledge, *Ships of the Royal Navy,* 135, 365; Boudriot and Berti, *La fregate,* 158, 166, 167, 179.

56. Boudriot and Berti, *La fregate,* 166, 167, 179; "Strength of the US *Constellation* and French Frigate *La Vengeance,*" from *Claypoole's American Daily Advertiser,* 28 April 1800, QW 5:163–64.

57. Letter, Stoddert to Truxtun, 13 September 1808, enclosing R. T. Lowes's letter to Stoddert, 13 September 1808, plus Truxtun's reply, undated, QW 5:70–72.
58. Letter, Stoddert to Thomas Fitzsimmons, 1 December 1800, QW 7:3.
59. Letters, Murray to Stoddert, 28 December 1800, QW 7:52; Stoddert to Murray, 30 December 1800, QW 7:56.
60. Letter, Murray to Capt. Prosper Sergente, Fr. Lugger *Mars,* 18 January 1801, QW 7:96.
61. Letters, Stoddert to Murray, 16 March 1801, QW 7:148; Murray to Stoddert, 21 March 1801, QW 7:152; Stoddert to Murray, 23 March 1801, QW 7:156; Murray to Stoddert, 1 April 1801, QW 7:170; Lt. Henry Caldwell to Lt. Col. William Burrows, 3 April 1801, QW 7:175.
62. Letters, Gen. Samuel Smith, acting secretary of the navy, to Murray, 11 April 1801, QW 7:186; Murray to S. Smith, 26 April 1801, QW 7:205: *Constellation* drew 22 feet 6 inches. USF *United States* drew 22 feet 6 inches, too. In 1804, in the Mediterranean Sea, *Constitution* drew 23 feet 3 inches.
63. Letter, Murray to S. Smith, 12 April 1801, QW 7:189.
64. Letter, Capt. James McKnight, USMC, to Comdt. William W. Burrows, 17 April 1801, QW 7:435–36.
65. Letters, Joshua Humphreys to S. Smith, 20, 22 April and 3 May 1801, Joshua Humphreys Letter Book, HSP.
66. Letters, Murray to S. Smith, 18 May; Smith to Murray, 23 May 1801, QW 7:227, 234.
67. Letter, Murray and Humphreys to S. Smith, 26 May 1801, Joshua Humphreys Letter Book, HSP.
68. Letters, Gen. H. Dearborn, acting secretary of the navy, to Humphreys, 27 June 1801, JHC, HSP; Humphreys to Dearborn, 7 July 1801, Joshua Humphreys Letter Book, HSP; Humphreys to Capt. Thomas Tingey, commandant, Washington Navy Yard, 7 August 1801, Joshua Humphreys Letter Book, HSP; Dearborn to Humphreys, 9 July 1801, JHC, HSP; Secretary of the Navy Robert Smith to Humphreys, 13 August 1801, JHC, HSP; letter, Samuel Humphreys to George Harrison, 22 May 1817, RG45, Entry 244, vol. 9, NARA. Humphreys reminded Harrison of the work Nathaniel Hutton performed on *Constellation* when she was repaired at Philadelphia.
69. Letter, Humphreys to Secretary of the Navy Robert Smith, with a general review of the condition of *Constellation,* 12 September, 7 October 1801, Joshua Humphreys Letter Book, HSP; letters, R. Smith to Murray, 30 September 1801, QW 7:289, and 27 October 1801, BW 1:609.
70. Letters, R. Smith to Murray, 31 October, QW 7:295; Murray to R. Smith, 4 November, QW 7:298–99, R. Smith to Murray, 9 November 1801, QW 7:301–2.
71. Letters, Murray to R. Smith, 1 December 1801, QW 7:304–5, R. Smith to Murray, 5 December 1801, BW 1:627; Murray to R. Smith, 16 December 1801, QW 7:308–9; Murray to R. Smith, 26 February 1802, BW 2:68; ASP 1:252. See chapter 3 for measurements of the masts and spars installed in *Constellation* by Joshua Humphreys in 1801.

72. *Constellation*'s Log, by Midn. Thomas MacDonald, 29 April through 9 May 1802, Delaware Historical Society (DHS), Wilmington; Murray's journal, 5, 13, and 21 July 1802, RG45, NARA; letters, Murray to R. Smith, 7 May, 5 July, BW 2:146, 192–93; Murray to Nicholas C. Nissen, Danish consul, 13 July 1802, BW 2:202.

73. *Constellation*'s Log (MacDonald), 22 July 1802; Murray's journal, 22 July and 11 August 1802, BW 2:209, 230; letter, Keith Spence to Polly Spence, 31 July 1802, Huntington Library and Art Gallery, San Marino, California.

74. Letter, Murray to R. Smith, 30 July 1802, BW 2:217–19.

75. Letters, Murray to R. Smith, 14 August 1802, BW 2:234–35; Murray to William Eaton, U.S. consul, Tunis, 18 August 1802, BW 2:238–39; Murray to Capt. Richard V. Morris, 20 August 1802, BW 2:242–43; Eaton to secretary of state, 23 August 1802, BW 2:248–49.

76. Letters, James L. Cathcart, ex–U.S. consul, Tripoli, to secretary of state, 8 October 1802, BW 2:287–88; Murray to Morris, 12 December 1802, BW 2:331; Murray to R. Smith, 13 December 1802, referring to Smith's letter of 23 October to Commodore Morris, ordering Murray home, BW 2:332; Murray to R. Smith, 20 December 1802, BW 2:336; Murray's journal, 26 January, 10 to 15 March 1803, RG45, NARA; letter, R. Smith to Murray, 31 July 1805, BW 6:199.

77. Letters, William Bainbridge to Cdr. Edward Preble, 23 October 1803, BW 3:170; Bainbridge to Lt. John Smith (*Vixen*), 31 October 1803, BW 3:171; Bainbridge to R. Smith, 1 November 1803, BW 3:171–72; Bainbridge to Preble, 6, 25 November 1803, BW 3:173, 175; R. Smith to Preble, 7 May 1804, BW 4:88; Edward Preble's diary, 27 November 1803, BW 3:240; journal of surgeon Jonathan Cowdery, BW 3:532; Leiner, *Millions for Defense,* 70–71.

78. Davies, "Robert Smith and the Navy," 305–22.

79. Letters, R. Smith to Preble, 7, 21 May 1804, BW 4:88, 114–15; R. Smith to Campbell, 29 May 1804, BW 4:127; R. Smith to Barron, 6 June 1804, BW 4:152–54.

80. Journal of William Eaton, June 9–26, Huntington Library, San Marino, California; letter, Campbell to Barron, 10 June 1804, BW 4:175; letter, Preble to O'Brien, 13 June, BW 4:183–84; Rodgers's journal (*Congress*), 4 July 1804, BW 4:247; battle report, Preble to R. Smith, 18 September 1804, BW 4:293–308; letters, Richard O'Brien to John Gavino, 5, 14 September 1804, BW 4:516–17.

81. Resumé, Captain Barron's squadron activities, July 1804–June 1805, BW 5:8–12; letters, Barron to Rodgers, 28 February 1805, BW 5:377, Campbell to Barron, 10 April 1805, BW 5:498; Campbell to R. Smith, 11 April 1805, BW 5:4–5.

82. Letters, Commo. John Rodgers to Campbell, 16 August 1805, BW 6:233; Captain Decatur and Master Commandants Stewart and Shaw to Campbell, 18 August 1805, BW 6:235; Rodgers to Campbell, 19 August 1805, BW 6:237; Rodgers to R. Smith, 21 and 27 August 1805, BW 6:240, 251; Rodgers to Campbell, 21 August 1805 (2 letters), BW 6:240–41, 243; Rodgers to William Higgins, naval agent, Malta, 22 August 1805, BW 6:245; journal of Hezekiah Loomis, USF *Congress,* 20 September 1805, BW 6:285; R. Smith to Rodgers, 12 October 1805, BW 6:290–91; R. Smith to John Cassin, 26 November 1805, BW 6:312; resumé of service, BW 6:36.

83. Davies, "Robert Smith and the Navy," 313–18; vessel repairs, ASP 1:252–53; report, Smith to speaker of the House of Representatives, 28 June 1806, BW 6:357–58; letter, constructor Josiah Fox to Capt. Thomas Tingey, commandant, Washington Navy Yard, 12 November 1807, BW 6:579; report, Edward Preble to President Jefferson, 1 January 1805 (incorrectly dated 1805; should be 1806), Thomas Jefferson Papers, CXLVI, folder 25411, Library of Congress.

84. Report, R. Smith to speaker, 28 June 1806, BW 6:357–58; Preble, report to Jefferson, 1 January 1806, Library of Congress.

85. Cost of repairs, ASP 1:252–53.

CHAPTER 3. TINGEY'S REBUILD, 1812

1. Eckert, *Navy Department in the War of 1812*, 15.

2. Congress, Act of 30 March 1812.

3. USS *Adams*, 24 guns, dimensions: length, 128 feet 4 inches and breadth, 35 feet, launched at Brooklyn, New York, 8 June 1799, at a cost of $76,622; act of 30 March 1812 authorized $60,000 to redesign and rebuild *Adams;* letter, Tingey to Hamilton, 13 June 1812, found in Dudley, ed., *Naval War of 1812*, 1:132: "I have carefully examined this ship and feel convinc'd from her extreme state of decay that to repair her afloat will be far more expensive than to build a new ship." A summary of the work done at the Washington Navy Yard appeared in the *National Intelligencer*, 29 December 1812: "A LAUNCH—Thursday last, about half past 11 o'clock was launched from the Navy Yard at this city, the frigate *Adams*, which had been hauled up, divided in the middle, lengthened fifteen feet, and almost rebuilt. She proudly swam into her destined element at the appointed time, amid the acclamations of hundreds, under a salute of artillery. After the launch many of the ladies and gentlemen assembled in a sail loft, which had been cleaned for the occasion, and spent a pleasant hour. The *Adams* is to be commanded by Capt. Morris." Morris, "The Autobiography of Charles Morris," 169–72: Captain Morris recorded in his journal that *Adams* sailed from the navy yard 8 May 1813, but she proved to be top-heavy and very unstable. After a survey by naval officers the ship returned to the Washington Navy Yard 12 August 1813 and was converted into a sloop of war. The navy sent her crew, consisting of 250 sailors and one hundred marines, to Annapolis to man Forts Madison and Severn against possible British attack. The yard had *Adams* ready once again 18 November. Letter, Captain Charles Morris, commander, USS *Adams*, to Secretary William Jones, 31 December 1813, Dudley, *Naval War of 1812*, 2:401–2. While still on the Potomac River just prior to his dash for the Capes, Captain Morris wrote the secretary affirming that the yard's work on his ship was still troublesome: "I regret that the ship gives but little satisfaction either to myself or officers, they are so little satisfied with her that they would willingly change to any other vessel that can get to sea, but will not apply for a removal while I remain in her. They do not consider her a safe vessel, owing to the motion of her rudder which I formerly mentioned—I believe myself

that this continual motion, which increases in violence in propertion [*sic*] to the ships way in the water, will materially affect the durability of the ship." On the night of 18 January 1814, with two inexperienced Potomac River pilots on board *Adams*, Captain Morris made a dash for the Capes and the Atlantic Ocean. He wrote that the wind blew hard, causing the ship to sail so fast that proper soundings could not be recorded: "We shoaled and almost immediately struck the ground two or three times." A change of course took the ship into deeper water and twelve knots carried *Adams* past the Royal Navy ships anchored in Lynnhaven Bay. "We were probably not even seen by them," Morris wrote in his journal.

4. U.S. Frigate *Chesapeake*, launched at Gosport Navy Yard, 1799, drafted and built by Josiah Fox; 36 guns, length bpp 152 feet 8 inches, breadth 41 feet 3 inches. Bearss, *Charlestown Navy Yard*, 1:95–108, 115, 116, 120, 121, citing letter, Hamilton to Bainbridge, 2 April 1812; Bainbridge to Hamilton, 6 April 1812, Bainbridge to Hamilton, 12, 13 April 1812; Bainbridge to Secretary of the Army Eustis, 25 May 1812, Bainbridge to Hamilton, 5, 10 Junes 1812; Hamilton to Bainbridge, 30 June 1812, Hamilton to Bainbridge, 7 August 1812; Bainbridge to Secretary of Navy William Jones, 14 April 1813. Also, letters, Bainbridge to Hamilton, 14 April, 5 and 10 June 1812, Dudley, *Naval War of 1812*, 1:91, 93, 130, 131. Captain Bainbridge took the position of superintendent of Charlestown Navy Yard on an interim appointment while waiting for war to be declared and while awaiting an assignment to ship out. Bainbridge commenced repairs on *Chesapeake* upon the receipt of instructions from Hamilton on 2 April 1812. The yard at Charlestown was small and rundown; most of the timber and planks available for repairs had rotted after years of neglect. The yard's lack of facilities forced Bainbridge to arrange for *Chesapeake*'s repairs at a private wharf at extra cost. He wrote that since the time of her repairs at Washington, the frigate had deteriorated badly while in ordinary in Boston. Cost of *Chesapeake*'s great repair was $105,991. Hamilton offered Bainbridge command of *Constellation*, but Bainbridge waited to exert seniority over Captain Hull, commander of *Constitution*. When Hull arrived in Boston after his narrow escape from the Royal Navy, Bainbridge was in Washington. Hull slipped out to sea again and successfully engaged *Guerrière* before Bainbridge caught up with the ship and replaced him.

5. Section two of the act of 30 March 1812; see also letter, Stewart to Hamilton, 12 November 1812, ASP 1:278–79. This act specifically instructed the navy to use the appropriation for "the purchase of timber suitable for rebuilding the frigates *Philadelphia, New York, General Greene* and *Boston*." However, though the legislation ordered the navy's first purchases of timber designated for the four ships named, Congress did not specifically authorize the repair or rebuild of *Philadelphia*, a frigate lost at Tripoli, and the other three ships considered by William Jones to be hulks. Jones, who replaced Hamilton, used this congressional oversight as reason for withholding his approval to rebuild any of these ships.

6. Letter, Charles Stewart to Secretary of Navy Jones, 2 March 1813, Dudley, *Naval War of 1812*, 2:49–50; report, Thomas Tingey to Jones, 15 October 1814, ASP 1:342.

7. Letter, Joshua Humphreys to Congressman Adam Seybert, 5 September 1812; Dudley, *Naval War of 1812,* 1:455–61.

8. Ibid.

9. Ibid.; also see Joshua Humphreys to Robert Smith, secretary of the navy, 10 August and 12 September 1801, Joshua Humphreys Papers (JHP), HSP. Though Humphreys seemed to blame foul odors as the source of rot, it is known now that failure to combat condensation trapped between ceiling and planking caused rot to spread.

10. Letter, Humphreys to Seybert, 5 September 1812; letter, Humphreys to R. Smith, 7 October 1801; JHP, HSP.

11. Letter, Humphreys to Seybert, 5 September 1812, JHP, HSP; Dudley, *Naval War of 1812,* 1:460.

12. Letter, R. Smith to Humphreys, 26 October 1801, JHP, HSP; letter, R. Smith to Alex Murray, 5 December 1801, BW 1:627.

13. Report, Hamilton to Henry Clay, speaker, ASP 1, no. 88, 253.

14. Letter, Humphreys to R. Smith, 12 September 1801, JHP, HSP; letter, Preble to Thomas Jefferson, received 1 January 1806; Jefferson incorrectly recorded receipt of the message 1 January 1805, Thomas Jefferson Papers, CXLVI, folder 25411, Library of Congress.

15. Report, Tingey to Secretary of the Navy William Jones, 15 October, 1814; ASP 1:342.

16. Chapelle, *History of the American Sailing Navy,* 234. This naval architect, draftsman, and author, presumably having read Tingey's report to the secretary of the navy, wrote that in 1812 *Constellation* was rebuilt and her beam was increased by fourteen inches and her appearance was much changed. Chapelle provides his readers with two choices: Tingey extended her beam by (a) doubling her planking or (b) padding out her frames. Chapelle does not present the alternative probability that the increased molded breadth at the dead flat of her newly rebuilt frame altered her hull shape after refairing her lines throughout the length of the frigate's hull. Either padding or altering the shape of the ship's frames would produce a modification in hull shape, but as Tingey replaced all of her futtocks, padding was unwarranted. Double planking would not contribute to the ship's stability but would add appreciably to *Constellation's* deadweight and draft. Chapelle and Polland, *Constellation Question,* 19. Chapelle revised his thinking here as he offered the argument that carpenters under Tingey's supervision double planked or girdled *Constellation* with seven-inch planks bolted to the ship's wales below her light load line to a point a little above her load waterline. Without citations supporting this bizarre method of increasing stability, Chapelle rested his case. Supporters and opponents of his position on the provenance of the ship have blindly accepted this position, including Polland, Chapelle's opponent in this published debate. "Samuel Humphreys," *Army and Navy Chronicle* (3 December 1840) 11, 358–60 (reprint of an article from the *New York Times* and *Star*). Humphreys points out in this article, which he signed H.S., that the French navy corrected instability of a number of its ships by doubling them with light wood a foot thick at the extreme breadth but ten feet under water. Humphreys notes that the cause of instability was evidently not the lack of extreme breadth but the diminishing breadth at the place of flotation, fore and aft. He wrote that

the form of the immersed body and the weight of the ship are the chief components of stability. Continuing, he argued that stability could be obtained by keeping the center of gravity as short a distance as possible below the water's surface. We must increase the area of the load water section so as to ensure a sufficient degree of stability. Increasing the breadth of a ship within the limits of the parts immersed and emerged by inclination, certainly adds to the stability. Later in the article Humphreys mentioned overgunning as one reason American warships (which, like *Constellation,* had been built with speed in mind) could be unstable; heavy armament placed on the spar deck of the ship, added to masts, spars and rigging, brought the center of gravity above the load waterline. Nowhere in this article does Humphreys suggest that a ship's stability can be improved by girdling it above the load waterline, as Chapelle argued Tingey did when rebuilding *Constellation.* In this discussion of instability, Humphreys never mentioned *Constellation* specifically, a ship his father designed for speed and which had been overgunned and overmasted before departing on her initial cruise. Letter, John Lenthall to Commo. William Skinner, chief of the Bureau of Construction, Equipment, and Repair, 18 December 1851 (included with letter to Secretary of the Navy Graham), RG45, MF-518, NARA. Discussing *Constellation*'s reputation for instability, Lenthall noted that it is no new discovery in naval architecture that large dimensions with a small displacement give brilliant qualities to ships—though speed is highly desirable, it is not the only quality required in ships of war. Here again is a veiled reference to *Constellation*'s sharp underbody and her difficulty in carrying heavy guns on two decks, perhaps the real cause of her instability. Lenthall's modifications in 1853 did not include significant alterations in her hull shape below the waterline but did include plans to razee her into an inferior sloop of war, which should have reduced her weight above the waterline. Wegner, *Fouled Anchors,* 2. To establish the integrity of this report's basic premise, that there were no alterations in *Constellation*'s hull design (shape) from the time Joshua Humphreys had drawings of her prepared in 1795 to the day yard crews commenced dismantling the ship in 1853, the framers of this navy-authorized report seemed unaware of Tingey's report to Jones concerning her rebuild of 1812, dated 15 October 1814. However, after reading unidentified documents about the increase in *Constellation*'s beam, the author of *Fouled Anchors* shrugged off this change as merely "some addition of thicker planks." Clearly, there was no reason to fasten an extra seven-inch outer layer of planks to her hull's wales as Tingey documents that the ship was "rebuilt up entirely new." But, assuming that *Fouled Anchors*'s undocumented opinion has merit, the weight of an added seven inches of planking to the ship's sides at the ship's wales alone would increase her deadweight by as much as 115 tons, causing her to settle deeper into the water though her draft previously equaled that of U.S. Frigate *United States,* a substantially larger ship. It is documented that *Constellation*'s draft actually decreased as a result of the 1812 rebuild. Wegner, "An Apple and an Orange," 88–89. Defending the conclusion of *Fouled Anchors,* published a year earlier, Wegner, writing about the 1812 rebuild, evidently had still not discovered Tingey's report to Jones of 15 October 1814 concerning the increase of *Constellation*'s breadth. He doggedly sticks to his undocumented claim that any increase in her beam was the result of adding an extra seven inches of planking to her top sides. He does state (on page 89, note 36, next to last line) that following the rebuild *Constellation*'s extreme breadth was the same in 1812 as the ship's extreme breadth dimension following her rebuild in 1854. Though an interesting comment, it is not true. Dunne, "The Frigate *Constellation*," appendix 1, 2–85, 95. Dr. Dunne's article was a rebuttal of *Fouled Anchors*'s conclusions, and he included in it the complete text of Tingey's report of 15 October 1814 to William Jones. Dunne's principal argument is that Wegner was wrong about the double planking and he accepts Tingey's report at face value. In addition to successfully undermining the unsupported data contained in *Fouled Anchors*, Dr. Dunne's article brought forward other primary source data that the authors of the navy report ignored. Wegner, "The Frigate Strikes Her Colors," 246. In his response to Dr. Dunne's article and of his interpretation of the contents of Tingey's report, Wegner provides his readers with the definition of "moulded breadth" and informs them correctly that a change in *Constellation*'s molded breadth would signal a change in hull form. Then, incredibly, Wegner writes that "if Captain Tingey meant *Constellation*'s molded or designed beam was increased, he would have said it," which is exactly what Dr. Dunne and most other historians, including this writer, believe that Tingey wrote in his report to Jones that he accomplished. Letter, John Rodgers, president of the Navy Board of Commissioners, to James Barron, commandant, Gosport Navy Yard, 16 July 1829, RG45, Entry 216, NARA. Rodgers reprimanded Barron in 1829 for replacing *Constellation*'s pine wales and top timbers used in Tingey's rebuild in 1812 with new pine wales in 1828. Barron pointed out that when Tingey used pine in 1812 pine was considered as durable as white oak and used on *Wasp, President,* and *Hornet,* as well as on *Constellation.* There was no hint in this correspondence that the pine wales replaced by Barron in 1828 were thicker than seven inches. Barron replaced pine with pine because of a shortage of white oak plank at Gosport in 1828. Georgia pine weighs, on an average, about 5 percent less than white oak.

17. Letter, Captain Alexander Murray to Acting Secretary of Navy Samuel Smith, QW 7:205.

18. Letter, Hugh Campbell to Samuel Barron, 10 April 1805, BW 5:498.

19. Letter, Truxtun to Secretary of War James McHenry, 23 June 1798, QW 1:132.

20. Letter, J. Humphreys to R. Smith, 7 October 1801, JHP, HSP. Humphreys wrote that in "the design and construction of our first frigates it was our object of the first importance to make them fast sailing."

21. Harry Bluff [M. F. Maury], "Our Navy," *Southern Literary Messenger,* January 1841, 16. Maury criticizes the Navy Department for selecting "a long legged, crank, 36 gun ship [*Constellation*] for the East Indies [China] cruise—of all the vessels in the Navy, the one least suitable for such a service." The term "long leg" was attached to vessels with keels that dragged downward significantly from bow to stern—a term usually applied to the keel design of Chesapeake Bay pilot schooners.

22. USS *John Adams,* a small frigate (28 guns) built at Charleston, S.C., in 1799. She was considered too sharp by Tingey and he ordered Josiah Fox to rebuild her at the Washington Navy Yard between 1807 and 1809. Chapelle, *History of the American Sailing Navy,* 233, 244: Chapelle confused *Adams* with *John Adams,* writing that work commenced on the

former in 1807 and was completed in 1812, whereas Josiah Fox repaired and converted *John Adams* into a sloop of war between 1807 and 1809. Also, letter, Josiah Fox to Thomas Tingey, 12 November 1807, BW 6:579. Fox reported that work on *John Adams* was considerably advanced at that date (1807). Work on *Adams,* as previously noted, did not start until April 1812. Tingey, the conservative ex–Royal Navy officer, also rerigged the U.S. Navy's Baltimore schooners *Nautilus* and *Enterprize* as brigs. The former was the first U.S. Navy vessel lost in 1812 and though observers considered *Enterprize* slow as a brig, she became "the lucky *Enterprize*" because of her good fortune during the war. *Vixen,* another Fells Point–built navy schooner, became a brig in 1804 and the Royal Navy captured her in 1812.

23. Franklin Buchanan, Journal No. 6, Dimensions U.S. Frigate *Constellation,* 1815, United States Naval Academy, Nimitz Library, Special Collections, Annapolis, Maryland; Joshua Humphreys, builder's draft (reprint, 1943), no. 408192, superseding 41-9-1-P (WD), RG19 Entry 126, NARA.

24. Buchanan Journal No. 6; also Humphreys' draft, no. 408192, RG19, Entry 126.

25. Josiah Fox Papers, Letter Book, PEM. Fox measured *Constellation* in 1806 and calculated the ship's maximum molded breadth at 40 feet, and located her dead flat section at a point 94 feet 2 inches forward of the rabbet of the post. This, the point of the dead flat, was 3 feet 5 3/4 inches forward of one-third of the length of the keel. Thus, Fox confirmed once again, that Stodder built *Constellation* in accordance with Humphreys' dimensions and specifications.

26. Ibid.; Buchanan Journal No. 6 and U.S. Frigate *Constellation* Orders, Muster Rolls, Stores & etc., Thomas Truxtun Order Book, 1798, MS-679–67, HSP; Humphreys' draft, no. 408192, U.S. Frigates *Constellation* and *Congress,* RG19, Entry 126. Also, USF *Congress's* measurements, QW 4:76, 140–42. A comparison of Franklin Buchanan's measurement of *Constellation's* keel (140 feet) with constructor James Hackett's measurements of *Congress's* keel, 145 feet (147 feet 7 inches extreme keel) suggests that *Constellation's* stem and post raked a total of seven and one-half feet more than her sister ship. This may account, in part, for *Congress's* less distinguished sailing reputation compared to *Constellation.* Hackett measured *Congress,* built from the same drawings as *Constellation,* in 1799. Others attribute *Constellation's* sweeping rake of stem to builder Stodder when in reality it was Joshua Humphreys' innovation, influenced by Chesapeake Bay schooner design, which he included in his original frigate design, afterwards adding diagonal riders to strengthen the ends of the long ships with relatively sharp ends.

27. Letter, Stewart to Jones, 2 March 1813, Dudley, *Naval War of 1812,* 2:49–50.

28. Letter, Humphreys to R. Smith, 7 October 1801, Joshua Humphreys Letter Book, HSP. Humphreys notified Secretary Robert Smith that he and Captain Murray agreed that *Constellation's* masts and yards "would be reduced to more closely match those of Congress."

29. Letter, Humphreys to R. Smith, 7 October 1801, Joshua Humphreys Letter Book, HSP. Humphreys concluded that *Constellation* was overmasted and he reduced the lengths of her masts and shifted their location. Tingey's changes, producing one-third greater sail area, would have overpowered the ship if she had not been redrafted first. Also,

Buchanan's Journal No. 6, which contains the length of *Java*'s foremast, 98 feet, main mast, 104 feet, and mizzenmast, 86 feet.

30. Letter, Murray to S. Smith, 26 April 1801, QW 7:205; also Log of U.S. Frigate *Constellation*, commanders William Crane and John Shaw, 1817, Huntington Library, San Marino, California; also, Log No. 2, RG24, NARA, Capt. Charles Morris, commodore, and J. J. Nicolson, flag captain, 15 September 1819. Prior to commencing a long cruise to Rio de La Plata in 1819, *Constellation*'s maximum draft measured 22 feet 3 inches in the Elizabeth River; as the ship was fully provisioned and watered on both occasions there is no explanation for the difference between the one in 1817 and the later one in 1819 except in the latter case *Constellation*, heavily loaded for a cruise to the east coast of South America, lay in Elizabeth River where September water temperatures often exceed 80 degrees.

31. Letter, Capt. Charles Morris to Secretary of the Navy William A. Graham, 15 November 1851, Letters of the Bureau of Construction, Equipment, and Repair to the Secretary of the Navy, RG19, Entry 49, 55.

32. U. S. House of Representatives, "Deficit in Naval Appropriations," 7 February 1813, ASP 1: 286–89.

33. U.S. House, *Condition of the Several Navy Yards*, 1 December 1814; ASP 1, 13th Congress, 3d sess., as cited by Agranat, "Thorough and Efficient Repair," 88–91.

34. *Niles Register*, 19 July 1829, profile of the U.S. Frigate *Constitution*.

35. *Niles Register* 5, supp. 5, profile of William Bainbridge; letters, Paul Hamilton, secretary of the navy, to Capt. Isaac Hull, 18 June 1812; Hull to Hamilton, 21 July 1812; Hull to Hamilton, 28 August 1812, Dudley, *Naval War of 1812*, 1:135, 136, 161–65, 231–33.

36. Letter, John Rodgers to Hamilton, 3 June 1812, Dudley, *Naval War of 1812*, 1:119–22.

37. Journal of Sailing Master William Laughton, commander of Gunboat 71, Sunday, 11 October 1812, Dudley, *Naval War of 1812*, 1:543; letter, Hamilton to Stewart, RG45, secretary letters to captains, MF-149, Nimitz Library, USNA.

38. Letters, Thomas Tingey to Hamilton, 1, 9, and 15 July and 3 December 1812, Dudley, *Naval War of 1812*, 1:183, 188–89, 613; also, Laughton's journal, 24 October 1812, Dudley, *Naval War of 1812*, 1:546.

39. Laughton's journal, entries from 6 to 26 November 1812, RG24, NARA.

40. Pratt, *Navy*, 211.

41. Letter, Charles Stewart to unknown correspondent, 4 February 1801. Governor Garcia to the president of the United States, 21 January 1801, QW 7:99, 100; list of vessels captured by Stewart, QW 7:312.

42. Eckert, *Navy Department in the War of 1812*, 14–15; Eckert references Irving Brant, *James Madison*, 6:125, 126.

43. Letter, Stewart to Hamilton, 12 October 1812, RG45, MF-125; letter, Stewart to William Jones, 23 January 1813, RG45, MF-125, Nimitz Library, USNA; letter, Lt. Charles Morris to Congressman Langdon Cheves, 9 January 1813, Dudley, *Naval War of 1812*, 2:20–24.

44. Chapelle and Polland, *Constellation Question,* 14, 16, 19. In 1970, more than two decades after he wrote *History of the American Sailing Navy,* Chapelle once again aggressively presented his position in the book cited on administrative rebuilding, herein defined as the United States Navy's clandestine policy of building new ships under the guise of rebuilding an old ship. Chapelle argued that a number of ships rebuilt between 1820 and 1855 (and he names them) were, in fact, ships built entirely new. His charge includes as a scenario a rogue navy conspiring to hoodwink Congress, the guardian of appropriations that closely protected its right to authorize new ships. Though under attack in 2000, his administrative rebuilding theory was unquestioned in 1970—even by his opponent, Leon Polland, the co-author of this book, as well as by most naval architects and historians. Writing in *Constellation Question,* Chapelle blocks out the earlier periods of U.S. Navy rebuilding activity as he describes Tingey's 1812 programs, including the rebuilding of *Constellation* and *Adams,* as a pre-rebuilding period and merely an introduction to the years (1820s) in postwar America when he declared that the navy commenced building new ships under the guise of rebuilding older ones. Obviously, *Adams* and *Constellation,* both redrafted in 1812, could not be considered new rogue ships, as Congress authorized and funded their repairs. Incredibly, Chapelle asks his readers to ignore these contradictions as he shapes his opinions on rebuilding, accepting that *Adams* was not only not new after her complete rebuild during which she was lengthened, but, according to his logic, not even a true rebuild as he refers to her as only partially rebuilt (14) even though Tingey added fifteen feet to her length. Writing about *Constellation* in 1970, Chapelle makes no mention of Tingey's report to Jones of 15 October 1814 but restates his conviction that *Constellation* was girdled in 1812 with no change to her molded breadth, and therefore, no change in her hull shape. He misleads his readers. By ignoring changes in the shape of *Constellation*'s hull, he hopes that her modifications in 1812, as well as her rebuilds of 1829 and 1839 which followed, would not impact on his argument that *Constellation*'s design between 1798 and 1853 was never altered. This denial allowed him to reach a conclusion that John Lenthall created a completely new design for a new *Constellation* in 1853, built administratively new without authority from Congress. The profound inconsistency of Chapelle's view on navy policy is a notion that the navy successfully carried through a secret program to replace ships for decades; that the navy hid from Congress plans and documents relating to ships included in its clandestine program for almost a half of century. This is, of course, absurd since the navy issued an annual report from 1823 onward in which it outlined for Congress its proposed activities each year. As an example, one may question the wisdom of the navy's decision to rebuild ships in specific instances such as its rebuild of U.S. Frigates *Macedonian* and *Congress.* One may even agree with Chapelle that rebuilding these two frigates stretched to the limits of common sense. But in the end, what Chapelle thought or anyone else believes today about the navy's rebuilding program as represented in these two instances, which Chapelle called administrative new ships, is immaterial, as Congress passed specific laws that authorized rebuilding of *Macedonian* and

Congress and appropriated funds to rebuild both ships. Neither Chapelle nor any other citizen has the right to overturn an act of Congress. Here then, Chapelle's rogue program, once exposed by its inconsistency, withers under scrutiny. Like a kid in his own backyard organizing a pickup game of baseball, Chapelle fashioned his rules for rebuilding according to the shape of the playing field. If readers understand his means or methods early on, then his ends or goals will not be hard to grasp in later chapters. The principal historically factual point made here is that by 1812, redrafting and making important alterations to ship hulls, spars, and equipment during the rebuilding process was a policy wholeheartedly embraced by the United States Navy with full knowledge of the executive and legislative branches of the government.

45. There are many examples of close cooperation concerning rebuilding as the navy, in its annual reports or by special communications, informed Congress of plans to redraft and rebuild specific ships. If nothing else, this multitude of reports, documents, and communications expose Chapelle's and Dana Wegner's failure to do research into the administration of the navy and its relationship to Congress between 1820 to 1842, at which time the Board of Commissioners was disbanded and the bureau system installed by the Navy Department.

46. Letter from Congress to the president, 26 August 1852, RG45, Entry 27, 67; also, Navy Annual Report, 1852, dated 4 December 1852. The Senate sent a letter to the president instructing the executive branch to revise annual reports to Congress and include, by the next session, abstracts of new projects of bureaus of different departments such as the Bureau of Construction, Equipment, and Repair of the Department of the Navy and in this manner highlight them for Congress's attention. When Secretary of the Navy John P. Kennedy of Baltimore presented his annual report in December 1852, he included Chief of the Bureau of Construction, Equipment, and Repair, W. B. Shubrick's, Abstract Report in which, in advance of any work performed, he notified Congress that "provision has been made in the estimate (for 1853) for repairing the *Franklin,* 74, reducing her to a razee of fifty guns, and the *Constellation,* frigate, of thirty six guns, reducing her to a first class sloop of war, by which two valuable cruising ships would be made available."

47. Lavery, "The Rebuilding of British Warships," pt. 1, 5–15, pt. 2, 113–27.

48. Letters, John Rodgers to John Branch, secretary of the navy, 2 August 1830; commissioners to secretary, RG45, Entry 28, NARA: 1,022. Rodgers informed Branch that the cost of a hull of a vessel of war estimated separately did not amount to more than one-third of a ship's total cost, when equipped and in a state of readiness for sea. A contemporary example of the difference between the cost of a ship and the cost of the hull, including masts, spars, and labor for sheathing the ship's bottom are in the figures for U.S. Frigate *Java,* a private contract. For the hull and extras listed above, builders William Parsons and William Flannigain received $94, 994.38; the navy's total cost for the ship was calculated at $232,767.38. The smaller amount, mostly representing the cost of her hull, amounted to 41 percent of the total cost.

49. Secretary William Jones's Report on the State of the Navy, presented to Congress, 22 February, 1814, *Niles Register* 6 (2 April 1814): 74.

50. Ibid.

51. Ibid.

52. Wegner, "An Apple and an Orange," 2–86. Wegner concludes that "the old *Constellation* was built essentially as designed by Humphreys and the hull form was not substantially or permanently altered before her demise." He wrote that there were no alterations to *Constellation*'s hull shape from the time that Humphreys/Doughty prepared the original drafts in 1795 until she was dismantled in 1853. If it is proved in this chapter that Wegner's conclusion is incorrect and that in fact Tingey altered the dimensions and shape of *Constellation*'s hull, it follows that the foundation on which Wegner based his thesis is flawed.

CHAPTER 4. THE LUCKY CONSTELLATION

1. Cooper, *History of the Navy,* 2:154n letters, Charles G. Ridgely to William Jones, 2 and 7 April, and Jones to Ridgely, 7 April, Ridgely to George de la Roche, 7 April 1814, ordering Roche to strip ship; Ridgely's Journal, Library of Congress. Cooper missed the blockade of USS *Erie* (Charles G. Ridgely, commanding) in the spring of 1814. Thomas Kemp, who built her under contract, delivered *Erie* to Ridgely, who sailed her down Chesapeake Bay for trials. Off the mouth of the Patuxent River he chased a Royal Navy brig down to Potomac River. Sighting a ship of the line, Ridgely reversed course and returned up the bay and immediately wrote to the secretary of the navy that since it was late in the season it might prove hazardous to attempt to run the blockade. Having received Secretary of the Navy William Jones's permission to lay up *Erie,* the much-needed sloop of war never attempted to break the blockade.

2. Van Horne and Formwalt, eds., *Correspondence and Miscellaneous Papers of Benjamin Henry Latrobe,* 3:448–50: letter, William Henry Latrobe to William Duane, 2 May 1813. Writing the month before the Battle of Craney Island but months after the Royal Navy trapped USS *Constellation,* Latrobe points out that Madison's underlying failure during the war was his inability to create any kind of sense that the country faced invasion or even blockade, particularly on Chesapeake Bay as a diversion for British forces in Canada. The navy possessed only eight frigates of thirty-two guns or more when Madison declared war. That Stewart, Hamilton, or even Madison held back one of the navy's best ships, completely rebuilt if not completely ready, at the navy yard, one day longer than necessary, is evidence enough of the mind-set of his administration. The only explanation of the Navy Department's failure to push Stewart to get out of Chesapeake Bay was the alarming passive attitude that affected the administration's handling of the crisis.

3. Letter, Latrobe to Isaac Hazlehurst, 13 December 1812, Latrobe Papers, 3:403–5. Hamilton resigned as secretary of the Navy Department 31 December, 1812. His replacement, William Jones, accepted the post 14 January 1813.

4. *An Act to Increase the Navy of the United States,* 2 January, 1813; the navy commissioned three ships of the line, *Independence, Washington,* and *Franklin,* after the war; of the total of six frigates authorized, *Columbia* burned at the Washington Navy Yard and *Java* and *Guerrière* were commissioned in 1815.

5. Orders, Lord Commissioners of the Admiralty to Adm. John B. Warren, 26 December 1812, Dudley, *Naval War of 1812,* 1:638.

6. Letter, Stewart to Hamilton, 29 December 1812, RG45, MF-125, Nimitz Library, USNA; George de la Roche's Journal, MHM 42:265. De la Roche recorded that floating ice already filled the bay when the ship left the Potomac 16 January.

7. Letters (2), Stewart to Secretary of the Navy William Jones, 23 January 1813, RG45, MF-125, NARA.

8. Letter, Jones to Stewart, 25 January 1813, RG45, MF-149, NARA.

9. Letter, Stewart to Jones, 5 February 1813, Dudley, *Naval War of 1812,* 2:311–12.

10. Ibid.

11. Letter, Stewart to Jones, 10 February 1813, RG45, MF-125, NARA.

12. Dudley, *Naval War of 1812,* 2:311, comments by the editor; Jones to commanders of ships refitting, 22 February 1813, Stewart to Jones, 2 March 1813, ibid., 2:48–50; there is no evidence to support the editor's statement that Stewart's ship was sea ready for a cruise in February 1813.

13. Letter, Stewart to Jones, 5 February 1813, Dudley, *War of 1812,* 2:311–12.

14. Ibid.; also, de la Roche Journal, MHM 42:265.

15. *Norfolk Herald,* 5, 8 February, 1813; also, Stewart to Jones, 5 February 1813, Dudley, *Naval War of 1812,* 2:311–12.

16. *Norfolk Herald,* 5, 8 February 1813; also Sailing Master Benjamin Brian to Jones, 13 November 1813, Dudley, *Naval War of 1812,* 2:393–94, concerning the events of 4 February, Stewart to Jones, 5 February 1813, and also Capt. George Burdett to Admiral Warren, 9 February 1813, Dudley, *Naval War of 1812,* 2:318–19: note 1 states that Captain Burdett arrived at Cape Henry 4 February 1813.

17. Stewart to Jones, 5 February 1813, Dudley, *Naval War of 1812,* 2:318–19.

18. Letter, Stewart to Jones, 17 March 1813, Dudley, *Naval War of 1812,* 2:315–16; also Rear Adm. George Cockburn to Adm. John B. Warren, 13 March 1813, ibid., 2:321.

19. Letters, Jones to Capt. John Cassin, 16 February, Dudley, *Naval War of 1812,* 2:313–14; Stewart to Jones, 17 and 22 March, ibid., 2:315–17; also Stewart to Jones, 24 March, RG45, MF-125, NARA, and Jones to Stewart, 27 March 1813, Dudley, *Naval War of 1812,* 2:317; also Hallahan, *Battle of Craney Island,* 38–43.

20. Letters, Stewart to Jones, 17 March 1813, Dudley, *Naval War of 1812,* 2:315–16; Cockburn to Warren, 23 March 1813, ibid., 2:326–29; also Holiday, "History of Portsmouth," an unpublished manuscript; John Lloyd Emmerson, "Some Fugitive Items of Portsmouth and Norfolk County History," an unpublished manuscript, Portsmouth Public Library, Portsmouth, Virginia.

21. Letter, Cassin to Jones, 20 March 1813, RG45, MF-125, NARA; Cooper, *History of the Navy,* 2:155–56.

22. Cooper, *History of the Navy*, 2:155-56.

23. Letter, Stewart to Jones, 22 March 1813, Dudley, *Naval War of 1812*, 2:316–17.

24. Letters, Stewart to Jones, 24 and 28 March 1813; Cassin to Jones, 18 and 20 March 1813, RG45, MF-125, Nimitz Library, USNA.

25. Letter, Jones to Stewart, 27 March 1813, Dudley, *Naval War of 1812*, 2:317.

26. Letter, Secretary John W. Croker to Warren, 17 May 1813, Dudley, *Naval War of 1812*, 2:356–57; also, "A List of Vessels Detained by the Blockade," undated, from the Papers and Letters of Moses Myers, Norfolk Archives, Chrysler Museum, Norfolk. Like the U.S. Navy, Royal Navy crews shared prize money, with the largest allocation awarded to commanders and fleet admirals. In addition to prize money for capturing *Constellation* and other navy craft, Warren and Cockburn could expect a large share of the prize cargoes of the commercial ships blockaded at Norfolk. There is evidence that a total of twenty-two ships lay at anchor above *Constellation,* with cargoes totaling in value approximately $360,000, plus the combined worth of all American vessels caught in the port.

27. Letters, Cockburn to Warren, 13, 23 March 1813, and Dudley, *Naval War of 1812*, 2:320–24, 326–29; also, letter, Robert Greenshow to Governor Barbour, 24 February 1814, H. W. Flournoy, ed., *Calendar of Virginia State Papers, 1 January 1808 to 31 December 1835,* (Richmond, Va.: Virginia State Library, 1892), 304–5. Greenshow informed the governor that soon after the Royal Navy fleet arrived in March, Cockburn, disguised as a waterman, landed at one of Norfolk's wharves and "possessed himself of every circumstance relative to our state of defense and the means in our power to resist their attacks." Later, Cockburn allowed local fishermen to continue to sail up Elizabeth River and deliver fish to Norfolk. He was rebuked by the admiralty for his leniency. Greenshow told the governor that fishing continued as watermen continued deliveries to Norfolk and the British fleet. Once again, according to Greenshow's letter, Cockburn availed himself of a daring means of gaining information. Disguised as a fisherman, the admiral hijacked a fishing boat, and casting a line as he paddled up river, he finally reached *Constellation* and entered into negotiations for fish with the crew. Once on board, he remarked on the superiority of "his" country's frigates to those of the "enemy." Though the depth of water between Sewell Point and Lambert Point in the vicinity of Tanner Creek, where the pilot in Cockburn's custody sounded, was only three fathoms, the main channel running up the middle of the river abreast of Craney Island reached a depth great enough to carry a ship of the line. Then, once above the island, the river's channel parallels its western shore until it reaches the mouth of the western branch, where the channel shifts to the western shore until the river narrows just below Norfolk, the spot Stewart selected to moor *Constellation.*

28. Cooper, *History of the Navy*, 2:156–58. Lieutenant Neale's observation that the alleged traitorous pilot conducted soundings for the channel inside the flats off Sewell Point at Tanner Creek, suggests that the American pilot misled his British captors. Cooper's writings on the plight of *Constellation* contain the ring of truth, though the sequence of

events became confused over time. While Cooper's history was published almost twenty years after the events of the War of 1812, several officers of *Constellation* still lived and, even more important, remained in naval service. For instance, Cooper states that Lt. William B. Shubrick, one of the navy's heroes of Craney Island, was a close friend. Cooper points out (159) that even though *Constellation* remained blockaded throughout the war, she survived to be treasured as one the navy's lucky vessels, along with *Enterprize* and *Constitution.* Letter, Stewart to Jones, 13 April 1813, RG45, MF-125, NARA; also, Cranwell and Crane, *Men of Marque,* 112.

29. Letter, Stewart to Jones, 13 April 1813, NARA RG45, MF-125, Nimitz Library, USNA.

30. Letter, Jones to Stewart, 27 March 1813, Dudley, *Naval War of 1812,* 2:317.

31. Letters, Stewart to Jones, 4 April, Jones to Stewart, 8 April 1813, Dudley, *Naval War of 1812,* 2:346–47. Once again Jones presented his strategy to Stewart: that the defense of one part (of the country) must be regulated by the whole. Locally, Stewart must make the best of what was available. Jones wrote that he did not believe that it was the enemy's intention to attack that place or the force in its waters. Jones, during these exchanges, exposed his lack of understanding of the importance of Norfolk, Portsmouth, Gosport, and *Constellation* and their connection to the free flow of goods shuttling between Hampton Roads via the Elizabeth River canal to North Carolina ports.

32. Letter, Stewart to Jones, no date, acknowledged received by Jones 22 April 1813, RG45, MF-125, NARA.

33. Letters, Jones to Stewart, 7, 17 May, 1813, RG45, MF-149, NARA.

34. Letter, Stewart to Jones, 12 May 1813, RG45, MF-125, NARA.

35. Letters, Charles Gordon, commander, USS *Constellation,* to Jones, 6, 12 October, Stewart to Jones, 18 October, Jones to Stewart, 28 October, sailing master Benjamin Bryan to Jones, 13 November 1813, Dudley, *Naval War of 1812,* 2:387–94; Joseph Tarbell to Jones, 7 December 1813, RG45, MF-125, NARA; Paullin, "Naval Administration," 42.

36. Letter, Jones to Master Comdt. Joseph Tarbell, 30 March 1813, RG45, M-149, NARA. Tarbell's original orders included his assignment to the Norfolk Flotilla under Cassin; Stewart's seniority gave him command of all naval activities in the Hampton Roads area.

37. Whitehorne, *Battle of Baltimore,* appendix B, 225.

38. Letter, Stewart to Jones, 13 May 1813, Dudley, *Naval War of 1812,* 2:347; letter, Capt. John Myers, aide to General Taylor, to Harry Heth, Richmond, date unknown, Moses Myers Papers, Norfolk Archives, Chrysler Museum, Norfolk; letter, Croker to Warren, 17 May 1813, Dudley, *Naval War of 1812,* 2:356–57; comments by the editor, ibid., 2:357.

39. Wertenbaker, *Norfolk,* 111; also, Hallahan, *Battle of Craney Island,* 42–43.

40. Letters, Stewart to Jones, 21 and 22 May 1813, RG45, MF-125, NARA; Latrobe to Robert Fulton, 6 June 1813, Latrobe Papers, 3:467–68.

41. Letters, Cassin to Jones, 13 May, 1, 10 and 15 June 1813, RG45, MF-125, NARA.

42. Hallahan, *Battle of Craney Island,* 54–56; Whitehorne, *Battle of Baltimore,* 57–60.

43. Letter, Cassin to Jones, 23 June 1813, Dudley, *Naval War of 1812,* 2:359–60; letter, Warren to Croker, 24 June 1813, ibid., 2:360–61.

44. Hallahan, *Battle of Craney Island,* 53, quoting letter, Taylor to Armstrong, 18 June 1813.

45. A true copy of the vote of the Council of War, 19 June 1813, James Maurice, recorder, Papers Defending General Robert B. Taylor's Actions in Defense of Craney Island, James Barron Papers, Box 2, Folder 17, Stem Library, College of William and Mary.

46. Letters, Capt. James Sanders (HMS *Junon*) to Cockburn, 20 June 1813; Cassin to Jones, 21 June 1813, Dudley, *Naval War of 1812,* 2:357–59.

47. A true copy of the vote of the Council of War, 20 June 1813, Barron Papers.

48. Deposition of Theo W. Maurice, Lt., Corps of Engineers, 26 December 1813, Papers Defending Robert B. Taylor, Barron Papers.

49. Letters, Cassin to Jones, 23 June 1813, Dudley, *Naval War of 1812,* 2:359–60; Sailing Master Benjamin Bryan to Jones, 13 November 1813, ibid., 2:393–94; also, Hallahan, *Battle of Craney Island,* 61–64; and James Jarvis Journal, *Virginia Historical Register and Literary Advertiser,* 1:138.

50. Jarvis Journal, 138; Hallahan, *Battle of Craney Island,* 64.

51. Letters, Warren to First Secretary of the Admiralty John M. Croker, 24 June 1813, Dudley, *Naval War of 1812,* 2:360–61; Lt. Col. Henry Beatty to General Taylor, 25 June 1813, *Virginia Historical Register,* 1:135–36; Hallahan, *Battle of Craney Island,* 65–73.

52. Beatty to Taylor, 25 June 1813, *Virginia Historical Record,* 135–36; letters, Cassin to Jones, 23 June 1813, Dudley, *Naval War of 1812,* 2:359–60; Capt. Robert Barrie (HMS *Dragon*) to Mrs. George Clayton, his mother: "Thank God *Dragon* had no share in the attack on Craney Island," ibid., 2:384–85.

53. Wertenbaker, *Norfolk,* 113–14; letter, Cockburn to Warren, 12 July 1813, Dudley, *Naval War of 1812,* 2:184–86.

54. Dudley, *Naval War of 1812,* 2:387, editor's comments on the condition of *Constellation* as brought to Secretary Jones's attention by Captain Gordon; letters, Jones to Charles Gordon, 6 October and 13 December 1813, Benjamin Bryan to Jones, 13 November 1813, ibid., 2:387–88, 393–94, 397–98; Joseph Tarbell to Jones, 7 December 1813, RG45, MF-125, NARA.

55. Letters, Stewart to Jones, 18 October 1813, Dudley, *Naval War of 1812,* 2:390–92; Jones to Stewart, 28 October 1813, ibid., 2:393.

56. Letters, Gordon to Jones, 28 December 1813, Dudley, *Naval War of 1812,* 2:400–401; Gordon to Jones, 3 and 11 February 1814, RG45, MF-125, NARA; *Niles Register,* 19 February 1814; letter, Gordon to Jones, 21 June 1813, RG45, MF-125, NARA. Captain Gordon previously commanded the Upper Chesapeake Bay Flotilla of gunboats, and for a period, four letter of marque Baltimore schooners, taken into the navy to bolster local forces when Cockburn threatened Baltimore in 1813. The young captain, still suffering the effects of a duel wound received in the aftermath of the *Chesapeake-Leopard* affair in 1807, seemed confused by the assignment. Jones appointed the veteran navy captain Joshua Barney to replace him. Napier, *Life and Correspondence of*

Admiral Sir Charles Napier, 91–93. Captain Napier, commanding HMS *Euryalus* (36 guns), smaller than *Constellation,* but about equal in armament, issued a challenge to Captain Gordon to come out and fight his ship, one on one, just as his hero, Captain Broke, commanding HMS *Shannon,* did with U.S. Frigate *Chesapeake.* Napier dated his letter 28 January 1815. Gordon, responding 8 February, provided Napier with the name of his representative, appointed to work out the details of the engagement. To an unknown correspondent Napier wrote that his challenge to *Constellation* was accepted and that the ships would meet in a few days. News of a peace treaty, worked out in Europe 24 December 1814, arrived before the battle took place, the good news reaching *Constellation* with Gordon's bad luck draped over her like a widow's veil.

57. J. D. Smith, "Commodore James Barron: Guilty as Charged?," U.S. Naval Institute *Proceedings* (November 1967), James Barron's File, Special Collections, Nimitz Library, USNA.

58. Ibid.; also Anthony, *Decatur,* 171–75.

59. Paullin, *Commodore John Rodgers,* 302. Rodgers, in 1815, assessing the leadership qualities of potential commissioners for the navy's new board, wrote that Gordon was a good seaman and qualified for command at sea, but his opinions were too flexible to qualify him for an appointment as commissioner.

60. Anthony, *Decatur,* 236–47.

61. Ibid.; also Ireland, "Rais Hammida," 187–96; also Decatur's Reports, ASP 1:396–97.

62. Letter, Decatur to secretary of the navy, 17 June 1815, Captain's Letters, RG45, MF-125, NARA; also, reports, Decatur to Crowninshield, ASP 1:396–97.

63. Allen, *Our Navy and the Barbary Corsairs,* 281–84.

64. Ibid.

65. Letter, Gordon to Rodgers, 26 November 1815, Rodgers Family Papers, Container No. 2, General Correspondence, 1814–19, Library of Congress (LC); also, letter, Gordon to Rodgers, 20 April 1815: Gordon brings to Rodgers's attention charges he has brought against Capt. Joseph Tarbell and others at Norfolk, Rodgers Papers, Container 9, 1815–23, LC.

66. Letter, W. Bainbridge to Crowninshield, 14 September 1815; Bainbridge to Gordon, 5 October 1815, RG45, MF-125, NARA.

67. Letters, Gordon to Mr. Norderling, son of consul of Sweden, 22 February 1816, Gordon to John Broadbent, U.S. consul, Messina, Gordon to Capt. O. H. Perry (*Java*), Gordon to Adam B. Kyle, 11 July 1816, Charles Gordon's Correspondence, MHM 67:389–418.

68. Letter, Gordon to H. Thorn, purser, New York, Gordon's Correspondence, MHM 67:392–93.

69. Letter, Gordon to an unknown friend or family member, 12 April 1816, Gordon's Correspondence, MHM 67:395–98, 418.

70. Letter, Commo. I. Chauncey to Secretary Crowninshield, 13 September 1816, RG45, MF-125, NARA; also, letters, board of commissioners to Cassin, 5 and 30 March 1818, commissioners to commandants, RG45, Entry 216, NARA.

CHAPTER 5. LIKE FISH OUT OF WATER

1. *Act to Create the Navy Board of Commissioners*, 7 February 1815, found in Homans, ed., *Laws of the United States*, 102.

2. Letter, Secretary of the Navy B. W. Crowninshield to John Rodgers, president, Board of Commissioners, 29 April 1815, RG45 Entry 8; also, letter, Crowninshield to Rodgers, 18 May 1815, in response to Rodgers's letter of 16 May, RG45, Entry 8, NARA.

3. Paullin, *Paullin's History of Naval Administration*, 171–74, also Paullin, *Commodore John Rodgers*, 306, 309.

4. Six secretaries of the navy served during the years between 1815 and 1837, the period in which Rodgers served as president of the board nineteen of the twenty-two years. No member of the executive branch except John Branch, President Andrew Jackson's first secretary of the navy, ever seriously questioned Rodgers's policies.

5. Paullin, *Commodore John Rodgers*, 324–25; also, ASP 1:616–17. A concise but complete outline of John Rodgers's program for the Navy Peace Establishment sent to Congress in 1819.

6. Report, Smith Thompson to Samuel Smith, 16th Congress, 2d sess., 25 January 1921, ASP 1: 712–13; also, letter, James Barron, commandant, Gosport, to commissioners, 27 July 1827, RG45, Entry 220, NARA: according to a report prepared for Samuel Smith, chairman of the House Ways and Means Committee, the six operating navy yards employed approximately sixteen hundred mechanics and laborers in 1820. At that time the commissioners assigned most repair work to Gosport Navy Yard and the New York Navy Yard with the Charlestown yard at Boston handling a lesser share. Washington Navy Yard built only new vessels in 1820 as the navy had started a process of converting it into a manufacturing facility for metal working, blocks, cables, and hemp products. The yards at Philadelphia and Portsmouth, New Hampshire, built new ships. Additionally, the navy established shore stations at Baltimore and Charleston and overseas. During one seven-year period the number of mechanics and laborers employed at Gosport increased from 383, reported to Congressman Smith, to almost 600. This expansion occurred mostly as a result of an increase in repair work. The cost (crew and provisions) of keeping U.S. Frigate *Constellation* at sea on a distant station for two years plus nine months totaled approximately $300,000; a ship of the line probably cost twice that amount for the same period.

7. David Porter, who grew up in Baltimore, entered the navy in 1798 as a midshipman on the original muster list of the U.S. Frigate *Constellation*, Thomas Truxtun, commander. Isaac Hull, already a merchant marine captain, received the appointment of lieutenant 13 March 1798 and served on U.S. Frigate *Constitution*, Silas Talbot, commander.

8. Homans, *Laws of the United States*, 106; the act of 29 April 1816, *Act for Gradual Increase of the Navy*. Congress authorized $1 million per annum for six years for construction of nine

ships of the line and twelve large frigates (44s); funds not to be used for other purposes nor carried to surplus. The act also authorized the building of three steam batteries.

9. Letter, Stewart to Hamilton, 12 November 1812, ASP 1:278–79: during the course of planning the expansion of the United States Navy in Washington in the autumn of 1812 as Congress considered legislation to increase the size of the navy, Secretary Paul Hamilton asked Capt. Charles Stewart to provide him with his opinion of the most suitable combination of new ships for an expanded navy. Stewart responded that a ship of the line was three times as effective as a large frigate, a large frigate worth two sloops. To fight the War of 1812, Stewart recommended ships of the line and frigates, seemingly unaware that small ships and schooners would prove most effective against the British forces including her merchant service. When Congress convened to consider the navy's postwar expansion program in 1816, John Rodgers and his colleagues, including Charles Stewart, pushed the same message, that big ships must be the mainstay of the postwar navy, though none of the ships of the line or frigates built as a result of Stewart's recommendations for use during the War of 1812 fired a shot and there was no reason to believe that battleships and frigates built as a result of Rodgers's advice and authorized by the act of 1816 would ever see action, which, of course, they did not. Ships built under the 1816 act included nine ships of the line: *Alabama, Columbus, Delaware, Virginia, New York, North Carolina, Ohio, Pennsylvania,* and *Vermont;* nine frigates of the *Constitution* class: *Potomac, Brandywine, Columbia, Cumberland, Raritan, St. Lawrence, Savannah, Santee,* and *Sabine;* and one frigate purchased, *Hudson.*

10. *Santee,* launched 16 February 1855 and commissioned 9 June 1861, and *Sabine,* launched 3 February 1855 and commissioned 23 August 1858, were the last new all-sail ships commissioned by the United States Navy. John Lenthall ordered these two frigates redesigned while still in the stocks but with hulls completed. The new drafts retained most of the ships' original midbodies but lengthened the two frigates overall twenty feet, principally at the bow, providing them with modern bows and steamship sterns, similar in the main to those Lenthall drafted for the frigate *Constellation* in 1853, though *Constellation,* like *Erie* in earlier years, had been dismantled first before carpenters rebuilt the ship.

11. Homans, *Laws of the United States,* 106, 143, act of 29 April 1816; act of 29 March 1827, *Act for Gradual Improvement of the Navy of the United States;* Wegner, *Fouled Anchors,* 3, 66, 88; Chapelle, *History of the American Sailing Navy,* 309, 310, 314; Agranat, "Thorough and Efficient Repair," 67; Navy Annual Report, 1826, 3–4. *Fouled Anchors* concluded that the workers of the Gosport Navy Yard took U.S. Frigate *Constellation* out of ordinary and destroyed her in 1853. The report then concluded that the navy built a new USS *Constellation* and that Congress authorized construction of a new sloop of war twenty-six years earlier under the title of the act of 3 March 1827, an Act for Gradual Improvement of the Navy of the United States. The authors recognized the need to identify specific legislation that authorized the navy to build a new sloop of war because the navy built no new ships without enabling legislation describing the class of ship authorized and source of funds allocated for the construction. Further, it

became necessary for *Fouled Anchors* to name a specific act as Wegner's report rejected as false Howard Chapelle's often repeated statement that the navy built *Constellation* as a new ship in 1853, hiding from Congress information that the service improperly used repair appropriations for funding new ship construction. The rejection of Chapelle's clandestine substitute shipbuilding scheme as unrealistic forced the authors of *Fouled Anchors* to find a law that Congress actually passed to authorize the building of a new sloop named *Constellation* in 1853. They attempted to solve this dilemma by reporting that Congress authorized the new *Constellation* of 1853 by the act of 1827, legislation passed in Congress one year before the U.S. Frigate *Constellation* was rebuilt at Gosport Navy Yard in 1828–29. *Fouled Anchors's* convoluted explanation is incorrect because the act of 1827 did not authorize the building of any new ships of war (other than steam batteries) and as an act to improve the navy's infrastructure, the legislation dealt only with matters such as building dry docks at Gosport and Boston, timber sheds at ship yards, and the purchase of timber and other materials for stockpiling. The acts of 1816 and an amending act, titled The Act of 1821, both dealing with increase of the navy, named specifically the types of ship and number authorized (nine battleships and twelve heavy frigates). Chapelle wrote with some confusion on the substance of the act of 1816, referring to it incorrectly as an Act for the Gradual Improvement of the Navy, which did not become law until passed by Congress in 1827. Furthermore, he incorrectly wrote that Congress authorized the ship of the line *Columbus* under the act of 1813 and authorized only six ships of the line by the act of 1816. The fact that Chapelle confused the act of 1816 (an Act to Increase the Navy) with the act of 1827 (an Act to Improve the Navy) and that he miscalculated the number of ships authorized, suggests that his incorrect analysis provided Wegner and his associates with the notion to associate the authorization of a second *Constellation* with the act of 1827. Secretary of the Navy Samuel L. Southward (Navy Annual Report, 1826) interpreted these enabling acts correctly, starting with the act of 1813, that legislation authorized the building of four ships, none with less than seventy-four guns each and six ships rated forty-four guns. He pointed out that the act of 29 April 1816 authorized building nine ships of the line and twelve frigates of not less than 44 guns each. According to Southard, the act of 1816 also included the one ship of the line and three frigates (44s) previously authorized by the wartime act of 1813 but not built during the war as well as allowing for the frigate (44) burned in Washington. Therefore, by these two laws, twelve ships of not less than 74 guns and fifteen frigates plus a replacement for *Columbia*, all not less than 44 guns, were actually authorized. Southward wrote that by 1826, the navy launched seven ships of the line and had five others under construction. He reminded those to whom his report was directed that one frigate, *Columbia*, authorized during the war that Tingey ordered burned, was replaced by the U.S. Frigate *Hudson*, purchased. Southward reported that four more frigates (44s) had been launched, seven were in the stocks, and frames had been ordered for the last three. The amount appropriated under the two acts discussed above totaled $10.5 million. Southward also pointed out that Congress combined the act of 1816 with an earlier act of 3 March 1816, which appropriated $600,000 for the purchase of timber. The year, 1827, when the Act to Improve the Navy passed, the total number of ships and classes authorized were twelve ships of the line, seventeen frigates, first class, three frigates, second class (*Constellation, Congress,* and *Macedonian*), sixteen sloops of war including USS *John Adams* and *Cyane,* and four schooners. The act of 1827 authorized no additional ships. In summary, the authors of *Fouled Anchors* incorrectly concluded that the building of a new *Constellation* was authorized by the act of 1827; also, they confuse the two acts when they state that the act of 1827 succeeded or amended the act of 1816. The Acts to Increase and Improve the Navy were not combined under a single appropriation heading until 1840, at which time funds for Increases, Improvements, and Repairs were combined as a single line item in the navy's budget. The fact remains that neither the act of 1813, the act of 1816, nor the act of 1827 authorized new second-class frigates or sloops of war; nor did Congress fund a new ship named *Constellation* in 1816, 1821, 1827, 1833, 1840, or by any other legislation passed by Congress.

12. Letter, Secretary of the Navy Crowninshield to commissioners, 12 April 1817, RG45, Entry 8, NARA: frame up all frigates to best preserve timber.

13. Commissioners' Report to the Senate Committee on Naval Affairs, 21 January 1819, ASP 1:616–17. Rodgers's report broke down the navy's requirements in ships into four classes: ships of the line, twelve (three in commission and nine authorized and under construction) and twenty frigates. Rodgers also covered the navy's needs for vessels of lesser size, twenty sloops of war, of which the navy had four plus two corvettes in 1819 (sloops *Erie, Ontario, Peacock,* and *Hornet* and the corvettes *John Adams* and *Cyane,* the latter a trophy ship); and twenty schooners, most of which would be built or purchased in subsequent years. Rodgers's report of 1819 is a remarkable document as his early recitation of the commissioners' wish list provides an accurate picture of a course upon which the navy had just embarked. Six years later the navy's fleet existed in classes and numbers closely paralleling this report. To the historian this document supports strongly the argument that Rodgers, as leader of the navy in 1819, led a group that held political power that determined the country's naval policy. Furthermore, pronavalists, led by Rodgers, included as part of a long-range program the retention of all historic and trophy ships in service indefinitely.

14. Navy Annual Report, 1826, 110–13, 124. Using the secretary's estimated budget for 1827 as an illustration, the total submitted to Congress for consideration amounted to $3,014,802.26. Of this total, the cost of wages for 4,648 officers and men on sea duty totaled an estimated $968,544 and the navy projected the cost of provisions at $579,148.54. The total of these two line items equaled approximately one-half the estimated budget. The amount submitted for repairs amounted to just $450,000. The budget figures were based on the following vessel requirements that year: one ship of the line, three first-class frigates, two frigates of the *Constellation* class, eleven sloops of war, and four schooners, a total of twenty-one ships.

15. Acts of 3 March and 29 April 1816, act of 5 January 1821, act of 3 March 1825, act of 1827, and act of 1833. All acts provided for purchasing live oak timber for new construction. The act of 3 March provided $200,000 annually for three years and was Congress's first postwar legislation for a permanent naval peace establishment; it was also the first of a number of appropriations to acquire live oak and other timber for stockpiling at navy yards. Congress later combined this appropriation with funds authorized by the act of 1816. Problems acquiring and storing live oak became important considerations affecting navy planning as existing technology for preserving timber did not provide methods for controlling the decay of lumber or the deterioration of live oak once it was cut and stockpiled. In the case of live oak, navy yards lost a significant percentage of the stockpiled timber to deterioration, splitting, theft, or water damage.

16. Paullin, *Paullin's History of Naval Administration,* 178; the act of 5 January 1821 amended the act of 1816 by reducing the amount of funds allocated each year for ships of the line and frigates authorized in 1816 from $1 million to $500,000, and a total of $8 million was appropriated. This act was supplemented by the act of 1827 and the act of 1833, Acts to Improve the Navy, but did not combine or amend either of the earlier two acts. As a result, the legislation allowed the navy to stretch out construction of ships in stocks indefinitely.

17. Navy Annual Report, 1826, 125. During fiscal 1826, the navy commissioned one new ship of the line, USS *North Carolina,* while six remained moored in ordinary. USS *Ohio,* launched in 1820 and in ordinary at the New York Navy Yard in 1826, unequipped and unrigged, reported advancing decay.

18. Report of the Navy and its Expenses, 16th Congress, 2d sess., Secretary Thompson to Samuel Smith, chairman, House Ways and Means Committee, 25 January 1821, ASP 1:712; Homans, *Laws of the United States,* 218–19; letter, James Barron, commandant, Gosport Navy Yard, to commissioners, 26 July 1827, RG45, Entry 220, NARA: number of employees, Gosport, 1820, 383; Barron reported this figure had increased to 594 in July 1827. Congress appropriated for repairs: 1821, $385,000; 1830, $770,380. In Homans's book he accounted for funds appropriated for rebuilding ships with those for new construction when Congress voted specific funds to rebuild a named ship, such as the special acts authorizing and funding rebuilding U.S. frigates *Macedonian* and *Congress.*

19. Homans, *Laws of the United States,* act of 15 May 1820, with documents accompanying the bill to authorize a certain number of small vessels; also, act of 20 December 1822. The navy's new schooners' estimated cost, including hulls of live oak frame of $4,500, totaled $15,500 each, not including the cost of crew or provisioning. Readers should note the cost of the hull, estimated at less than one-third the vessel's total cost. This percentage, thought to be fairly consistent with navy experience, is an extremely important concept for students and historians to grasp because, like many otherwise informed individuals, many modern naval architects incorrectly equate the total cost of a navy ship with its wooden hull. Schooners purchased for the suppression of piracy included *Beagle, Fox, Greyhound, Ferret, Jackal, Terrier, Weasel,* and *Wildcat;* other small craft were purchased, including a small steamboat.

20. Long, *Sailor-Diplomat*, 85–89; letter, B. W. Crowninshield to James Biddle, commander, USS *Ontario*, 21 July 1817, RG45, MF-149; James Biddle's Journal, 4 October 1817–22 March 1819, RG45, MF-902, NARA.

21. Long, *Sailor-Diplomat*, 85–89; also Hopkins and Hargreaves, eds., *Papers of Henry Clay*, 2:817–18.

22. McKee, *Gentlemanly and Honorable Profession*, 339–41. Captain Lawrence's contemplated deal had the support of John Rodgers, Stephen Decatur, and Isaac Chauncey, suggesting that many senior officers would agree to carry naval freight regardless of tradition or executive orders.

23. *Norfolk Beacon*, 3 January 1818; also letter, Crowninshield to Rodgers, 28 March 1818, RG 45, Entry 8, NARA; Mills, *Oliver Hazard Perry*, 246–59.

24. Mills, *Oliver Hazard Perry*, 246–59.

25. Morris, "The Autobiography of Charles Morris," 192–94.

26. Log of the U.S. Frigate *Constellation*, 12 November 1819 to 30 June 1820, signed by John B. Nicolson, commander, Charles Morris, commodore, Huntington Library, San Marino, California.

27. Morris, "The Autobiography of Charles Morris," 192–94.

28. Ibid.

29. Log of the U.S. Frigate *Constellation*, 4 March 1820, RG 24, NARA; also, Capt. J. J. Nicolson's report concerning the Sailing Qualities of U.S. Frigate *Constellation*, signed but undated, Vessels Sailing Qualities, Subject Files, AQ, Box 88, RG45, Entry 464, NARA.

30. de Kay, *Chronicles*, 158 –73. Letter, Capt. John Downes, commander, USF *Macedonian*, to Secretary of the Navy Smith Thompson, 18 June 1821, with enclosures, RG45, MF-125. Journals kept on board USS *Macedonian* by Lts. Charles Gauntt and Charles J. DeBlois, RG45, Appendix D, nos. 35 and 36, NARA.

31. de Kay, *Chronicles*, 143–44; also Dudley, *Naval War of 1812*, 2:696–99, 701.

32. de Kay, *Chronicles*, 158 –62; letter, Downes to Smith Thompson, 18 June 1821; also, Gauntt and DeBlois Journals, RG45, Appendix D, NARA.

33. Letter, Downes to Thompson, 18 June 1821.

34. Ibid.

35. Letter, Charles G. Ridgely to Secretary Thompson, 21 July 1820, Ridgely Letter Book, Library of Congress, Washington, D.C.

36. Letter, Ridgely to Thompson, 11 August, 3 October, and 11 November 1820, Ridgely Letter Book; also, Captain Ridgely's Journal, Library of Congress, Washington, D.C.

37. Ridgely's Journal, USF *Constellation* Log No. 2, RG24, NARA; also letter, Ridgely to Thompson, 11 November 1820, Captain's Letters, RG45, MF-125, NARA.

38. Ridgely's Journal, USF *Constellation* Log No. 2, RG24, NARA.

39. Ibid.; also letters, Ridgely to Thompson, 7 and 8 March 1821, RG45, MF-125, NARA.

40. Letters, Ridgely to Thompson, 31 March, 3, 7 April, and 18 May 1821, Ridgely's Letter Book; Ridgely's Private Journal; *Constellation*'s Log No. 2, RG24, NARA.

41. Ridgely's Private Journal; letter, Michael McBlair to Ridgely, 15 January 1823, MS 1355, MHS.

42. Letter, Ridgely to Don Pedro Flibadia, 20 January 1822; also, letter, Ridgely to Commodore Stewart, 2 February 1822, Ridgely's Private Journal.

43. "I am on board *Constellation*." Letters, Vice King Joaquin de la Pezuela to Ridgely, 7 June 1821; "All right but it is against the rules." Ridgely to de la Pezuela, 8 June 1821. "I arrive to take your friends out of the country." Ridgely to Capt. L. Smith, 17 February 1822, Ridgely's Private Journal.

44. Letter, Ridgely to Thompson, 27 April 1822, RG 45, MF-125, NARA; letter, Ridgely to commissioners, 30 July 1822, Ridgely's Letter Book; also, letter, Hugh G. Campbell to Samuel Barron, 10 April 1805, BW 5:498.

45. Letter, Ridgely to McBlair, 19 May 1823, McBlair to Ridgely, 3 December 1823 and 17 March 1824, MS-1355, MHS.

46. Charles Stewart's court-martial, convened 18 August 1825, ASP 2:487–597.

47. Ibid.; also letter of Secretary Samuel L. Southward to Stewart, 5 September 1825, Captains' Letters Sent, RG45, MF-149, NARA.

48. Letter, Secretary Crowninshield to Charles Morris, 27 February 1817, RG45, MF-149, NARA.

49. Letter, Secretary Thompson to John Downes, 27 April 1819, RG45, M-149, NARA.

50. Letter, Thompson to Stewart, 8 September 1821, RG45, MF-149, NARA, and ASP 2:538–39.

51. Letters, Ridgely to Secretary Jones, 2 and 7 April 1814; Ridgely to George de la Roche, 7 April 1814: orders to strip ship, Ridgely Letter Book.

52. Agranat, "Thorough and Efficient Repair," 192–202; John Branch, Navy Annual Report of 1829, 189; also, letter, Branch to Rodgers, 2 November 1830, RG45, Entry 8, NARA. President Jackson mediated an argument between Secretary of the Navy John Branch and Rodgers, then rendered an executive order stating that repairs and rebuilding were, in fact, different, but also that rebuilding differed from new construction. Therefore, henceforth, funds appropriated and used to rebuild specific ships must be covered by separate acts of Congress. Commissioners complied with these procedures during Jackson's terms in office.

53. Geoffrey M. Footner, "The Turbulent History of Fells Point," unpublished manuscript; also, Fox Papers, PEM.

54. W. M. P. Dunne, The Navy Scribe, Resource Data File, USS *Erie*, 13; also, Emmons, *Navy of the United States*, 112. When assigned to William Bainbridge's squadron in the Mediterranean Sea, the commodore recorded in his journal that *Erie* was his dullest sailer; Emmons wrote: "very crank, requiring close watching; stays badly and makes a great deal of lee way."

55. Construction Plan for Sloop of War *Erie*, As Rebuilt, RG19, Entry 126, NARA.

56. Letters, William Doughty to David Porter, 9 September and 18 October 1822, RG45, Entry 224, NARA.

57. Chapelle, *History of the American Sailing Navy,* 336. the title of the revised draft of *Erie* signed by William Doughty states that it should be used if the ship was to be rebuilt. This plus the Doughty-Porter correspondence and the New York Navy Yard's detailed records for that period made it impossible for Chapelle to state that she was a new ship. Though he acknowledges that the sloop was rebuilt, Chapelle used *Erie*'s rebuild as a cornerstone upon which to build his Administrative Rebuilding Scheme, writing that the practice of "rebuilding" ships on a new design may be said to have started with *Erie.* This statement, typical of Chapelle's convoluted manner of expressing a contrived conclusion, was a wish rather than a fact. He proceeded to write that redesigning of *Erie* was partial, but it was an easy step to use a completely new design, producing an entirely different model and even class of ship in the guise of rebuilding. Chapelle endeavors to set a stage with *Erie* upon which he would develop a narrative about several secretaries of the navy falsely notifying Congress over a period of more than four decades, and by their action had successfully hoodwinked legislators for decades, substituting new ships for old ones under a clandestine program of replacement. Chapelle needed to clearly establish *Erie*'s rebuild of 1822 as similar to the rebuild of *Constellation* in 1853, shaping the story of the earlier rebuild (which included redrafting her hull) as the departure point from which a program of substitute ships became an illegitimate activity. He ignored the redrafted and rebuilt navy ships before *Erie.* Chapelle also ignored correspondence, historical documentation, the navy's annual reports, and congressional legislative records and reports on naval affairs, most of which reveal a well-informed Congress closely working with presidents and secretaries of the navy but particularly with the Navy Board of Commissioners. Congress passed several acts authorizing the expansion of the navy including ten new sloops of war in 1825. If the nation's legislative body freely authorized funds for new ships, why would the navy risk political disaster and its officers risk disgrace by clandestinely building a new *Erie* without Congress's authorization? The historical record discloses the opposite, that Congress closely controlled the activities of the navy, playing a major role in expanding its construction, repair, and rebuilding facilities as local congressmen worked to increase navy yard employment for the benefit of constituents. The suspicion develops, as one familiar with the historical record reads Chapelle's writings, that as he writes about *Erie,* he starts a process that has as its final chapter or goal, the undermining of the historical and physical provenance of the U.S. Frigate *Constellation.* Cleverly, he wove his story about a period (1820–55) into the mainstream of naval thought, a period of naval history that most naval historians and naval architects avoid, leaving a blank shelf in naval history. Chapelle gambled, when he formulated his theory of Administrative Rebuilding, that contemporary naval historians and naval architects would accept his charge that his colleagues remained unaware of the navy's clandestine administrative rebuilding activities for almost 120 years until he exposed his version of navy administration under the Board of Commissioners. One who casually reads the record of relations between the navy and Congress between 1820 and 1855 will be pro-

vided ample proof that Chapelle's Administrative Rebuilding Scheme consisted of events staged to fit a fictitious ending—a new *Constellation,* secretly built in 1853–55. Chapelle and Polland, *Constellation Question,* 15–16; also, Wegner, *Fouled Anchors,* 66, 88. Chapelle presented his Administrative Rebuilding Scheme in a bold fashion in this written debate, published in 1970, having discovered that few historians contradicted his theory in the years between 1945, when it was first presented, and 1970. Though many historians believed that documents held in naval archives supported a conclusion that the navy rebuilt the U.S. Frigate *Constellation,* downrating her to a sloop of war, Chapelle wrote in 1970 that ships rebuilt after *Erie* in 1822 were not "great repairs" or alterations to old ships but these so-called rebuilds were, in fact, new construction. Chapelle, without important dissenters in 1970, felt strong enough to overwhelm the feeble voices of opposition. His undocumented dogma succeeded in holding his disciples in camp until his most fervent supporters, the authors of *Fouled Anchors,* repudiated his theory.

58. Navy Annual Report, 1854. Lenthall reported that U.S. Frigate *United States'*s repairs in 1822 cost $223,083.
59. Agranat, "Thorough and Efficient Repair," 147–53.
60. Letter, Secretary of the Navy Thompson to James Pleasant, chairman of the Senate Committee on Naval Affairs, 2 February 1822, and Rodgers to Pleasant, 8 February, 1822, ASP 1:786.
61. Letter, Rodgers to Secretary of the Navy John Branch, 11 August 1830, RG45, Entry 28, NARA; also, Emmons, *Navy of the United States,* 1775–1853, 10–11.
62. Letter, Rodgers to Branch, 11 August 1830, RG45, Entry 28, NARA.
63. First Annual Report of the Secretary of the Navy, 1823; Agranat, "Thorough and Efficient Repair," 169; Secretary of the Navy Thompson to Samuel Smith, chairman, House Ways and Means Committee, ASP 1:801–2.
64. Homans, *Laws of the United States,* 136; act of 3 March 1825: Congress authorized the building of ten sloops of war, carrying not less than twenty guns; also, ASP 1:898–900: a ship of the line crew including officers totaled just under eight hundred men; the new sloop-ships' crews would total less than two hundred men each.
65. Letter, Samuel Humphreys to Commodore Bainbridge, 4 December 1826, RG45, Entry 224, NARA; Agranat, "Thorough and Efficient Repair," 160–61; Paullin, *Paullin's History of Naval Administration,* 181. Pensacola Navy Yard opened during the administration of John Quincy Adams.
66. Letter, Fox to Benjamin Talmadge, congressman from Connecticut, 15 April 1810, Fox Papers, PEM.
67. Morris, "The Autobiography of Charles Morris," 200.
68. Ibid., 201.
69. "Exhibit of Expenses for Labor and Materials of every Description of the Ships Built or Building under the Law of Gradual Increase," Navy Annual Report, 1825, no page number; also, letter, Rodgers to Thompson, 5 September 1822, ASP 1:835.

70. *Portsmouth, Va.: 200 Years of Service* (Norfolk, Va.: Norfolk Naval Yard, 1967), 12; Alexander Murray took the position as commandant at Philadelphia rather than go on half-pay status and he remained until his retirement in 1821.

71. Morris, "The Autobiography of Charles Morris," 207; also, Grant, *Isaac Hull*, 306–7, 323–24. Though Morris proved to be one of the better commandant-administrators, nevertheless it is a fact that he took the position at Boston for reasons of health; Bainbridge (see chapter 4) took the position between assignments; Hull received appointments to Washington and Charlestown Navy Yards, where he suffered through investigations and financial troubles and some official criticism.

72. *Norfolk Beacon*, 2 March 1839: an announcement of the organization of the Gosport Navy Yard Mutual Assistance Society, Francis Grice, president; the directors consisted of thirteen master workmen including Charles A. Grice, the constructor's brother, and James Jarvis, inspector of timber. "Clerks and porters are on salary—they degrade us." Charles A. Grice to James Barron, 14 February 1831, Barron Papers, Box 9, Folder 64.

73. Letters, constructor Francis Grice to James Barron, 23 January 1826; Barron to Lieutenant Smoot, 29 May 1829, Barron Papers, Box 7. "High price of labor and other inconveniences and disadvantages (at Gosport) beyond the power of the Commissioners to remedy." Letter, Rodgers to Smith Thompson, 5 September 1822, responding to Senate Resolution of 5 April 1822, RG45, Entry 213, NARA.

74. *Norfolk Beacon*, 17 April 1828: Francis Grice appointed to anti-Jackson committee. "To the Victors Belong the Spoils—John L. Porter, once a Whig, replaces John Brownley, both master carpenters; Dr. Robert W. Boykin has been appointed naval storekeeper at Gosport Navy Yard." *Norfolk Beacon*, 28 April 1853 headline.

75. *Dictionary of American Naval Fighting Ships*, 3:181, 508–9: U.S. Frigate *Guerrière*, launched in Philadelphia, 17 June 1815, broken up at Gosport Navy Yard, 1841; U.S. Frigate *Java*, launched at Baltimore in 1815, broken up in 1842.

76. Paullin, *Commodore John Rodgers*, 339, 352–53, 358; Lubbock, *Opium Clippers*, 85–87; Geoffrey M. Footner, "The Turbulent History of Fells Point." American merchants purchased opium which moved in volume from Smyrna to China or to Baltimore and other east coast ports for transshipment to China. USS *Porpoise* and other navy ships convoyed these commercial vessels during this period while in the eastern Mediterranean. Evidently, other missions of Rodgers's large fleet, which remained in the Mediterranean over two years, included ceremonial exchanges of gifts with Turkish officials, a program to improve navy discipline on board ships and an improvement in Rodgers's health. Other official reasons for the cruise remain obscure. When Rodgers returned from the Mediterranean, the only cruise he took between 1815 and the year he retired, he resumed the position of president of the Board of Commissioners.

77. *Constellation* Repairs, Subject Files AR, Box 92, RG45, Entry 464, NARA; also, Operational History of U.S. Frigate *Constellation*, unpublished, prepared by the Ships

History Section, Division of Naval History, Office of the Chief of Naval Operations, Washington Navy Yard, 5.

CHAPTER 6. 1829 HULL MODIFICATIONS

1. Letters, Captain Warrington to Secretary of the Navy Southard, 15 February, 10 March, 22 June 1825, RG45, MF-125; letter, Southard to Warrington, 24 May 1825, RG45, MF-149, NARA; Secretary of the Navy's Annual Report, 2 December 1825; also, Warrington to commissioners, 20 February 1826, RG45, Entry 221, NARA.

2. Navy Annual Report, 1826, 7; Thomas H. S. Hamersly, *Complete General Navy Register of the United States of America, 1776–1887* (New York: W. K. Boyle, Printer, 1888), 2.

3. Letter, Ridgely to commissioners, 16 February 1827, RG45, Entry 213, NARA.

4. Letter, Lieutenant Williamson, Gosport, to commissioners, 17 July 1827, RG45, Entry 213; also, letter, commissioners to James Barron, commandant, Gosport, 24 July 1827, RG45, Entry 216, NARA. *Constellation, John Adams* and *Macedonian* were scheduled to be rebuilt at Gosport. A large number of ships required extensive repair in 1827–29, placing a strain on the annual appropriation for repairs. Further stress on the budget developed at this time as ships of the line such as USS *Ohio,* unfitted and as yet not commissioned, began to draw down repair funds to replace decayed planking, etc. In a real-life version of Howard Chapelle's charge, that the navy used its repair fund for administrative rebuilding of a new ship, as it happened in the case of *Ohio* and other new ships in stocks or in ordinary, but unfinished, unequipped, and not commissioned, repair funds became mixed with construction funds as new ships rotted before they were finished, consuming repair wear and tear funds and funds for new construction at the same time as the navy completed the ship.

5. Letter, commissioners to Barron, 24 July 1827, RG45, Entry 216, NARA.

6. Board of Commissioners circular letters, 26 June 1819 and 26 May 1825, RG45, Entry 212, NARA.

7. Letter, Rodgers to Bainbridge, 20 August 1829, RG45, Entry 216, NARA; also circulars, 29 March and 22 July 1830, RG45, Entry 212, NARA.

8. Annual Survey of Naval Public Stores, 1 October 1828, Gosport, RG19, Entry 8, NARA. This report highlights procedures in effect controlling surveys and the storage of equipment taken out of *Constellation* while she remained at Gosport's ordinary; these rules and regulations covered ships in ordinary and outside the control of the yard's storekeeping department. Later, the inventoried equipment was returned to the ship after undergoing repair or reconditioning as necessary. Officers in charge of ships in ordinary accounted separately for masts, sails, casks, cordage, cables, chain, and extra anchors held by the shop or department charged with the reconditioning or repair of specific equipment and stored outside of the storekeeper's jurisdiction.

9. Homans, *Laws of the United States,* 143–44; the act of 3 March 1827, titled *Act for the Gradual Improvement of the Navy;* also, letter, Barron to commissioners, 27 July 1827, RG45, Entry 220, NARA. It should be emphasized again that this legislation authorized

no new warships of any class; Congress limited the use of all timber and other materials purchased by funds appropriated under this act for the construction of new ships authorized by specific acts. The legislators controlled the deposition of funds and did not give the navy authority to transfer the money appropriated each year ($500,000) for other purposes. As an example, no new ships of the line were ever authorized again. Timber purchased, cut, and molded into frame pieces for ships of the line, potentially surplus, would eventually rot or deteriorate unless the law was amended at some later date. The navy gained some flexibility as timber purchased for new construction could be used for repairs if the proper account, Gradual Increase (1816) or Gradual Improvement (1827), received credit with a transfer of repair funds by the Treasury Department. Yards kept stockpiles of equipment and materials purchased for repairs by designated appropriations. As an example, Barron notified the commissioners that he already had on hand at Gosport a supply of copper sheets "for Repairs" available for *Constellation.* Because of the congressional controls placed on specific appropriations (Gradual Increase, Gradual Improvement, Ordnance, Ten Sloops [1825]), regular annual line item appropriations in the budget, advances to contractors, multiyear contracts, repair and construction projects, and yearly overruns made the navy's finances a hot issue never resolved by several administrations or Congress.

10. *Act for the Gradual Improvement of the Navy,* 3 March 1827.
11. Letter, commissioners (Warrington) to Barron, 19 September 1827; also, commissioners (Rodgers) to Barron, 17 October 1827, RG45, Entry 216, NARA.
12. Letter, Comdt. James Barron to commissioners, 14 November, 1827. RG45, Entry 220, NARA. Rodgers became president of the Board of Commissioners again in the fall of 1827.
13. Letter, Barron to Rodgers, 22 November 1827, RG45, Entry 220; also, letter, Rodgers to Barron, 26 November 1827, RG45, Entry 216, NARA.
14. Letters, Rodgers to Barron, 19 and 26 November 1827, RG45, Entry 216, NARA; also, Navy Annual Report, 1827, 235.
15. Navy Annual Report, 1828, 159; also, commissioners to Barron, 6 December 1827, RG45, Entry 216, NARA.
16. Letter, commissioners to Barron, 7 December 1827, RG45, Entry 216, NARA.
17. Letter, Rodgers to Barron, 7 December 1827, RG45, Entry 216; also letter, Barron to commissioners, 10 December 1827, enclosing letter, Grice to Barron, 8 December, 1827; letter, Barron to Rodgers, 15 December 1827, RG45, Entry 220, NARA.
18. Vessel Repair Costs, one volume, RG19, Entry 5, 171–72, NARA.
19. Letters, Samuel Humphreys to Rodgers, 1, 2 January 1828, with reports on condition of *Constellation* and *John Adams* (reports missing), RG45, Entry 224; letter, Rodgers to Barron, 5 January 1828, RG45, Entry 216, NARA.
20. Letter, Barron to Rodgers, 21 February 1828, RG45, Entry 220, NARA.
21. Letter of Transfer of Relics from the U.S. Naval Shipyard, Boston, Massachusetts, Leonard F. Cushing to the *Constellation* Committee of Maryland, Neil H. Swanson, pres-

ident, 9 September 1955, four pages, forty-five items; item 34: series of letters and offsets for *Constellation,* 1828, with notes on her original construction and a record book (journal) kept by Mr. Saltonstall at Gosport 1828–29; photocopy of Cushing's transmittal letter in possession of author. Photocopy of drawing signed by Francis Grice is located in Ship's Papers, Naval Historical Center Washington, D.C., and Leon Polland Papers, Nimitz Library, Special Collections, USNA.

22. Letters, commissioners to Barron, 22 July and 1 August 1828, RG45, Entry 216; circular to commandants, 24 September 1828, RG45, Entry 212; letters, Rodgers to Southard, 6 November 1828, RG45, Entry 213; Barron to Rodgers, 23 February 1829, RG45, Entry 220, NARA.

23. *Niles Register,* 11 October 1828; letters, Barron to Rodgers, 6 December, Francis Grice to Barron, 16 December, and Barron to Rodgers, 16 December 1828, RG45, Entry 220; letters, Rodgers to Barron, 19 December 1828, 17 January and 26 February 1829, RG45, Entry 216, NARA; also Navy Annual Report, 1829. Most historians who touch on the history of this period believed that Gosport Navy Yard scheduled *Constellation*'s great repair in 1829; the correspondence and yard records of 1828–29 confirm that the yard completed most of her modifications and work in 1828. As readers will have an opportunity to see, her hull at the midsection and above the waterline was altered, presumably on orders of the commissioners, resulting in the refairing of the ship's hull from stem to stern. The drafts covering the modifications to *Constellation* in 1828 as well as those for *John Adams* during her rebuild in 1829 are missing from the National Archives.

24. Letter, commissioners to Barron, 20 May 1829, RG45, Entry 216, NARA; also letter, Barron to John Branch, secretary of the navy, 27 May 1829, Barron Letter Book, Box 8, Folder 49, James Barron's Papers; also, letters, Branch to Rodgers, 19 May 1829, Entry 8; Rodgers to Barron, 20 April 1829, RG45 Entry 216, NARA, *Niles Register,* May 30, 1829, citing the *Norfolk Herald:* Rodgers ordered Barron to prepare *Constellation* for sea; Branch ordered her ready by July 1; Rodgers arranged the transfer of Barron to Philadelphia Navy Yard, a smaller yard with a limited amount of repair work. The bitter relationship between Rodgers and Barron flared up once again because of Barron's resistance to the commissioners' orders to commence rebuilding Stephen Decatur's trophy ship, U.S. Frigate *Macedonian.* Barron, who killed Decatur in a duel in 1820, remained a target of the dead naval hero's political faction, led by his widow, Susan Decatur. The fight to retain *Macedonian* on the navy list as a rebuilt ship with a new hull built of American live oak frame from the keel up was intense. Decatur supporters made it a momentous political issue, placing heightened emotional pressure on trophy and sentimental rebuilding, the core reasons for retaining *Macedonian* in service. Congress stepped into the fray and put a legal stamp on the trophy ship by authorizing her rebuild and providing the navy with funds to accomplish it.

25. *Returns of Repairs to Vessels,* RG19, Entry 5, 1:171–72, NARA.

26. Letter, Barron to commissioners, 15 December 1827, RG45, Entry 220; letters, commissioners to Barron, 6 December 1827, RG45, Entry 216, Humphreys to Rodgers, 1, 2 January, RG45, Entry 224, and Rodgers to Barron, 5 January 1828, RG45, Entry 216, NARA.

27. *Returns of Repairs to Vessels,* RG19, Entry 5, 1:171; also, *Constellation* Repairs, 1828–29, Subject Files PI, Box 520, Folder 2, RG45, Entry 464, NARA. With the semimonthly returns listing the progress of *Constellation*'s repairs in 1828–29, there is a breakdown by month of the number of men employed on the ship and the total days worked each month. Also recorded is the total cost of labor for the 1828–29 repairs, $86,565. The average paid for a day's wage was $1.40. Dividing the daily average wage into the total labor cost, the result is an approximate figure for the total days worked, 61,832. According to these records about two-thirds of the total days worked fell between 1 January 1828 and 1 February 1829. The record of employment for January 1829 states that 121 men worked 15,403 days, which makes no sense. Presumably, the yard clerk did not keep employment dates and figures on a current basis.

28. Grice's drawing of Constellation's midsection, 1 January 1839, Ship's Papers, Naval Historical Center, Washington, D.C.

29. Wadsworth/Pearson Watch Bill, RG45, Entry 406, NARA, and Buchanan's Journal No. 6, Nimitz Library, USNA. James Miller's Journal, MHS.

30. Randolph, *"Fouled Anchors? Foul Blow,"* 100; Dana Wegner, curator of ship models, David Taylor Research, is the principal author of *"Fouled Anchors,* Query and Response," *American Neptune* 52, no. 4: 262. Randolph's article brought to *American Neptune's* attention Grice's drawing. It is accurately drawn only to the level of *Constellation*'s gun port sills. Readers' attention is directed to Wegner's letter, written in response to Randolph's suggestion that Wegner missed Grice's drawing. To this, Wegner responded that the drawing Randolph referred to "was one of many items deemed likely forged" and that he had found its primary copy among Leon Polland's papers. Wegner suggested in his *American Neptune* letter that Polland "specifically chose not to utilize it in his defense of the 1797 origin of the ship." Here Wegner suggests that he could read Polland's mind even though the naval architect was dead and though Polland frequently left out of his presentations many authentic documents (and possibly some forged ones too, for as Wegner realizes, he never knew any were fakes). Because of this oversight, Polland failed to establish *Constellation*'s provenance. Both Polland and Wegner, who never knew Polland, remained caught in the similarly narrow box they placed around their investigations as both endeavored to prove that *Constellation*'s modifications between 1795 and 1853 were minimal. Both probably left this drawing out of their reports because drawings like Grice's completely undermine the conclusions of Wegner in *Fouled Anchors* as well as Polland's arguments in publications such as *Constellation Question.* Wegner, in *"Fouled Anchors,"* takes great pains and much space to describe the origins of paper tests performed to prove the authenticity of the materials and documents used to support his thesis. Did he check the authenticity of Francis Grice's signature with a handwriting expert? Did he provide any analysis on the logic of his conclusion that the Baltimore forger prepared this drawing? Chapelle attempted to prove his conclusions by stating that there existed no documentation to disprove them. Wegner plants the concern that documents uncovered that disagree with his conclusions are fraudulent. How could Grice's drawing possibly fit into the work of revisionists who minimize the extent

of *Constellation*'s alterations prior to 1853? This study will continue to demonstrate that the ship modifications, including those in 1829, were significant, and yets part of the navy's normal process of redrafting and rebuilding many navy wooden ships prior to the Civil War.

31. *Returns of Repairs to Vessels,* 1:171, RG19, Entry 5; *Constellation Repairs, 1828–1829,* Box 520, RG45, Entry 464, NARA; also, Wegner, "An Apple and an Orange," 86–27n; Wegner, "The Frigate Strikes Her Colors," 246–47; and Wegner, *Fouled Anchors,* 139–43. Defending his denial in the original report, *Fouled Anchors* insists that no alterations to *Constellation*'s stern occurred in 1828–29. The fact is the navy reporters substitute stem for stern in the first article and in the second, deny, without supporting evidence, that the ship received other than light work on her stern, centered around "carving, priming and painting, not rebuilding." In his article defending *Fouled Anchors*'s position, Wegner missed important points available to him in the ship's recorded history, this time failing to uncover the cost of rebuilding *Constellation* in 1828–29, which totaled at least $167,683.02, a cost greater than his statement implied when he claimed that the frigate's repairs represented the cost of only light work. It was but one of several occasions that Wegner missed cogent records, particularly documents that suggest conclusions different from those of his carefully shaped report. See also Dunne, "The Frigate *Constellation,*" 86–88.

32. Chapelle, *History of the American Sailing Navy,* 364–65.

33. *Returns,* RG19, Entry 5, 171; *Army and Navy Chronicle,* 2 July 1840; also, DeRoos, *Personal Narrative;* Barley, *British Sailor;* Dunne, ed., "Navy Scribe," April 1993, 2, unpublished manuscript concerning the writings of Lieutenant DeRoos,

34. Wines, *Two Years,* 32; also, Wegner, *Fouled Anchors,* 139–43. The *Fouled Anchors* report is handicapped because the author was unaware that in 1828–29 *Constellation* had received a new stern section, including galleries, taffrail, and rudder assembly. An attempt is made to distort the archival evidence by suggesting that an original drawing of a side view of the frigate's stern, now listed as stolen from the National Archives, was faked, since only a printed copy of it in *Constellation Question* survives. The drawing, marked both 1829 and 1840, is a side view of a stern section carved C O N S T. The author of *Fouled Anchors* argues that the illustration shows not an elliptical stern, but rather a square one; then Wegner asks the question, is the drawing genuine? To these choices, one can only respond that it is a good drawing of a round stern, much the same model as the type John Lenthall designed for USS *Germantown,* built at Philadelphia 1843. Samuel Humphreys or John Lenthall drafted USS *Raritan* in 1820–21, and she is believed to be the first navy ship with a round stern. It is assumed that Humphreys drafted, with Francis Grice, *Constellation*'s stern assembly in 1828, though no draft survives.

35. Wines, *Two Years,* 15, 28; letters, Rodgers to Barron, 18 June, Warrington to Barron, 22, 23 June 1829, RG45, Entry 216, and Barron to commissioners, 25 June 1829, RG45, Entry 220, NARA.

36. Letters, Barron to commissioners, 27 June 1829, RG45, Entry 220, and Warrington to Barron, 1 July 1829, RG45, Entry 216; also, letter, Barron to commissioners, 18 September 1827, RG45, Entry 220, NARA.

37. Wines, *Two Years,* 15; letters, commissioners to Barron, 26 May 1829, RG45, Entry 216, and Barron to Warrington, 28 May 1829, RG45, Entry 220, NARA.

38. Letters, Barron to Rodgers. 23 May 1829, RG45, Entry 220, NARA, and Barron to Secretary Branch, 30 May 1829, Letter Book, Barron Papers.

39. Letter, B. Homans for Branch to commissioners, 7 June 1829, RG45, Entry 8, NARA.

40. Letter, Barron to commissioners, 19 June 1829, RG45, Entry 220, NARA.

41. Wines, *Two Years,* 32–40, 74; also, Long, *Sailor-Diplomat,* 143–49.

42. Wines, *Two Years,* 75–102.

43. *Niles Register,* 24 October, 7 November 1829.

44. Wines, *Two Years,* 127, 141–43.

45. Wheelock, "Henry Eckford," 177, quoting James Ellsworth de Kay, *Sketches from Turkey,* 312–13; also *Constellation*'s Log No. 8, 26–27 July 1831, 8 A.M. to meridian, RG24, NARA.

46. Wines, *Two Years,* 337–338, Navy Annual Report, 1831, 260; also, Vessel Repairs, RG19 Entry 5, 1:172: lists repairs including to outside copper, air ports, and channels on starboard side of ship; cost $3,037.

47. Navy Annual Report, 1842, Estimates of the Amount Required to Keep in Commission for One Year—Frigates, Sloops of War and Brigs or Schooners.

48. Letter, John Lenthall to Captain Skinner, chief, Bureau of Construction, Equipment, and Repairs, 18 December 1851, RG45, NARA. Lenthall noted the total cost of *Constellation*'s repairs in 1829 were $181,000 and the cost of hull modifications and repairs, $114,000. Various publications listed different totals: $167,000, $170,000, and the figure John Lenthall used.

49. Ibid.; also, Ship Repairs, Subject Files AR, Box 92, July 1829, RG45, Entry 464, NARA.

50. A rough estimate of the total cost of repairs received by *Constellation* between March 1812 and July 1838 is $450,000 or $17,000 "wear and tear" depreciation for each of twenty-six years, a figure just half as great as the official "wear and tear" figure used ($30,000) to calculate the cost allocated for depreciation of first-class frigates for each year in commission.

51. Agranat, "Thorough and Efficient Repair," 182–90.

52. The first surveys of *John Adams*'s condition took place in December 1827 when Humphreys came to Gosport to view *Constellation*. At the time that *Constellation*'s repairs started, repairs to the smaller ship stopped and did not resume until early 1829, just before Branch took office. Rodgers successfully demonstrated to Branch that he had the previous secretary's authority to rebuild *John Adams*.

53. Letter, Louis F. Linden, director, Constellation Foundation, to the author, 29 January 1998. Linden, who at that date headed the Baltimore group charged with rebuilding *Constellation,* promoted with great enthusiasm the notion that the sloop-ship in Baltimore's harbor was built new in 1853–55. After being presented with evidence that

she was rebuilt in 1853, Linden wrote: "The debate over whether this [*Constellation* today] is a rebuild of an 18th century frigate or a sloop new in 1854 strikes me as simply one of definition. Define a term broadly enough and you can make it mean whatever you want it to mean." Then, he added that the fact that some people in the nineteenth century may have thought differently is a matter of their frame of reference and should be understood in that context. "That, as they say, is why they call it history." Branch's rejection of contemporary explanations of the navy's definitions and policies of rebuilding, based as it was on his ignorance of naval operations and policies, strikes the historian as similar to the confusion created by Linden's simplistic definitions presented without independent historical documentation. History as a subject of study should never be reduced to merely a definition or a set of drawings.

54. Act of 3 March 1825; also, letter, Rodgers to Branch, 31 March 1829, RG45, Entry 213, NARA; letter, Secretary Southard to B. W. Crowninshield, 6 March 1822, ASP 1:898–900; also report to House of Representatives, 4 May 1832, Section F, ASP 4:135: a concrete example of the rising cost of work done at navy yards may be observed in the returns of the costs of building ten sloops of war authorized in 1825. The commissioners received an estimate per ship of $85,000. The average cost overrun amounted to $39,000, a 46 percent increase for the cost of each ship; see also Homans, *Laws of the United States,* 128, 147, 159, and 160, acts of 15 May 1820, 3 February, 1831, 30 June 1834. The estimated cost of a schooner rose from $15,000 in 1820, to $29,120 in 1831, to $35,000 in 1834.

55. Letters, Rodgers to Barron, 19 December 1828, 2, 17, and 24 January, and 2 March 1829, RG45, Entry 216, NARA; Navy Annual Report, 1830, 188; letter, Branch to Rodgers, 30 July 1829, RG45, Entry 8, NARA; Agranat, "Thorough and Efficient Repair," 193–98.

56. Navy Annual Report, 1930, 188; letter, Branch to Rodgers, 30 July 1829, RG45, Entry 8, NARA.

57. Letters, Rodgers to Branch, 2, 6, 11, 17 August, RG45, Entry 28, and Branch to Rodgers, 6 and 16 August 1830, RG45, Entry 8, NARA; also Bassett, *Correspondence of Andrew Jackson,* 4:172: letter, Branch to Andrew Jackson, 14 August 1830.

58. Letter, Branch to Rodgers, 2 November 1830, RG45, Entry 8, NARA; Chapelle, *History of the American Sailing Navy,* 359, 360. The architect of the theory that new ships were substituted for old under the guise of rebuilding chose *John Adams* as the ultimate case, accusing the commissioners of rebuilding her with a new design, new dimensions, and a new rate, downrating her from frigate to sloop of war. Chapelle weaves into a narrative his version of the treatment of *John Adams* as he leads his readers toward a preconceived conclusion, that, like *John Adams,* the navy built *Constellation* as a new ship in 1853–54. But Chapelle wrongly states that *John Adams*'s rate changed, because the navy carried her as a 24-gun ship before and after her 1829 rebuild. Second, the modification of her dimensions and draft upgraded the ship's design to more closely match that of the sloops of war built after 1825, considered the most modern ships of that rate available to the navy. Chapelle faults Congress for not controlling the commissioners' "administrative fiction" but ignores the fact it was an intraservice navy battle involv-

ing Branch and Rodgers, not the navy and Congress. Further, Chapelle overlooks the outcome of the Rodgers-Branch argument—an order by President Jackson that authorized the rebuilding of *John Adams* as well as returning the contentious problem of deciding when a repair should be considered a rebuild back to Congress, which originally conceived and legitimized the policy prior to the War of 1812. One of the less obvious attributes of the Board of Commissioners but nevertheless an important one throughout its existence under Rodgers's leadership, related to its knowledge of naval legislation and its subservience to the will of Congress as well as the board's consistent adherence to the laws that governed the administration of the navy.

59. An act to complete the rebuilding of the Frigate *Macedonian*,10 July 1832; an act to purchase timber to rebuild *Java* and *Cyane,* 10 July 1832; an act to provide for the rebuilding of U.S. Frigate *Congress,* 30 June 1834.

60. de Kay, *Chronicles,* 191–206.

61. Agranat, "Thorough and Efficient Repair," 247–48.

62. Ibid.; also, *Congress* Repairs, Subject Files AR, Box 69 and 76, RG45, Entry 464, NARA; *An Act Giving the President of the United States Additional Powers for the Defense of the United States, in Certain Cases, Against Invasion, and for Other Purposes,* 3 March 1839; also, act of 20 July 1840; letter, John Lenthall, chief constructor, to Charles W. Skinner, chief of Bureau of Construction, Equipment, and Repair, 18 December 1851, RG45, NARA, Navy Annual Reports 1839, 573; 1840, 411; 1841, 401; 1852, 351; Agranat, "Thorough and Efficient Repair," 350; Chapelle, *History of the American Sailing Navy,* 402–4. *Congress, Constellation*'s sister ship, was surveyed and condemned by Francis Grice and Samuel Humphreys; the yard broke her up in 1834 following the passage of the act by Congress that authorized the navy to rebuild her. The commissioners delayed work on rebuilding *Congress* until the Harrison-Tyler administration lifted a cap on building or rebuilding ships previously authorized, concurrent with the passage by Congress of the War Powers Act of 3 March 1839. The commissioners dropped plans to rebuild her as a second-rate frigate in favor of a new draft for a frigate-44, and it was by these drawings that the Portsmouth yard rebuilt her. Specific authority to alter her rate and dimensions was not considered a legislative problem as there existed an opening under the legal cap placed on the number of frigate-44s authorized by Congress. If the navy needed additional authority to rebuild *Congress* as a frigate-44, Congress provided for it under the act above and by the act of 20 July 1840, which combined "all remaining balances of appropriations, heretofore made for *building, rebuilding, replacing, purchasing or repairing, vessels of war, or other vessels, for the use of the Navy, or for purchase of timber, ordnance,* etc.," transferring all previously granted authority to a single line item of appropriation. The navy had no interest in rebuilding her as a frigate-36 because of the unpopularity of the smaller-sized frigate with senior captains, and more important, because the navy stockpiled several sets of live oak frames molded for larger frigate-44s following the passage of the act of 20 July 1840, and they could be used for rebuilding *Congress.* Because the navy built her hull new, resulting in a ship of higher rating,

with greater dimensions, skeptics including Chapelle use *Congress* as an example to prove their premise that rebuilds were actually new ships. By doing so, Chapelle ignored the role of Congress, which authorized this and other rebuilds in the Jackson administration. These acts never were challenged in federal court or by anyone else during that period. As set by prior precedent in the case of *Philadelphia,* Congress could designate for rebuild any ship it so wished. Chapelle, probably unaware that Congress approved legislation to rebuild U.S. Frigate *Congress,* called her replacement an "administratively" rebuilt ship, though as outlined above, Congress sanctioned her rebuild just as it had the rebuild of *Constellation, Adams,* and *Philadelphia* and a group of other ships prior to the War of 1812.

Congress extended the acts of 1816, 1821, and 1827 six years in 1833, resulting in a mammoth stockpile of timber at Gosport and at other navy yards. Some of the stored timber consisted of live oak promiscuous pieces, but much of it was cut and molded to size as frame sections for ships of the line, frigates rated forty-four guns, and for smaller sloops of war. As the act of 20 July 1840 combined monies appropriated under previous acts to increase, improve, repair, or rebuild into a single line item containing all previously appropriated funds, this made the combined appropriation available for any of the purposes listed above. The change in policy allowed shipyards to draw down on the stockpile of live oak timber frames formerly reserved only for new ships and not previously available for repairs or for rebuilding ships such as *Congress;* this gave them a flexibility not available for the rebuilding of *Macedonian.* As the commissioners never sought authority *to build* any new second-class frigates, Congress never authorized funds to purchase live oak frames for smaller frigates of thirty-six guns for stockpile. The navy never purchased molded frame pieces for smaller-sized ship-frigates except in the case of the *rebuild* of *Macedonian,* for which the navy purchased a complete frame with specific funds supplied by Congress. Though the navy purchased a new frame molded specifically for Decatur's trophy ship, there existed no similar strong, politically active group agitating to rebuild *Congress* on her original lines, so with several complete frames for frigates-44 on hand, the commissioners found it more expedient to rebuild *Congress* as a first-class frigate-44 to the lines of a new draft when a decision was made to rebuild her in 1839 under the authority of the act of 30 June 1834. More than a decade later, when the navy began considering the fate of *Constellation, Congress*'s more historically significant sister, a new set of circumstances prevailed. First, in 1852, when Secretary John P. Kennedy approved the decision to rebuild *Constellation,* she had extensive rebuilds in 1829 and 1839; during both of those occasions, the first at Gosport and the second at Boston, the yards replaced many of the live oak timber pieces that formed her frames above her floors with new live oak futtocks. John Lenthall wrote in 1851 that he believed that her bottom was sound, and one might add, probably many of her upper frame pieces, since they were new in 1829 and 1839. This meant that, on a practical basis, unlike the old *Congress,* many of *Constellation*'s live oak timber pieces, of a size not replaceable from stockpiles, could be reused in 1853. Second, because of strong sentimental attachment of the navy and the country for its historic first frigate, rebuilding her as a frigate-44 with a new frame was not acceptable as an alternative, nor did the navy design or build any new frigates following the rebuild of *Congress.* Moreover, Lenthall never requested funds for a new frame for *Constellation* in 1852. For those reasons and because other frigates-44 remained in stocks, a decision was made to modernize and modify the frigate *Constellation,* reducing the number of guns in her main battery, which placed her in a new class of ships, a first-class sloop of war. When the navy modified and razeed *Constellation,* it eliminated the class of second-class frigates, as it razeed *Macedonian* before modifying *Constellation.*

63. Letter, Commo. Daniel T. Patterson to Secretary Levi Woodbury, 6 January 1834, Captain's Letters, RG45, MF-125, NARA; also Emmons, *Navy of the United States,* 94.

64. Letter, Read to Dickerson, 30 November 1834, Captains' Letters, RG45, MF-125; also, *Constellation*'s Log No. 10, RG24, NARA.

65. Court-martial of George C. Read, 22 June 1835, RG45, M-273, 622, NARA.

66. *Norfolk Herald,* 1 July 1833.

67. *Norfolk Herald,* 1 July 1833, 11 August 1837; Vessel Repairs—*Constellation,* RG19, Entry 5, 172; also *Constellation* Repairs, 1834–35, Subject Files PI, Box 521, RG45, Entry 464, NARA.

68. Vessel Repairs, *Constellation,* RG19, Entry 5, 172, and *Constellation* Repairs, 1834–35, Subject Files P I, Box 521, RG45, Entry 464, NARA. It is difficult to interpret exactly what corrective measures constructor Grice did to minimize the effects of the frigate's hogged keel without affecting the ship's sailing qualities. He filled the hollows in her floors and added hog streaks on the ship's bottom and then coppered over the work. If in this process he reduced the area of the keel that extended below the ship's bottom without adding a cap to the keel to compensate for that loss, this would have affected *Constellation*'s ability of work up wind under sail.

69. Navy Annual Report, 1835, 368, 379–80; Navy Annual Report, 1836, 442–43; also letter, Dallas to Dickerson, 8 October 1835, RG45, MF-125, NARA.

70. Cooper, *Ned Myers,* 238–39; Dudley, "James Fenimore Cooper's *Ned Myers,*" 326. Dudley informs us in this article that Myers transferred to USS *St. Louis* sometime during his cruise on *Constellation.* Dallas, continually faced with a shortage of men among ships of the squadron, made a decision to moor *Constellation* permanently at Pensacola, and transfer members of his flagship's crew as needed to other navy vessels and revenue cutters assigned to him; see also letter, Dallas to Gen. Francisco Caravano, 28 November 1835, RG45, MF-125, NARA.

71. Letters, Dallas to Dickerson, 5, 7, 14 February, 10 April 1836, RG45, MF-125, NARA.

72. Letters, Dallas to Dickerson, 6 January, 7 February 1836, RG45, MF-125, NARA.

73. Letter, Dallas to Taylor, 9 May 1836, RG45, MF-125, NARA.

74. Letters, Dallas to Charles Boarman, commander, USS *Grampus,* 14, 16 May; letter, Dallas to Dickerson, 17 May 1836, RG45, MF-125, NARA.

75. Letter, Dallas to Dickerson, 20 May 1936, RG45, MF-125, NARA.

76. Letter, Master Commandant Rousseau to Dallas, 6 July 1836, RG45, MF-125, NARA.

77. Letters, Master Commandant Mix to Dallas, 6 July, and Dallas to Dickerson, 3, 6 July 1836, RG45, MF-125, NARA.

78. Letters, Mix to Dallas, 23 July and 5 and 6 August; Dallas to Acting Secretary of the Navy John Boyle, 11, 31 August, RG45, MF-125; Master Commandant Dulany to Dallas, 28 August 1836, RG45, MF-125, NARA.

79. Letters, Dallas to Boyle, 31 August, 6, 12 September, 6 October 1836, RG45, MF-125, NARA.

80. Letters, Dallas to Dickerson, 4, 10 October 1836, RG45, MF-125, NARA; Navy Annual Report 1838, 39; see also chapter 7, endnotes 1–9. Dallas pleaded with the secretary for a large frigate—*Columbia, United States,* or *Raritan*—none of which could navigate the bar at the entrance to Pensacola harbor, an amazing oversight on Dallas's part. This suggests that Commodore Dallas's ambition to have as flagship a frigate-44 darkened his condemnation of *Constellation. Macedonian* 36, replaced *Constellation* in 1838.

81. *Constellation*'s Log No. 12, 12 February 1837 to 15 August 1838, RG24, NARA.

82. Letters, Dallas to Secretary J. K. Paulding, 9, 17 July, 7 August; James M. McIntosh, flag captain, *Constellation,* to Paulding, 18 August 1838, RG45, MF-125, NARA. Dallas transferred his flag to USS *Vandalia* and placed Lieutenant McIntosh in command of *Constellation;* he delivered her to the Charlestown Navy Yard. See also *Constellation*'s Log No. 10, RG24, NARA: *Constellation*'s speed reached eight knots on one occasion between Pensacola and Boston.

83. Letters, Dallas to Paulding, 3 August, 2 September, 15 November 1838, RG45, MF-125; also letter, John Boyle, acting secretary of the navy, to Board of Commissioners, 29 October, 1838, RG45, Entry 8, NARA.

Chapter 7. 1839: Modifying Prior Modifications

1. Letter, Dallas to Secretary Dickerson, 6 January 1836, RG45, MF-125, NARA.

2. Ibid.

3. *Constellation*'s Log No. 12, 15 February 1837 to 15 August 1838, RG24, NARA; also, Navy Annual Report, 1836, and Ferguson, *Truxtun,* 202–5.

4. Letter, Dallas to Dickerson, 20 May 1836, RG45, MF-125, NARA.

5. Letter, Dallas to Dickerson, 29 September 1836, RG45, MF-125, NARA.

6. Letter, Dallas to Dickerson, 23 February 1837, RG45, MF-125, NARA.

7. Letter, Dallas to Paulding, 3 August 1838, RG45, MF-125, NARA.

8. Paulding to Chauncey, 17 August 1838, RG45, Entry 8, NARA.

9. Letters, Dallas to Paulding, 2 September 1838, RG45, MF-125, and John Boyle, acting secretary of the navy, to commissioners, 29 October 1838, RG45, Entry 8, NARA; *Army and Navy Chronicle,* 1 November 1838 (article reprinted from the Boston *Statesman*); also, *Constellation*'s Log No. 10, 16 August to 4 November 1838, James M. McIntosh, commander, RG24, NARA; also, letter, Commandant Downes to commissioners, 24 October 1838, RG 181, NARA, Waltham, Massachusetts.

10. Circular to All Commanders—List of the Vessels of the U.S. Navy with their respective designating numbers, 1 October 1838, from the commissioners, 5 October 1838, Geisinger Papers, MS1283, MHS.

11. Bearss, *Charlestown Navy Yard,* 2:755–57; letter, Commissioner Morris to Downes, 30 October 1838, RG181, NARA, Waltham; also, *Army and Navy Chronicle* (July–December 1835), 256–57.

12. Charlestown Navy Yard Journal, 24 October to 27 November 1838; letters, Downes to Morris, 3, 15 November 1838, RG181; NARA, Waltham.

13. Letter, Downes to Morris, 11 December 1838, RG181: Downes included the survey, which had no date or signature, with this letter. A photocopy of the report is located in the Leon Polland Papers, Special Collections, Nimitz Library, USNA, where the naval architect, working on the preservation of USS *Constellation* in the 1960s, placed a set of his papers and drawings. The photocopy without citation may be authenticated by matching the work required specified in the survey with the running log kept by the yard clerk and available at the National Archives, Washington, D.C.; RG45, Entry 464, Subject File AR, Box 92, Folder 5, NARA.

14. Survey with letter, Downes to Morris, 11 December 1838, RG181, NARA.

15. "Letter received enclosing drawings of shape of U.S. Frigate *Constellation,*" Inbound Letter Log (with summaries), Bureau of Construction, Equipment, and Repair, from Gosport Commandant Breese, 2 February 1853, RG19, Entry 60-A, NARA; Chapelle and Polland, *Constellation Question,* 29: "The plan (107-13-4B) was probably made [February 1853] when planking was stripped from the hull and was intended to inform the Bureau of hull distortions resulting from excessive hog." John Lyman, "The *Constellation* and Her Rebuilding," *Sea History* (July 1975), 26: Lyman writes that Chapelle suggests that these offsets (107-13-4B) were taken (February 1853) when planking was stripped from the hull. However, Lyman concludes that the drawing was prepared while the planking and copper were still on her; thus the positions of the frames were not known. Lyman writes that ballast was left in her to avoid any chance of capsizing while being hauled from dry dock to the north slip. *Constellation* did not enter dry dock at Gosport in 1853; "therefore Lyman's concepts are flawed." Wegner, *Fouled Anchors,* 78: "Another drawing on linen dated Norfolk, February, 1853 (107-13-4B) was prepared—probably after the ship was in the slip." What slip? When? How? Also Wegner, "The Frigate Strikes Her Colors," 347: Wegner wrote that just before the ship was destroyed in 1853, hull drawings were made for bracing her while in dry dock and the docking plans confirmed that between 1795 and 1853 the shape of *Constellation*'s hull below the waterline was not altered. The last statement is incorrect because the drawing in question shows that *Constellation*'s breadth differed from the 1795 Doughty draft. The ship was not taken into dry dock prior to hauling her up, as Wegner wrote. As a matter of fact it makes no sense to prepare the drawing if the ship is about to be broken up, nor would a ship have been hauled out as in the case of *Constellation* if it was not the plan to reuse her timbers and equipment.

16. *Constellation's* Survey, 1838, Boston; Polland's Papers, Nimitz Library, USNA.

17. Ibid.; also *Daily Journal*, Charlestown Navy Yard, RG181, NARA, Waltham; *Constellation's* Repairs, Boston, 1838–40, RG45, Entry 464, Subject AR, Box 92, Folder 5, NARA.

18. *Daily Journal*, RG181, NARA, Waltham; *Army and Navy Chronicle* (article reprinted from the Boston *Transcript*), 28 February 1839; also, Truxtun's Muster, Order, and Signal Book, 1798, HSP.

19. *Constellation's* Bimonthly Repair Report, Subject File AR, Box 92, RG45, Entry 464, NARA; Daily Journal, RG181, NARA, Waltham; Transverse Sections of Frigate *Constellation*, no. 107-13-4B, RG19, Entry 126, NARA, College Park, Maryland.

20. Letter, Morris to Downes, 31 December 1838, RG181, NARA, Waltham; act of March 3 1839; act of 20 June 1840.

21. Letter, Charles Stewart, for the commissioners to Secretary Woodbury, 19 November 1832, RG45, Entry 213, NARA; also, ASP 1:44; Harry Bluff [Lt. M. F. Maury], "More Scraps from the Lucky Bag," 7, 327. Maury charged that timber removed from timber ponds, hewn or sawed, and placed in sheds to dry, frequently split, causing large losses to the total stockpile. Of the 75 percent of the weakened timber that survived wet storage, he believed that another large percentage would be lost to theft, rents, and other damage when stored in open sheds. In the case of *Constellation*, add to the percentages lost to damage, waste caused by hewing larger shaped frame pieces cut for ships of the line and first-class frigates or from unmolded promiscuous pieces into a frame for a smaller second-class frigate.

22. Letters, Downes to Morris, 18, 19 February 1839, RG181; also, Morris to Downes, 8 April 1839, RG181, NARA, Waltham.

23. *Constellation's* Repairs, Boston, 1838–40, Subject File AR, Box 92, RG45, Entry 464, NARA; Drawing of *Constellation's* Bow, No. 107-13-4, RG19, Entry 126, NARA, College Park.

24. Letter, Downes to Morris, 28 August 1839, RG181, NARA, Waltham: Drawing of *Constellation's* Keel, No. 107-13-4A, RG19, Entry 126, NARA, College Park, Maryland. Original not found at archives; copies located in the collection of Leon Polland, Special Collections, Nimitz Library, USNA; see also Chapelle and Polland, *Constellation Question*, 28.

25. *Constellation's* Repairs, Boston, 1838–40, Subject File AR, Box 92, RG45, Entry 464, NARA; Chapelle and Polland, *Constellation Question*, 96; there is also a copy of this drawing in Polland Collection, USNA.

26. Transverse Sections of the Frigate Constellation, No. 107-13-4B, RG19, Entry 126, NARA, College Park. The script and print in these drawings of *Constellation's* bow, keel, transverse sections, and a drawing of her load plan made at Boston are prepared in the same handwriting.

27. Bearss, *Charlestown Navy Yard*, 777–79; letters, Paulding to Downes, 12, 22 October 1839, 28 September 1840, RG45, MF-149; Downes to Paulding, 15 October 1839, RG45, MF-125, NARA.

28. Letters, Downes to Paulding, 8, 11, 22 October 1840, RG45, MF-125, and Paulding to Downes, 17 October 1840, RG45, MF-149, NARA.

29. Letters, Downes to commissioners, 30 December 1839, 23 March 1840, RG181; also, Boston Yard's Daily Journal, 11, 12 March and 9 November 1840, RG181; letter, commissioners to Downes, 5 August 1840, RG181, NARA, Waltham.

30. Letter, Downes to commissioners, 23 November 1840, RG181, NARA, Waltham.

31. Letter, Downes to commissioners, 30 December 1839, RG181, NARA, Waltham.

32. Harry Bluff [M. F. Maury], "Scraps from the Lucky Bag, of Reorganizing the Navy," *Southern Literary Messenger* (January 1841), 17. Lieutenant Maury calculated that the navy wasted $250,000, a figure higher than the ship's original cost, following the discovery of decay in U.S. Frigate *United States* after the ship received $80,000 in repairs at Boston. In addition to that $80,000, he included in the $250,000 the cost of manning the ship for four months by her five hundred crew members, shifting the ship from Boston to New York and then from New York to Norfolk, plus repairs, pay, and provisioning at Norfolk.

33. Letters, Storer to Downes, 9, 10, 12, 15 November 1840; also, Downes to Captain Ward Marsten, 9 November 1840, Miscellaneous Papers, Charlestown Navy Yard, RG181, NARA, Waltham; Bearss, *Charlestown Navy Yard,* 790: Secretary Paulding's Circular Letter, dated 13 September 1839.

34. Letters, Storer to Downes, 16 (2 letters), 17, 24 November and 7 December 1840, RG181, NARA, Waltham.

35. Letter, commissioners to Downes, 2 March 1842, Misc. Documents, RG181, NARA, Waltham; letter, Downes to Commissioners, 25 November 1840, containing Storer's letters and surveys and copy of survey ordered by Downes, 25 November 1840, RG45, Entry 220, NARA.

36. Letters, Storer to Paulding, 9 December; Abbot to Downes, 28 November; Storer to Lieutenant Jones, et al., 23 December 1840; Jones et al. to Storer (2 letters), 11 January 1841, Misc. Documents, RG181, NARA, Waltham; Storer to Paulding (2 letters), 26 January 1841, RG45, MF-125, NARA; surveys, Lieutenant Pinkney to Kearny, *Constellation*'s guns, 23, 26 February 1841; Kearny to Paulding, 24 December 1840; Ridgely to Paulding, 5 February; Ridgely to Kearny, 11 February 1841; Kearny to Paulding, 26 February, 6 March 1841, RG45, MF-125, NARA; Bearss, *Charlestown Navy Yard,* 2:836–37; letters, Kearny to Paulding, 25 February 1841, RG45, MF-125 and to commissioners, 4 March 1841, RG45, Entry 220, NARA.

37. Survey of Rigging, 6, 12 April, by Commander Long et al., USS *Boston* and *Constellation*; letter, Kearny to Secretary Badger, 21 April, East Indies Squadron Letters, RG45, 26 February 1841 to 18 May 1844, Roll 1, NARA; letter, M. G. L. Claiborne to A. P. Maury, 16 April 1841, copy in author's files.

38. Letter, Kearny to Secretary Badger, 11 June, 20 July 1841, East Indies Squadron Letters, RG45, Roll 1; also, letter, Downes to commissioners, 21 January 1842, RG45, Entry 220, NARA.

39. Abstract of *Constellation*'s Journal; letter, Kearny to Secretary of the Navy Abel P. Upsher, 26 March 1842, East Indies Squadron Letters, RG45, Roll 1, NARA.

40. Alden, *Lawrence Kearny*, 131–39.

41. Letter (orders), Paulding to Kearny, 2 November 1839, East Indies Squadron Letters, RG45, Roll 1, NARA.

42. Lubbock, *Opium Clippers*, 32–35; Geoffrey M. Footner, *Tidewater Triumph*, 134, 163; Alden, *Lawrence Kearny*, 168–69.

43. Lubbock, *Opium Clippers*, 32–35, 147, 158, 166, 173; also, Geoffrey M. Footner, *Tidewater Triumph*, 132–35, 163. Delano, Snow, Hunter, and King all worked for Russell & Company; Sturgis's employer in 1842 is not known; his father was a mariner and long associated with the opium trade and at one time a principal in the firm of Russell, Sturgis & Company. Extract from U.S. laws on navigation, art. 1362: "but no such vessel shall be entitled to registry, or, if registered, to the benefits thereof, if owned in whole or part by any citizen usually residing in a foreign country, during that residence, unless he be a consul of the United States, or an agent for, and a partner in some house of trade."

44. Letters, Kearny to secretary of the navy, 23 September, 15 November, 13 December 1842, and 16 January 1843, with attachments; Kearny to Ke, governor of Canton, 8 October; Ke to Kearny, 15 October, consul Snow to Kearny, 20 October 1842, East Indies Squadron Papers, RG45, Roll 1, NARA. The treaty opened specific ports that included Canton, Amoy, Foo-chow foo, and Shanghai to British trade and ceded the island of Hong Kong to Her Majesty's Government. It also awarded the British $20 million including $6 million for the opium destroyed by Lin at Canton.

45. Letters, Kearny to secretary of the navy, 25 February, Augustine Heard & Co. to Edward King, vice consul, 5 January, King to Kearny, 5 January, Kearny to Heard, 9 January, Kearny to King, 9 January, Kearny to James P. Sturgis, vice consul, 14 January, Sturgis to Kearny, 15 January, Kearny to Governor Ke, 15 March, Governor Ke to Kearny, 15 March, and Kearny to Governor Ke, 13 April 1843, East Indies Squadron Papers, RG45, Roll 1, NARA.

46. Letters, Kearny to Secretary of the Navy, 5, 19 May 1843, East Indies Squadron Papers, RG45, Roll 1.

47. Alden, *Lawrence Kearny*, 173–82; letter, Kearny to secretary of the navy, 21 April, Kearny to Daniel Webster, secretary of state, 21 April 1843, East Indies Squadron Papers, RG45, Roll 1.

48. Circular Letter, Kearny to American Merchants and Others, 18 May 1843, Squadron Papers, RG45, Roll 1; Geoffrey M. Footner, *Tidewater Triumph*, 135, 137, 166–68, 232; see also, Layton, *Voyage of the* Frolic, 1–109.

49. Letter, Kearny to secretary of the navy, 19 May, Kearny to Sturgis, 21 May 1843; extract of Log of the *Ariel*, East Indies Squadron Papers, RG45, Roll 1, NARA.

50. Alden, *Lawrence Kearny*, 217: letter, Kearny to his children, 12 March 1843; letters, Kearny to the secretary of the navy, 27 July and 23 November 1842; abstract of *Constellation*'s Journal, East Indies Squadron Papers, RG45, Roll 1.

51. Abstract of *Constellation*'s Journal; letters, U.S. commercial agent, Sandwich Islands, to Kearny, 7, 11 July 1843; Kearny to Rt. Hon. Lord George Paulet, commanding HBM ship *Carysfort,* 17 July, Kearny's protest to King Kamehameha, 11 July; commercial agent William Hooper to Kearny, 14 July; Kearny to Governor Kekaulluohi, 14 July; Kekaulluohi to Kearny, 15 July; King Kamehameha to Kearny, 19 July 1843, East Indies Squadron Papers, RG45, Roll 1, NARA.

52. Letters, Kearny to secretary of the navy, 2 September 1843 and 16 March and 1 May, 1844; abstract of *Constellation*'s Journal, East Indies Squadron Papers, RG45, Roll 1, NARA. The ship *Seaman,* built at Baltimore about fifty years after *Constellation,* made the run between San Francisco (slightly farther) and Valparaiso in 1854 in thirty-five days. *Constellation,* in 1844, three years out of dry dock at Boston, leaking, poorly rigged, and obviously badly in need of rebuilding from keel to rail, covered 8,007 miles between Monterey and Valparaiso in sixty-one days, averaging five knots per hour.

53. *Constellation*'s Log, Lawrence Kearny, commander, 12–17 May 1844; *Constellation*'s Log, Lts. G. G. Williamson and B. W. Hunter, 6 June 1844 to 12 July 1845, RG24, NARA; Young's Log, Gosport Navy Yard, from 10 May 1844, RG71, Entry 91, NARA, Philadelphia; Storekeeper Returns, Gosport, RG19, Entry 320, vol. 166, NARA. It should be noted that, according to shipyard procedures, at no time during the process of stripping a ship entering ordinary did the ship's equipment come under the jurisdiction of the yard's storekeeping department. Naval regulations required that naval officers attached to the navy yard assume responsibility as custodian of a ship's equipment while in ordinary. By cross-checking with the storekeeper's inventory, it may be verified *Constellation*'s equipment never passed through the storekeeper's log or inventory; for example, between January and June, 1845, the storekeeper had no anchors in his stores; see Return to Stores, RG19, Entry 320, vol. 166.

54. Harry Bluff [M. F. Maury], "Scraps from the Lucky Bag," *Southern Literary Messenger,* January 1841, 16.

55. Agranat, "Thorough and Efficient Repair," 310–11; *Act to Reorganize the Navy Department of the United States,* 31 August 1842, *Laws of the United States,* vol. 10, chap. 464, 393–96; Paullin, *Paullin's History of Naval Administration,* 209–10.

56. Act of 17 June, 1844, limiting enlistments to seventy-five hundred, Navy Annual Report, 1844, 515; act of Congress of 4 August 1842, limiting the number of officers and men on the active duty; the act of 31 August 1842 withdrew the right of the navy, granted in 1840, to transfer appropriations for different uses; see also Paullin, *Paullin's History of Naval Administration,* 227.

57. Navy Annual Report, 1844, 516; Agranat, "Thorough and Efficient Repair," 341–60. Agranat provides a complete analysis of the treatment Lieutenant Maury's reforms received between 1842 and midcentury; see also *Army and Navy Chronicle and Scientific Repository* (6 April 1843) 1:411; also see vol. 3, 28 March, 405; 6 June, 712; 20 June, 781; and 27 June 1844, 822–27.

58. *Army and Navy Chronicle and Scientific Repository* (18 May 1843) 1:599, 601, 609; Agranat, "Thorough and Efficient Repair," 356–57; Harry Bluff [M. F. Maury], "Scraps," *Southern*

Literary Messenger (January 1841): 22, also November 1841: 369; Chapelle, *History of the American Sailing Navy,* 436, 438.

59. Letter, John Lenthall to Chauncey, 12 February 1838, RG45, Entry 277, NARA; Navy Annual Report, December 1854, 475. The secretary of the navy appointed John Lenthall navy constructor, Philadelphia Navy Yard, in February 1838. Lenthall drafted and supervised the construction of USS *Germantown* in 1845–46. As chief navy constructor in 1853, he was charged with redrafting *Constellation.* As chief of the Bureau of Construction, Equipment, and Repair, he assumed direct supervision of the conversion of frigate *Constellation* to a sloop of war in December 1853. There are writers, principally Howard I. Chapelle (*History of the American Sailing Navy*) and Dana Wegner (*Fouled Anchors*), who have concluded that John Lenthall drafted and built under his watch a new ship named USS *Constellation* when chief of the Bureau of Construction, Equipment, and Repair. It is important to note the statement by Lenthall, included in the Navy Department's Annual Report for 1854 and addressed to the secretary of the navy, the president of the United States, and ultimately to Congress, refutes their conclusion. Lenthall wrote in 1854, the year that Gosport launched the rebuilt *Constellation,* that the sloops of war (which included *Germantown,* drafted by him) "which were launched from 1842 to 1845 are the sailing ships of the latest date that have been built in the Navy." This statement survives in this report as his indisputable testimony that rebuts Chapelle and Wegner's undocumented conclusion that the navy constructed a new sailing ship named *Constellation* in 1853, ten years after Congress authorized and funded this final group of new sailing ships.

60. Navy Annual Report, 1844, 465, 467. *United States* cruised the coast of Africa in 1846 and *Constitution* was in ordinary in Boston that year.

61. Log of *Constellation* to 12 July 1845, RG24; Young's Log, 8, 15, 16, 17, 22 July and 16 August 1845. RG71, Entry 91, NARA.

62. *Baltimore Patriot,* 10 July 1845.

63. *Niles National Register,* 19 July 1845.

64. Letter, Bureau of Construction Chief Shubrick to Secretary of the Navy George Bancroft, 8 July, and Shubrick to Commandant Wilkinson, Gosport, 11 July 1845, Bureau Letters, MF-518, RG45, NARA; letters, Capt. Robert F. Stockton to secretary of the navy 11, 18, 24, 27 July 1845, MF-125, RG45, NARA; also, Charles H. Haswell's estimate of cost of *Constellation*'s engines, etc., dated 22 July 1845, Bureau Letters, RG45, MF-518, NARA; and Samuel Humphreys Survey (with Foster Rhodes), dated 19 July 1845, Leon Polland's Papers, Special Collections, NARA.

65. Letter, Stockton to secretary of the navy, 29 July 1845, RG45, MF-125, NARA; also, Humphreys/Rhodes Survey, Leon Polland Papers, Nimitz Library, USNA.

66. Instructions for Preparing *Constellation* for Ordinary, dated 1846, Subject File AL, Laid-up Ships, Box 68, RG45, Entry 464; Young's Log, Gosport, 23 July 1846, RG71, Entry 91, NARA, Philadelphia; letter, Stockton to secretary of the navy dated 29 July 1845, RG45, MF-125, NARA; and Humphreys/Rhodes Survey, Leon Polland's Papers, NARA.

67. Navy Annual Report, 1850, 231–32.

68. Letter, Skinner to Graham, 25 February 1851, with John Lenthall's letter of 6 February to Skinner attached, RG19, Entry 49, No. 30, NARA.

69. Letter, Bureau Chief Skinner to Secretary Graham, 16 April 1851, Bureau Letters, RG45, MF-518, NARA.

70. Letter, Bureau Chief Skinner to Graham, 20 June, and Report of Board, consisting of bureau chiefs, Morris, Warrington and Smith, 1 July 1851, Bureau Letters, RG45, MF-518, NARA; Navy Annual Report, 1851, 77; also, letter, Skinner to Graham, 2 April 1852, Bureau Letters, RG45, MF-518, NARA.

71. Letter, Bureau Chief Skinner to Graham, 19 December, 1851, with Chief Naval Constructor John Lenthall's letter of 18 December 1851 attached, Bureau Letters, RG45, MF-518, NARA.

72. Ibid.; In his 18 December letter, Lenthall referred to *Constellation* as an inferior ship. Though he mentioned her reputation for instability, by referring to her as inferior, he directed his comment to her classification as second-class frigate not to her sailing qualities. But Lenthall also pointed out that the smaller ship's large dimensions with small displacement provided her brilliant qualities; he noted, too, that though speed is highly desirable, it was not the only quality of a ship of war. Chapelle and Polland, *Constellation Question,* 33–37: Chapelle got it correct when he stated that Lenthall's letter presented his views only and could only be considered recommendations. He evidently did not see Skinner's covering letter that limits his recommendation, at that specific point the conversion of *Constellation* into a sloop of war, if she is worthy of repair, a decision that Skinner could not or had not been prepared to make either.

73. *Portsmouth Beacon,* 26 May 1849; Navy Annual Report, 1849, 461; Chapelle, *History of the American Sailing Navy,* 349, 358–59. Chapelle ignored the fact that the navy rebuilt *Vandalia,* which included extending her length fifteen feet.

Chapter 8. From Frigate to Razee-Sloop of War

1. Navy Annual Report, 1854, 475; Martin, *Most Fortunate Ship,* 311–12; Chapelle, *History of the American Sailing Navy,* 464, 468. John Lenthall, after drafting the conversion plans for *Constellation,* stated in his initial report as chief of the Bureau of Construction, Equipment, and Repair that Congress authorized the last new sailing ships designed and built by and for the United States Navy in 1843. Commander Martin discusses the modifications made to *Constitution* during her rebuild of 1858, following which, he states, her rate changed from first-class frigate to second-class ship. As the navy had no such rate as a second-class ship, Martin seemed reluctant to admit that the navy reclassified *Constitution* an inferior sloop of war. However, Chapelle states that the navy downrated the ship to corvette (sloop of war), and then contradicts himself later in his book, stating that *Constitution* always maintained her form, rate, and original dimensions. Sentiment for the nation's first three frigates remained high and the navy never ordered

the destruction of USF *United States;* she stayed in ordinary at Norfolk until destroyed to keep her out of the hands of the Confederate Army.

2. Letters, Lenthall to Skinner, 18 December, and Skinner to Graham, 19 December 1851, Bureau Letters, RG45, MF-518, NARA.

3. Letter, Skinner to Graham, 21 January 1852, RG19, Entry 49, NARA; Navy Annual Report, 1850, 231; Wegner, "An Apple and an Orange," 78, 79, n. 3. Wegner cites Skinner's remarks from Navy Annual Report, 1850, 231, to support his statement that the navy decided to break up *Constellation* and replace her with a new ship. It is a fact that Skinner limited his remarks to a suggestion that *Constitution, United States,* and *Constellation* should no longer be prepared for sea duty, but should be returned to the ports where they were built to become receiving ships. The navy never acted on Skinner's suggestion. Wegner's statement is incorrect.

4. Letter, Skinner to Graham, 21 January 1852, RG19, Entry 49, NARA; letter, W. Branford Shubrick to Capt. Francis Henry duPont, 30 March 1852, Captain duPont's correspondence, W9-6309, Box 20, Hagley Museum and Library, Wilmington, Delaware; Paullin, *Paullin's History of Naval Administration,* 207, quoting Tuckerman, *Life of John Pendleton Kennedy,* 21–22: "His name gracefully designates a channel of the lonely Arctic Sea and is identified with the initial experiment which established the electric telegraph; with the opening of Japan to the commerce of the world; with the exploration of the Amazon and the China Sea; with the benefactors of [George] Peabody and the loyalty of Maryland." President Pierce selected Shubrick to replace Skinner after taking office but the new chief did not assume control of the bureau until 1 July 1852.

5. Sailing Master H. A. F. Young, yard clerk, Gosport Navy Yard Log, 3 November 1852, RG71, Entry 91, NARA, Philadelphia; letter from Congress to J. P. Kennedy, 16 April 1852, RG45, Entry 27; letter, Bureau Chief W. Branford Shubrick to Kennedy, 18 August 1852, RG19, Entry 49, NARA. Concerning converting *Constellation* or any other warship from sail to steam power, Shubrick responded to this inquiry by enclosing John Lenthall's earlier correspondence on the subject. His letter provided the navy's final judgment on this issue—that it would be more economical to build a new ship rather than convert *Constellation* or any other warship from sail to steam power. He limited his letter to advice and issued no order to destroy *Constellation.* Wegner, *Fouled Anchors,* 3, 94 n. 5, 132, 147 n. 3; Wegner, "An Apple and an Orange," 78–79, n. 3. In three separate instances, Wegner cites Captain Shubrick's letter of 18 August 1852 to substantiate his statement that the navy "decided to replace *Constellation* with a new ship." What Shubrick actually wrote 18 August consisted of a restatement of Lenthall's recommendations: "With respect to the particular application to the case of a propeller for the frigate *Constellation,* now at Norfolk, I submit a letter from the Naval Constructor marked (1) and a letter from the Constructor marked (2) from which the question between building a new propeller ship of the class of *Constellation* or repairing that ship and fitting her with a propeller is stated that the cost of converting the old ship with propeller would be the same as building a new one." No order was issued to destroy *Constellation.*

6. Tuckerman, *Life of John Pendleton Kennedy,* chap. 10.

7. Charles Henry Bohner, *John Pendleton Kennedy* (Baltimore: Johns Hopkins University Press, 1961) 205, 211 n. 5, quoting letter, Kennedy to Elizabeth Gray Kennedy, 28 July 1852.

8. Secretary of the Navy Kennedy's Annual Report, dated 2 December 1852, 320, 321, 326, 350, 351, 352, 357-C&D, and 630. Kennedy's thoughtful and detailed report, supplemented by Bureau Chief Shubrick's report for the Bureau of Construction, Equipment, and Repair, outlined navy intentions to repair *Constellation* and provided verification that the Bureau of Construction, Equipment, and Repair notified the Senate of the United States that the navy would request funds to repair her in the budget for the fiscal year 1853–54. Shubrick also referred to the bureau's request for authorization to build six new steamships which Congress authorized by the act of 6 April 1854. This act confirmed that by 1853–54 Congress and the navy had moved beyond the sailing ship era; additionally, the navy had no legal authority or even a strong interest in building new sailing vessels. See also Navy Annual Report, 1854, 475, in which Bureau Chief Lenthall reported that the navy did not design, build, or authorize any new sailing warships after commissioning sloops of war *Jamestown, Germantown,* and *St. Marys* in 1846.

9. In the Senate of the United States, 26 August 1852, Letters from Congress, RG45, Entry 27, no. 67, NARA.

10. Letter, U.S. Department of State to J. P. Kennedy, secretary of the navy, 19 October 1852, RG45, Entry 27, no. 68, NARA.

11. Navy Annual Report, 1852, 320, 326. On page 320 of Kennedy's report, the secretary directs the attention of Congress to the recommendations of the bureau; again, on page 326 at the very end of his summary report, Kennedy directs attention to attached abstracts of chiefs of bureaus, as required by the Resolution of the Senate of 26 August, 1852.

12. Navy Annual Report, 1852, 350, 351, 630.

13. Ibid., 351, 630.

14. Ibid., 351.

15. Ibid., 630.

16. Ibid., 351; letter, Board of Review, consisting of Capts. Charles Morris and Joseph Smith, plus Samuel Hartt, Charles W. Copeland, and John Lenthall, to Secretary Dobbin, 31 August 1853, and memorandum of same board, dated 21 January 1854, Bureau Letters, RG45, MF-518, NARA; Agranat, "Thorough and Efficient Repair," 402–4. The navy built USS *Franklin,* new, one of six steam frigates authorized by the act of 6 April 1854.

17. Summary of Letters Received by Chief Shubrick, Bureau of Construction, Equipment, and Repair, from Commandant, Gosport Navy Yard, sent 3 November, received Washington, D.C., 5 November 1852, RG19, Entry 60-A, NARA. Gosport yard wanted two crabs from the Washington Navy Yard for drawing up *Constellation.* Young's Log, 18, 19, 23, 25, 26, 29 November, 4, 6, 7, and 14 December 1852, and 23 February 1853, RG71, Entry 91, NARA, Philadelphia; also, Navy Annual Report, 1853, 546: Young reported that laborers were hoisting up *Constellation's* ballast and/or hauling out iron tanks.

18. Chapelle, *History of the American Sailing Navy,* 468. Chapelle summarized his conclusion concerning the navy's intentions for *Constellation* and in the process discussed Congress's alleged ignorance of the navy's real intent in 1853; he wrote: "The rebuilding of the *Constellation* in 1853–1854 represents a different situation from that of the numerous rebuilding of such naval monuments as *Constitution* and *British Victory*. In the case of the corvette [*sic:* sloop of war *Constellation*], she was rebuilt into what was then a modern ship of war without any attempt to preserve the original, and the only reason her register was maintained, by means of an administrative fiction, was to enable the work to be done without the need of applying to Congress for authority and funds to build an entirely new ship." Nothing that happened between 1850 and January 1853 supports Chapelle's hypothesis. Proponents of an argument that the navy intended to build a new ship without receiving congressional approval did not avail themselves to Senate resolution of 26 August 1852 and therefore accept suppositions put forth by Chapelle though they are proven false. Certainly, those who support the two-*Constellation* dogma failed to take into consideration the sentiments of Congress, of the navy, and of the nation in 1852, and to gauge the importance of their combined considerable interest in the fate of *Constellation*. The Chapelle conclusion is based on the false premise that Congress operated with little knowledge of the content and scope of United States naval policies. The opposite is true as legislators demonstrated constant interest in naval affairs, a subject treated in detail in previous chapters.

19. Storekeeper's Returns, Gosport, vols. 165–69, January 1844, June, 1847, RG19, Entry 320; General Orders, Regulations, and Circulars Regulating the Activities of Navy Yard Storekeepers, 22 June 1830, 26 November and 15 December 1842, 16 March and 25 September 1843, 21 January 1844, 14 April and 14 May 1845, 18 May and 18 August 1848, and 8 August 1851, Secretary of the Navy Circulars to Commandants and Bureau Chiefs, RG45, MF-977, NARA; Young's Log, 4–7 and 14 December 1852, RG71, Entry 91, NARA, Philadelphia; Equipment Held for *Constellation* in Ordinary, RG19, Entry 8, NARA. Items of equipment held in storage for *Constellation* included sails, spars, and rigging, furniture, boats, casks, anchors, cables, cordage, iron tanks, and tools. When the ship moved out of ordinary for repairs, she came under the direct control of the Bureau of Construction, Equipment, and Repair. The ship's ordnance was the responsibility of the department of ordnance storekeeper and a special storekeeper controlled surgeons and hospital supplies for that department. An ordinary crew placed *Constellation*'s iron tanks, specially fabricated at the Washington Navy Yard in 1839 to fit her sharp angle of deadrise, in storage or sent them to Washington to be reconditioned. The only control exercised by Gosport's storekeeper over a ship's own equipment when under repair, according to navy rules and regulations in effect in 1853, covered the management of the movement of that ship's equipment between departments, yards, and shops as it was repaired, to arrange transportation to another yard if necessary, and to keep account of value added to equipment repaired in a yard's shop. Storekeepers tracked each item belonging to *Constellation* as it moved from storage to shop and finally to the con-

struction site. Storekeepers passed these returns to the bureau concerned as each department or shop kept track and accumulated costs of repairs. In this manner all of the
equipment belonging to *Constellation* remained charged to her throughout the period
as her hull and her equipment underwent repair or until the master mechanic determined it unsuitable for further use to the ship. The navy considered the hull, valued at
approximately one-third of the value of a fully equipped ship, as only one of several
parts of a ship, which included all the equipment, material, and provisions that would
make up an operational gun platform. The principal duties of the yard's storekeeping
department included receiving all newly purchased items into stores, making reports on
inventories of those stores, and delivering out new equipment and materials to authorized personnel by requisitions. The yard assigned several clerks to Gosport's storekeeper's office and duties became specialized over time. One man would be charged with
records of live oak timber and other wooden materials, another for metal supplies, and
so on; there was also a traffic manager whose duties included tracking movements of
Constellation's equipment between Gosport and Washington or between the ship and
repair shops, to the sail loft, and so forth.

20. Young's Log, 17 January 1853, RG71, Entry 91, NARA, Philadelphia; letter summary,
Breese to Bureau of Construction, Equipment, and Repair, 24 January 1853, RG19 Entry
60-A, NARA, enclosing drawing of *Constellation*'s keel.

21. See chapter 7 for information concerning the keel drawing made at Boston and sent to
the Board of Commissioners and the controversy over the origin of this drawing and its
companion, Transverse Section Drawing.

22. Letter, Commandant Breese to Capt. Joseph Smith, chief, Bureau of Yards and Docks,
28 January 1853, RG71, Entry 5, NARA.

23. *Portsmouth Daily Transcript*, 2 February 1853, Huntington Library.

24. Drawing No. 107-13-4B, RG19, Entry 126, NARA, College Park; Wegner, "An Apple and an
Orange," 80. Wegner's article reached several conclusions without supporting citations. He
asked his readers to accept his unsupported statement that the navy made no decisions concerning *Constellation*'s future prior to hauling her; that the Gosport Navy Yard prepared the
Transverse Section Drawing just prior to hauling the ship; and also that the drawing
reflected *Constellation*'s hull shape in 1795, which it did not. He may have presumed that his
readers would overlook two other important facts: constructor Delano did not consult
Constellation's 1795 drawings because the navy altered the ship's shape three times prior
to her haul out in 1853. Second, Delano, then Lenthall, consulted the drawings made of
Constellation in Boston in 1839 and 1840 because they provided them with the ship's shape
in 1853. Wegner knew or should have known that *Constellation*'s dimensions no longer
matched Humphreys' draft, which, of course, is the reason Lenthall requested that the yard
send the Boston drawings to Washington. With these drawings, he made his set of modifications, using Drawings 107-13-4, 4A, and 4B as reference points of departure.

25. Summary of letter enclosing drawing of shape of *Constellation*, Breese to Bureau of
Construction, Equipment, and Repair, 2 February 1853, RG19, Entry 60-A, NARA;

Drawing 107-13-4B and 107-13-4, RG19, Entry 126, NARA, College Park. It is believed that the other draft the yard sent Lenthall was of *Constellation*'s bow, also drafted at Boston in 1839. Wegner, *Fouled Anchors,* 4. In his outline of the sequence of events at Gosport in January and February, 1853, Wegner concluded that Gosport's draftsman prepared the Transverse Section Drawing just before the yard hauled *Constellation.* Wegner's conclusion, originally conceived in this report, is incorrect as the yard did not take *Constellation* into dry dock. The Boston Navy Yard prepared drawings 107-13-4 and 4A and 4B in 1839.

26. Young's Log, 11, 12, 14, 15, 17, and 18 February 1853, RG71, Entry 91, NARA, Philadelphia.
27. Ibid., 22 February 1853.
28. Ibid.; also, summary of letter, Commandant Breese to Bureau of Construction, Equipment, and Repair, 23 February 1853, RG19, Entry 60-A, NARA.
29. Young's Log, 24 February 1853, RG71, Entry 91, NARA, Philadelphia; also, Breese to chief of Yards and Docks with constructor's report on the efficiency of iron capstans, 24 February 1853, RG71, Entry 5; Gosport Storekeeper's Returns, April–June 1853, RG19, Entry 320, NARA.
30. *Portsmouth Daily Transcript,* 25 February 1853, Huntington Library.
31. Letters, Secretary Dobbin to Chiefs of Bureau, 18 and 22 April 1853, RG45, MF-518, NARA; Young's Log, 22 and 25 April, 1853, RG71, Entry 91, NARA, Philadelphia; Gosport Storekeeper's Log, vol. 175, RG19, Entry 320, NARA; Navy Annual Report, 1853, 546; letters, Samuel Hartt to Dobbin, 17 November 1853, RG45, MF-518; Dobbin to Hartt, 17 November, and Dobbin to John Lenthall, 18 November 1853, secretary's letters to bureaus, RG45, MF-480, NARA; Coletta, *American Secretaries of the Navy,* 275, 279–88. After congratulating President Pierce, Kennedy received assurances from the new president that his innovations in the Navy Department would be continued. James C. Dobbin was a respected lawyer and administrator from North Carolina but inexperienced in naval affairs. Samuel Hartt's two-page report for the Bureau of Construction, Equipment, and Repair, written 1 November 1853 and included in Secretary Dobbin's first Annual Report, 1853, offered little new information concerning *Constellation* except that her repairs continued at Gosport. He resigned 17 November and John Lenthall replaced him, providing Secretary Dobbin with sound administration of the Bureau of Construction, Equipment, and Repair throughout the secretary's four-year term of office.
32. Letters, Shubrick to Dobbin, 9 March 1853, RG19, Entry 49; Dobbin to Shubrick, 10 March 1853, enclosing his letter to the president referring to act of Congress, dated 3 March 1853; also Dobbin to Shubrick, 1 July, and Dobbin to Hartt, 2 July 1853, RG45, MF-518, NARA.
33. Young's Log, 27 April 1853, RG71, Entry 91, NARA, Philadelphia.
34. Bureau of Construction, Equipment, and Repair, Statement of Expenditures, Norfolk Section, 1851–53, RG19, Entry 31, NARA. The expenses commenced with the decision to remove the ship from ordinary in October 1852. With intense pressure on appropriations for fiscal 1852–53 and 1853–54, the Bureau of Construction, Equipment, and Repair

would not expend a large amount of money to prepare *Constellation* for destruction. The amount spent, $20,328.47, did not include the additional cost of dismantling the ship's hull.

35. Navy Annual Report, 1852, 362, item 1; letter, Graham to Shubrick, 8 May 1852, RG45, MF-518, NARA. Congress gave only the president authority to dispose of *Fairfield,* this authority granted by sec. 5, act of Congress, 21 April 1806; letter, E. H. Delano to Samuel L Breese, 19 March 1853, RG71, Entry 5, NARA. The newspaper *Argus* reported 20 May 1852 that *Fairfield* would be sold at auction. The same paper announced 17 June that the navy had bid in the ship for $8,500. From the amount of public and navy attention given to the disposal of *Fairfield,* one may conclude that had *Constellation* been scheduled for sale or destruction, the reaction would have amounted to a national scandal.

36. Gosport Storekeeper's Returns, vol. 175, RG71, Entry 320; Record of Cost of Labor and Repairs for Vessels, April 1849 to June 1855, Washington Navy Yard, vol. 1 of 1, RG19, Entry 29, NARA; also, Circular—Rules for Auction, 8 December 1842, Secretary of the Navy, Circulars to Bureaus and Commandants, RG45, MF-977, NARA.

37. Storekeeper's Returns, vol. 175, 1853–54, April 1853, RG19, Entry 320, NARA.

38. Letter, Chief of Bureau of Construction, Equipment, and Repair John Lenthall to Secretary Dobbin, 17 December 1853, RG19, Entry 49, NARA. Lenthall points out that because of budget cuts by Congress in the 1852–53 fiscal year to the appropriation for repairs, inventories stores and supplies were much reduced. Though the yard had a large force of carpenters and other mechanics working or seeking work, the storekeeper's returns and the yard log reflect the information that fourteen months passed between the time that it laid *Constellation*'s new keel until her launching August 1854. Over a period of approximately seven months, carpenters fit the frame together at an economical pace. This stretched-out building schedule used old frame pieces and lower-cost promiscuous timber to save money. However, the commandant had to measure these labor savings against the higher cost of labor of building a frame with reshaped old frame pieces and promiscuous live oak timber, most shaped and cut for ships of the line and large frigates. Promiscuous live oak timber are pieces sided to various thickness, and of a variety of lengths and widths, hewn to different sizes as required for each class of ship, but not molded or hewn into frame pieces.

39. Young's Log, 9, 16 May 1853, RG19, Entry 71, NARA.

40. For Captain Kearny's problems with *Constellation*'s leaks, see chapter 7; consult chapters 6 and 7 for data concerning the number of futtocks replaced at Gosport and Boston in 1829 and 1839.

41. Young's Log, 24 May 1853, RG71, Entry 91; letter, Shubrick to Dobbin, 28 May 1853, RG19, Entry 49, 141, NARA.

42. Young's Log, 24–28 May, 1, 2, 8–15, 25 June 1853, RG71 Entry 91; letter, constructor Delano to Commandant Breese, 11 June 1853, RG71, Entry 5, NARA; *Southern Daily Argus,* 11 July 1853; Wegner, *Fouled Anchors,* 4, 95 n.10. An article in the Norfolk newspaper, *Southern Daily Argus,* following the laying of the ship's new keel, mentioned that the yard had

torn to pieces the "old" frigate preparatory to building a "new" *Constellation*. Young's Log recorded hauling out new timber and the laying of a new keel for the "frigate" *Constellation;* Delano wrote of the old and rebuilt hull as the "old" and "new" *Constellation.* Taking these comments out of context, though they were not of an official nature, concerning the disposition of the frigate or the building of a sloop of war, *Fouled Anchors* cites Delano's note to Breese mentioning old and new *Constellation*s as "proof that *Constellation* was destroyed in 1853." There exist no official or unofficial documents that directly relate to an order to destroy *Constellation* nor are there any official documents referring to the construction of a new ship. The language of the yard was often determined by custom, such as substituting the word "frigate" instead of *Constellation*'s new rate. Often the words "old" and "new" were used informally to clarify the location of the workers. It should be noted that the navy considered both sites and both hulls as parts of a single repair project.

43. Young's Log, 8–15, 21, and 25 June 1853, RG71, Entry 91, NARA. Commodore Smith visited Gosport 21 June; Young recorded in his log that on 25 June the yard laid the frigate *Constellation*'s new keel.

44. *Norfolk Daily Southern Argus,* 23 July 1853; Wegner, "An Apple and an Orange," 83–84. Attempting yet again to inflate the significance of unofficial news articles, Wegner wrote that the newspaper is accurate in the content of this article, but he failed to note that the reporter wrote that *Constellation*'s new keel measured 176 feet in length, which is, of course the ship's length between perpendiculars. Moreover, the newspaper's acceptance of a carpenter's comments that the live oak timber used to rebuild *Constellation* was fresh and sound after twenty years immersed or stored in sheds flies in the face of a dozen or more navy reports on the condition of live oak after long periods of time submerged and placed in open-air sheds. The facts, discussed in previous chapters, are that while it may not have decayed in the normal way of oak, live oak dryrotted, cracked, and split, leaving a high percentage of any quantity taken out of stockpile unusable. One bad piece in four was the calculation used by Lt. Matthew Maury in his widely accepted reports.

45. Young's Log, 25 June 1853, RG71, Entry 91, NARA.

46. Storekeeper's Returns, daily and monthly reports, vol. 175, 1853–54, RG19, Entry 320; Rules and Regulations for Storekeepers, Secretary of the Navy Circular, 26 October 1818 and 7 December 1841, RG45, MF-977, Roll 1. Storekeepers tabulated materials drawn from stores by master mechanics assigned to *Constellation,* charging requisitions to the navy's general appropriation account under the heading "Increase, Repairs, &c." The commandant accumulated the returns of the ship's repairs and passed them on to the Bureau of Construction, Equipment, and Repair. The bureau charged the navy's current appropriation for repairs (Wear and Tear account) for the costs of labor in the yard, including reconditioning *Constellation*'s equipment, the cost of replacement equipment provided the ship, new ordnance, replacement of or new warrant officer outfits, surgeon supplies, provisions, and other expenses and charged the Increase, Repair &c. account

at Gosport for the services provided through the storekeeper's office or from inventory. These procedures applied only for ships under repair. If Gosport built a new *Constellation* in 1853, all of her materials and equipment would be drawn from the Storekeeper Department and eventually charged to the special appropriation that Congress funded following the passage of the act that authorized a new ship. Under no navy regulation would a new ship be built with funds from the navy's Wear and Tear account. To prove that *Constellation* was, indeed, repaired, all that must be demonstrated is that used materials and equipment from the old hull moved across the yard to Ship House B or from a repair shop to the site where labor was building the ship. If the navy built a new ship, all materials and equipment originated from the storekeeper's inventory or from vendors and then sent to the site of the new ship, after which the navy agent or storekeeper charged the specific appropriation under which the navy built the new ship. Wegner, *Fouled Anchors,* 3, 66, 88. In his report, after rejecting Chapelle's theory of a navy clandestine substitute ship policy, Wegner endeavored to tie authorization and funding for a new sloop of war named *Constellation* to the Act to Improve the Navy (act of 1827) and then combine this act with the act of 1816, an Act to Increase the Navy, under which Congress authorized new ships of the line and frigate-44s. But as neither of these two acts as passed or as later amended authorized a first-class sloop of war or a new ship to replace *Constellation,* the report's attempt to uncover legislation under which Congress authorized a new *Constellation* bore no fruit. But it should be noted that funds authorized under the act of 1816 had, in 1853, been spent except for a few thousand dollars.

47. Letter, Delano to Breese, 11 June 1853, RG71, Entry 5, NARA. Most historians accept as authentic the trail of archival navy documents that prove that the navy ordered *Constellation* repaired in 1853. Navy historians agree that reusable materials moved freely between two sites, just as it moved from shops back to ship in the course of a repair project. That reusable equipment and materials repaired at distant locations such as Washington or a shop at Gosport were returned to USS *Constellation* at Ship House B without passing through the storekeeper's records is clearly covered by shipyard rules and regulations.

48. The *Portsmouth Daily Transcript,* 28 August 1854; Wegner, "An Apple and an Orange," 82 and n.11. Wegner insisted that no material moved from the site where the original hull was dismantled to Ship House B and invoked Chapelle's statement that there exists no evidence that workers transferred any material. Wegner obviously did not know the procedures in shipyards and seemed unaware of the newspaper's account of such transfers. But Wegner commits greater errors, stating that 16,387 cubic feet of live oak framing timber was withdrawn from stockpiles, when actually about 78 percent of the total live oak timber withdrawn consisted of promiscuous pieces, miscellaneous timber of far less ($1.00 per cubic foot) value and cut and sided for general use, not necessarily for frames. He compounds these errors with the statement that 16,387 cubic feet of live oak timber when taken out of stockpile totaled about 150 percent of the quantity required to

build an entirely new sloop of the size of *Constellation*. As he distorts the facts his conclusions become blatantly inaccurate and misleading. First, timber molded and hewn for frames is far different than promiscuous timber pieces. Use of large promiscuous timber pieces caused a great increase in the percentage of wasted timber when carpenters shaped them into futtocks. Second, because most live oak timbers, framing pieces, or promiscuous timber drawn out of stocks were precut for ships of the line and first-class frigates, ships larger than *Constellation,* and none cut for second-class frigates or ships the size of Lenthall's new dimensions for *Constellation,* carpenters lost a higher percentage of these larger timber pieces as they sawed or hewed them for the smaller vessel. Finally, as the yard took this timber from stockpiles, on hand for up to twenty years, it is estimated that another 25 percent proved unusable because of splitting and other deterioration. According to an estimate made by William Doughty, a completed frame of a second-class frigate consisted of about 16,500 cubic feet of live oak timber. The total cubic feet of live oak for constructing a frame for *Constellation,* 176 feet between perpendiculars in length but only inches more in breadth than her previous model, is estimated to be about 2,500 cubic feet more than required for a second-class frigate. Wegner's assumption that the gross quantity requisitioned, 16,387 cubic feet of live oak timber, mostly promiscuous pieces for larger ships, after twenty years of being submerged and stored in open-air sheds, unmolded and not yet hewn for this hull, was 150 percent more than required to rebuild *Constellation*'s frame, is wrong, and many thousands of cubic feet short of the gross amount required to build a frame of approximately 19,000 cubic feet.

49. Wegner, "The Frigate Strikes Her Colors," 248 n. 22, 23, 249 n. 27. Here Wegner makes a final effort to convince historians of Chapelle's conclusion when he wrote that there were two wooden sailing warships named *Constellation.* He denies the possibility that used framing pieces and other materials moved freely between the two sites as workmen rebuilt *Constellation.* He makes this conclusion without citations. Then, in the same article he contradicts his position, admitting to the authenticity of the *Portsmouth Daily Transcript* article of 28 August 1854. He brushes this evidence aside when he suggests that the incident occurred outside of Gosport's storekeeping system which ignores the fact that none of *Constellation*'s reused materials or equipment passed through the storekeeper's records. Clearly, he did not understand navy rules and procedures that controlled the activities of the yard's carpenters and storekeepers as they repaired or rebuilt a vessel.

50. Gosport Log, 25 June, 29 August, 6 September 1853, and 26 August 1854, RG71, Entry 91.

51. Crothers, *American-Built Clipper Ship,* 119–303. This book is the textbook on the nomenclature and construction plans of large wooden ships at mid–nineteenth century.

52. Gosport Storekeeper Returns, vol. 175, April 1853 to July 1854, RG19, Entry 320, NARA. The volume covering fiscal 1854–55 is now missing, and there are other breaks in the returns between 1845 and 1855; letter, Lenthall to Dobbin, 17 December 1853, RG45, MF-518, NARA; Navy Annual Report, 1853, 318, 545, and 548.

53. Recapitulation of Timber on Hand at Gosport, 1 July 1844, RG19, Entry 8, NARA. This is a record of live oak and other timber stockpiled at Gosport in 1844; neither Gosport nor any other yard stored live oak timber frames, frame pieces, or promiscuous timber hewn for second-class frigates or for a ship of the dimensions of *Constellation* as modified by Lenthall's drafts. Gosport's ponds and sheds held in storage only $7,336 worth of timber purchased under the (1816) Act to Increase the Navy. The yard stockpiled $397,975 worth of timber purchased under the Act to Improve the Navy, all of it shaped for 74s, 44s, and sloops of the Germantown class. Timber purchased and stored for repairing ships inventoried at $421,152 but none stocked for ships of *Constellation*'s class or dimensions. Timber held for repairs included 77,587 cubic feet of timber cut to the molds of 74s, 44s, and smaller sloops and steamers, as well as 143,134 cubic feet of promiscuous timber stockpiled for repairs to those classes of ships. The yard held thousands of feet of keelson timber and beams of live oak and yellow pine, none of sizes usable in *Constellation*'s hull without reworking.

54. Recapitulation of Timber on Hand at Gosport, RG19, Entry 8, NARA. Cost of framing timber shaped to molds: $1.60 per cubic foot; cost of promiscuous pieces, $1.00 and $1.20 per cubic foot. *Army and Navy Chronicle and Scientific Resources* (6 April 1843) 1: 411: "Live oak, though more durable, is almost as hard as iron and exceeding difficult to be cut and hew into shape, so that the expense of working it is many times the expense of working white oak."

55. Navy Annual Report, 1854, 476–77. Despite huge accumulations of live oak and other timber from 1820 to 1840, stockpiles had become somewhat depleted by 1853 when repairs commenced on *Constellation*. In the Bureau of Construction, Equipment, and Repair section of the Navy Annual Report of 1854, Chief Lenthall pointed out that the appropriation for General Increase, Repairs &c. was exhausted, complete hull frames acquired under the Act to Improve the Navy, broken up, and stocks of specific preshaped items such as keels, posts, stems, floors, and keelsons nearly exhausted. He noted that the bureau needed to purchase 170,000 cubic feet of live oak each year to maintain the navy but the service had acquired far less than that amount each year. Lenthall made note once again of the rising cost of labor and materials in 1853–54, explaining that for that reason "the appropriation for the present fiscal year may be expected to fall short."

56. Ibid.

57. Agranat, "Thorough and Efficient Repair," 331–34; Harry Bluff [M. F. Maury], "More Scraps from the Lucky Bag," *Southern Literary Messenger* 7 (May–June 1841): 367; Haines, "Ship Preservation," 290–94; letter, Humphreys to the commissioners, 11 November 1835, RG45, Entry 224, NARA. Samuel Humphreys provided commissioners with the estimated quantity of live oak timber used in each class of ship. He noted that navy builders used several thousand cubic feet of live oak timber for structural parts other than the hull's frame.

58. Letter, Capt. Charles Stewart to Secretary Woodbury, 19 November 1832, RG45, Entry 213, NARA; Wegner, *Fouled Anchors*, 5, 96 n. 12. When Gosport Navy Yard began to rebuild *Constellation*'s hull in 1853, as modified by John Lenthall's drafts, the bureau

ordered no complete frame for the ship nor did it order any new frame pieces specifically molded and cut to *Constellation*'s offsets. And of course, storekeepers at Gosport (nor anywhere else), stockpiled no live oak timber hewn to her dimensions. It is of particular note that the Bureau of Construction, Equipment, and Repair did not contract for a complete new frame for *Constellation* at the time of her rebuild because this would have been the most economical method to build *Constellation* if the navy intended to build her new. The author of *Fouled Anchors,* using computers, compiled a list of live oak timbers requisitioned from Gosport's stockpiles by ship carpenters working on *Constellation*'s hull in 1853–54. He concluded that "some 16,387 cubic feet of live oak framing timber was withdrawn" for her frame. According to the report, of the total taken from stockpile for the frame, 22 percent of 16,387 cubic feet consisted of stockpiled timber molded and cut by timber contractors to sizes for the frames of ships of the line or 44-gun frigates, ships of larger dimensions than *Constellation,* plus a small quantity cut for sloops of war of smaller dimensions. The other 78 percent of the timber drawn out of stockpile for use building the frame of *Constellation* consisted of promiscuous timber in sizes hewn to specifications for the same classes of larger ships. For the second-class frigate's new keel, stern post, and stem, carpenters drew from the storekeeper 150 percent of the ship's needs, according to *Fouled Anchors,* which allowed for 33 percent waste. Therefore, the total of 16,387 cubic feet requisitioned for the frame, the gross quantity, already deficient of the 19,000 cubic feet required for the frame, should be reduced by 33 percent to account for waste according to the report's own calculations. Wegner evidently did not realize that *Constellation*'s frame consisted of approximately 3,000 cubic feet more than 16,387 cubic feet, the gross amount requisitioned. Nevertheless, using the report's 33 percent calculation for waste the remaining quantity amounted to 10,925 cubic feet of the total 19,000 required in the finished frame. Wegner's conclusion demonstrates that the yard's workmen transferred up to 40 percent of the rebuilt *Constellation*'s frame timbers from her dismantled hull. And the author of *Fouled Anchors* admits that "much material was lost converting bulky ship of the line timbers for the smaller dimensioned sloop's [*sic, Constellation*'s] requirements." He failed to prove his point because he was evidently unaware that *Constellation*'s finished frame consisted of approximately 19,000 cubic feet of molded and hewn timber. The figures provided by Captain Stewart in the case of *Guerrière,* that 39 percent of the live oak timber was waste, is a reasonable comparison with *Constellation*'s situation at Gosport in 1853. The situation with *Constellation* duplicated in large measure *Guerrière*'s, as for neither of these rebuilds had the Navy Department stockpiled frames or frame pieces. Using *Fouled Anchors*'s figure, 16,387 cubic feet, representing the amount drawn from stockpile for *Constellation*'s frame and Stewart's 39 percent wastage figure, the total net usable amount for *Constellation*'s frame, after waste loss of 6,391 cubic feet, would be just 9,996 cubic feet. But, a frame for a ship of *Constellation*'s modified breadth and length and built according Lenthall's offsets, consisted of 19,000 cubic feet. Therefore, if

Wegner's estimates are accepted, Gosport reused as much as 50 percent of *Constellation*'s old frame timbers.

59. Letter, Samuel Humphreys to Board of Commissioners, 1 January 1827, RG45, Entry 224, NARA.

60. Letter, William Doughty to Board of Commissioners, 18 November 1817, RG45, Entry 224, NARA.

61. USS *Constellation* Table of Offsets, 1853, Document No. 142-1-7, RG19, Entry 126, NARA, College Park.

62. USF *Congress:* Cost of Various Ships, RG45, Entry 276: *Congress*'s complete frame molded in accordance with her offsets and purchased as a prefabricated unit, cost just $30,164.23. It consisted of approximately 22,000 cubic feet of live oak timber when finished at $1.36 per cubic foot. The total cost of materials for her new hull, $132,400, exceeded total labor costs of the hull, $77,172, almost two to one. USF *Constellation*'s repairs at Gosport 1828–29, which included replacing 213 top timbers and stanchions, 148 futtocks, and many other components of her hull, totaled approximately $170,000. As would be expected, labor exceeded material costs, $86,565 to $81,118. The point taken is that by using promiscuous and other timbers not shaped for the ship's offsets and by reusing the hull's old frame pieces, labor costs for rebuilding *Constellation* added more to the cost of repairing the hull than the yard saved using lower-priced promiscuous timber. This was true in 1853–54 as nearly always in the past when repairing a navy ship built with live oak. Therefore, those who would claim that the use of lower-priced promiscuous timber pieces caused the reduction in total cost ($277,116) of rebuilding *Constellation* in 1853–54 are wrong.

63. Gosport Storekeeper Returns, 1853–54, RG45, Entry 320, NARA.

64. Ibid.; also Minute Book of Bureau of Construction, Equipment, and Repair, 26 January 1854, RG19, Entry 60-A, NARA. Further evidence that the breaking up of *Constellation*'s hull proceeded at a pace that paralleled the rebuilding of the hull is illustrated by the fact that the commandant did not transmit the costs for dismantling *Constellation*'s hull to the bureau until 26 January 1854, one month after carpenters turned in the last lot of scrap to Gosport's storekeeper.

65. Gosport Storekeeper Returns, vol. 175, July–December 1853, RG19, Entry 320, NARA.

66. Ibid., April–December 1853.

67. Ibid., December 1853, January–February 1854.

68. Ibid., July 1853–March 1854.

69. USF *Macedonian, Act to Rebuild Macedonian,* 1832; *Act to Rebuild USF Congress,* 30 June 1834; *Act to Consolidate Navy Appropriations,* 1840.

70. Chapelle, *History of the American Sailing Navy,* 536. USF *Congress,* launched 1841, 44 guns, 179 feet between perpendiculars by 47 feet 8 inches extreme beam (46 feet 6 inches molded beam) and 1,867 tons; USS *Constellation,* relaunched 1854, and 176 feet between perpendiculars by 44 feet extreme beam (41 feet molded beam); burden 1,400 tons.

71. Gosport Storekeeper Returns, 1853–54, vol. 175, RG19, Entry 320, NARA; returns for 1854–56 are missing.

72. USF *Congress,* Costs of Various Ships, RG45, Entry 276, NARA.

73. Ibid.

74. Letter, Lenthall to Dobbin, 12 July 1854, RG45, MF-518, NARA; Navy Annual Report, 1850, 240, and Navy Annual Report, 1854, 485. Labor wages and costs of timber and other materials rose sharply during this period, but perhaps falling productivity caused the greatest change in costs of repairs as well as new construction at navy shipyards. Protected from outside competition, they became increasingly inefficient and costly to operate.

75. Navy Annual Report, 1854, 485.

76. Ibid.; letters, Grice to Barron, 8 December 1827, RG45, Entry 220; Humphreys to Rodgers, 29 April 1834, RG45, Entry 224, NARA. When preparing an estimate for a new hull for *Constellation* in 1827, constructor Grice used the figure of $100 per ton; Samuel Humphreys used $109 in 1834; in 1841 the actual cost of *Congress*'s hull reached $112.25 per ton as shipyard costs rose. Adding the 19 percent increase in costs between 1841 and 1854 to obtain the total cost of a new ship in 1854, the estimated cost of a new hull for *Constellation* would be $187,012. Double the estimated cost of the hull (as in the case with *Congress,* since no allocation for crew provisions is included) and the total is $374,024 for a new ship of *Constellation*'s revised tonnage of 1,400 tons. This figure, $374,024, calculated on the basis of the hull-only cost, proves to be comparable to the previous calculation of the cost per ton for a complete ship, using the cost per ton figure of $268.71 times a "new" *Constellation*'s tonnage of 1,400 for the total cost of $376,194 in 1854. The difference, about $2,000, provides a margin of error in the different ways of calculating a "new" *Constellation* of less than 1 percent. Readers are reminded that the cost of rebuilding *Constellation* in 1855 totaled $277,116.

77. Report of Cost and Time of Repairs to Vessels of the Navy, prepared in response to Senate resolution, 27 May 1858, RG19, Entry 49, NARA.

78. Young's Log, RG71, Entry 91; Storekeeper Boykin's Returns and Inventory, RG19, Entry 320; Record of Equipment Held for *Constellation,* RG19, Entry 8; Record of Costs of Labor and Repairs for Vessels, 1849–55, RG19, Entry 29; *Constellation*'s Logs (Kearny and Williamson), RG24, NARA.

79. *Constellation*'s Log (Kearny), 12–17 May 1844, RG24; Young's Log, 1 June 1844, RG71, Entry 91; *Constellation*'s Equipment, RG19, Entry 8; Gosport's Storekeeper Returns, 1853–54, RG19, Entry 320, NARA.

80. USF *Congress*'s Returns, RG45, Entry 276; *Constellation*'s Log (Kearny), 12–17 May 1844, RG24; Young's Log, 7 and 12 February 1855, RG71, Entry 91, NARA. Warrant officer outfits, an expensive item of equipment, may have been sent to Washington Navy Yard for reconditioning.

81. *Constellation*'s Log (Kearny), RG24; *Constellation*'s Log as Receiving Ship, kept by Lt. G. G. Williamson, 19 June 1844, RG24; Record of Equipment held for *Constellation,* RG19, Entry 8; Young's Log, 9, 17 July 1845, RG71, Entry 91, NARA.

82. *Constellation's* Log (Kearny), RG 24; *Constellation's* Log (Williamson), RG24; Record of Equipment Held for Constellation, RG19, Entry 8; letter, Lenthall to Dobbin, 17 December 1853, RG19, Entry 49; Record of Equipment held for *Constellation*, RG19, Entry 8, NARA.

83. Record of Cost of Labor and Repairs for Vessels, 1849–1855, one volume, RG19, Entry 29; Commandant's Responsibilities, commissioners to secretary of the navy, 26 March 1828, RG45, Entry 28, NARA.

84. *Constellation's* Log (Kearny), RG24; *Constellation* Equipment, RG19, Entry 8, NARA.

85. Circular from the Board of Commissioners, 22 June 1830, Rules Regarding Ships in Ordinary, RG45, Entry 212, NARA.

86. Letter, Lenthall to Dobbin, 17 December 1853, RG19, Entry 49; Bill of Lading and Invoice, covering the shipment of *Constellation's* running rigging from Boston to Gosport, 8 May 1854, RG19, Entry 4, NARA.

87. Young's Log, 15 July 1845 and 18, 19, 23, and 25 November 1852, 24 February 1853, and 5 September and 29 December 1854, RG71, Entry 91; RG19, Entries 8 and 29, NARA.

88. *Constellation's* Equipment, RG19, Entry 8; Young's Log, 17 October 1854, RG71, Entry 91: anchors and cables returned from Washington; 12 December, labor getting out *Constellation's* cables; 18 December, labor recoiling *Constellation's* hawsers; 20 December; stowing *Constellation's* chain cable; 5 February 1855, labor employed getting *Constellation's* anchors down; 19, 21, and 22 February 1855, stowing *Constellation's* anchors. None of this equipment was requisitioned from the yard's storekeeper.

89. Chapelle, *History of the American Sailing Navy,* 468. Chapelle, discussing the rebuilt *Constellation,* states that "she was rebuilt into what was then a modern ship of war *without any attempt to preserve the original* [italics added]." He was unaware of the care taken to preserve her equipment as well as timber from her condemned hull. And, having written this, the question has existed unanswered since 16 March 1948, following a navy announcement that *Constellation* would be restored: Why did Howard I. Chapelle publicly claim that *Constellation* was built in 1854 just three days after the navy's decision to restore the ship, an act that embarrassed the navy and ruined the opportunity for the ship to be restored with navy and congressional support? Chapelle's testy revelations built around his concept of rebuilding old ships, which in essence, accused the navy of a series of cover-ups reaching back to the post–War of 1812 period. In 1945 he charged once again that the navy had decided to hoodwink Congress as it intended with its current announcement to restore the ship. Chapelle antagonized the Navy Department by accusing the service of duplicity, scared off Congress, and ruined the ship's chances of being funded properly. Fortunately for the navy, since then, naval historians, inside and outside the service and including the author of *Fouled Anchors,* concluded that Chapelle's charges, based on flawed research, are too narrowly drawn to reflect nineteenth-century naval policy.

90. Report of Cost and Time of Repairs to Vessels of the Navy, prepared in response to Senate Resolution, 27 May 1858, RG19, Entry 49; also, Statement of Expenses, Norfolk Section, 1851–53, RG19, Entry 31, NARA.

91. Sheads, *Fort McHenry,* appendix H, 149–50.

92. Kevin Lynaugh, in Wegner, *Fouled Anchors,* appendix B, 157–58, 172–73. Naval architect Lynaugh adds computer technology to the *Constellation* controversy by preparing a series of computer comparisons and conclusions. In the section of *Fouled Anchors* containing his findings, he compares Lenthall's 1853 drawings of *Constellation* and the Transverse Sections Drawing prepared at Boston in 1839. His conclusion is that "discrepancies between the frames are noticeable [in the drawings] and in his opinion, [they] are not of the same vessel." His conclusion that one *Constellation* was destroyed and a new one built is based solely on the fact that the two drawings are not identical. This, of course, is the function of computers, to illustrate the differences in two images electronically where once architects overlaid one drawing on another by hand. Like a dictionary, a computer defines. Without the systematic addition of reams of historic, architectural, and construction data, covered in the seven preceding chapters of this book, including three rebuilds and three new hull shapes before 1853, one could expect no more than the simplistic conclusion such as Lynaugh reached. Perhaps sensing his tool's inadequacy, Lynaugh offers to provide a discussion of the possibility of converting the hull from frigate to sloop of war. Finding nothing on the subject in paragraph 4.3, page 157 of the report to which he directs the reader, one must assume that paragraph 3.1.1 on page 158 is the correct one. Here, without aid of computers or historical data concerning *Constellation, Sabine,* or *Santee* (the latter two frigates' hulls having been completely planked by 1853), Lynaugh states that it is unlikely such a conversion (of *Constellation*) occurred. He explains that an examination of her hull substantiates his conclusion that he found no scarf zones, providing proof that there was no conversion. One must assume that Wegner failed to make Lynaugh aware that the yard first dismantled *Constellation*'s hull to lay a new keel before the hull was rebuilt at Gosport in 1853–54. With a composite drawing of Joshua Humphreys' body plan of 1795 and Lenthall's body plan of 1853 (page 173, Figure 18), Lynaugh demonstrated his points—but in reality he proves that Lenthall's design modifications are not only possible but a reality. Lynaugh made an unfortunate choice for another comparison (page 172, Figure 17) when he compares Humphreys' 1795 drawing with Lenthall's drafts of 1853, though the 1795 draft of the shape of *Constellation* is superseded by the Transverse Drawing of 1839. He compared apples and oranges. Nevertheless, from the base line to the twenty-foot line the midbody sections illustrated by both his printouts, Figures 17 and 18, show the same small variations which are the result of refairing the ship's lines by Lenthall. One must assume that the historical data provided to Lynaugh by his coauthors did not include information of the drafting and construction plans of Lenthall as they related to *Constellation, Santee,* and *Sabine.* The navy concentrated the planned modifications of the three ships on their modernization: decks for improved armament, bow extensions for speed and increased stability, easy working of guns, and round steamboat sterns for strength and comfort of crew. Regardless of these oversights, Lynaugh's decision to limit his investigation to a comparison of line drawings resulted

in conclusions which are abstract in essence and far removed from the multilayered conditions surrounding the great repair of *Constellation* at Gosport in 1853–54. Moreover, his conclusions fail to illuminate the complicated circumstances surrounding the drafting and rebuilding of *Constellation*. Like Chapelle's single-sentence claim that *Constellation* was new in 1855 because her model changed—whatever a change in model means—Lynaugh attempts to reduce the history of a navy ship to computer images.

93. Letter, secretary of the navy to Committee on Naval Affairs, U.S. Senate, 23 December 1854, Letters to Congress, RG45, NARA: attesting to Lenthall's genius; Martin, *Most Fortunate Ship,* 299, 321, 358, 360; Chapelle, *History of the American Sailing Navy,* 468–69. Commander Martin, discussing Captain Skinner's suggestion in 1850 to return the nation's historic frigates to permanent stations to ports where built, writes (299) that this did not happen, and as it turned out, neither of the other frigates (*United States, Constellation*) saw active duty again. He concludes (321) that *Constellation* was "the 1854 corvette that had succeeded to the name of an earlier frigate." Martin repeated his version of history, writing (358) that [Roosevelt] "saw the 1854 sailing corvette *Constellation.*" Again in a caption of a photograph on page 360, in which the sloop of war is cropped out of view, readers are informed that berthed alongside *Constitution* is the "1850s vintage corvette, *Constellation.*" Without citations to support these statements, first written in 1980 when the navy listed *Constellation* as its oldest ship, Commander Martin indulges in what public relations people and others refer to as "spin." There is no inference in this manuscript that any single person or group conspired or conspires today to undermine *Constellation*'s position in American naval history. Only Chapelle knows why he chose the ship as his victim. Most of his writing about substitute ships and administratively built new ships reads as preamble to his position on *Constellation* in the latter pages of *History of the American Sailing Navy.* It is convenient for others with differing goals than Chapelle to perpetuate his position that the navy establishment conspired to build new ships by subversive means and that USS *Constellation* was a new ship built without the authority of Congress. Underneath all of the furor over *Constellation* is the undeniable fact that she survives as a shrine and that her bond of provenance to the navy's first ship-frigate is strong and uneffected by the current controversy. Commander Martin takes foolish risks, advancing negative propaganda directed at *Constellation* as he spins and respins Chapelle's fable.

94. Though no correspondence or other records passing between the chief constructor's office and the Bureau of Construction, Equipment, and Repair survive today to explain the process by which the decisions concerning *Constellation*'s conversion and rebuild were reached, readers are reminded that in 1853 Lenthall, as chief constructor, had no line or executive authority as a staff member of the Navy Department. Captain Shubrick, followed by Samuel Hartt, chiefs of the bureau in 1853, approved Lenthall's plans and directed the project from the time of her removal from ordinary.

95. de Kay, *Chronicles,* 194, 313–15.

96. Author's conversations with Paul G. Powichroski, ship's manager, USS *Constellation,* Baltimore; supplemented by records of measurements and data compiled in connection with the ship's restoration.

97. Ibid.

98. Crothers, *American-Built Clipper Ship,* 48, 50, 53, 54.

99. Colan Ratliff, "*Constellation* Evidence and Warship Design," Appendix A of Wegner, *Fouled Anchors,* 131–32, 144, 146; also, letter, Shubrick to Kennedy, 18 August 1852, RG19, Entry 49, NARA. Ratliff's choice of language makes his treatise difficult to follow to its conclusion. He states that Lenthall rebuilt the navy's old ships, including *Constellation.* Then he changes direction, stating that only *Constellation* was replaced by a new ship. He cites Shubrick's letter about abandoning the idea of providing *Constellation* with a propeller as proof that the navy destroyed her. Then, reversing himself, Ratliff acknowledges that *Constellation* could have been converted into a sloop of war. Yet again, supporting Wegner's conclusions, Ratliff writes that, as two sets of offsets do not exist, that fact is proof enough that *Constellation* was not rebuilt, ignoring that Lenthall consulted the takeoffs incorporated in the Transverse Section Drawing when he prepared drafts and new offsets. But, unfortunately, like Lynaugh's computer report, Ratliff's conclusions are irrelevant as he limits his considerations to a discussion of a new ship versus the imaginary jumbo-izing of *Constellation*'s old hull at midship. As the leader of the group producing the *Fouled Anchors* report, Wegner knew that *Constellation* was dismantled and rebuilt from the keel up, but by eliminating this and other data from consideration, he is able to present a one-dimensional conclusion, that the navy destroyed the ship-frigate and built a new ship-sloop.

100. I want to stress the point that my thesis does not take the position that modifications to *Constellation*'s hull as redrafted by John Lenthall resulted in retention of the original hull lines of the ship of 1795 or 1839. Chief constructor Lenthall's modifications required refairing of her hull from stem to stern. What is concluded here is that Lenthall's modifications were just that—modifications—and though they were extensive, he made each specific in its extent and purpose and therefore, to repeat, were modifications. He did not draft a new hull of a new design. Because Lenthall retained the original hull's integrity as the navy intended, combined with the reuse of materials and equipment, Gosport Navy Yard successfully carried out Congress's and the navy's intent. But again, to underscore the facts concerning *Constellation*'s rebuilt hull, the discussion in this chapter is limited to a discussion of Lenthall's modifications to her hull. But readers should never forget that navy wooden ships consisted of much more than just a hull.

101. Wegner, *Fouled Anchors,* 78; Lynaugh, Appendix B of Wegner, *Fouled Anchors,* 158; Chapelle and Polland, *Constellation Question,* 27, 29–30. Perhaps to obscure Lenthall's purposes for conferring with the Transverse Section Drawing (107-13-4B) as he redrafted *Constellation*'s hull, Wegner informs his readers that the drawing was prepared (in Norfolk) after the ship was hauled out as its purpose was limited at the shipyard to guide carpenters preparing shoring to hold the ship upright. Such explanations camouflage

simple truths. Like those of his associate Lynaugh and earlier, Chapelle, Wegner's dis-jointed explanations for the Transverse Section Drawing ignored the altered dimensions of the body sections that Boston Navy Yard prepared in 1839. By overlooking *Constellation*'s modifications in 1839, both Wegner and Chapelle left their readers with the incorrect conclusion that the ship's dimensions in 1839 (and 1853) were exactly the same as in Humphreys' original 1795 drafts. They were not.

102. *Constellation*'s maximum molded breadth was 40 feet 7 inches, when Gosport disman-tled the ship in 1853; this was approximately a 7-inch increase over her designed breadth in 1795. Tingey increased her breadth 14 inches to 41 feet 2 inches in 1812 and when Gosport Navy Yard rebuilt her hull in 1829, Francis Grice redesigned the hull once again, increasing her maximum molded breadth to 42 feet 7 inches. Constructor Barker redrafted her midbody sections in 1839 at Boston, reducing maximum molded breadth to approximately 40 feet 7 inches, according to the Transverse Section Drawing (107-13-4B).

103. Captain Truxtun, following his victory over the French frigate *l'Insurgente,* in 1799, replaced *Constellation*'s heavy 24-pound guns of her main battery with 18-pounders; he also reduced the lengths of the frigate's masts and yards, in recognition of the fact that the too-tall masts he designed for her, along with the heavier guns, had caused most of the problems in the ship's performance. The only other commander to detect that the continuous criticisms of *Constellation*'s instability related to overarming was Capt. Charles Ridgely, who recommended to the Board of Commissioners in 1822 that the number of guns carried on her spar deck be reduced.

104. Navy Annual Report, 1854, 475.

105. de Kay, *Chronicles,* 252.

106. Ratliff, "*Constellation* Evidence," 146; Lynaugh, Appendix B of Wegner, *Fouled Anchors,* 158; Plans of Proposed Alterations to *Santee* and *Sabine,* nos. 138-13-12, 79-10-7B, 107-10-9M, RG19, Entry 126, NARA, College Park. The navy scheduled *Sabine* and *Santee,* hulls completely built, but still in stocks and obsolete after three decades, for modifications after *Constellation.* Lenthall directed that the two first-class frigates were to be length-ened and rebuilt with new bows and sterns. When they were launched, only their mid-bodies remained intact after modifications and modernization. Ratliff points out that when the navy rebuilt *Sabine* and *Santee* only one-third of their amidship section [*sic,* the midbody] was retained. Discussing the modifications of these frigates, Lynaugh wrote that not only were the frigates still in stocks but when rebuilt, "no planking or major construction had taken place in the forward and aft frames," which confirms that Wegner failed to inform the naval architect of the state of their construction and con-sequently, of the dismantling of those frigates before they were rebuilt. Wegner, lead writer of *Fouled Anchors,* evidently failed to inform Ratliff or Lynaugh that the navy dis-mantled *Constellation, Santee,* and *Sabine* before reconstruction. Perhaps Wegner felt it necessary to avoid mentioning the similarity of the navy's plans for modernizing the three ships.

107. Navy Annual Report, 1851, 77; Opinions, Attorney General, 1857, 8:504–11; Agranat, "Thorough and Efficient Repair," 384–89; de Kay, *Chronicles,* 262–64. The Attorney General's opinion that the navy could not reduce *Macedonian* and *Constellation* in rate without congressional authorization places final closure on arguments that *Constellation* was a new ship in 1855. The attorney general's ruling not only confirmed that *Constellation* was not a new ship in 1855, but that she legally remained a frigate following her conversion as she carried guns mounted on two decks. The navy drew up new Rules and Regulations governing the service in 1858 and when they were approved by Congress, the navy then reduced the two ships in rate from frigates to razee-sloop, also called first class-sloop of war or corvette.

Bibliography

Public Documentation

Navy Department Documents

Dictionary of American Naval Fighting Ships. Washington, D.C.: Ships History Division, Department of the Navy, Navy Historical Division, 1959–81.

Dudley, William S., ed. *The Naval War of 1812: A Documentary History.* Vols. 1, 2. Washington, D.C.: Naval Historical Center, 1985, 1992.

Knox, Dudley W., USN (Ret.), ed. *Naval Documents Related to the Quasi War between the United States and France.* Vols. 1–7. Washington, D.C.: Government Printing Office, 1940.

———. *Naval Documents Related to the United States Wars with Barbary Powers.* Vols. 1–7. Washington, D.C.: Government Printing Office, 1940.

Naval Affairs. American State Papers: Documents, Legislative and Executive, Vols. 1–4. Washington, D.C., 1832–61.

Secretary of the Navy's Annual Reports, 1823–58 (Navy Annual Reports).

National Archives (NARA), Washington, D.C. (except as noted)

Record Group 19. Bureau of Construction, Equipment, and Repair

Entry 4. Invoices and Bills of Lading.

Entry 5. Returns of Repairs to Vessels.

Entry 7. Cost of Building and Repair of Vessels, 1826–42.

Entry 8. Inventories of Stores, Gosport, 1844.

Entry 20. Tables of Allowances.

Entry 29. Costs of Labor and Repairs, 1849–53.

Entry 31. Statement of Expenditures, Norfolk, 1851–53.

Entry 49. Letters to Secretary of the Navy.

Entry 60-A. Inbound Letter Log.

Entry 126. Vessel Plans, NARA, College Park, Md.

Entry 127. Index of Vessel Plans, NARA, College Park, Md.

Entry 229. Reports of Ships under Construction and Repair, 1837–96.

Entry 231. Records Relating to Disposal of Vessels, 1845–76.

Entry 320. Returns to Storekeepers, Gosport.

Record Group 24. Logs and Journals

Laughton's Journal.

USS *Constellation*'s Log Books.

Record Groups 36 and 41. Pre-Federal and Federal Vessel Registers

Record Group 45. Navy Administration

Entry 1 (Microfilm M-149). Letters to Officers from Secretary.

Entry 3 (Microfilm M-209). Miscellaneous Letters Sent by Secretary.

Entry 5 (Microfilm T-829). Letters to Congress.

Entry 8. Secretaries' Letters to Commands, Agents, and Commissioners.

Entry 13 (MF-480). Letters to Bureaus.

Entry 23 (MF-147). Letters Received by the Secretary from Commanders.

Entry 24 (MF-125). Letters Received by the Secretary from Captains.

Entry 25. Letters between Officers and Agents of the Department of State.

Entry 27. Letters Received by the Secretary from Congress.

Entry 28. Letters Received by the Secretary from Commissioners.

Entry 30 (MF-89). Letters Received by Secretary from East Indies, Mediterranean, and African Squadrons.

Entry 32 (MF-518). Letters Received by Secretary from Bureaus.

Entry 33. Letters Received by Secretary from Naval Agents and Storekeepers.

Entry 34. Letters Received by the Secretary from Commandants.

Entries 41 and 42. Directives Sent by Secretary.

Entry 46. Inventory of Stores in Navy Yards, 1794–1800.

Entry 57. Letters to Secretary from Fourth Auditor and Comptroller.

Entry 169. Lists of Vessels of the Navy, 1797–1816.

Entry 209. Journal of Board of Commissioners.

Entry 211. Letters Sent by Commissioners.

Entry 212. Circulars Sent by Commissioners.

Entry 213. Letters Sent by Commissioners to Secretary.

Entry 214. Letters Sent by Commissioners to Officers.

Entry 216. Letters Sent by Commissioners to Commandants.

Entry 217. Miscellaneous Letters Sent by Commissioners.

Entry 218. Letters Sent by Commissioners to Constructors.

Entry 220. Letters Received by Commissioners from Commandants.

Entry 221. Letters Received by Commissioners from Officers.

Entry 222. Letters Received by Commissioners from Secretary.

Entry 224. Letters Received by Commissioners from Constructors.

Entry 270. History of the Boston Navy Yard by Preble.

Entry 276. Costs of Building Various Navy Vessels.

Entry 277. Sailing Qualities of Various Vessels, 1825–53.

Entry 320. Annual Survey of Articles on Hand, Gosport.

Entry 374 (MF-739). War Department Letters Concerning Naval Matters.

Entry 392 (Appendix D). Journals of Officers.

Entry 395 (Appendix E). Letter Books of Officers.

Entry 406. Watch, Quarter, and Station Bills of Various Vessels, 1829–96.

Entry 463 (MF-625). Area Files.

Entry 464. Subject Files, Boxes 1 and Up.

Record Group 71. Inventory of Records of Yards and Docks

Entry 5. Letters Received by Chief of Bureau.

Entry 6. Minutes of Bureau.

Entry 7. Register of Correspondence, 1842–99.

Entry 62. Stores Returns, Norfolk, 1844–69.

Entry 91. Journal of Daily Transactions, Norfolk Navy Yard, NARA, Philadelphia, Pa., 1844–58.

Entry 93. History of the United States Navy Yard at Gosport, Va.

Record Group 74. Records of the Bureau of Ordnance

Record Group 94. Records of the Adjutant General's Office, 1780–1917

Entry 19. Returns and Receipts of Naval Stores, Navy Yard, Baltimore, Md., 1794–98.

Record Group 181. Records of the Boston Navy Yard, Constellation Repairs, 1839–41, NARA, Waltham, Mass.

Record Group 200. Log of the USF Constellation, 1799

Record Group 217. Records of the Treasury Department

United States Attorney General, Opinions, Vol. 8.

UNPUBLISHED MANUSCRIPTS AND DOCUMENTS

DELAWARE HISTORICAL SOCIETY, WILMINGTON, DEL.

Thomas MacDonald's Journal, USF *Constellation*

HAGLEY MUSEUM AND LIBRARY, WILMINGTON, DEL.

Francis Henry du Pont's Correspondence

HISTORICAL SOCIETY OF PENNSYLVANIA, PHILADELPHIA

USF *Constellation,* Orders, Muster Rolls, etc.
Dreer Collection
Joshua Humphreys' Correspondence and Letter Books
Jones and Clarke Papers
John Rodgers Papers
Smith Papers
Thomas Truxtun Papers, Letter Books, and Journals
Truxtun-Biddle Papers
Truxtun-Hare Papers

HUNTINGTON LIBRARY AND ART GALLERY, SAN MARINO, CALIF.

William Eaton Papers
Log of the USF *Constellation,* William Crane and John Shaw, commanders
Keith Spence Correspondence
Thomas Truxtun Letters

LIBRARY OF CONGRESS, WASHINGTON, D.C.

Leonard Cushing Papers
Thomas Jefferson's Papers and Correspondence
Charles G. Ridgely Journals and Letter Book
John Rodgers Papers, 1814–19
Snow Collection
Thomas Truxtun Papers

MARYLAND HISTORICAL SOCIETY, BALTIMORE

USF *Constellation* Papers
Geisinger Papers
William Kelly Papers
James McHenry Papers
James Miller's Journal
William Patterson Papers

MYSTIC SEAPORT MUSEUM, G. W. BLUNT WHITE LIBRARY, MYSTIC, CONN.

John W. Mason's Journal

Bibliography

NEW JERSEY HISTORICAL SOCIETY, NEWARK

Charles Stewart Papers

CITY OF NORFOLK ARCHIVES, CHRYSLER MUSEUM, NORFOLK, VA.

Moses Myers Correspondence

PEABODY ESSEX LIBRARY, SALEM, MASS.

Josiah Fox Papers

INDEPENDENCE SEAPORT MUSEUM, PHILADELPHIA, PA.

John Lenthall Papers

SPECIAL COLLECTIONS, NIMITZ LIBRARY, UNITED STATES NAVAL ACADEMY, ANNAPOLIS, MD.

James Barron Papers
Franklin Buchanan Journal No. 6
Leon Polland Papers

VIRGINIA STATE LIBRARY, RICHMOND

Calendar of Virginia State Papers

STEM LIBRARY, COLLEGE OF WILLIAM AND MARY, WILLIAMSBURG, VA.

James Barron Papers

NEWSPAPERS AND JOURNALS

HUNTINGTON LIBRARY AND ART GALLERY, SAN MARINO, CALIF.

Portsmouth (Va.) Daily Transcript

MARYLAND HISTORICAL SOCIETY, BALTIMORE, MD.

Baltimore American and Federal Gazette
Baltimore Federal Gazette
Baltimore Federal Register
Baltimore Patriot
Baltimore Sun

Federal Gazette and Baltimore Advertiser
Maryland Historical Magazine
Maryland Journal
Niles Register
The (Fells Point) Telegraphie

PORTSMOUTH (VA.) PUBLIC LIBRARY

Norfolk Herald
Norfolk Beacon
Portsmouth Argus
Portsmouth Beacon
Portsmouth Daily Globe

NIMITZ LIBRARY, UNITED STATES NAVAL ACADEMY, ANNAPOLIS, MD.

Army and Navy Chronicle

PUBLISHED HISTORIES, COLLECTIONS, MEMOIRS, AND BIOGRAPHIES

Agranat, Brina J. "Thorough and Efficient Repair: Rebuilding in the American Navy." Master's thesis, East Carolina University, 1991.

Alden, Carroll Storrs. *Lawrence Kearny: Sailor-Diplomat.* Princeton: Princeton University Press, 1926.

Allen, Gardner W. *Our Navy and the Barbary Corsairs.* Cambridge, Mass.: Houghton Mifflin, 1905.

Anthony, Irvin. *Decatur.* New York: Charles Scribner's Sons, 1931.

Barley, Frederick (Commander, R.N.V.R.). "A British Sailor Looks at the United States Navy of the Nineteenth Century." *American Neptune* 21 (1961): 57–69.

Bassett, John S. *Correspondence of Andrew Jackson.* Washington, D.C.: Carnegie Institution, 1926–35.

Bearss, Edwin C. *Charlestown Navy Yard.* 2 vols. Washington, D.C.: U.S. Dept. of Interior, 1984.

Bluff, Harry [M. F. Maury.] "Our Navy." *Southern Literary Messenger,* 1839–41.

Brewington, Marion V. "The Designs of Our First Frigates." *American Neptune* 8 (1948).

———. *Shipbuilding in Maryland, The Old Line State: A History of Maryland.* Annapolis, Md.: Hall of Records, State of Maryland, 1971.

Brugger, Robert, et al. *Maryland: A Middle Temperament.* Baltimore: Johns Hopkins University Press, 1988.

Chapelle, Howard I. *History of the American Sailing Navy.* New York: W. W. Norton & Co., 1949.

Chapelle, Howard I., and Polland, Leon D. *The Constellation Question*. Washington, D.C.: Smithsonian Institution Press, 1970.

Coletta, Paolo E. *American Secretaries of the Navy*. 2 vols. Annapolis, Md.: Naval Institute Press, 1980.

Cooledge, J. J. *Ships of the Royal Navy*. Annapolis, Md.: Naval Institute Press, 1969.

Cooper, J. Fenimore. *History of the Navy of the United States of America*. 2 vols. 2d. ed. Philadelphia: Lee and Blanchard, 1840.

———. *Ned Myers: A Life Before the Mast*. New York: G. Putnam Sons, 1899.

Cranwell, John P., and William B. Crane. *Men of Marque*. New York: W. W. Norton, 1940.

Crothers, William L. *The American-Built Clipper Ship*. Camden, Me.: International Marine/Ragged Mountain Press, 1997.

Davies, George E. "List of Members of the First Presbyterian Church, 1766–1783." *Maryland Historical Magazine* 35 (1940): 256–61.

———. "Robert Smith and the Navy." *Maryland Historical Magazine* 14 (1919): 305–22.

de Kay, James Tertius. *Chronicles of the Frigate* Macedonian, *1809–1922*. New York: W. W. Norton & Co., 1998.

DeRoos, Frederick Fitzgerald. *Personal Narrative of Travels in the United States and Canada in 1826 with Remarks on the Present State of the American Navy*. London: Privately printed, 1827.

Dudley, William S. "James Fenimore Cooper's *Ned Myers: A Life Before the Mast*." *American Neptune* 57 (1997).

Dunne, William M. P. "The Frigate *Constellation* Clearly Was No More: Or Was She?" *American Neptune* 53 (1993).

Eckert, Edward K. *The Navy Department in the War of 1812*. Gainesville: University of Florida Press, 1971.

Emmons, George F. *The Navy of the United States, from Commencement, 1775–1853, with a Brief History of Each Vessel's Service and Fate, as Appears upon Record*. Washington, D.C.: Gideon & Co., 1853.

Ferguson, Eugene S. *Truxtun of the* Constellation: *The Life of Commodore Thomas Truxtun, U. S. Navy, 1755–1822*. Baltimore: Johns Hopkins University Press, 1956.

Footner, Geoffrey M. *Tidewater Triumph: The Development and Worldwide Success of the Chesapeake Bay Pilot Schooner*. Mystic, Conn.: Mystic Seaport Museum, Inc., 1998.

Footner, Hulbert. *Sailor of Fortune: The Life and Adventures of Commodore Barney, USN*. Annapolis, Md.: Naval Institute Press, 1998.

Grant, Bruce. *Isaac Hull: Captain of Old Ironsides*. Chicago: Pellegrini and Cudahy, 1947.

Haines, Charles. "Ship Preservation in the Old Navy." *American Neptune* 42 (1982).

Hallahan, John M. *The Battle of Craney Island: A Matter of Credit*. Portsmouth, Va.: St. Michaels Press, 1986.

Hamersly, Thomas H. S. *Complete General Navy Register of the United States of America, 1778–1887*. New York: W. K. Boyle, Printer, 1888.

Holiday, Mildred M. "History of Portsmouth (Va.)." Portsmouth, Va. Unpublished manuscript, no date.

Homans, Benjamin. *Laws of the United States in Relation to the Navy and Marine Corps to the Close of the Second Session, 26th Congress.* Washington, D.C.: J & G. S. Gideon, 1843.

Hopkins, James F., and Mary Hargreaves, ed. *The Papers of Henry Clay.* Lexington: University of Kentucky Press, 1963–73.

Hoxse, John. *The Yankee Tar: An Authentic Narrative of the Voyages and Hardships of John Hoxie and the Cruises of the US Frigate* Constellation. Northampton, Mass.: Printed by John Metcalf for the author, 1840.

Humphreys, Henry. "Who Built the First United States Navy?" *Pennsylvania Magazine of History and Biography* 40 (1916): 385–411.

Ireland, J. de Courcy. "Rais Hammida, Last of the Great Algerian Corsairs." *Mariners Mirror* 60 (1974): 187–96.

Jarvis, James. "A Narrative of the Attack on Craney Island on the 22nd June 1813." *Virginia Historical Register and Literary Advertiser* 1 (January 1848):137–41.

Lavery, Brian. "The Rebuilding of British War Ships, 1690–1740." *Mariners Mirror* 66 (1980): 5–14, 113–27.

Layton, Thomas N. *The Voyage of the* Frolic: *New England Merchants and the Opium Trade.* Stanford, Calif.: Stanford University Press, 1997.

Leiner, Frederick C. *Millions for Defense: The Subscription Warships of 1798.* Annapolis, Md.: Naval Institute Press, 2000.

Long, David F. *Sailor-Diplomat: A Biography of Commodore James Biddle, 1783–1848.* Boston: Northeastern University Press, 1983.

Lubbock, Basil. *The Opium Clippers.* Glasgow: Brown, Son & Ferguson, Ltd., 1933.

Martin, Tyrone G. *A Most Fortunate Ship: Old Ironsides.* Annapolis, Md.: Naval Institute Press, 1997.

———. "USS *Constitution:* A Design Confirmed." *American Neptune* 57, no. 3 (1997).

McKee, Christopher. *Edward Preble: A Naval Biography, 1761–1807.* Annapolis, Md.: Naval Institute Press, 1972.

———. *A Gentlemanly and Honorable Profession: The Creation of the U.S. Naval Officer Corps, 1794–1815.* Annapolis, Md.: Naval Institute Press, 1991.

Mills, James Clark. *Oliver Hazard Perry and the Battle of Lake Erie.* Detroit: John Phelps, 1913.

Morris, Charles. "The Autobiography of Charles Morris." Naval Institute *Proceedings* 6, no. 12 (1880).

Napier, Elers. *The Life and Correspondence of Admiral Sir Charles Napier.* London: Hurst and Blackert, 1862.

Owens, Hamilton. *Baltimore on the Chesapeake.* Garden City, N. Y.: Doubleday, Doran & Co., 1941.

Palmer, Michael A. *Stoddert's War: Naval Operations during the Quasi War with France, 1798–1801.* Columbia: University of South Carolina Press, 1987.

Paullin, Charles Oscar. *Commodore John Rodgers: Captain, Commodore and Senior Officer of the American Navy, 1773–1838.* Annapolis, Md.: Naval Institute Press, 1967.

———. "Naval Administration under Secretaries Smith, Hamilton and Jones, 1801–1814." Naval Institute *Proceedings* 32, no. 1, 306 (December 1906).

———. *Paullin's History of Naval Administration, 1775–1911.* Annapolis, Md.: Naval Institute Press, 1968.

Pratt, Fletcher. *The Navy: A History*. New York: Garden City Publishing, 1941.

Radoff, Morris N., ed. "(Letter of) Captain Gordon of the *Constellation*." *Maryland Historical Magazine* 67 (1972): 389–418.

Randolph, Evan. "*Fouled Anchors*? Foul Blow." *American Neptune* 52 (1992).

Semmes, Raphael. *Baltimore as Seen by Visitors, 1783–1860*. Baltimore: Historical Society, 1953.

Sheads, Scott. *Fort McHenry*. Baltimore: Nautical & Aviation Publishing Co., 1995.

Stanton, Elizabeth Brandon. "Builder of the First American Navy." *Journal of American History* 2 (1908): 101–12.

Steiner, Bernard C. *The Life and Correspondence of James McHenry*. Cleveland, Oh.: Barrows Bros., 1907.

Strott, Howard J., ed. "A Seaman's Notebook: The Travels of George de la Roche." *Maryland Historical Magazine* 42 (1947): 261–69.

Syrett, Harold C., ed. *Papers of Alexander Hamilton*. New York: Columbia University Press, 1967.

Tuckerman, Henry T. *The Life of John Pendleton Kennedy*. Baltimore: G. B. Putnam's Sons, 1961.

van Horne, John C., and W. F. Formwalt, ed. *The Correspondence and Miscellaneous Papers of Benjamin Henry Latrobe*. New Haven, Conn.: Yale University Press, 1988.

Wegner, Dana. "An Apple and an Orange." *American Neptune* 52 (1992).

———. *Fouled Anchors: The Constellation Question Answered*. Bethesda, Md.: David Taylor Research Center, 1991.

———. "The Frigate Strikes Her Colors." *American Neptune* 55, no. 3 (1995).

Wertenbaker, Thomas J. *Norfolk: Historic Southern Port*. Durham, N.C.: Duke University Press, 1962.

Westlake, Merle. "The American Sailing Navy: Josiah Fox, Joshua Humphreys, and Thomas Tingey." *American Neptune* 59 (1999).

Wheelock, Phillis de Kay. "Henry Eckford, 1775–1832." *American Neptune* 17 (1957).

Whitehorne, Joseph A. *The Battle of Baltimore, 1814*. Baltimore: Nautical & Aviation Publishing Co., 1997.

Wines, E. C. *Two Years and a Half in the Navy: Journal of a Cruise in the Mediterranean and Lavant on Board US Frigate* Constellation, *1829–1831*. Philadelphia: Carey and Lee, 1832.

Wood, Virginia Steel. *Live Oaking: Southern Timber for Tall Ships*, Annapolis, Md.: Naval Institute Press, 1981.

Index

Myers, Ned, 162–63

Mystic, 258

Napier, Charles, 93, 95, 96

Natchez, 162, 165, 195

National Archives at College Park, Maryland, 174

National Register of Historic Vessels, 266

Nautilus, 59, 60, 73

Naval Historical Center, 262

Naval Sea System Command, 263

navy: administration, 105–7, 194–95, 228, 256; attitude toward *Constellation,* viii–ix; diplomatic missions, 113–18; expansion of, 37–38, 75, 83–84, 104–13, 195–96; mobilization of, 33–34; permanent establishment of, 104–5; policy on hull modifications, 72–73; preparation for war, 62; role in restoration, 261–63

Navy Act, 3

Navy Board of Commissioners: administrative changes (1827), 131; creation, 106–9; live oak, purchase of, 177–79; personnel restrictions, 123; repair/rebuild/construction work assignments, 127–28, 133–34; on repair/rebuild estimates, 136–37; replacement by bureau system, 194; and surplus ships, 129–30

Neale, Benedict I., 95

new construction: approval (1839), 177–79; cost, 226–27; and personnel issues, 123; policy, 75–78, 133–34, 157–58, 214–15; reduction after Algerine Treaty, 28

New York, 60, 63, 78–79

New York Navy Yard, 259

Nicholas, John S., 257–58

Nicholson, John B., 116–17

Nicholson, Joseph Hopper, 99

Nicholson brothers, 99

Nonsuch, 113, 115–16

Norfolk, Va., 85–91, 97, 98

Norfolk Navy Yard, 259

North Carolina, 126, 129

O'Brien, Richard, 59

O'Donnell, John, 4

Ohio, 112

Oliver, Robert, 4, 7

Olsson, Lloyd A., 145

Ontario: cruise to Mediterranean Sea, 100; cruise to South America, 114–15, 117; effort to keep in service, 111, 130; at Pensacola, 165; repair requirements, 112, 123

operating costs (1829), 153

Opium War, 188–92

ordinary, 58, 132–33, 196–98

orlop deck plan, 181 fig. 7.3

Packet, 163

Patterson, Daniel T., 159–61

Patterson, William, 27

Paulding, James K., 169, 181

Paulet, Lord George, 193

Peacock, 112, 123, 130

Pearson, William, 141, 143–44, 146 fig. 6.2, 178 fig. 7.2

Pechell, Samuel J., 92

Penetreau, P. J., 45

Penrose, Thomas, 3

Pensacola, Fla., 165, 168–69

Perry, Oliver Hazard, 115–16

Peru, 114–18, 120–22

Pezuela, Royalist Vice King, 121

Philadelphia, 56, 58–59, 63, 78–79, 124

Philadelphia Navy Yard, 127–28

Phillips, Benjamin Hammell, 50–51

Pickering, Timothy, 9, 15, 26–27

Pickering Brothers, 190

Pierce, Franklin, 210

Pitot, Captain, 48–51

Pleasant, James, 125

Plymouth, 196

Pooks, James, 135

Porpoise, 113

Porter, David, 74–75, 108, 113, 117, 119

Porter, John L.: frame construction, 237; at Gosport Navy Yard, 210; timber requisitions, 216, 218, 220, 224–26, 242–43

ports, shipbuilding, 3–4

About the Author

Geoffrey M. Footner served during World War II as a naval officer in the Pacific and European theaters. Before and after the war, he attended various colleges, including Johns Hopkins and Columbia universities. During the seventies and eighties, Footner worked in international shipping, where he pioneered combined land, air, and sea transportation between the United States and Europe and Africa. With associates in America and abroad, his companies developed the concept of international intermodal service, using selected domestic transportation companies along with international air and ocean transportation companies for American exports. He left this segment of his career in 1980 to tend his vineyards on the Eastern Shore of Maryland. During the next decade, Footner turned his attention to writing about the Chesapeake Bay. His articles and books on sailing craft, ship building, pilot boats, and Baltimore schooners have been published in the United States, as well as in France and Great Britain.

Footner lives in Fells Point, the original port for Baltimore, in an eighteenth-century house where several prominent shipbuilders lived. William Price, who built USS *Experiment* (1799), USS *Maryland*, and USS *Hornet* (1805), lived there until he built his mansion across the street, and Lewis de Rochbrune, who built USS *Patapsco* (1799), and John Price, who built Baltimore privateer schooners during the War of 1812, lived there, too, early in the nineteenth century. Evidence suggests that all three shipbuilders worked on the U.S. Frigate *Constellation*.